3/2000 28^{50}

D1474584

English Origins of
AMERICAN COLONISTS

From The New York Genealogical and
Biographical Record

English Origins of
*A*MERICAN *C*OLONISTS

From The New York Genealogical and
Biographical Record

Selected and Introduced by

HENRY B. HOFF

Genealogical Publishing Co., Inc.

Excerpted and reprinted from
The New York Genealogical and Biographical Record
with added Introduction and Index by
Genealogical Publishing Co., Inc., Baltimore, 1991.
Added matter © 1991 by Genealogical Publishing Co., Inc.
Baltimore, Maryland. All Rights Reserved.
Library of Congress Catalogue Card Number 91-71006
International Standard Book Number 0-8063-1309-9
Made in the United States of America

Introduction

~~~~~~~~~~~~

Because we are a nation descended from immigrants, American genealogy has been a two-part process: the American part and, if discovered, the pre-American part. The family founder in this country is the focus of many of our genealogical publications, of our standard numbering system and superscripts, and of many hereditary societies.

Identifying an immigrant's place of origin and parentage frequently becomes a long search involving years of work. Many successful searches have begun with a single clue found in English probate records or depositions.

Between 1903 and 1916 *The New York Genealogical and Biographical Record* published four series of abstracted English records that are reprinted in this book. All four series were inspired by Henry FitzGilbert Waters (1823-1913), who described his method as searching English records "between certain dates, *seriatim,* keeping a sharp look out for everything possibly indicative of the slightest connection with known American families." Most of the records contained in this book are wills of the seventeenth and eighteenth centuries, often mentioning one or more of the Thirteen Colonies. The contributors were two Americans (Lothrop Withington and J. Henry Lea) and two Englishmen (J. R. Hutchinson and William Gilbert).

The two Americans (both of whom died soon after Waters) were among a small group of researchers who, by applying Waters' methods of working with English probate records and depositions, have made remarkable contributions to genealogy. Best known of this group are the following, Waters first:

Henry FitzGilbert Waters. His series, "Genealogical Gleanings in England," was published in *The New England Historical and Genealogical Register* between 1883 and 1899, then collected and published with an index in 1901, and reprinted in 1969 by the Genealogical Publishing Company (GPC), along with a new series of "Gleanings" originally published in 1907.

Lothrop Withington. His series, "New York Gleanings in England," was published in *The New York Genealogical and Biographical Record* between 1903 and 1908, and is reprinted in this book. His series, "Virginia Gleanings in England," was published in *The Virginia Magazine of History and Biography,* 1903-1919, and was reprinted with additional material in 1980 by GPC. Another of his series, "Abstracts of English Wills," was published in *The New England Historical and Genealogical Register* between 1897 and 1901, and was reprinted in volume 3 of *English Origins of New England Families,* 1st series, published in 1984 by GPC.

J. Henry Lea. His series (with J. R. Hutchinson), "Clues from English Archives Contributory to American Genealogy," was published in *The New York Genealogical and Biographical Record,* 1900-1905, and is reprinted in this book. A parallel series, "Genealogical Gleanings Among the English Archives," was published in *The New England Historical and Genealogical Register,* 1900-1905, and was reprinted with Lothrop Withington's series in 1984.

George Sherwood. His two-volume work, *American Colonists in English Records* (1932-33), was reprinted as one volume in 1969 by GPC.

Frank Smith. His *Immigrants to America Appearing in English Records* was published in 1976.

Peter Wilson Coldham. His series, "Genealogical Gleanings in England," has appeared in the *National Genealogical Society Quarterly* since 1971. His *Lord Mayor's Court of London Depositions Relating to Americans 1641-1736* was published in 1980 by the National Genealogical Society. Also in 1980 his *English Estates of American Colonists* was published by GPC, one volume for the seventeenth century and one for the eighteenth century. A third volume, covering the first half of the nineteenth century, appeared the following year. These three volumes were reprinted with additional material in 1989 as one volume—*American Wills & Administrations in the Prerogative Court of Canterbury, 1610-1857.* His two-volume *English Adventurers and Emigrants* was published in 1984-85 by GPC, and his subsequent two-volume work, *The Complete Book of Emigrants,* published in 1987-90 by GPC, contains some depositions.

Not mentioned here is the fine work of the many genealogists to use English probate records and depositions for finding the origins of specific American families. When extensive abstracting has been done (e.g. by Noel Currer-Briggs on the Kirby family of Virginia), clues on unrelated American colonists have sometimes been discovered.

There has been some overlap among records abstracted. For example, Peter Wilson Coldham's *English Adventurers and Emigrants* includes Admiralty depositions for the period 1609-1733, yet it does not include all the depositions in this book, some of which are verbatim rather than abstracts. And the careful researcher will want to look at all versions, especially for the genealogical commentary that makes many of these works particularly valuable and for abstracts of records no longer available for inspection.

Henry B. Hoff

New York City, 1991

Contents

English Origins of
*A*MERICAN *C*OLONISTS

From The New York Genealogical and
Biographical Record

CLUES FROM ENGLISH ARCHIVES
CONTRIBUTORY TO AMERICAN GENEALOGY.

BY J. HENRY LEA AND J. R. HUTCHINSON.

It is well known that the English records contemporary with the landing of the Pilgrim Fathers contain a wealth of information concerning the family history of the early colonists, not only of the New England but of the Southern settlements. The searchers of the Probate and Chancery Records, Feet of Fines, Manorial Court and Plea Rolls, Inquisitions Post Mortem, Star Chamber Court, Ship Money Tax, Subsidies and Parish Registers have found these documents a veritable treasure mine of genealogical information. It is proposed in this and succeeding articles to extract, digest and place before the reading public as much of this invaluable matter as can be found from the period of 1600–1675, exclusive of what has already been published, and to thus establish beyond reasonable doubt the kinship of many of the early American families with their English ancestors.

29 July, 1655, I Sir EDMUND PLOWDEN of Wansted, co. Southhampton, Knight, Lord Earle Palatine, Governor and Captaine Generall of the Province of New Albion in America, and a peere of the Kingdome of Ireland, being in perfect health of body. To be buried in Lidbury church in Shropshire, in the Chappell of the Plowdens, neere Plowden, with a monument of Stone with brasse plate engraved with my Armes and Inscription and brasse plates of my eighteen children, affixed to ye said monument at thirty or fourty pounds charges, together with my p'fect pedigre as is drawne at my house. To the eleven parishes in Hampshire, Sussex and Shropshire wherin my lands lye 40s. each. To Mr Edward Weedon late of Aston on the Walls, Northants, £40 for pious uses. And whereas my eldest son Francis Plowden hath been extremely disobedient and vndutifull vnto me for these eighteen yeares past, setting division, strife and debate between me his father and my wife his own mother, whereby many yeares, suites, scandall and greate expences have been expended and she carryed away and hid from me, with diverse of my cattle and goods purloined by them, and by their practises I was wrongfully and cruelly imprisoned in the ffleete vntill by the Pords Peeres Committees in Parliament about fifteen yeares since I was freed, and she ordered to returne and cohabite with me, my said son being specially forbid to meddle with my estate or rents did nevertheless when I was in Ireland report I was dead and took diverse of my rents . . . riotously and forcibly . . . and brake upp my closet and took away or lost one deed of revocation of Submission to Arbitrators betwixt me and my father and one Bond of £400, for want of which, and other sinister practices of him and his mother, I was barred of £10,000 due to me from my father, and since my residing in America and Albion six yeares, my said son being expressly forbidden my house and lands . . . did nevertheless many yeares reside in my house at Wansted and forcibly received my rents and stocks, giving out I was dead, and by acting therein . . . and his mother's practise to sequester my estate in my absence in America, I am barred of six yeares rent and engaged in many suits to recover my estate, so as by his vndutifull carriage I have been damnifyed by him, in these last eighteen yeares time, fifteen thousand pounds, and his mother being a mutable woman and by him alienated in affection from me, and set on in a new suite scandallously and wickedly to refuse to cohabite and live with me, but to sue for alimony, and forcibly to kepe my house etc. to the value of three hundred pounds, and secretly to pilfer, steal and sell my goods, though since the said Peeres order she had a child by me, And whereas by mediation of friends, and to winne him by kindnesse, five yeares since I received him to my house for two full yeares, in which tyme he could not be brought to acknowledge his grevious

2

offences, and hath threatened to shorten my life, and hath basely married his mother's chambermaid after having had an illegitimate child by her, Therefore I think him not fitt to make mine heire nor any of his issue by . . . his nowe wife soe meanly borne, And I think it fitt that my English lands shall be vnited to my Honor, County Palatine, and Province of New Albion, and doe conceive that his mother will sufficiently provide for him, to whom I leave five hundred pounds a yeare in lands and jointure for her life, namely Wansted and all other lands heretofore her father Mr Peter Mariner's, which I purchased of her and her mother . . . and walled out the sea and improved the lands, in all neare £4,000 charges, and payments to her mother, who lived twenty yeares afterwards; which lands, with Herrierd Grange and parsonage in Hampshire, I doe confirm to my wife for her life, on condition that neither she nor my son Francis oppose this my will or sell any of the said lands. To my wife £150 in household stuff, to be vsed in my Manor house of Wansted. To my daughter Winifred Plowden the lease I have made her for one and twenty yeares of Bedenham Farme. To my son Thomas his daughter £300 out of Stansted lease lands. I devise all my lease land in England to be sold and with the proceeds free lands to be bought and entailed as the rest of my lands are. To Thomas my son and Thomasine his wife all such estates as I have assured to them vppon their marriage. To Anne, wife of one Carter in Barkshire, if she be living, or else to her children—she being the daughter of one Thomas James of Burfield—£10. And whereas I am seised of the Province and County Palatine of New Albion as of free Principality, and held of the Crowne of Ireland . . . and of the Manor and capitall messuage of Wansted, the moiety of the Manor of Bedenham, and of diverse lands in Hampshire, and of the Manor of Stackstedd in Farley, etc., all which are entailed on my second son Thomas and the heirs males of his body, with diverse remainders over vnto my brother Francis and his son Edmund, Nowe in accordance with the powers to me reserved in the said settlement I doe annul all the said remainders, and doe devise all the said Province, Manors, lands, etc. vnto my son Thomas for the term of his naturall life, with remainder therein to his heires males, or in default of such to my nephew Edmund Plowden for life, with remainder to his heires males, or in default of such to the heires males of my son Francis not begotten on the body of his nowe wife Margaret, or in default to Winifred my daughter for life, with remainder to her heirs males, soe as they stile themselves by the name of Plowden. To my sister Dame Anne Lake and others, golde rings. Executor in trust, Henry Sharpe, my late servant. Overseer, Benedict Hall, Esq., my kinsman, or, if he be dead, his eldest son my cousin. I appoint as my Trustee for the planting, fortifying, peopling and stocking of this my Province of New Albion, Sir William Mason of Grey's Inn, Knt., who shall summon all my undertakers to transplant thither and there to settle their number of men which such of my estate yearly can transplant, namely, Lord Monson, 50; Lord Sherrard, 100; Sir Thomas

3

Danby, 100; Captain Batts his heir, 100; Mr. Eltonhead, a Master in Chancery, 50; his eldest brother Eltonhead, 50; Mr. Bowles, late Clerk of the Crown, 40; Captaine Cleybourne in Virginia, 50; Viscount Muskery, 50; and many others in England, Virginia and New England subscribed, and by direction in my manuscript bookes since I resided six yeares there, and of policie and government there, and of the best seats, profits, mines, rich trade of furrs, and wares, and fruits, wine, worme silke and grasse silke, fish and beastes there, rice and flotable ground for rice, flax, naples, hempe, barley and corne twoe cropps yearly. To build Churches and Schools there, and to indeavour to convert the Indians there to Christianity, and to settle there my family, kindred and posterity. (*Signed*) Albion. Witnesses, W. H. Smith, R. Minshull, Gilbert Jones, George Penne, Fr: Ewre of Bucknall in Oxfordshire near Brackley, Philip Clarke late Bayly of Ludlo, Roger Raven of Andover, gent, Evan Griffith my clarke, Anthony Foxcrofte of Halifax in Yorkshire. Proved 27 July, 1659, by Henry Sharpe, executor in trust. (P. C. C. Pell 432.)

This long and interesting will of the unfortunate emulator of Smith and Raleigh in the endeavor to found a colony on the Delaware, is of much value, not only as confirming such historical records as exist regarding him but also in furnishing details, hitherto unknown, in the life of this most strenuous and turbulent gentleman. Born of one of the most ancient of English families, the Plowdens of Plowden, in Salop., who had been there seated before the earliest extant records, his first known ancestor was Roger Plowden who accompanied King Richard to Palestine in the 12th Century. He was himself grandson of the eminent jurist of his own name,* by his second but only surviving son, Francis Plowden, Esq., whose second son he was.†

He married, about 1610, Mabel,‡ daughter of Peter Mariner of Wanstead, Hants., a lady who brought him an ample jointure but, we fear, little domestic peace or happiness, and, although she bore him eighteen children, as we learn by his will, he was twice divorced from her and spent two years or more in the Fleet prison rather than pay her alimony,§ while in his will he makes a scathing arraignment of her conduct, tempered by an ample provision for her future.

His life seems to have been an adventurous one: in 1634 he was in Ireland, as we learn from the Visitation of Oxon. for that year.‖ In 1642 he came with Evelin to Virginia, and in 1643 with two faithful retainers, was marooned on Smith's Island, off the coast, by his mutinous crew¶ of servants, from which he was rescued by a passing vessel, and fell into the hands of the Swedish

---

* *Dict. Nat. Biog.*, XLV, 428.
† Burke's *Commoners*, III, 251.
‡ Called " Mary " in *Complete Peerage* by G. E. Cokayne, I, 67.
§ See *Penn. Hist. Mag.*, V, 424-5, for details of this suit.
‖ *Harl. Soc.*, V, 3.
¶ Account by Gov. Printz, see Niell's *Va. Car.*, pp. 180-183, and *Penn. Hist Mag.*, VII, 50.

Governor on the Delaware. He had had four years' travel in Germany, France, Italy and Belgium, served as an officer five years in Ireland and had been seven years in America before 1648.*

The son, Thomas Plowden, seems to have inherited under the will of his fatner and his own will, proved in the Prerogative Court of Canterbury in 1698, and the certified verbatim copy of the Patent to New Albion may be found in the article by Prof. G. B. Keen in the *Pennsylvania Magazine* in 1883.† His third son, Francis Plowden, succeeded his father by his will and came to America to prosecute his rights and died in Maryland. His descendants registered their pedigree in 1774 at the College of Arms in London, but the title of Earl of Albion was never assumed after 1659. There is no trace of any such earldom to be found in the Irish records either as Albion or Plowden.‡

I CHRISTOPHER LAWNE of Blanford in the Countie of Dorset, nowe lying in Charles Citie in Virginia, beying sicke of bodie. My debts in Virginia and England first to be paid. I give to Anne Oliffe my daughter in lawe £50 at marriage, being her portion. To Robert Olife, being his portion, £20 at marriage. To my wife Susanna £30, to be paid unto her at the first sale of my goods now in Virginia to be sent into England. My will is that all my Bills of Adventure be discharged at the rate of fower for three. To my wife Susanna £20 a year for life out of my goods now to be sent out of Virginia into England. All the rest of my goods I give to my two sons Lovevell and Symon Lawne, whom I make my executors, the increase of my stock to be bestowed for their maintenance and bringing up in learning until they come to the age of fower and twentie yeares. I entreate my loving freinds Captaine Nathaniel Powle, Mr. Samuel Macocke and Captain Ralph Hamor to be Overseers of this my last will and my debts owing to pay and the remainder to send over into England to my loving Friends Mr Lawrence Anthony of the Poultrie in London, Mr Richard Ellis of St. Sythinges Lane in London, Mr John White of Ockford in Dorset, and Mr Wm Willis of Moore in Dorset, whom I request to be Overseers of this my will. I give power to my overseers in Virginia to sell all my goods there and to send the proceeds, together with the rest of my Tobacco and Sasafras, unto my overseers in England. Dated 2 Nov., 1619. Witnesses, Nathaniel West, Pharao Flynton. 17 June, 1620, commission to William Willis, one of the supervisors, to administer during the minority of Lovewell and Simon Lawne, sons of deceased. (P. C. C.   Soame 56.)

The testator was a very prominent and picturesque figure in the early history of the Puritan movement, joining the Brownists or Separatists, he repaired with them to Holland, and we find him there marrying, 6 Feb., 1610, to a Susanna,§ whose surname is not given in the record, but the internal evidence of the above

---

* *Penn. Hist. Mag.*, VII, 50-66.
‡ *Complete Peerage* by G. E. Cokayne, I, 67.
§ Amsterdam Marr. Records, see in *Mass. Hist. Soc. Pro.*, 2d Series, Vol. VI, p. 56.

will shows her to have been a widow of the name of Oliffe, with two unmarried children, Ann and Robert Oliffe, while he himself had also had two children by a former marriage. He was excommunicated in Jan., 1611–12, in company with John Fowler, Clement Sanders and Robert Bulward,* who united with him in the authorship of a fierce attack on their former associates which was issued in July, 1612, entitled "The Prophane Schisme of the Brownists," etc., and in May, 1613, followed this by "Brownisme turned inside out."†

He was sent out to Virginia by Richard Wiseman, Nathaniel Basse and others‡ and perhaps accompanied Sir Francis Blackwell in 1619§ although, as he represented his settlement (afterwards called the Isle of Wight Plantation) in the Assembly of Virginia in July of that year, it may have been earlier. The probate of his will informs us that he soon succumbed to the malarial climate of the Colony.

8 Julye, 1606, I RICHARD MODYE of Garesdon in the Countye of Wilts, Esquyer, being sicke in body. To be buried in the parish church of Gareston. And for soe much as I have already taken order for the disposing of my lands vnto mine heir, and for the meyntenaunce of my wife, the greatest part of my goods I purpose to leave vnto my children. To my daughter Anne Modye £1500 over and above the £500 in the hands of Mr John Bancks of London. Poor of Gareston £20. Nephew Mr Richard Love, bachiler of divinitie, £20. Thomas Harrison in whose howse I nowe remaine, £3-6-8, to be paid before my body be removed out of his howse. Peeter Hawkins my man £6-13-8. Residuary leagtee, my sonne Sir Henry Modye, Knt., whome I make sole executor. Witnesses, Edward Underhill, William Bell, William Reddinge, John Hollway, Townclerke of Oxon. Proved 16 July, 1614, by the executor named. (P. C. C. Lawe 74.)

The testator was father of Sir Henry Moody of Garsdon, Knt. (the executor), who was created a Baronet 11 March, 1621-2, having been Sheriff of Wilts 1618–19, and M. P. 1625–26 and 1628-9. He married Deborah, daughter of Walter Dunch of Avebury, Wilts., by his wife Deborah, daughter of James Pilkington, Bishop of Durham, 20 Jan., 1605-6, and died 23 April, 1629. His widow, Lady Deborah, being a Puritan, came with their young son, Sir Henry Moody, Bart., to New England before 1638. They settled first at Lynn, but getting into trouble with the ecclesiastics, removed to Salem, and later, between 1646 and 1654, to Long Island, N. Y., where she became one of the patentees of Gravesend. She died before 11 May, 1659, when administration on her estate was granted to her son.‖

---

* Morton Dexter's *England and Holland of the Pilgrims*, p. 536.
 † Arber's *Pilgrim Fathers*, pp. 110-119; Dexter's *England and Holland of the Pilgrims*, pp. 204, 545, 546; Dexter's *Congregationalism*, p. 332, App. p. 25.
 ‡ *N. E. Hist. Gen. Reg.*, XXXI, p. 397. Hotten's *Lists*, pp. 184, 241, 272.
 § Bradford's *Hist. Muc.*, pp. 24-26.
 ‖ *Complete Baronetage* by G. E. C., I, 191; *Notes and Queries*, 7th Ser., V, 415; *Winthrop's Hist.*; Savage, *Gen. Dict.*, III, 225.

3 February, 1656-7, I RICHARD WHEELER, Cittizen and In-holder of London, being aged and weake in bodie . . . give and bequeath vnto my grandchild Richard Moye £150, and to his brother John Moye nowe residing in Virginia, if he be living at the time of my death, £50, to be paid vnto them at their severall ages of one and twentie yeares; and my will and pleasure is that my executor shall not pay my said grandchild John Moye his legacie unless he come over into England and demaund the same. To my sister Margaret Wheeler 40s. a yeare for tenne yeares out of my rents in Moorfields, Cosin Stephen Wheeler of Chelsey £8, and his sonne Arthur Wheeler 40s. Kinsman John Langford 40s. and his sonne Cecill 20s. Katherine Freeke and her sonne John Freek 20s. apeece and her daughter 10s. Kinsfolkes Thomas Kelsey, Anne Kelsey and Elizabeth Kelsey 40s. apeece, and Susan Kelsey that lives with me £3. Joan Wheeler my brother's daughtet 40s. The nowe wife of Richard Smith, my kinswoman. 20s., and her son Hayes my godson 40s. Brother in lawe Hitchcock in Wiltshire 10s., his three sonnes 5s. apeece, and his daughter 10s. George Cooke and Arthur his brother 12d. apeece. And whereas I am possessed in my owne right of a lease messuage in Moorfields called the Cocke in the Hole, and of severall other small tenements therevnto adjoin-ing, wherein I have some twenty five years yet to come, worth neare vppon fortie pounds per annum, nowe I doe give the said yearly rent (the aforesaid legacies being paid) as follows: To my grandchild Richard Moye £10 per annum after he come to his age of one and twentie; to Susan Kelsey whom I brought upp, the brock tenement next to the Ditch, wherein John Francklyn doth dwell; and to my brother George Kelsey, whome I do make my executor, £5 and £5 per annum for his paines. Overseers, my cosin Stephen Wheeler of Chelsey and William Cunningham of Moorfields, victualler. Witnesses, Wil-liam House, John Slater, William Hall, scr. Proved 1 January, 1657-8, by the executor named. (P. C. C. Wootton 2.)

Power of Attorney of Richard Wheeler, Citizen and Jnholder of London, dated 1 Oct., 1649, to John Goodwin of Ratcliffe in Co. Middx., Marryner, for the Constituant (as grandfather of the sons of the late John Moye in Virginia, dec'd., who was killed by the Last massacre of the Indians) his said two grandchildren, sons of the said John Moye, the elder of whom called (*blank*) Moye to settle in Va., the younger called (*blank*) Moye to be brought to England by said Goodwin.* In October, 1650, the eldest son, John Moy, was in tuition of Robte Davyes who petitions Court for his charges for same.† (Lower Norfolk, Va., Court Records in *Certf. of Head Rights* by J. H. Lea, *op. cit.*, in *N. E. Register*, XLVII, p. 353.)

---

* Recorded 27 Feb., 1649-50. Ct. Rec. Lower Norfolk Co., Va., *op. cit.*
† *Ibid. Reg.*, XLVII, p. 353.

7

CLUES FROM ENGLISH ARCHIVES
Contributory to American Genealogy.

By J. Henry Lea and J. R. Hutchinson.

19 February, 1656-7, I Elizabeth Lloyd of Elizabeth River in Lower Norfolke in Virginia, widdowe, being sicke of bodie, give and bequeath vnto my worthy friend Leiutenant Colonell Thomas Lambert to Thousand pounds of Tobacco as a Testimonie of my Thankfullness for all his respects towards mee; vnto Mr William Davies one thousand pounds of Tobacco; vnto Mr William Shipp fourty shillings to buy him a ring; vnto Mr Richard Pinner's sonne, my godchild, and vnto Mr Sayer's sonne, my godchild, each one haifer with a calfe by her side. My will is that Nedd a molatto shall be a freeman at the expiration of his tyme with Mr Sanderson, and I give vnto him one heifer calfe; vnto Rachell Lambert, daughter of the aforesaid

Thomas Lambert, five pounds to buy her a goune and five pounds more to pay for her passage into Virginia, and I doe order my executor to pay this money vnto James Matts of the Citty of Bristol within one Twelve month and a day for the use of the said Rachell, and I doe appoint the said Rachell to live with the said James Matts vntill she doe goe to Virginia. Whereas I have given alreadie vnto Mr Nicholas Harte seaven thousand pounds of Tobacco for looking after my business in Virginia, I doe give him five thousand pounds of Tobacco more as a token of my remembraunce. All the rest of my goods cattells plantations within Virginia I give vnto my brother in lawe Thomas Eavans of Kilkenny in Ireland, gent, for the only proper vse of my deare sister Mary Eavans his nowe married wife, whom I make and ordaine my whole and sole executor, he paying to Doctor Collins of Bristol all the money I doe owe him. Overseers, my friends Lieut.-Col. Thomas Lambert and James Matts. Witnesses, Will: Pyner, Jane Mansfield, Sarah Matts, Ja: Matts. Proved 15 June, 1657, by Thomas Eavans the executor named. (P. C. C. Ruthen 249.)

She was widow of Cornelius Lloyd who, by Patent No. 222, had 800 acres of land on Elizabeth River and Merchants' Creek. He had had Head Rights for 16 persons (*not named*) in 1635, for 60 persons (*named*) in 1642, for 5 persons (*named*) in 1647, and 6 persons (*named*) in 1653, then called "Leift. Col.,"* in Patent of 1636 described as "of London, merchant."† He was born about 1608, being 38 years of age in deposition of 1 Sept., 1646,‡ and was in Virginia before 1640, Burgess for Lower Norfolk Co., 1642 to 1652, Lieut.-Col., 1653, and Colonel.§ He died before 10 Dec., 1654, when we find Power of Attorney from Elizabeth Lloyd (the testatrix), relict of Cornelius Loyd, to friend Nicholas Hart of New England, merchant, with witnesses Thomas Lambert and William Turner.‖ Power of Attorney was granted 28 April, 1658, to Thomas Evans of Citty of Kilkenny, in Ireland, to kinsman John Bellgraue of Kilkenny, gent., to collect all dues in Virginia which "did belong to my late sister, Mrs. Elizabeth Loyd of Elizabeth River, etc." And, later, we have an agreement between William Carver of the County of Lower Norfolk, Attorney for mʳ. Nicholas Hart of Rode Jland in New England, for an estate left by Mrs. Elizabeth Loyd of county aforesaid and (*blank*) unto Thomas and Mary Evans of kilkeny in Jreland, by which all differences are settled with mʳ. John Belgraue of Kingdom of England, Attorney for Thomas and Mary Evans, dated 26 July, 1661.¶

---

* See *Certificates of Head Rights in Va.*, by J. H. Lea, in *N. E. Gen. & Hist. Reg.*, XLVII, pp. 63, 65, 69, 194.

† *Critic*, 25 Jan., 1890.

‡ Court Records, Lower Norfolk, Va.

§ *Virginia Caroloum*, by E. D. Niell, pp. 168, 185, 189, 199, 226, 232.

‖ Recorded 12 Dec., 1654.

¶ Recorded 15 Feb., 1661–2.

The connection shown above with Nicholas Hart is most interesting. He was of Taunton, Mass., in 1643, was excommunicated there, went to Boston and was in trouble again in that place in 1644, as was Sarah, wife of Benjamin Keayne, daughter of Gov. Thomas Dudley, who was also excommunicated.* In January, 1648, he was in Warwick, R. I., and in 1651 at Portsmouth. His widow, Jane (or Joan), daughter of Edward Rossiter of Mass., petitioned the General Court for aid being then 70 years old.† Hart's exact relationship with the Evans and Lloyds is not apparent.

Edward Lloyd, brother of Cornelius, was perhaps of Elizabeth City in 1623,‡ he was Burgess of Lower Norfolk, 1644-46, and removed to Maryland before 1659.§ The Col. Thomas Lambert who was Overseer of the will of Elizabeth Lloyd may be identified with "Coll: Lambert" whose Banns of marriage with Dorothy Mason, both of the Parish of Lynhaven, were published in Court, 17 May, 1661.‖ She was probably a daughter of Col. Lemuel Mason, but if so, predeceased him, as she is not named in his will, dated 17 June, 1695.¶

Queene Camell 22 August 1652. IN THE NAME OF GOD AMEN I JAMES ROCHE of Warras Sweeke alias Warwicke Sweeke in the Isle of Wight in Virginia, planter, but nowe in Queene Camell alias Est Camell in the Countye of Somersett in the Kingdome or Commomwealthe of England being sicke of body but of perfect memory (thanks be to God) Doe make this my last will and Testament in manner and forme following Inprimis I bequeathe my soule to God the ffather of Spirits my Maker my Redeemer and only Saviour and my bodie to the Earthe whence it was taken to be decentlie buried in Christian buriall Item whereas I sett sayle out of Virginia for England on the first day of January one thousand six hundred forty nyne and left behind mee a Stocke of Cattle Vizt: seaven Kine one Ox and one Steere in the hands and care of Thomas North my servant to be managed to the best Improvement for my vse Item whereas I left certeine Debts vnreceaved and Due to mee att and before my departure out of Virginia The wryteings by which they are to be demanded being in the Custodie of Captaine George Fadding alias ffawdin of Warras Quirke aforesaid which were comitted to him as my Attorney in trust for my vse as it will appeare by the testimony of Thomas Taberer and Thomas Northe Planters there Item whereas I received a letter from Thomas Taberer dated the tenth day of May one thousand six hundred fifty and twoe att Warras Quicke signifieing the sending vnto mee out of Virginia eight or tenne hogsheads of Tabaccoe this present sumer as my owne and for my owne proper vse All which goods above menconed being my owne pper goods to witt seaven kine one Oxe one Steeere

---

* Savage, II, 367.
† Austin's Gen. Dict. of Rhode Island, p. 316: Pope, 392.
‡ Hotton's Lists, 182.
§ Niell's Founders of Maryland, p. 137.
‖ Court Records, Lower Norfolk Co., Va.
¶ Certf. Head Rights, by J. H. Lea, op. cit. Reg., XLVII, p. 70.

and the encrease by breed of those seaven kyne from the first of January one thousand six hundred forty nine to the day of my death and vntill such time as satisfaction shall be made for them to my executors And all Debts due before my coming over and eight or tenne hogsheads of Tobaccoe alreadie sent into England or to be sent this sumer And whatsoever things else are my proper Goods Chattles or Cattles either in Virginia England or elsewhere I doe will and bequeathe them and by theis p'sents doe give them and all of them vnto my eldest brother Roches* viccar of Queene Camell aforesaid whome I make my full and whole Executor To which I have sett my hand and seale the twoe and twentieth day of August in the yeare of our Lord God one thousand six hundred fiftie and twoe 1652 (*James Roche*) Signed sealed and delivered in the presence of vs Ed: Gillmore John Marten William Stephens. Proved at London 18 September, 1652, by Robert Roche the brother of deceased and sole executor named in the will. (P. C. C. Bowyer 237.)

Will of JOHN BLY, dated 3 January, 1662-3. I release £4 I was to have at my mother's death. As for the £130 that is in the hands of Master Richard Booth, merchant, I desire that it may be shared according to the order I left in the hands of my brother Giles Bly. I release my brother William of the £20 he owes me. My brother Giles shall pay £3 for a silk rug I received from Richard West, and keep the rest of the money that is in his hands. To my wife the produce of 50 hogshead of tobacco that is to be shipped home for England in the "Frederick," and I desire that care may be taken that there be shipped home for England this present year, if tobacco may be procured, the quantity of 220 hogsheads, of which my third part shall be conveyed to my wife in such goods as she shall desire. Also to my wife all the goods that I brought over in this year to furnish my house, and I desire her father to make satisfaction for the goods I bought for him in England. To Master William Bough, junior, a chest. To my brother George Hunt a chest, and if he desire to return back for England I desire my wife at his return to pay him the quantity of ten hogsheads of tobacco. The produce of certain hogsheads of tobacco to be divided between my mother and my brothers and sisters. Whereas I left in the hands of my father in law Abraham Wood Esq. £26 and certain goods, I desire that they may be returned to my wife. To Master Ceristopher Branch,† senior, one hogshead of tobacco for writing my will. To

* Robert Roche instituted Vicar of East Camel, 16 Feb., 1635. He held the living until 1666. He was of Magd. Coll., Oxford, matriculated 16 March, 1626-7, aged 18, son of Robert Roche, Vicar of Hilton, Dorset, 1617-1629. The father was also of Magdalen.

† Christopher Branch of Kingsland, Henrico Co., Va. (now in Chesterfield Co.), who was brought to Virginia as an infant about 1613. There is no connection between this family and the Peter Branch from Holden, Co. Kent, England, who died at sea on the ship *Castle* on the way to New England. (See his will dated 16 June, 1638, in *N. E. Hist. & Gen. Register*, II, 183.) I have a long pedigree of the Virginia family which I would be pleased to communicate to any worthy descendants. J. H. L.

Christopher Branch, junior, one hogshead of tobacco. Executrix, my wife Mary Bly here in Virginia. Executor in England, my brother Giles Bly. Witnesses: Thomas Branch, John Gardner. Proved 23 March, 1662-3, before the Governor etc. of Virginia. Proved at London 16 May, 1664, by Giles Bly, executor.

(P. C. C. Bruce 46.)

WILL of PHILIP MALLORY lately resident in Virginia and now in London, clerk, dated 23 July, 1661. To be buried at the discretion of Captain John Whitty, one of my executors. To my nephew Mr Roger (*sic*) Mallory and his heirs all my plantations, lands, etc. in Virginia or elsewhere. To Mrs Elizabeth Mallory my mother and to Mr Thomas Mallory my brother £10 each. To my nephew Thomas Hawford £10. Towards the erecting of a college in Virginia £10. Legacies to friends. To my niece Frances Pidgeon ten head of cattle to be delivered to her or her assigns in Virginia. The residue of my estate either in England or Virginia I give to my said nephew Mr Richard (*sic*) Mallory. Executors, the said Roger (*sic*) Mallory and Capt. John Whittie. To my cousin William Mallory £20. Witnesses: Warham Horsmanden, Benjamin Sheppard, scr. Proved 27 July, 1661, by John Whitty one of the executors power being reserved to Roger Mallory. (P. C. C. May 114.)

Not in Waters, who, however, names a Philip Mallory of Virginia as marrying a Catherine Batt (see *Virginia Caroloum, in note infra*).

Rev. Philp Mallory was son of Dr. Thomas Mallory, Archdeacon of Richmond, 1603, and Dean of Chester (1607-1644),[*] and was born about 1617, being matriculated at Corpus Christi College, Oxford, 28 May, 1634, *aged 17 years;* he was B. A. from St. Mary's Hall, 26 April, 1637, and A. M. 16 Jan., 1639-40; Vicar of Norton, Co. Durham, 1641. He married Catherine, daughter of Robert Batt, vice-master of Oxford University. He was in Virginia in 1656, and probably much earlier, in 1657 he was a member of the Assembly, at which he also officiated in 1658-9, and at the religious services when Charles II was proclaimed at Jamestown, 20 Sept., 1660.[†] In March, 1660-1, he was appointed, "having been eminently faithful in the ministry," in company with Sir William Berkeley, the Governor, to solicit in England for the church in Virginia on which mission he evidently died, in spite of the fact that he is said to have been minister at Elizabeth City in 1644 and 1664 as "Mr. Mallory."[§] The first of these dates probably refers to the testator, the second *certainly to some one else*, as the date and probate of his will prove conclusively that he died between July 23d and 27th, 1661, in England, nor could this have been his brother Thomas, as he had then been presented for four years as Prebend of Chester (30 July, 1660),[‖] but it may

---

[*] Le Neve's *Fasti Ecclesiæ*, III, 264, 267.
[†] Neill's *Va. Caroloum*, p. 238.
[‡] *Op. cit.*, p. 283; Tyler's *Cradle of the Republic*, pp. 90-91.
[§] Meade's *Old Churches and Families of Va.*, I., 230-31.
[‖] Le Neve's *Fasti Eccl.*, III, 271.

12

have been his nephew "mr." Roger Mallory, who is called his son in error by Mr. Tyler* and who, later (1668), had grant of land from York County "for the use of Mr. Philip Mallory."† This Roger settled in King and Queen County and had a son William, who may have been the "cousin William Mallory" named in the will.

William Batt, brother of Catherine, the wife of Rev. Philip Mallory, entered land on Mobjack Bay, Gloucester Co., as early as 5 Sept., 1643,‡ and was a member of the Assembly in 1654 from Surrey. John Batt, elder brother of the above, being son and heir of Robert Batt of Okewell in Birstall, by his wife Mary, daughter of Mr. John Parry of Hereford, was Captain of Foot in Regmt. of Aybrigg and Morley and J. P. of the West Riding, Yorkshire; he married Martha, daughter of Thomas Mallory, Dean of Chester, and had John (lost in the Irish Sea, coming from Virginia with his father), William, Thomas and Henry (in Virginia 1667), and Martha.§

Deare wife and wellbeloved, with all our deare and sweet children, I (RICHARD HUNT) waiting daylie for my change and dissolucon am willing to leave with you this my last will and testament, (having) written it with my owne hande in the time of my health, least the omitting of it should trouble me at the howre of death when thoughts of other things wilbe more needful. . . . And touching my bodie, I commit it to the earth whence it came, but if otherwise the Lord hath disposed of me, his holy will bee fullfilled. . . . According to the custom of this honourable Cittie I devyde my estate into three parts, whereof I bequeath one part to my wife Jane, which I hope will amount to £1800 besides her jewells and rings; also I bequeath unto her my great silver bason and ewer with two faire flaggon potts and the lease of my house in Hackney parish. One other third part I bequeath amongst my children, vizt., to my eldest sonne Josia Hunt £800 at 21, to my eldest daughter Sarah Hunt £500 at 21 or marriage, to my daughter Katherine £500 in like manner, to my young son Nathaniel £500 at 21, to my son Richard £500 at 21, and if my wife be with child, to such child £400. To my brother John Hunt £60, and to my brother William Hunt £20, for the use of their children. To my sister Ellen's children, vizt., William Thompson £10, George Thompson £20, Richard Thompson £10, Thomas Thompson, if he returnes from the warres, and setts up trade, £10, and to the other two in the country £5 apeece. To my sisters Jane, Elizabeth and Anne, for their children £40 apiece. To my brother John Watkin 40s., and to my sister 20s. Tobias and Arthur Watkin £5 each. Brother Richard Kent £5. My master Capt. Edward Ditchfield, one of the best friendes that

---

* *Cradle of the Republic*, pp. 90, 91.
† *Ibid.*
‡ Virginia Ld. Records, I, p. 901.
§ Water's *Gleanings*, I, 105, from Harl. MS., 4630, p. 26, and *Richmond Standard*, 4 June, 1881.

ever I had in the world, £10. Mr William Greenhill my deare friend £5. Mr Feake, lecturer of Wolchurch, £3. Ten other ministers, Mr Trebitt and Mr Rawlinson being two, £30. Mrs Mary Gray and Mrs Catherine Midleton 30s. each. Mr Hugan Hovill, Mr Hooper and Mr Wilson 20s. each. Mr Isaac Knight and Mr John Carter £3 each. Mrs Alice Allen 20s., Thomas Stivers the elder 40s., Joseph Mordocke 20s., William Sawyer £3, and Edward Hiller if he serve his time out 40s. Mrs Katherine Exelby £5, Richard Pierson 20s., and Mrs Jane Laney 20s. The Artillerie Company £20. Poor of Mary Wolchurch 20 nobles. Sibill Jones £5. I give the land I adventured for in Ireland, if it be gained, to my eldest son Josias. To my deare wife £1000. To my brother John's children £300 if they be Protestants. To my brother William's child £200 upon the like terms. To Ralph Hunt my brother William's son £50, Item to New England towards a library twentie poundes. Residuary legatee and executrix, my deare wife. Overseers, Capt. Edward Ditchfield, Mr Hugan Howell and Mr Thomas Wood. Dated 22 Aug., 1643. Witnesses: William Medley, John Peace. Proved 30 Jan., 1643-4, by the executrix. (Commissary of London, vol. xxix, fo. 213.)

Will of SAMUEL BELLERS of the parish of St. Botolph without Aldersgate, co. Middlesex, baker, dated 17 January, 1748-9. To Thomas Ibell of the parish of St. Giles Cripplegate, baker, and Thomas Milward of the same, cornchandler, £500 interest in the Joint Stock erected by act of Parliament in the 18th year of his present Majesty, in trust for the benefit of my daughter Martha Scott* wife of John Scott late of the parish of St. Giles Cripplegate, baker, but now in parts beyond the seas, during her life, for her sole and separate use; and after her death, in case she shall then leave only two or one female children or child, the said sum to be applied for their education and maintenance. Son Samuel Bellers. Sister Margaret Coxon, wife of John Coxon of St. Giles Cripplegate, pawnbroker. Kinsmen Benjamin Jennings, William Jennings and Sarah Jennings, children of my kinsman John Jennings of Alcester, co. Warwick, butcher. Residuary legatees and executors, upon trust, the said Thomas Ibell and Thomas Milward. Witnesses: John Paukeman, Fra: Beck, Peter Jopson. (Consistory of London, 1720-51: fol. 209.)

30 September, 1656, I JEREMIAH NOREROSSE (sic), being sicke of an ague Which I thincke tendeth to my death, doe commit my body to the earth to be decently buried with as little cost as may be, and my soule into the hands of my faithfull Creator. And concerning my Estate in New England, vizt., The dwelling house, barnes, cowes, horses and lands and cattell, the will I made there, wch I lefte in the hands of my friend Charles Chaddocke of Newe England, shall stand to a tittle; And conceringe the goods that I have in this land, out of them ffirst I give vnto my sonne Captaine Mazye my gold girdle and to his wife Sarah

---

* A Martha Scott owned ye Covenant and was baptized at Farmington, Conn., 16 March, 1706-7.—*Register*, XXXVIII, 276, 412.

Mazye my scarlett mantle, and to my twoe grandchildren Scarfes (*sic*) and Sarah Mazye each one imbroydered scarlett cushion, and to my twoe grandchildren Jeremie and Marie Norcrosse, borne to my sonne Richard Norcross, to each of them the like. Granddaughter Mary Norcross, daughter to my son Nathaniel, the long cushion; and to my sonne and daughter Nathaniel and his wife each a gould ring. To my beloved wife 20 shillings in gould. Residuary legatee and executor, my sonne Nathaniel in trust for his mother, soe thanking him and his wife for their loving duetye and care of us, soe I comitt her to him and his wife, to have a care of her. Witnesses, John Baxter, Honor Baxter, Margaret Uring. Proved 5 April, 1658, by the executor named. (P. C. C. Wotton, 152.)

Chas. Chadwick of Watertown is certainly intended by this mention (Chaddock being a well known variant of that name). He came probably in Winthrop's fleet. Freeman, May, 1631; Selectman, 1637; Representative, 1657, and died 10 April, 1682, aged 85.*

Nathaniel Norcross, son of the testator and his residuary legatee and executor, returned to England and became parson of St. Dunstan's in the East, London, and died there in August, 1662.†

I MARY CONY of Boston, co. Li..coln, widow, being weake in body. To my reverent and deare brother Mr John Cotton of New England the sum of twentie shillings, and also to my sister Cotton and my sister Makepeace twentie shillings apeece as a small testimonie of my endeared love and affection towards them. To John and Elizabeth Hawcrid, the children of my late brother Samuel Hawcrid, (*sic*) £3 apiece at 21. Mary wife of my son Samuel Cony my best tabby gowne and peticoate. Anne daughter of my son John Cony my best wrought cushion. Elizabeth Hawcridge (*sic*) one paire of redd curtains. Hannah Simpson my servant 40s. Cousin Adlard Pury 20s. Cousin Doctor Tuckney 20s. Mr Naylor and Mr Anderson 20s. each. Residuary legatees and executors, sons Samuel and John Cony. Dated 29 April, 1652. Witnesses: John Cony, Elizabeth Hadocke. Proved 23 May, 1653, by the executors named. (P. C. C. Brent, 88.)

Rev. John Cotton, son of Roland Cotton, Esq., was born in Derby, England, 4 Dec., 1585; grad. Emanual College, Cambridge, and was Vicar of Boston, England, 1626–1633. He came to America in the *Griffin*, arriving 4 Sept., 1633. Installed teacher of the church of Boston, Mass., 17 Oct., 1633. His second wife, Mrs. Elizabeth Story, widow, survived him at his death in 1652, and, four years later, married Mr. Richard Mather of Dorchester. His will, dated 30 Nov., proved 27 Jan. (11 mo.), 1652, mentions his brother Coney, his sister Mary Coney and their son John

---

* Savage, I, 351; III, 286. Bond's *Watertown*, p. 376.

† See his will in P. C. C. (Laud, 129) printed, with valuable note by John Ward Dean, in Waters' Gleanings, II, 1041.

Coney.* His first wife's name was Elizabeth Harcocks of Cambridge, as we learn from the following entry of his marriage:

"1613, Johannes Cotton de Boston cler' in Theolog' Bacalaurius et Elizabetha Harcocks de Cantab singel' nupti Julij 3°.†"

---

* Savage, I, 462; Pope, 119-120.
† From Parish Registers of Balsham, Cambridgeshire. In Pope and other authorities she is called Horrocks.

CLUES FROM ENGLISH ARCHIVES

CONTRIBUTORY TO AMERICAN GENEALOGY.

BY J. HENRY LEA AND J. R. HUTCHINSON.

29 March, 1638, I ROBERT ESTREY of the parish of Eᵈmunton and county of Middlesex, yeoman, being in good health . . . bequeath my body to be buried within the parish church of Edmunton; to the poor of Edmunton 40s. in monie or bread; to my daughter Mary all the moveable goods which were her husband's, mentioned in a certain inventory thereof taken in *anno* 1632, also the great press standing in the chamber over William Chapman's hall; to Prudence Littlepage, daughter of Humphrey Littlepage by my said daughter Mary, £20; to my son Edward Esery (*sic*) and heirs all my freehold land in Edmunton, or in default to my daughter Marie's two children James Littlepage and Robert Littlepage equally. All the rest of my goods I give to my son Edward Estrey, whom I make executor. My daughter Mary shall have her dwelling in my house for one whole year after my decease, and shall enjoy the strawberry garden for two years. Overseer: Humphrey Littlepage my son in law. To Judith Alstone, wife of Penning Alstone, one silver-gilt salt, and to Agnes Williams her sister one gilt beaker. Witnesses: Humphrey Littlepage, William Dible.

11 April, 1639, commission to Humphrey Littlepage, overseer, during the absence and for the use of Edward Estrey, now dwelling in parts beyond the sea. (Commissary of London, Vol. 28, f. 33.)

9 April, 1639, I TIMOTHY CANNON, citizen and draper of London, being very weake and sicke of bodie . . . give and bequeath unto Thomas Johnson my nephew my old furd gowne; to my good friend Mrs Moore one of my black mourning gowns; to my neighbour Nicholas Meeking my black truncke; to my friend Thomas Fosket 10s.; to my cosin Edward Jones my great bible; to my sister Anne, now wife of Richard Nash, my half-head bedstedd, and to her husband my sage-colour suit. All the rest of my goods I give to my son John Cannon who is now at Bermoodas in the parts beyond the seas, provided alwaies that if he be dead, or die before he receive my goods, then I bequeath the same unto my cosin John Cannon to divide the same amongst all his children. Executors, my son John Cannon and my neighbours Thomas Hough and Nicholas Mekins. Witnesses: William Johnson, scr., Daniel Mercer.

Codicil dated 10 April, 1639, bequeathing 20s. to Thomas Hough. Witness: Nicholas Mekin.

Proved 18 April, 1639, by Thomas How and Nicholas Meekins, power being reserved to John Cannon the son. (Commissary of London, Vol. 28, f. 34.)

A John Cannon came in the *Fortune* in 1621, but his name is not found in the division of cattle in 1627. There was a Cannon of Sandwich in 1650, perhaps identical with Robert of New London, 1678.* In the church records of Scituate and Barnstable, 19 April, 1691, occur the baptisms of John, Philip, *Timothy*, Nathan and Elizabeth, children of Joanna Cannon, probably a widow, who had but recently removed there.†

Memorandum that EDWARD MARSHALL of the parish of St. Peter's neere Paulswharfe, London, who died on or about the fifth day of December, 1639 . . . did utter and speake these words following, that is to say "Cosen (hee then speaking unto Anne Cossens, widdow), I pray see mee buried well, and take all my goods that I have and keepe them for the benefit of my sonne Thomas Marshall," who was then and is now beyond seas, "and if hee come not home again, then I give all my goods unto you." Witnesses: John Cosens, Sara wife of Michael Barnett, Anne wife of Isaac Finch.

10 Dec., 1639, commission to Anne Cosens to administer for the use of Thomas Marshall, son of deceased, now dwelling in parts beyond the seas. (Commissary of London, Vol. 28, f. 92.)

Four persons of the name Thomas Marshall appear in New England prior to the date of this will: Thomas, planter, Dorchester, freeman 4 March, 1634–5 (name sometimes spelled Marshfield); Thomas, Boston, admitted to the church there 3 June, 1634; Thomas, shoemaker, Boston, came in the *James* in 1635, aged 22; and Thomas, tailor, Lynn, proprietor, 1638; but there is a good deal of confusion in the accounts of these persons as given by Savage and Pope.

I THOMAS MALTHUS of Enfield, co. Middlesex . . . give my grey gelding to Thomas Cullenben; to my two sisters 40s. apiece; to the poor saints of God £5; for the use of those poore children that are to be conveyghed into New England 40s.; and to my wife all my lands in Edmonton and Enfield, for the term of her life, and afterwards to my daughter Elizabeth and her heirs. Witnesses: John Cornish, Joshua Birling. Proved 12 Oct., 1643, by Joan Malthus, relict and executrix. (Commissary of London, Vol. 29, f. 140.)

22 April, 1639, I WILLIAM THOMPSON, Citizen and Haberdasher of London, being at this present in reasonable health . . . give one third of my personal estate to my wife Joan as her due according to the custom of the City of London, one other third amongst my children Samuel, Peter, John and Mary, equally, for that I have already sufficiently advanced my eldest son Richard sufficiently, and out of the other third part, reserved to myself, I give the following legacies:—Towards the maintenance of a weekly lecture in the parish church of St. Katherine Creechurch. London, 20s. per annum for twentie years; to the poor of Thorpe Market, Norfolk, 6s.8d. yearly for seven years, to be distributed

---

* Savage, I, 332.
† *N. E. Hist. Gen. Register*, X, 347.

by the discretion of my executrix or of my brother John Thompson now dwelling at Colby, Norfolk; to the poor of St. Katherine Creechurch 6s. 8d. a year for 20 years; to my servant Edward Turner and to Margaret Cordwell sometime my servant; to my sister Elizabeth Thompson, wife of my said brother John, 20s., and to my cousin Martha Thompson her daughter 20s.; to Widow Mayle, heretofore wife of John Prowd, joyner, 6s. 8d. per annum for life; to my brother Rowland Thompson 20s. a year for life; to my son Richard Thompson £5 in money in full of his portion, in regard I have already sufficiently advanced him; and to my aforesaid four children Samuel, Peter, John and Mary as residuary legatees of my said third part; provided always that the £200 which my daughter Mary, now wife of Jasper Clayton, hath already received shall be accompted as part of her portion. I doe give and bequeath unto my said four children and their heirs all my lands, interests and adventures in Virginia, St. Christopher's, and any other the parts or islands in the West Indies. To my son Richard Thompson and his heirs all my freehold messuages, lands, etc. in Thorpe Market, Roughton and Gunton, co. Norfolk, charged with certain payments to the preaching ministers of Thorpe Market and Antingham, otherwise St. Margaret's and with the following legacies:—my brother Rowland 20s. a year: my grandchild William Clayton £50; my grandchild Jasper Clayton £30; my other grandchildren Mary, John, Rebecca and Elizabeth Clayton £25 each at age of one and twenty; each of my three sons Samuel, Peter and John £80 at said age. Executrix, my wife Joan, or, if she will not enter into bond for the due administration of my estate, my son Peter Thompson. Overseers: Mr Thomas Free in Mark Lane, Mr George Dunn, and Mr Richard Glover, apothecary. Witnesses: William Frith, John Frith, John Brand, John Bassano, John Hare, servant to said William Frith. Codicil dated 23 Aug., 19 Charles I., devising lands, etc. called Bartletts, purchased since the making of the above will, lying in Goldhanger and Little Tothem, co. Essex, to my grandchild William Thompson, son of my son Richard, and to his heirs, or in default to my grandchild Richard Thompson, brother of said William. Witnesses: Rowland Thompson, Hen: King, scr. Proved 28 Oct., 1643, by Joan Thompson, relict and executrix. (Commissary of London, Vol. 29, f. 149.)

I Sarjant Major JUDE LEIGH, being weake in body, ordaine my last will in manner following, vizt., I give and bequeath all that mansion in Cawdwell, in the parish of Erkinton, co. Darby, now in the occupation of William Leigh, gent, my father, which was conveyed to me and my heirs by my said father in lieu of my redeeming the said estate, it being mortgaged, by deed dated 12 April, 1633, unto my said father for the term of his naturall life, and after his decease to my brother William Leigh, gent, and heirs. I give to my said father and brother my eighth part of the good shipp called the John of London, which cost me £54 by deed under the hand of Henry Catlin of London, merchant, bearing date 15 Oct., 1641. To my said father and brother £200 odd due unto me from William Flesher of Laurance Lane, London, linendraper. And whereas I entrusted Capt. William Elvin as my attorney to receive for me 15000 weight of tobacco due from Thomas Laurance, to whom I sould my plantacon, now my will is that Mr Edward Thompson shall receive thereof 4000 weight in lieu of so much due to him, and that the remainder be equally divided between my said father and brother. I give all that my parcel of tobacco, amounting to 17,600 weight, due to me from George Sterill by order of Court, which order was left in the hands of Capt. Jeremiah Hartley, unto my said father and brother; also the benefit of the 2000 weight of tobacco in the hands of John Coughland of Penny come quicke in Cornwall, which was sold by him to Mr Stoone of Plymouth. Executor: my brother William Leigh. Overseers: my friends and kinsmen George Sitwell, Esq. and Lieut. John Ivie. Dated 13 Nov., 1643. Witnesses: Hen: Buckle, Judith Francklyn, John Ivie. Codicil of same date: To Capt. William Emerson £3 in lieu of his charges in going down to my Lord General's army about my warrant. To Lieut. John Ivie £4 for procuring the said warrant. Further to the said Lieut. Ince (*sic*) £10 with my new plush jumpe and my rapier and dagger. To Capt. Francis FitzHughes my gorgett. To Mrs Francklyn for her care of me in my sickness £20. To my father my watch and seal. Proved 20 Dec., 1643, by the executor named. (Commissary of London, Vol. 29, f. 186.)

The testator was evidently a cadet of the family of Leigh of Eggington in Derbyshire, whose pedigree is recorded in the Visitations of 1569 and 1611,* but unfortunately omitted from that of 1663–4,† which would probably have enabled us to place the testator with certainty.

I MARY SCRIVEN of the parish of St. Sepulchre's without Newgate, London, widow, being somewhat visited in body . . . commit my body to be buried soe neere my late husband as may bee . . . and give unto the poor of the said parish £5; to my daughter in law Elizabeth Scriven £20; to Elizabeth Hughes £5; to Mary Hughes my god-daughter £5; to Nicholas Cleggett and his wife 20s. each; to Mr. Burton and Mr. Robinson, sons in law of said Cleggett, and to their wives, 20s. each; to John Leadall and Rose his wife 20s. apiece; to Robert Austin 20s.; to my god-daughter Katherine Hollis 40s.; to my god-daughter Mary Frier 40s.; to my god-daughter Ellen Clarke 10s.; to my god-daughter Mary Danson 10s.; to my god-daughter Mary Heaven 20s.; to Mary Hawkeswell and Ellen Haifeild, sisters of my late deceased husband, 20s. apiece; to my cousin Robert Browne, carrier, 20s.; to George Priest and Alice his wife 20s. apiece; to Mary, wife of Thomas Hudson, 20s.; to Jane wife of Rice Hughes 20s.; to my cousin James Armitage and Katherine his daughter 20s. apiece; to Mary, wife of said Robert Browne, my white cloth gowne; to my cousin Anne Hayfield my serge gown; to Ellen, wife of said Robert Austin, my red cloth petticoat; and to Judith

---

* *Genealogist, N. S.*, VII, 231.
† Sir Thomas Phillipps' edition, 1854.

Hopkins my servant my red stuff petticoat. I forgive Richard Stanton the debt he owes me. I give to Edward Birkett sometime my servant 20s.; to Jane, wife of Robert Carrington, my silver tankard; to Margaret, wife of (*blank*) Nurse, smith, my little silver cupp. I give and bequeath unto my brother John Ayres if he shall bee living at the time of my decease, or doe in his own person demand the same, the sum of twentie pounds to be paid unto him upon such his demand. Cousin John Hayfield my seal ring and my bible and all the meal, etc. belonging to the trade of a baker which shall be in my dwelling house in Fleet Lane. Residuary legatees, Thomas Hudson and my cousin John Hayfield, whom executors. Dated 20 Dec., 1643. Witnesses: John Lawrence, Judith Hopkins, Nath: Hudson, son of Antho: Hudson, scr. Proved 28 Dec., 1643, by the executors named. (Commissary of London, Vol. 29, f. 188.)

John Ayers was of Salisbury, Mass., 1640. He had wife Hannah, and children John, Nathaniel, Hannah (married 1663, Stephen Webster), Rebecca, Mary, Obadiah, Robert, Thomas and Peter, and died 31 March, 1657. Compare will of James Eayres, below.

I WILLIAM HOLLIS of Fleetlane, in the parish of St. Sepulchre's Citizen and Cutler of London, being very sick and weake . . . give my body to be buried in the churchyard of the aforesaid parish . . . and such worldly wealth as it hath pleased God to bless me with as followeth. Inprimis I give and bequeath unto my son Richard Hollis, who about two years since went beyond the seas, if hee bee living, tenne shillings of lawfull English money; to my friend Robert Austin of Fleetlane, pewterer, 20s.; to my brother Robert Hollis of Gothurst, co. Bucks, cook to the Lady Digby there, my gold ring which I daylie weare on my finger, having thereon a W and an H; to my godson Edward Clark, son of Richard Clark of Seacole lane, merchant taylor, 2s. 6d.; to said Richard Clarke and his wife 12d. each, and to their daughter Ellen Clark 6d.; and to my daughter Katherine Hollis £30 at 18. Residuary legatee and executrix, my wife Mary. Dated 30 May, 1642. Witnesses: Richard Clark, Richard Wallis, Robert Austin, Silvanus French, scr. Proved 8 Jan., 1643-4, by the executrix. (Commissary of London, Vol. 29, f. 198).

See collection of Hollis wills, and others related to this family, in Water's Gleanings, (*N. E. Reg.*, vol. XLV, p. 51, etc.), having direct reference to the well known benefactors of Harvard College. It is probable that the testator was also a member of this family.

I HENRY TIMBERLAKE of Chilling in the parish of Tichfield, co. Southampton, gent, being sickley in body and lame in my limmes, this 10th day of July, 1625, make this my last will and testament. Poor of Tichfield £3. To Thomas Timberlake my eldest son and his heirs all such lands and tenements and shares or parts of land as I am now seised of in the Somer Islands or Virginia in the parts beyond the seas, and one parcel of land called Hobbs or Madam Land, lying in Barking, co. Essex. To Henry Timberlake my youngest son and his heirs one cottage and parcel of land called Mount Marsh lying in Pricklewell, co. Essex, and two cottages in Lambehith Marsh near London. And as touching my goods and chattels, personal estate and adventures beyond the seas, whereas I am indebted in divers great sums of money for most of which my friend Arthur Bromfield Esq. standeth bound, and whereas Sir William Cope of Hauwell, co. Oxon, Knight and Bart., is indebted to me in £3,947, for the securing of which he did convey unto me certain lands in the said county and in Essex, and whereas in respect of some defect in the title of said lands I have obtained a Decree in Chancery for receiving the said debt out of rents due unto the said Sir William out of Custom House Key, London,—now my will is that out of the same my debts shall be paid and Arthur Bromfield be discharged of his undertaking, and that Sir William be reassured of the said lands. I give unto Sarah my daughter, now wife of Timothy Blyer of Tichfield, clerk, £200; to my daughter Hester, now wife of Thomas Williams, for the better maintenance of her and of Thomas and Judith Michell, two of her children now living with her, £30 yearly out of my leasehold tenements in London; to the said Judith Michell £120, to John Michell her brother, my grand-child, £120, and to Thomas and William Michell her brothers £20 apiece in addition to the £50 each given unto them by the will of my said daughter Hester's former husband,—all these legacies to my said grandchildren to be paid at their respective ages of one and twenty years. To Benjamin Burrowes and Katherine his wife, my sister, £10 yearly soe long as they shall live together. To Rebecca, daughter of my said sister and now wife of Ralph Radford, £10. To Henry Burrowes, son of my said sister, £20, and to Michael Burrowes her son, if he be now living, £10. Legacies to Samuel Breach, Agnes Ratcliffe, Rich-ard Falder, Margaret Dodde, Arthur Bromfield my godson, Wil-liam Dartnall my godson, Timothy Blyer the younger, my apprentice, the Company of Browne Bakers whereof I am a mem-ber, Margaret Copland my servant, Henry Copland her brother, Henry Laundy my godson, Mary, wife of Arthur Bromfield, Eliz-abeth his daughter, William Beeston, gent. and my kinsman Jas-per Dartnall and wife. To Dorothy Pescod, a poore innocent that I keepe, £5, and my executors shall provide some fitt place for her, that she may neither wander nor begge. Old servant Joan Riever a cowe. Kinsmen John Carter and Richard Walker £5 each. Residue of all goods and of my adventures beyond the seas to Margaret my wife. Executors: my wife and William Styant of the Inner Temple, gent. Overseers: Arthur Bromfield, Esq. and William Beeston, gent, Witnesses: Arthur Bromfield, Anthony Erfield, Tho: Greenhill, William Styant. 30 January, 1643–4, commission to Sarah Bellecre *alias* Timberlake, daughter of deceased, to administer, the executors being dead. (Commis-sary of London, Vol. 29, f. 211).

Henry Timberlake of Newport R. I., was Corporal there 1644. By his wife Mary he had William, Henry, Joseph and John. He died before 1680, and his widow 10 Sept., 1705. It may be that he was the youngest son Henry, named in the will, the connection shown with the Bromfield family indicating a connection with New England rather than with Virginia.

20 Dec., 1641, I Rowland Thomson of London, esquier, being in good and perfect health . . . give and bequeath unto my worthy friends John Collinson, skinner, and Alexander Pollinton, haberdasher, citizens of London, £5 apiece. The rest and residue of my goods, chattles, shares of land, plantacons and estate, as well on this side as in any other parts or places beyond the seas, I give to my only son Edward Thomson and his heirs. Executors in trust, John Collinson and Alexander Pollinton, until my said son attain his age of 23 years. Witnesses: Chr: Townsend, scr., John Alsope his servant. Proved 2 Feb., 1643-4, by the executors named. (Commissary of London, Vol. 29, f. 217.)

I Alice Dobson of London, widow, late wife of William Dobson late of St. Albones, co. Hertford, Esq., deceased, being sicke in body . . . give and bequeath unto my son John Dobson the sum of ten pounds to be paid unto him within three months after he shall return from beyond the seas into England, if he shall live to return; to my son Edward 20s.; to my daughter Katherine Lile £5, and to Katherine Lile her daughter a pair of sheets; to Ellen my daughter my silk grogram gown; to my daughter Frances my scarlet petticoat and the sugered sateen gown that was my mother's; to Marie my daughter, for seven years after my decease, my messuage wherein I lately dwelt, lying in the town of St. Albones, and then to William my son and his heirs; to my daughter in law Jane my best tapestrie coverlett and four needlework cushions which were her mother's; to Benjamin my son £60; to Abraham my son £50 and my silver tankard with cover and the letters A.D. upon it; to my daughter Hammond a cubbard cloth; to Elizabeth my daughter in law a carpet; to my daughter Mary Burchinshawe six silver spoons and my watch; and whereas Catherine Baron my mother did by her last will bequeath unto me and others the lease of certain houses in Honie Lane, London, holden of the Company of Drapers, and did bequeath the residue of her estate to her executors and me equally, now I do hereby give unto my said daughter Mary Burchinshawe all the said residue of my mother's and my own estate. Executrix, said Marie Burchinshaw. Overseers: friends John Ellis of St. Albanes, gent, and my godson John Ellis of London, draper, his son. Dated 6 Dec., 1943. Witnesses: John Ellis, Steph: Massey, John Chapman, Hester Meadeaw. Proved 5 Feb., 1643-4, by the executors named. (Commissary of London, Vol. 29, f. 219.)

I Phillip Kekewich of London, marchant, being sick and weak in body . . . give unto my brother Peter Kekewich all my estate in the ship Unicorn of Flushin, Capt. Peter Marcus commander, together with the produce of my goods aboard the Flowerdeluz of London, Barnaby Stanfast master, what money shall be remitted by Edward Zalmonds, marchant at the Madera, and all my lands which I have in Cornwall. To the parish of Mihimot in Cornwall £20. John Ballowe junior £5. And as concerning my debts in Virginia, left in the hands of John Webb, merchant, I give the same to my said brother, except 5000 lb. of tobacco which I give to my countryman John Webb. John Mercer, chyrurgeon of the ship Flowerdeluz, £10. Augustine, Alexander and Abraham Smith, master's mates of the said ship, the 400 lb. of tobacco due me from John Ballowe, junior. My boy George Parish. Thomas Towers, boatswain of said ship. Residuary legatee and executor, brother Peter Kekewich. Dated in Virginia 4 April, 1644. Witnesses: John Ballowe, junior, John Webb, Abraham Smith, John Mercer. Proved 8 July, 1644, by the executor named. (Commissary of London, Vol. 29, f. 310.)

The last will and testament of Mr. JAMES EAYRES: All my tools belonging to a carpenter I give to my friend Edward Clements, and my clothes to my friend Margaret Clemence. My wages shall be paid to my brother William Eayres living in Farnum, or, if he be deceased, to his son Thomas. My debts due from the companie of the shipp America I give to my friend Margaret Clemence. For 50s. which Robert Ballard owes me I will that he pays only 30s. My shoes to Francis Vernam. £7 which my brother John Eayres owes me shall be paid to Margaret Clemence, as also £3 which William Terrill, ropemaker, in Redriffe, owes me. Debts owing by James Johnson, John Davis, John Brewin, Richard Smith and Lewis Davis to be abated. My calking tolls. What my master Mr William Hadock has had of me is to be paid to Margaret Clemence, together with the 500 weight of tobacco he owes me. My pistols and sword to Daniel Morgan, whom I put in trust to see my will performed. Dated 28 June, 1644. Signed, *James Eyres.* Witnesses: Daniel Morgan, Francis Vernam, Thomas Banforde. 30 July, 1644, commission to Margaret Clemence, principal legatee, to administer. (Commissary of London, Vol. 29, f. 319.)

A James Ayers was of Dover, N. H., 1658. Compare will of Mary Scriven, above.

Memorandum that the 24th day of May, 1644, I JESPER STANES of Epping, co. Essex, tallow chandler, being sick and weak in body . . . give and bequeath my house and cottage in Epping, where I now dwell, after my now wife's decease, unto my son John Stanes, if he be then living . . . upon this condition, that he the said John doe come in to inherit within seven years after my wife's decease, but if he doe not come home from beyond sea, or happen to die before the said seven years be expired, then I will the said house unto the children of my sister, wife of John Lucke the elder, that is to say, unto Raphe and Elizabeth Lucke and their heirs. Residuary legatee and executrix, my wife Grace. Witnesses: Nicholas Archer, senior, William Bamett, Nich: Archer, junior. Proved 1 Aug., 1644, by the executrix. (Commissary of London, Vol. 29, f. 319.)

8 March, 1639–40, I JOHN BROTHERTON of the parish of St. Gabriel Fanchurch, Citizen and Skinner of London, being sick . . . will my body to be buried in the churchyard of the said parish . . . and doe give to my cozen Thomas Jackson, my

cozen Joan Jackson his sister, my cozen Margaret Morlace, and my cozen John Sutton resident in Virginia 12d. apiece. Residuary legatee and executrix, my wife Margerie. Witnesses: John Woolston, scr., William Warren, Thomas Williams. Proved 11 Dec,, 1644, by the executrix. (Commissary of London, Vol. 29, f. 382.)

13 Dec., 1643, I SARAH COOKESON of St. Sepulchre's without Newgate, London, widow, being sick . . . commit my body to the earth, to be buried in the parish church of St. Sepulchre's . . . (*and*) give to the poor of said parish £3 in bread; to my three loving friends Richard Reeve, John Wilcocks and James Mason and their wives Margaret Reeve, Rebecca Wilcocks and Dorothy Mason, 20s. each; to my god-daughters Sarah Reeve 20s. and Sarah Mason a small silver trencher salt; to Philip Wingfield and his wife 20s. each, and to their three children each a silver spoon; to my brother James Mason's three children each a silver spoon; to my sister Alice Chappell, widow, 20s.; to my sister Ballard 10s.; to my niece Elizabeth Oakley 20s.; to my nephew Stephen Chappell, brother to my said niece Elizabeth, 20s.; to my nephew and godson John Chappell, brother to said Steven, 40s.; to Amy Hodgson 40s.; to my son James Cookeson my bigger death's-head which hath my brother Wingfield's name on it, and my lesser death's-head to my daughter in law Susanna Cookeson: and all the rest of my goods to my aforesaid friends Richard Reeve, John Wilcocks and James Mason in trust, and them I ordain executors. And whereas I have surrendered two customary tenements holden of the Manor of Acton to the use of my said executors, and have likewise surrendered a messuage and land holden of the Manors of Edgware and Kingsbury to the use of the same, Now I do give and bequeath the said messuages in Acton to my son James Cookeson and the heirs of his body, or in default to my nephew and godson John Chappell, he or they paying thereout the following legacies: to my nephew Francis Chappell £100; to my niece Ellen Thornton and her two children £20 each; to my sister in law Margaret Chappell £5; to my my brother John Chappell £10; to my nephew Francis Chappell's three childen £5 each; to my brother Thomas Chappell's daughter £10; to Richard Cookeson now living in Virginia £50; to Frizell Cookeson, sister to said Richard, £20, to be paid unto Stephen Chappell, clerk, son to my late brother Steven Chappell, deceased; and to John Wilcocks, son to my brother John Wilcocks, £10. And as to the messuage and lands in Edgware and Kingsbury, I give one moiety thereof unto Sarah Mason, one of the daughters of my brother James Mason, and to her heirs, or in default to Grace Mason, Dorothy Mason and Anne Mason, other daughters of my said brother; and of the other moiety I give the rents to the use of Elizabeth Wingfield, now wife of Philip Wingfield, for the term of her life, and after her decease the said moiety shall be and remain unto my goddaughter Sarah Wingfield and her heirs. Witnesses: Roger Reeve, Thomas Greene, William Hodgson, William Piers. 4 February, 1644-5, commission to James Cookeson, son of deceased, to administer,

the executors having renounced. (Commissary of London, Vol. 30, f. 12.)

10 November, 1644, I MARY KNIGHT of Wapping, co. Middlesex, widow, being sick . . . give and bequeath unto my mother in law Sarah Knight, now resident in New England (in case she be living), twenty pounds; to my brother Robert Knight now resident in Holland £20 and all my late husband's wearing apparel, his sea clothes only excepted, and if my said brother die before the proving of my will, the said £20 shall be divided amongst his children then living; to my brother Philip Knight £5 and all my husband's sea clothes and instruments; to my brother William Bradbank £10; to my brother Henry Harris £10 at 21; to my father in law William Harris £5 he oweth me; to my sister Anne Wilson £10 by 20s. per year; to the putting forth of my kinswoman Anne Chamberley to be apprentice £15; to the poor of Gravesend 40s. and to the poor of Wapping £3; to Katherine Townsend 20s.; to Goodwife Scamity and Goodwife Cock 10s. each; to Goodwife Armstrong and her mother 15s.; to Anne wife of John Babb 5s.; to my friend Francis Caly, scrivener, 20s.; to John Waterton, shipwright, a piece of black silk to make him a dublet, and to his wife my best scarlet peticoat with galoone lace; to Samuel · Waterton his son 20s.; to Richard Elstone his son in law 20s.; to Jonathan Meridith £5, and to his wife linen; to my sister Anne Bradbank all the rest of my goods, and her I make executrix. Overseers: John Waterton, Francis Calley and Jonathan Meredith. To William Chamberley my kinsman £5 when he come out of his time or be married. Witnesses: Henry Ward, Robert Mutton. Proved 5 Feb., 1644–5, by the executrix. (Commissary of London, Vol. 30, f. 15.)

In this most valuable will we are enabled to locate three of the name in New England, all evidently brothers, of whom the deceased husband of the testatrix, who seems to have been Alexander, was of Ipswich, Mass., in 1635, and had been an innkeeper at Chelmsford, Essex, in Old England, before his emigration.* That he was also a mariner is clearly indicated by the mention of his sea clothes and instruments—a fact that also accounts for the absence of his name from the shipping list in which those of his wife Sarah, aged 50, the testatrix, and daughter (or sister) Dorothy, aged 30, appear.†

Philip, the next brother, who had under the will the sea clothes and instruments above mentioned, was of Charlestown, Mass., in 1637. He was there a cooper, and by wife Margery had five children who, at his death in 1665, were of ages varying from eleven to twenty-six years.

Robert, who was in Holland at the time of the making of the will, was perhaps that Robert, formerly of Bristol, England, merchant, who was appointed attorney for Abraham Shurt of Pemaquid in 1647, and who married, about 1651, Anne, widow of

---

* Vincent's *Hist. of the Pequoit War.*
† Savage, III, 35.

Thomas Cromwell, a wealthy privateersman, rather than that Robert of Marblehead, carpenter, who came in the *Bevis* in 1638.*

Will Nuncupative of THOMAS MATHEWES of Merchants hope in Virginia, chirurgion, who deceased in Wapping at Mr Baker (the chirurgion's) house on the 16th day of June, 1645, (*and*) who before his death, in presence of Alexander Eaton of Wapping, apothecary, and Rebecca Pope of the same, widow, declared these words following:—I owe (*certain sums*) unto Mr Sadler, Mr Coyny,† Mr Abraham Redman, and my brother Knowles for a small birding piece. I have in my cheste a pair of muske codds of Mr Dickeson; Mr West sent them him. I have now in London 35 hogsheads of tobacco in Capt. Andrewes his warehouse, whereof I give one to Mrs Converse and three to my sister Redman. Mr Wilson oweth me £22–14–0, which I paid for him to Mr Menefree‡ in Virginia. Two empty cases I owe to one John Carey of Ratcliffe. I give to Mr William Baker's daughter for their love to me £15. Let John Cole have again the bill he turned over to me. I desire that my will I made in Virginia may stand. To Mr Pidgeon 10s. To the minister, Mr Jones, £5. Witnesses: Alexander Eaton, Rebecca Pope, William Baker, Anne Baker. 3 July, 1645, commission to Thomas Wilson, creditor, to administer, no executor being named. (Commmissary of London, Vol. 30, f. 50.)

3 July, 1645, I KATHERINE MORLEY of Stanmore Magna, co. Middlesex, widow, being somewhat weak in body . . . give to the poor of Stanmore 40s.; to my daughter Mrs Anne Gate a portugal piece, value three or four pounds; to my youngest son James Morley and heirs my messuage and land at Lucas-end in Cheshunt Leyes, co. Hartford, in as full and ample manner as they were to me surrendered long since by my son in law Thomas Gate of the Inner Temple, London, Esq., provided always that he the said James Morley do pay or cause to be paid unto my eldest son John Morley, now living in New England, three fourth parts of the real rent thereof from time to time, being lawfully demanded, during the natural life of my said son John Morley, and if the said James shall make default of such payment, then the said premises shall be to the use of the said John Morley, his heirs and assigns for ever, he or they paying unto the said James a like fourth part in like manner. I further will and bequeath unto my said son John Morley a Bible, desiring God to give him grace to make good use thereof, As also the sum of £10 in money, besides a nest of drawers with old lynen and other necessaries for household stuff (*sic*), which I past over to him in my life time. To my grandchild Judith Gate a cupboard cloth, and to her sister Katherine Gate a

---

* Savage, III, 38, 39; Pope, 273–4.

† Cf. will of Mary Cony of Boston, co. Linc., widow (P. C. C. Brent 88) in RECORD, July, 1909, Vol. XL, p. 184.

‡ *i. e.:* George Menefie, merchant, of James City, Va., came July, 1623, in the *Samuel;* was Councillor under Gov. Berkeley, 1642. He was the first to introduce the cultivation of the Peach into America (Neill's *Virginia Caroloum*).

cushion cloth, both of mine own making, desiring them to accept of them as the widow's mite. To my grandchild (*blank*) Morley, resident at Norremberg, son of my late son Thomas Morley deceased, £5. Residuary legatee and executor, my son James, willing him to remember the servants in the house of my brother Mr Thomas Burnell for their pains in this my long and heavy visitation. Overseers: my said brother Mr Thomas Burnell, desiring him to be ayding and assisting to my son James, as also to my poor son John Morley now in New England. Witnesses: Thomas Burnell, Hester Burnell, Mary Thomas. Proved 6 August, 1645, by the executor named. (Commissary of London, Vol. 30, f. 58.)

Katherine Morley, the testatrix, was widow of Thomas Morley of London, merchant, and daughter of John Burnell of London, merchant, by his wife Anne, daughter of William Seabright of London, town clerk. See the pedigrees of both families in the Visitation of London, 1634,* which indicate clearly the relationships shown in the will. Arms of Morley: *Sable, a leopard's head argent, jessant de lys gules, charged with three mullets.* Crest: *A talbot at gaze.*†

John Morley of Braintree, Mass., freeman, May, 1645, removed 1658 to Charlestown, where he was received into the church 6 August. He died there 24 Jan., 1661, and his widow, Constant Starr, in 1669. His will gives her all his estate in New England, and lands in Cheshunt, Hertfordshire, Old England, with remainder to her sister Anne Farmer.‡ In this will he refers to the will of his mother Katherine Morley, now first discovered. He was a legatee in the will of his uncle Thomas Burnall, citizen and clothworker of London, his mothers brother, 19, Aug., 1661, although then deceased.

Will of THOMAS HART of the parish of Stepney, co. Middlesex, gent, dated 3 Sept., 1661. Being weake in body. To Mr Richard Darnell who married my daughter (*blank*) the sum of fourscore pounds, being the remainder of £100 promised to him in marriage. My executors shall give my daughter Susan lodging and dyet during her life, and she shall have the benefit of the doors of the bowling greens as formerly. To my daughter Jane, wife of John Clopton (now beyond seas) my executors shall give her lodging and dyet until it pleaseth God to send her husband home. To the said John Clopton £5. Daughter Elizabeth Stevens, widow, £5. My two sons Henry Hart and Thomas§ Hart 20s. each to make them rings. Executors and residuary legatees, my son in law Mr Thomas White and Mary his wife. Witnesses: Humphrey Brooke, Andrew Middleton, Nath: Johnson, John Burnford. Proved 15 Jan., 1662–3, by the executors named. (Commissary of London, Vol. 31, f. 197.)

---

* Harl. Soc., XV, 123, and XVII, 111.
† *Ibid.*, XVII, 111.
‡ Savage, III, 233; Pope, 319.
§ Not in Waters, but see his later will of a Thomas Hart, perhaps the son Thomas above named (*Gleanings*, II, 914).

CLUES FROM ENGLISH ARCHIVES
Contributory to American Genealogy.

By J. Henry Lea and J. R. Hutchinson.

I Peeter Hooker of London Tallow Chandler the sixth day of August, 1636, intending a voyage to Verginia in the good shipp called the Globb of London . . . doe declare my last will and testament in manner and forme followinge. . . . My body I comit to the sea or land as God shall dispose of it. I give to the poore of Chilcombe parish in the county of South (*ampton*) twentie shillings. I give out of my Adventure to my Aunt Stroud three pounds; to my vncle Eger's children twentie shillings apeece; to my cusen Anne Hooker my vnckle Richard's daughter three pounds; to her brother Richard fortie shillings; to Henry Hooker my vnckle Peeter's sonne fortie shillings at his age of one and twentie; to his brother Nicholas Hooker the like sume; to Sibell Hooker my vnckle Peeter's daughter twentie shillings; to Richard Wood his children Hannah, John and Samuell twentie shillings apeece; if my aunt Stroud die before her legacy be due, then it shall be paid to her sonne and his children. I give to my brother John Hooker all my goods that I left in his hands and thirtie pounds; but if he die before the legacy be paid, I will it goe to his sonne John Hooker. I doe ordeine my beloved brother Edward Hooker my sole executor, vnto whom I doe bequeath all the rest of my estate, and I doe entreate my vnckle Edward Hooker and my cusen John Wood to be my Overseers, to whom tenne shillings apeece to buy a paire of gloves. Witnesses: Edward Hooker, Richard Potter, George Stretton. Proved 22 Nov., 1639, by the executor named (as will of Peter Hooker, deceased abroad, unmarried).‡ (P. C. C. Harvey, 187.)

21 March, 1608-9, I John Whale, nowe of the parishe of St. Mary the Virgin at the Walles of the towne of Colchester in the Countie of Essex, yeoman, beinge somewhat acrased (*sic*) in body . . . doe yeeld my body to be buryed in the chauncell of the

---

‡ Probate Act Book.

parishe church out of which parishe it shall please God to call me to his mercy. I give and bequeath vnto my sister Johan Biscoe £40; to the nowe wife of Philemon Whale my brother £20; to Jonas Whale, son of the said Philemon, £200; to Henry Whale, sonne of my said brother,£200; to Philemon Whale, one other of the sonnes of my said brother, £66-13-4 at his age of one and twentie or marriage; to Mary Whale, daughter of my said brother, 100 marks at 19 or marriage; to Elizabeth Whale, another of the daughters of my said brother, 100 marks at 19 or marriage; to (*blank*) Ingram, firstborne childe to Sarah Ingram my neece, £10 at 19 or marriage; to Mr. Thomas Waldgrave of Elmeswell 10s.; to Mr John Waldgrave of Bures St. Mary in Sufflolk 10s.; to Mr. Daniel Syday the Elder of Bures 10s.; to Mr. Thomas Higham's wife the elder, now or late of Withermonford, 10s.; to Anthony Colman of Wandringfeild 10s.; to Mr. Edward Shelton of Bures St. Mary 10s.; to Anne Chitter *alias* Potter of Bures 20s.; and to Elizabeth her daughter 20s. at 19 or marriage; to William Fisher the younger of Bures 20s. at 19; to Joan Priestman of Colchester, widow, 20s.; to William Grome (of which child Joan Priestman is grandmother) 20s. at 19; to Robert Wildes of Sudbury in Sufflolk 20s.; to John Tue my godchild 10s.; to Francis Johnson of Bures my godchild 10s.; to my fellow servants vnto Sir William Waldgrave 40s. wherewith to make a breakfast after my funeral; to Rachel Wade, Barbara Mytch, and Harry Lewcock, servants to my sister Joan Biscoe; to the poor of the parish wherein I dye £4; to the poor of Colchester 10s. each parish; to the inhabitants of the Alms Houses in Balcon Lane in St. Peter's 20s.; poor prisoners in the Castle 20s.; to Lawrence Leede 5s.; to Mrs. Elizabeth Waldgrave, daughter to Mr. Thomas Waldgrave, 10s.; to Sir William Waldgrave my master £100 of the money he owes me; to Sir William Waldgrave the younger 40s.; to Lady Waldgrave, wife of Sir William the younger, 40s.; to Lady Cooke, my master's daughter, 40s.; to Sir Edward Cooke, son of Lady Cooke, 20s.; to my Lady Beckingham, my master's daughter, 40s.; to Mrs. Anne Waldgrave my master's daughter, 40s.; to Mr. Henry, Mr Thomas and Mr Francis Waldgrave, my master's sons, 40s. each; and to Mrs. Avice, Mr. Stephen and Sir Thomas Beckingham. Executors, Mr. Robert Wade, Alderman of Colchester, my brother Philemon Whale and William Hudson of Stoke juxta, Nayland. Supervisor: William Fissher of Bures St. Mary. If my sister Joan die, her portion shall go to James Biscoe her husband. Legacies to Richard Mason, Mathew Browne the elder, Francis George, John Broman, Jonas Whale, Harry Whale, James Cadman, William Peper, Goodman Briscoe and Goodman Dickson. Witnesses: James Cadman, John Dyxon, William Pepper, Richard Mason. Proved 4 May, 1609, by the executors named. (P. C. C. Dorset, 39.)

Philemon Whale, weaver, of Sudbury, Mass.,1643, and Freeman there in 1648,* has been supposed to be connected with

---

* Pope p. 488.

Theophilus Whale of Kingstown, R. I., who came there with wife Elizabeth and children about 1676.* Both may have been connected with the well known General Edward Whalley of Shadwill in Essex,† the Regicide, who, with his son-in-law, Col. William Goffe, fled from England on the Restoration and finally took refuge in New Haven where he died.‡

Decimo quinto die Junij Annoque Dni 1636 Memorandum that I JOHN BEHEATHLAND beinge about to goe to my Mother at Virginia and beinge not well assured of my returne and havinge some small meanes cominge to me from my grandfather Mr. Richard Beheathland deceased doe by these p'sents acknowledge to give and leave all and eu'y such meanes that shall and is to accrewe or growe hereafter to me if I neu' returne vnto Charles Beheathland my kinsman for the naturall loue and affection that I beare to him beinge my gardian And for the true p'formance hereof I the aforesaid John Beheathland have hereunto put my hand Yeoven the day and yeare first above written in presents of Pollider Pen Samuell Eslake Thomas Voyley. 22 Oct., 1639, commission to Charles Beheathland kinsman and sole legatee of John Beheathland late of St. Endillion, Cornwall, but deceased abroad unmarried, no executor being named in the will.§ (P. C. C. Harvey 157.)

24 July, 1608, I SYMON YOUNGES of the parishe of Ringwood, in the countie of Southamton, yeoman, being sicke . . . doe bequeath my body to be buryed in the churchyarde of Ringwood, and give to the poore there 10s., to my parishe church 2s., to the two bridges 2s., to my wief one fetherbedd and other household stuffe, and to my sonne John one cow that I bought of Burton. I will that my copyhold called Viers, now in the hands of John Hinde, minister, in the right of his wife, and of Thomas Fuller, be vnto my sonnes Christopher and Richard, but if Christopher will give vnto Richard £30, then it shalbe vnto Christopher whole; if not, then it shalbe wholie vnto Richard. I give vnto my daughter Joan Batt's children, Elizabeth £13, Anne £10, and Dorothy £6-13-4. The stuffe in my house at Kingstone shalbe wholie to my son Christopher. To my son in lawe John Batt all my household stuffe nowe in his dwelling house at Longmore; also £6 out of my living at Burlie. Moneys due to me from Mr. Felix Hunt, John Wiseman, Henry Dymott, Richard Belbin, Laskue of Lungton, Christopher Saunders, Edmund Neate, John Norden, Mr. Robert Willowbie, John Reade of Kingstone, Mr. John Weekes of Harbridge, William King of Burley, and John Hurst. Residuary legatees, my son in lawe John Batt and my

---

* Savage, IV, 493, 494.

† Shadwill and Colchester are both in Essex but some 50 miles from one another.

‡ See his pedigree in Visit. Notts in Harl. Soc. IV, 117-118. See also note by John Ward Dean in Water's Gleanings, I, 495.

§ Location from Probate Act Book.

sonne Christopher, whom executors. Overseers: William Becon-
sawe, Esq., Edward Willmott, gent, and Martin Saunders, yeoman. Witnesses: William Jenkins, Roger Allee, Hugh Hinton,
Robert Bound. Proved 7 July, 1609, by the executors named. (P.
C. C. Dorset 69.)

The names in this will are very suggestive to students of
Long Island genealogy. The founder of the family of Youngs of
of Southold was Rev. Christopher, whose sons Rev. John and
Christopher came to America. Joan is also a family name in this
family. It should be noted that Symon Yonges owned a "living
at Burlie," meaning no doubt an ecclesiastical "living." If connection between the testator and the Youngs of Southold family
can be shown, this fact may be of great interest because of Rev.
Christopher's vocation.

There was a John Bats in 1681 at Huntington, L. I.; William
King an early settler of Salem and Southold; and Weekes is also
a familiar Long Island name. While no connection with the
testator can be established from this will without more light, it
undoubtely suggests a further examination of records in County
Southampton for the long-desired Youngs and King ancestry.
(F. E. YOUNGS.)

Will of THOMAS FEERING of Cambridge in the County of Cambridge, barber, dated 1 June, 1652. To be buried in St. Michael's
churchyard in Cambridge, neere the place where my children
were buried. Executrix: my wife Alice Feering. To my son
Thomas four score pounds at 21. To my son John the like sum
at said age. To Sarah Ivatt my sister and to her child or children
£120, after the decease of Alice my wife in case both of my
sons die before 21. "Also I give and bequeath unto my Brother
John Feering the sume of fortie poundes of lawful money of
England. . . . at any time within five years after the decease
of Alice my wife if in case my said brother John Feering shall
come over from beyond the seas within the space of five years
next coming after the decease of the said Alice Feering my wife
But in case he doth not come over from beyond the seas by the
time aforesaid, then said sum to be paid to heirs of wife Alice
and of Sarah Ivatt my sister." If my wife marry her husband
shall give good security to Thomes Lindsell of Newton, co.
Cambridge, clerk, and to Thomas Yates of Haslingfields in
the said county, gent, whom I desire to be superviors of this my
last will. Residuary legatee: Alice my wife. Witnesses: James
Dickinson, William Buggin, Thomas Daye Titus Edwards.
Proved 23 Sept., 1652, by the executrix. University Court, Peter-
borough Wills, Vol. III., fol. 303.

Cambridge St. Giles :—
 1615: Sarah dau: of John and Sarah Feering* bapt 30 Ap.

---

* The above John and Sarah are without doubt the parents of John the
emigrant. Compare above extracts with will of Thomas, 1652. Transcripts
for St. Michael's were not examined for this name.

1616–17: Thomas son of John and Sarah Feering bapt 24 Feb.
1619: Elizabeth dau: of John and Sarah Feering bapt 12 Dec.,
    buried 11 April 1624.
1625–6: John Feering buried 30 Jan. (no will found).
1638: John Ivatt and Sarah Feering married 9 Ap.

John Feering, servant of Matthew Hawk of Cambridge in England, came with him in 1638 and settled at Hingham, but had been a proprietor there three years earlier. Freeman 26 May 1652, Selectman and Deacon. Had wife Margaret, married here, and children John, Israel, Mary and Sarah. He died 14 May 1665, his will proved 16 June following (*see N. E. Register XIII, p. 331*).

26 June, 1658, I ELIZABETH JENNINGS of Hatfeild Broadoake in the county of Essex, widow, late wife and executrix of Thomas Jennings of the same place, gentleman, deceased, being at this present in bodilie health. . . . To be decently interred in the parishe churche of Hatfield, soe neare my late deare husband as convenientlie may bee. To my kinsman Daniel Foote of Trinitie Colledge in Cambridge £10 and to his sister Mary Foote £10. To my kinsman Joshuah Foote of London, ironmonger, £10, and to his brother Cales Foote £5, and to Mary Foote and Hannah Foote their sisters £5 a apiece. To Leonard Foote of Shawford, co. Essex, £10, and to Mary Cornewell his sister £5, and to Elizabeth Lyon his Sister £5. To Sarah, wife of Gabriell Angell, 40s., and to their daughter Sarah Angele £3. Elizabeth Angell £10 and all such moneys as shall be owing vnto me by Michael Grevill, gent., at my death. Sister in law Elizabeth Foote a 20s. piece of gould to buy her a ring. My other sister in law Elizabeth Foote, wife of my deceased brother Joshuah Foote, the like. Joseph Miles 20s. Elizabeth Goddard my little silver salte. Residuary legatee: my nephew Mr. John Foote of Stratford Langton, co. Essex, whom I appoint mine executor. Witnesses: John Kendall, Robert Marsh. Proved 28 March, 1660, by the executor named. (P. C. C. Nabbs 10.)

Joshua Foote, Citizen and Ironmonger of London, had extensive business connections here from 1644 to 1652 and was a member of the Iron Works Co. He came to New England in 1653, resided for a time at Boston but soon removed to Providence, R. I., where he died in 1655, his will dated 2 October, was proved 31 October of that year and mentions wife and children but does not name them.*

I JOHN LYON, heretofore of New England beyond the Seas, nowe of late belonging vnto the Elizabeth ffrigott in the States Service, marriner, vnder the command of Captaine Colman, in consideration of the love and and affection which I bear vnto

---

* Registered at Boston. See abstracts in *N. E. Register* V, 444 and (inventory) IX, 272.

Alice Linsey my loveinge Landladie for the great care she hath taken in my sickness, have given, graunted and confirmed vnto her all and singular my goods, etc.; provided always that if I live and escape this sickness, this present Deed of Guift shall be voyd. Dated 29 Oct., 1657. Witnesses: William Sheare, Thomas Raistone, Francis Hodgson, Geo. Wyatt, scr. 30 October, 1658, admon to Alice Linsey, universal legatee. (P. C. C. Wotton 559.)

There were two John Lyons in New England of whom the testator was very evidently that John who was taxed at Marblehead in 1637 and of Salem the following year, a proprietor in 1649 and disappears from the records after that date. The other John was son of William of Roxbury (who came in 1635, aged 14, in the Hopewell) and was born here in 1647, married, had children and died here in 1698.*

I ROBERT COCHET of Mickle Over in the countie of Derby, gent., being in good health. . . . To Anne my wife one third part of all such lands and tenements as I have in the counties of Stafford and Derby for the term of her life, for an addition to her jointure. Daughter Anne Cochet £500. Daughter Sarah Cochet and son Nathaniel Cochet £400 each and all my Debenturs for service done to the Commonwealth by myself and others of whom I have purchased them, amounting in all to £534. To my Son Thomas and heirs all my lands etc. in Titburie and Castlehay Parke, co. Stafford, within the Manor of Melbourne and the Manor of Barwardcoate, co. Derby, except my wife's third part as aforesaid. If any of my children, vizt., Anne, Nathaniel and Sarah, die before the age of one and twenty, the portions of him, her or them soe dying shall goe to my sonne and heir. I give and bequeath vnto my sister Dorothy Joyce, wife of one John Joyce of New England, or to their children, if my sister their mother be dead, the summe of five pounds. Niece Rebecca Ridgeway £5. Maimed souldiers and poor widows of souldiers of this countie £5. Twenty Bibles to 20 poor householders in Mickle Over. Brother in law Joseph Swetnam, and my friend Samuel Berisford, ministers in Derby, 20s. each. Residuary legatee and executrix, my wife Anne. Dated 5 Sept., 1657. Witnesses: James Wright, William Newton, Stephen Wall. Proved 5 April, 1658, by the executrix. (P. C. C. Wotton 128.)

John Joyce of Lynn before 1637, when he removed to Sandwich, Mass. and proprietor there 1638, removed to Yarmouth 1643, Constable 1646. Had daughter Abigail bapt. at Barnstable 1 June 1646. His will dated 20 November, proved 5 March 1666,† names wife Dorothy, only son Hosea and daughters Mary and Dorcas.‡

---

* Savage III, 137, Pope 297.

† *N E. Register* VI, 188

‡ Savage II, 573, Pope 264.

CLUES FROM ENGLISH ARCHIVES
Contributory to American Genealogy.

By J. Henry Lea and J. R. Hutchinson.

The collection of gleanings which follows will, the writers hope and believe, be found of unusual interest owing to the large proportion of Southern wills (Virginia and South Carolina) which they are able to offer to the readers of the Record, while those of the family of the first Governor of the Massachusetts Bay Company must take high rank for their historical as well as genealogical value.

The twenty seventh day of April, 1634, I Robert Bradford of Longload in the parish of Martock, (co. Somerset), husbandman, being sicke of bodie, do make and ordaine this my last will and testament in manner and form following: First I give to my daughter Alice Feele two acres of arable land in Long Sutton after the crop of barley (*is*) taken away by my wife, which was late in the custody (*?occupation*) of Edward Lide. I give to my daughter Alice's two children £4 apiece; to my daughter Grace Bradford £40; to my son Robert Bradford £20 to be paid in six weeks after he shall come into England and demand it of his mother, and he to discharge her of all bonds wherein (I) his father stand bound for him. To John Bradford my brother £3, three years after my decease. The residue of my goods I give to my wife, whom I make sole executrix of this my will. Witnesses: James Flinte, John Bradford. Proved 31 May, 1634, by Elizabeth Bradford, relict and executrix.

(Cons. Wells, Book xlvii, fo. 62.)

Robert Bradford of Boston, Mass., tailor, was an inhabitant there in 1639, and was admitted to the Church 4 July, 1640. By wife Martha had children Moses, born 1644, and Martha, born 1645, died 1661, another Martha who married Peter, son of Elias Maverick of Charlestown, and Robert, who in 1664 deposed that he was aged 32, may also have been a son. His will, dated 16 November, 1677, was proved 28 December, 1680, he left his second wife, Margaret, his widow.*

Will of William White of London, lynnen draper, dated 20 August, 1622. I give all my lands in Virginia, with all my

---

* *Savage*, I, 231; *Pope*, 63.

servants, goods, debts and whatsoever else I have, unto my beloved brother John White of London, Esquire, whom I constitute sole heir and executor of this my will. Signed: *William White.* Witnesses: Erasmus Ferior, John Wade. Proved 26 June, 1627, by the executor named. (P. C. C. Skynner, 65.)

This may have been that William White who was buried at Elizabeth City, Virginia, 12 September, 1624.*

I JOHN WHITE, Vicar of Cherton *alias* Cheriton in the countie of Wilts, being in good health. . . . bequeath my bodie to be buried soe neare as may be vnto my deare wife. I forgive vnto the persons vndernamed all such moneys as they doe owe me, vizt., my brother Goodwin, my cousin Lapworth, Samuel Roman of Woodborough, Henry Lighe, and all suche my brothers in lawe and sisters who are deceased. Item I give to my deceased brother's children in Virginia, to his eldest sonne John White £5, to his whole sister 50s., and to the rest of his children 50s. between them if they shall demand the same, or if my executor shall opportunely send the same vnto them. To my sisters Judith and Margaret all such goods of mine as are at Culnes Aylwins. The Herriot due to the Lord there. The money Richard Cripps doth owe me I give vnto Jane his nowe wife. To the children of my sister Joan Lapworth deceased 20s. apeice. To my cousin Phyllis Broadhurst the threescore poundes her father John Broadhurst doth owe me. To my nephew Edward Broadhurst £10 yearly towards his maintenance at Oxford or elsewhere, out of my lands at Bushton. And whereas a deede of guift was made vnto me by my sister Anne Beale, to the intent that I might receive debts due vnto her from George and John Beale and Robert Constable, which said George and John are not responsibly to be found, and whereas there is security from the said Robert Constable, now I doe assign the same assurance vnto my sister Anne Beale, charging my executors to provide her with houseroom, chamber and fireing fit for my aged deare sister. To my grandnephews trinepotes, Charles and Samuel Broadhurst, £20 apiece at one and twentie. To Richard Barnes, whose wife is lately deceased, the use of the money he oweth me for two years, when I give thereof to my two godchildren William and Mary, his children, 50s. each, and appoint that the other £5 be paid by the said Richard Barnes vnto Jane and Mary Bridges my goddaughters, who both are deafe and dumbe; and if either of them decease, I will that their other deafe and dumbe sister shall have their portion. To the poore of Cherton six large white woolen wastcoates worth 40s. Residuary legatees: my nephew and niece John Broadhurst and Phyllis his nowe wife, whom I make my executors. Overseers: my sister Anne Beale and my trinepotes John and Edward Broadhurst their sons. Dated 1 February, 1659–60. Witnesses: Francis Smith, Anne Smith. Proved 6 Feb., 1671–2, by the executors named.†

(P. C. C. Eure, 23.)

---

* *Hotton's Lists,* p. 257.
† Partial abstract only.

I GEORGE MENEFIE of Buckland in Virginia, Esq., being sicke and weake in body. To be interred at the discrecon of my wife in the parish church of Westover. My will is that whatever debts cann be iustly proved by any person within this country of Virginia shalbe first satisfied. My will is that all Tobacco etc. in England be referred to my bookes. The Shippe Desire nowe lyeinge before Buckland shall with all possible expedition be dispatched for England, part loaded with what Tobacco is ready hereabout, and shall receive the remainder of her ladinge belowe, vizt., twoe hundred hoggsheads on the partable accompt, one hundred on mine owne particular accompt, and the rest by direcon of a noate to be founde in a small Booke of Tobacco shipt and to be shippt abroad. The one hundred hoggsheads shipt on my accompt shalbe consigned to Captaine Peter Andrews, as alsoe my part of the shipp Desire and cargoe, with my sixteenth part of the William and George. To my daughter Elizabeth Menefie all the severall parcells of land belonging to me at Westover, James Citty and Yorke River. To my brother John Bishopp all that some of money for which he standeth engaged to me and one third part of the Cropp of Tobacco made the last sumer on my plantation at Buckland. All my stocke of sheepe that I have at Buckland to be a joint stoacke between my daughter Elizabeth and my son in law Henry Perry. Mr Jo: James £20 and one thousand pounds of Tobacco to preach a sermon att my funerall. Mr Jo: Converse, chirurgion, for his paines in my sickness, twoe thousand pounds of Tobacco. Brother Roger Booker £50, requesting him to be assisting vnto Humfrey Lister in the collecting of my debts. Jo: White, merchant, £50 provided he continue one yeare longer in Virginia and receive in my debts as formerly. What present ready Tobacco can be received more than shall freight the Desire, shalbe laden uppon the Flower of London, provided it may goe for £4 a tunn. The goods consigned to me in the William and George shalbe returned in kinde. Executrix and guardian to my daughter, my wife Mary Menefie. Residuary legatees as to my goods, parts of shipps, servants, negroes, etc. my wife and my daughter Elizabeth Menefie. The Tobacco due from me to Captaine Tho: Varvell shalbe satisfied by Mr Walter Aston out of that part of the levies to me assigned. Satisfaction shalbe made to Mr Humfrey Adlington for his care and paines in my business concerning Chamberline by Captaine Peter Andrews, whom I request to be one overseer of this my will and my friend Richard Bennett, Esq., the other, and that the latter take care that all tobacco that is upon accompt of the Richard and Judith be sent home this yeare, and that he take the said vessell to his owne accompt though with some losse to my estate. Dated 31 Dec., 1645. Witnesses: Howell Prise, Humfrey Lister. Proved 25 Feb., 1646-7, by Mary Menefie the relict and executrix.

(P. C. C. Fines, 31.)

George Menefie, merchant of James City, came to Virginia in July, 1623, in the *Samuel*, was Councillor under Gov.

Berkeley in 1642 and said to have introduced the peach tree into Virginia.*

I EDMUND MOORECROFTE of Virginia, merchant, being weake in body. . . . give vnto my sister Anne Thurmer £20 to buy her a piece of plate; vnto John Thurmer the younger twoe heifers; vnto Elizabeth Thurmer my god-daughter twoe heifers; and vnto Joan Thurmer the younger a heifer and a bull calfe, the latter to be exchanged as the stocke increaseth. I appoint my executors my sisters Elisabeth and Marie Morecrofte, who shall enioy all the goods belonging vnto me in Virginia or England. I do desire my brother in lawe John Thurmer, and Robert Hatt and Cornelius Lloide† to administer uppon my estate here in Virginia in the behalfe of my sisters, and to send the produce thereof into England for their accompt, and alsoe to take an accompt of Mr William Thomson of what shalbe due to me either in the ffowerths or in seavenths, and to deliver the same to my sisters as aforesaid. I give vnto my brother John Thurmer for his paines £30, and to Robert Houlde £10. My will is that Mr Jeremie Blackman and William Church doe make sale of all such goods as are in the stores belonging to my marchants or any other Adventurers. Dated 18 Dec., 1638, "in Virginia." Witnesses: Nich: Stallinge, Richard Handson, John Webb. Proved 20 June, 1639, by Elizabeth Morecrofte, sister of deceased and one of the executrices, power reserved to Mary Morecrofte the other. (P. C. C. Harvey, 102.)

There were Morecrofts of Ormeskirke in Lancashire with connections in Barbadoes, shown in will of James Fletcher, citizen and haberdasher of London, proved 22 May, 1656. (P. C. C. Berkley, 140.‡)

Cornelius Lloyd had 800 acres on Elizabeth River and Merchant's Creek by Patent No. 222, as Head Rights for sixteen persons, not named, in 1635. In Patent of 1636 he is called "of London, Merchant."§ He was born about 1608, being aged 38 in a disposition of 1 September, 1646. Burgess for Lower Norfolk County, 1642 to 1652, Lieutenant-Colonel in 1653, and afterward Colonel.‖ He died before 10 September, 1654, when power of attorney was given by his widow, Elizabeth Lloyd, to Nicholas Hart of New England,¶ merchant, which was recorded 12 December, 1654. Witnesses: Thomas Lambert and William Turner.** His widow died before 28 April, 1658, when power of attorney was given by Thomas Evans of Kilkenny in Ireland, to kinsman John Belgraue of same, gent., to collect dues, etc., in Virginia, of "late sister Mrs. Elizabeth Loyd of Elizabeth River," etc.††

---

* Neill's *Virginia Carolorum;* cf. also will of Thomas Matthews of Merchant's Hope, Va., in RECORD, Oct., 1909, Vol. XL, p. 239.
† Water's *Gleanings*, I, 85.   ‡ Waters, I, 394-6.
§ *Richmond Critic*, 25 January, 1890.
‖ Niell's *Virginia Carolorum*, pp. 168, 185, 189, 199, 226, 232.
¶ Cf. will of Thomas Hart in RECORD, October, 1909, Vol. XL, p. 240.
** Cf. the *Thurmers* named in the will.
†† See Certificates of Head Rights in Lower Norfolk County, Va., by J. H. Lea, in *N. E. Hist.-Gen. Register*, Vol. XLVII, pp. 63, 65, 69, 194.

I HENRY JACOB (of St. Andrew Hubbert, London*), dated 5 October, 1622, being well in health, do ordayne and appoynt my last will and testament in manner and forme following: I bequeath all my goods to my wife Sarah Jacob, yet so that she give to each of my children an equal part if she happen to die before she come into Virginia, whither my desire and will is that she shall go (if God permits it) before the last day of May next ensuing, by cause I myself, with some of my children, are (by God's help) now going thither before. Moreover I will that my children shall have their parts when they come to one and twenty years old. Howbeit I will and ordaine that not any of my children shall have any part of my goods at all unless they go to Virginia before the end of May next. And I will that Nathaniel Page who now dwelleth with me shalbe in accompt as one of my children and shall have a part with them at his age of 23 years. Witnesses: James Page, George Crouch. 5 May, 1624, commission to Sarah Jacob the relict to administer. (P. C. C. Byrde, 38.)

I, ROBERT WILSON, son of Richard Wilson, chirurgeon, deceased, being in my perfect sense though weak of body, do make and ordain this my last will and testament, that is to say, First I ingeniously confesse myselfe debtor to my father Andrew Jacob in 1580 pound of tobacco, for the which I do allow him £15-16-0. I also owe him £12 for goods bought of him. I give to my mother Katherine Jacob £41-4-0; to my friend Henry Walker 20s. for the pains he hath taken in my business; to my brother John Wilson £30, to be put to good use for his schooling; and the residue I give to my said father and mother. (Undated.) Witnesses: Henry Walker, George Smith. 1 June, 1651, commission to Catherine Jacob, natural mother and residuary legatee named in the will of Robert Wilson late beyond the seas in the parts of Virginia, bachelor, deceased, to administer.

(P. C. C. Grey, 135.)

Holograph will of William Moulte of Virginia:

Deare and loveinge brother I have received your Letter as willing as a ioyfull heart can expect with my sister Lince token, the which I give her kinde thankes for the same, and this is to let you vnderstand that my Tobacco is sould at Plymouth, but at a very lowe rate for I had as much in London for one hogshead, as I have there for two, but now it cannot be helpe, and soe wee must be content, for the Seas are soe dangerous wee could not get it about to London without hazarding or loosening of all. And I hope this weeke I shall receive my moneys for the said Tobacco, And I received the Twentie shillings of George Mairill the carrier, And I hope I shall hare from you once more by Marill, and that will be all the while I shall bee in London, for the Shipps falls downe to Gravesend every day but yet I may bee in England this month, or more, but writing one to the other will bee one retorne of the carrier, but when I come to Varginaye, and God blesse me but with life and health I shall not faile in

---

* In Probate Act Book.

writing vnto you and all our freinds, Neither I hope will you. The little Estate the Lord hath blessed mee withall in Virginia is most on it, is Cattell and bede with pote cetall guine (or gnive) and some hoges And if I should doe any other than well, you must write to James Jones and give him order to sell this goods and turne them in Tobacco for he cannot in one yeare get saile for all Therefore you must write vnto him, and he will advise you for the best, but you must satisfie him in some measure to, and then he will not neglect to be sure, for he is a very honesty man, and one that you may trust. Deare brother before you write to James Jones to sell any thinge, write vnto him what there is, and what to doe, and howe hee should advise you for the best, And then when you have his Answere, you will the better knowe what to doe in it, for I give you but this instructions that the best of every thinge might be made of it, and the care I take that if I should dye single that you should have it all, and I likewise if I should dye at sea, and not be taken, that you should have the little I take with mee to Sea, And if please God this should happen, you must write to him to whom in England he shall consine it over vnto for your vse, And if please God that this bee, Helpe our deare Mother and our good sisters and brothers If there be any occasion for I give you it with this intent, and I doubt noe lesse of you but that you will performe if such a thinge should ever happen and the Seas are so trouble-some that I dare not venter to take my sister Dorothie over with mee, but I would not have you to thinke it is for want of good will, for I vow to God it is not, nor to none of you all that is not wanting, but shall doe for any of you, the vtmost of my power. I cannot choose but to tell you that since the last letter I have bin dangerous sicke, the Doctor and Apothecary hath had of mee sixe pounds, but (thanks bee to God) I am well recovered, and soe with my love to my brother Edmon, my cozen Anne, my brother John wife, and to all our freinds in generall, and my humble duty to my deare Mother and my love to our good brothers and sisters and my deare love vnto yourselfe with my prayers to God for all your health and happiness I rest, your poore brother to his power *William Moulte* London the Queenes Armes the eighteenth of September, one thousand sixe hundred ffiftie three. (James Jones at Accomack in Northampton County, Nasswadax Crick.) ffor my deare brother ffrancis Moulte att Ashby ffawell in Leicester shire give this.*

20 June, 1657, commission to Francis Moulte, natural and law-ful brother and universal legatary named in this will of William Moult, deceased, to administer, etc. (P. C. C. Ruthen, 249.)

The five and twientieth daye of June, 1659, I Luke Johnson of Virginia, Planter, being weake in bodie. My funerall charges shall not exceed twentie markes. To my loving unckle John Turton of West Bromwich, co. Stafford, gent, and to James Carie, Citizen and Salter of London, 20s. each. Elizabeth, wife of said James Carie, 20s. Friends Mr John Banester and Elizabeth

---

* Spelling and punctuation as in the registered copy.

his wife 40s. each for rings. I give and bequeath unto my god-son John Banester, son of John Banister of Yorke River in Virginia, planter, one cowe. I give and bequeath unto my god-son Robert Bryen, son of Robert Bryen of Virginia, planter, one cowe. Residuary legatee: Anne my wife. Executors: my uncle John Turnton and my friend James Cary. Witnesses: Richard Morton, Pr: Stedman, servant to Thomas Russel, scr. Proved 1 Aug., 1659, by the executors named. (P. C. C. Pell, 450.)

It seems probable that the James Carie, citizen and salter, named in the above will, was a cousin or other near relative of Miles Cary, the well known founder of the family of that name in Virginia, who was killed in the fight with the Dutch at Point Comfort, 10 June, 1667. Miles Carey was descended from William Cary, Mayor of Bristol in 1546, who left a prolific family of merchants and adventurers, many of whom found their way to America during the 17th century. A James Cary, first cousin of Miles, was of New England at this period,* but evidently not the James named in the will.

16 August, 1593, I RICHARD CRADOCKE of London, merchant, being sicke of bodye. To be buried in the parish church at St. Tantlyns in London,† where I am now resident. To the Bailives and Burgesses of the town of Stafford £100 to be lent to tenne yonge men, occupyers of the said towne, for the space of twoe yeares, then to other tenne; also £100 towards the mainteyninge of some godly preacher to reade in the High Church there one Divinitie Lecture or Sermon every Sondaye in the forenoone for euer. Poore of Stafford £20. Sister Emme Cradocke now servant with Mr Alderman Offley of London £600. Sister Mary Cradocke £500. Sister Sara Cradocke £500. Brother Thomas Cradocke at this present resident in Bayon in France £500. Sister Anne Cunney £100. Sister Katherine St. Quyntyne £100. Sister Alice Ridley £100. Jane Mannering servant to Thomas Offley, son of said Alderman Offley, £100. The daughters of my sister Mannering £200. My mother Elizabeth Cradocke £200, she paying to my cosen Mathew Flier all such sume as were due to him from my father Mathew Cradocke deceased. Alice Ball, servant with my mother, £20. Brother Mathew Cradocke £200. Mathew Cradocke, son and heir to my brother George Cradocke of Stafford, £100. Walter Cradocke, son and heir to my brother Francis Cradocke, £100. Uncle Martin Nowell of Stafford £50. Joseph Jackson of Bayon £200. Arthur Jackson and John Jackson £200. Brother William Cradocke £400, so as he marry an English woman borne within the Realme of England. Brother George and his wife £20. Brother Francis and his wife £20. Brother Mannering and his wife £20. Brother Mathew Cradocke and his wife £20. Cosen Jane Mannering £6-13-4. Cosen Mr Alderman Offley £10. Cosen Mr Robert Offley the elder £10, and his son Robert £10. Arthur

---

* Stow MS., 670, fo. 229-30, in Brit. Musuem.
† St. Antholins, Budge Row.

41

and John Jackson and their wives. My aunt Hallingbury £30. Thomas Stevens servant to Alderman Offley £30. Nicholas Clarke, Citizen and Merchant Taylor of London, £50. Thomas and Robert, sons of Alderman Offley, £10 each. Cosen Mathew Flyer and wife £20. Cosen Edward Flier £10. Jarvis Hall servant to my brother Francis £40. Mrs Offley, wife of Alder-Offley, £10. Mrs Offley, wife of Thomas Offley, Mrs Offley, widow, late wife of Thomas Offley deceased, and Mrs Offley, wife of Robert Offley the younger, £10 each. Brother Francis Cradocke £100. Residuary legatees: my sisters Emme, Mary and Sarah Cradocke and my brother Thomas Cradocke. Executors: brother Francis Cradocke and Arthur Jackson. Overseers: Mr Alderman Offley and Mr Robert Offley the elder. Thomas Fitche, scr., £10. Witnesses: John Bovyatt, Robert Cocke, Thomas Stevens, Thomas Fitche, scr. Proved 25 Aug., 1593, by Thomas Ward, Not. Pub., proctor for the executors named.*

(P. C. C. Neville, 62.)

5 Nov., 1608, I GEORGE CRADOCKE of Stafford, co. Stafford, gent, whole of body. Poor of Stafford. £50 to be lent out to townsmen there, who shall take one of the children of my cousin Weldon, and the children of George Ranshawe, William Ranshawe and Francis Ranshawe, and teach them their trade. Sister Manwaring and her children 10s. apiece. Sister Ridley 10s. Sister Palmer and her children 10s. apiece. Sister St. Quintin and her children 10s. apiece. Sister Dorington and daughter 10s. each. Brother Thomas Cradocke 10s. Brother Mathew Cradocke and children 20s. apiece. Brother Coynes children which he had by my sister 20s. apiece, Godson Humfrey Weldon 20s. Johan my wife, for life, one third of all my lands and leases. Residuary legatee: my son Mathew Cradocke, with all his mother hath after her decease; or in default to my cousin Walter Cradocke, or my brother Thomas Cradocke, or my brother Mathew Cradocke, or my brother William Cradocke. Executor: son Mathew. Overseers: brother Thomas Cradocke and brother in law Thomas Jollye of Leeke. Witnesses: none. Proved 11 Oct., 1611, by the executor named. (P. C. C. Wood, 83.)

27 Julye, 1618, I THOMAS CRADOCKE of the towne of Stafford, merchant, being sicke in bodie. . . . To be buried in St. Mary's church in Stafford. To Dorothie my wife for life the house wherein I dwell and three other houses in Stafford, in Westgate street there, and all those my lands at Syclemore in the parish of Caytell *alias* Castell, which I lately purchased of my nephew John Cowper, son and heir of Edmond Cowper late of Dunstow in the said county, gentleman, deceased; with remainder (except as regard one house in Stafford) to my nephew Walter Craddocke, son and heir of my brother Francis Craddocke, and to his heirs males; with divers remainders over, in male tail, to my nephew Matthew Craddocke, son and heir of my brother

---

* Richard Cradock, merch‡, buried out of Mr. Jackson's house, Aug. 18, 1593. (Register of St. Antholin's, Budge Row, London.) Cf. the Jacksons named in the will.

George Craddocke, and to my nephew Mathew Craddocke, second son of my brother Mathew Craddocke deceased. Dorothy my wife £800. To my six sisters Jane Manwaring, Emme Dorrington, Katherine St. Quentin, Alice Ridley, Mary Palmer and Sarah White, each £40. To my nephew John Cowper fourscore pounds. To my niece Elizabeth Craddocke, wife of my nephew Mathew Craddocke, £10. To George Craddocke, son of the said Mathew, £20. To Anthony Dyott, son of my nephew Dyott, £10. To my niece Dorothy Sawyer, wife of Thomas Sawyer of Suffolk, mercer, £10. My nephew and servant Thomas Newton £20. Sister Margaret Nelson £5. Nephew Edward Manwaring, Esq., £20. Old servant Isabell Robinson £5. Poor of Stafford £5. Residuary legatee: my wife. Executors: my wife and the said Edward Manwaring. Witnesses: John Chelwarde, Thomas Whitegrave, John Lee, Thomas Thurstans. Proved 31 Oct., 1618, by the executors named.   (P. C. C. Meade, 93.)

Will of SAMUEL CRADOCK, Rector of Thiselton, co. Rutland, dated 24 Sept., 1652. Son Mathew £20. Son Samuel my brasse clocke and Mr Perkins his works and all my manuscripts. All the rest of my estate I bequeath to my wife Elizabeth, intreating her to provide for the rest of my children as God shall enable her. Sole executrix: my wife; and I enjoin her to give £10 apiece to all my children at their marriages in consideration of £100 given to my daughter Jorden (being the legacy of my daughter Mary deceased), which should have been divided amongst them. Witnesses: William Redish, Edward Caunt, Richard Ridall. Proved 26 Aug., 1653, by the executrix.
(P. C. C. Brent, 79.)

In the above most interesting wills we have much light thrown on the pedigree and connections of Matthew Cradock, the first Governor of the Massachusetts Company—Richard, George and Thomas Cradock being the uncles, and Samuel, Rector of Thistleton in Rutland, the elder brother of the Governor. The will of Matthew Cradock himself has been already printed.* Pedigrees of the family will be found both in the British Museum and the College of Arms,† and these are considerably amplified and corrected by the wills, as may be seen by comparison with the authorities cited.

The family arms were: Argent, on a chevron azure, a mullet charged with a crescent for difference. Crest: A bear's head couped sable, muzzled gules.‡

Governor Cradock himself never came to New England but his interest in the Colony was unfailing and generous; besides many mercantile ventures here, he built no less than two houses in Marblehead and Medford§ which were sold after his death.

---

* See *Hist. of Medford* by Charles Brooks, Boston, 1855, pp. 90-92, and W. H. Whitmore in *N. E. Hist.-Gen. Register*, IX, 124.

† Add. MS., Brit. Mus., 19125, fo. 124, printed in *Register*, *loc. cit.* and Visitation London, 1634, in Harl. Soc., XV, 198.

‡ Loc. cit. supra, see also Whitmore's *Heraldic Journal*, I, pp. 4-5, 15.

§ Brook's *Hist. Medford, Mass.*, p. 46.

The date of his decease is uncertain, but the following entry probably refers to him:

"May 27, 1641, Matthew Cradock, merchant, one of the Members of Parliament for ye city of London, dies."[*]

Although Winthrop gives the date as probably 1644.[†] His will, however, was not probated until 1662 owing, in all probability, to the disturbed condition of the country during the Civil War and the ensuing period of the Commonwealth.

A George Cradock, who was of Boston, Mass., about the middle of the eighteenth century, was possibly a descendant of the Governor, and it is stated by Hutchinson that he was so,[‡] but he was more probably of a comigerous family and perhaps derived from one of the five or more uncles of that distinguished man, from whom, however, we may with great certainty eliminate Francis Cradock of Wolverhampton, and George Cradock of Stafford, thus leaving either John, Thomas or William as his most probable ancestors.

Of the very suggestive Offley connection shown in the will of Richard Cradock in 1593, we may have more to say later, as it seems to indicate relations of another early New England family of high standing with that of Governor Cradock.

See also the Chancery Proceeding (Andrews vs. Glover[§]) recently printed in the *New England Historical-Genealogical Register*,[||] with most interesting note by Mr. Walter K. Watkins. This valuable document completes our knowledge of the children of Rev. Samuel Craddock, Rector of Thistleton, and supports and supplements the information contained in the above wills.

Know all men by these presents that I, SAMUEL DALE of Braintree in the county of Essex, Gent, being now advanced in years, do make this my last will and testament in manner and form following: First, I give and devise unto my cousins John Ruggles of Bocking in the said county, clothier, and Thomas Heckford of Braintree, draper, all that my messuage in the occupation of Moses Griffith, surgeon, situate in Bocking, and all those my lands lying in Little Leighs, in the occupation of William Drake, Robert Schooling and James Shonke, for the term of sixty-nine years in case Christian Dale my daughter shall so long live, in trust that they the said John Ruggles and Thomas Heckford shall provide for the said Christian; and after the decease of the said Christian I give and devise all the aforesaid premises unto my nephew John Dale and his heirs for ever, subject to the payment of £10 yearly to my nephew Francis Dale during the term of his natural life, to which Francis Dale I give also one shilling to be paid when demanded. I give and devise unto my said nephew John Dale and his heirs my messuage called Wigly-house lying in Ovington, co. Essex, now in the several occupations of Samuel Kempe, Richard Smith and John Ingham; also my messuage in the parish of St. Gregory in the town of Sudbury,

* *N. E. Hist.-Gen. Register*, XI, 296.
† Winthrop's Journal, Savage's Edition, I, 2.
‡ Hutchinson's *Hist. Mass.*, p. 23.
§ Chan. B. & A., Chas. I, A. 51/60.
|| January, 1910, Vol. LXIV, pp. 84–86.

co. Suffolk, now in the occupation of Samuel Wiatt, Mary White, widow, and Sarah Cox; and also my messuage in the occupation of Francis Little, victualler, in Braintree, called the White Horse. To Samuel Clapham my servant and his heirs my cottage in Braintree in the occupation of Henry Spooner. And whereas John Clapham of Felsted, wheelwright, stands indebted to me in the sum of £41-6-6, I do hereby forgive to him the half part of said sum, and the other half part I give unto the said Samuel Clapham. I give unto my nephew Francis Dale my History of Harwich and the third edition of my Pharmacologia, as they are in my Library. And whereas at the request of my great-nephew Thomas Dale, then of Bishopgate, London, but now of James Towne in South Carolina in America, I became bound unto William Leigh of St. Olave, Southwark, co. Surrey, skinner, in the sum of £40 for the payment of £20 by obligation dated 11 Nov., 1731, which said sum of £20 I paid to the said William Leigh, and which sum hath not been repaid me notwithstanding that the said Thomas Dale, together with one Peter Goudett, did become bound unto me for the repayment thereof, now my mind is that the said sum shall be forgiven the said Thomas Dale, and that my executors do deliver the said bond unto him my said nephew when demanded. To the Master, Wardens and Society of Apothecaries of London all such my books in Botany as at present they have not, and also all my Hortus Siccus or collection of dryed plants, including those collected by my kind friend and neighbour the late learned Mr John Ray, on condition that the said Master and Wardens shall erect proper conveniences in their Physick Garden at Chelsey for the reception thereof, and shall make such regulations for the preservation thereof as shall be approved by Sir Hans Sloane, Bart, M.D., President of the Royal Society. To my daughter Christian all the furniture in my chamber except the Buroy. To my nephew William Grey all my woolen wearing apparel, and to his sister one shilling. The rest of my goods I give to my nephew John Dale, whom I appoint executor. My kinsman Thomas Heckford to be supervisor of my will and assistant unto my executor in seeing my body buried in the Tomb with my two Wives in case my executor should not be here in time. Dated 5 August, 1738. /Signed: *S. Dale*/ Witnesses: Robt: Swift, Wm: Whitehead, Ralph Peers. Codicil dated 17 March, 1738-9, devising the messuage in Ovington, called Wigly-house unto my daughter Christian Dale for life, with remainder to my nephew John Dale, and giving unto my servants and assistants John Clapham, junior, Jeremiah Clapham, Thomas Clapham and William Bowes a guinea apiece. Witnesses: William Rayment, Thos: Sturgeon, Jno: Yeldham, junior. Proved 6 April, 1739 by the executors named. 16 Feb., 1769-70, commission to Sarah Dale, spinster, daughter and administratrix of John Dale, deceased, whilst living nephew and executor of above testator, to administer goods of the said testator, left unadministered by the said John Dale, who died intestate.
(Commissary London, Essex and Herts, Register Bull., folio 212.)

CLUES FROM ENGLISH ARCHIVES
CONTRIBUTORY TO AMERICAN GENEALOGY.

BY J. HENRY LEA AND J. R. HUTCHINSON.

The 19th day of April, 1634, I JOAN PATTEN of Crewkerne, co. Somerset, being weake of bodie, do make and ordain this my last will and testament in manner and form following: I give to every one of my brothers twenty shillings apiece; to my sister Sarah my best gown, and to every of her children twelve pence; to my sister Elizabeth twenty marks; to William Gaylard in New England five pounds to be bestowed for him as my executor shall think fit; to Richard Pore forty shillings; to Giles Browne twenty shillings; to Henrie Brooke twenty shillings; to the widow Arundell five shillings; and all the rest of my goods I give to my sister, whom I do make sole executrix of this my will. Memo that if it be so devised and expressed by my father's last will that my portion given (*by*) my father shall after my decease be equally divided between my sisters Marie and Elizabeth, then the twenty marks before given to my sister Elizabeth shall cease and not be paid. Memo also that Marie the sister of Joan Patten was nominated by the said Joan for her executrix. Witnesses: John Bull, Elizabeth Patten, widow. No Probate.

(Cons. Wells, Book 47, f. 11.)

The above most interesting will serves to give us a clue to an important family of Pitminster, in the County of Somerset, of which the founders (so far as at present known) were Nicholas Gayler (*i. e.*, Gaylord) and Joan, his wife (afterwards married to Giles Alwyn), whose wills follow, supplying the children of Nicholas, whose names he very inconsiderately omitted in his own will.

Joan Patten, the testatrix, was probably a daughter of one of the five sons Christopher, Hugh, William, John or Edmund, thus obtained but, as none of their wills have been discovered, it is, from the present view-point, impossible to say which. It seems evident that the William named in her will was that William of Dorchester, Mass., who died in 1673, aged nearly 88 years, and could not, therefore, have been her brother as both the putative parents had long been dead in 1585, and therefore he and his brother John, also of Dorchester, were probably her nephews. John was probably dead at the time of the making of her will (the last mention of him in our records being 1632), which accounts for his omission and strengthens the probability of the connection. Hugh Gaylord, of whom later, who remained in England but whose daughter Alice, wife of Richard Treat, came to America, could not for similar reasons of age, have been the brother Hugh of the will, but must also have been a nephew and probably a brother of the Dorchester emigrants. A brief sketch of what is known of these three may be of interest to the reader.

William Galler (as he signs himself in the Dorchester records) was a deacon at the gathering of the Church in Plymouth, England, in 1630. He came in the *Mary & John* the same year and made application for admission as Freeman, 19 October following, being admitted 18 May, 1631. He was Representative for Dorchester, 1635, 1636 and 1638. Removed to Windsor, Conn., and was Representative from that place for nearly 40* semi-annual sessions to 1664, and died 20 July, 1673, in his 88th year.

John Gaylord of Dorchester, Mass., brother of the above, was chosen by the town in 1632 to meet the Court of Assistance be-

---

* *Savage*, II, 238; Stiles' *Hist. Windsor*, II, 278; Hibbard's *Hist. Goshen, Conn.*, 452.

fore any system of Representatives had been formed. His name does not occur again and he probably died soon after, corroboration of which is found in his omission from Joan Patten's will.*

Hugh Gaylaud of Pitminster, co. Somerset, in 1573 held lands in Poundisford, Smalecross and Lakemead in the Tything of South Trendle (now the parish of Trull), late of Nicholas Gaylerd, and held lands in Southgrove, in said tything, by surrender of Johane, widow of said Nicholas, for his residence. On 4 October, 1608, he had surrendered the close called Smalrest (*sic*, but see above), in the tything aforesaid, to his son George Gaylard.† His daughter Alice was baptized at Pitminster, 10 May, 1594, and married there, 27 April, 1615, Richard Trott (*Treat*), and came to America with her husband and their nine surviving children in 1630.‡ They settled at Dorchester but soon removed to Wethersfield, Conn. Hugh Gaylord died at Pitminster and was buried there 21 October, 1614, His will, deposited in the Archdeaconry of Taunton, has unfortunately perished.§

Will of NICHOLAS GAYLER of Pytmyster, (co. Somerset), dated 25 March, 1546. Being sick of bodie. My bodie to the holie sepulture of Pytmyster. Maintenance of the Church there viijd. Mayntenance of our Ladie service there viijd. To the light before the sacrament of the Aulter viijd. To the High Cross light viijd. To the sepulture light viijd., to the Torches viijd, and to the Belles viijd. I give to my ghostly father Sir Thomas Bicknam, to pray for me, xijd. I am in debte to John Parson of Pitmister xijs. xiijd., to Richard File of Trull iijs. iiijd., to William Finche of Wells vjs. viijd., to a thatcher of Wells iiijd., to John Spursaie of Pitmister xiijd., to John Shute of Trull vijs., and to John Morcombe of Trull vjs. viijd. I make Johan Gayler my wife my executrix of all my goods. Witnesses: Sir Thomas Bicknam, John Parson, John Durston. Proved 8 April, 1546.
(Arch. Taunton, Book I, f. 349.)

Will of JOAN ALVYN of Pitmister, (co. Somerset), dated 29 August, 1572. To be buried in the churchyard at Pitmister. To Christopher my son £6-13-4. To William Gaylard my son a cow called Culver. To Mary Gaylard, daughter of William Gaylard, a cow called Tyttymus, the same to remain in the kepinge of Robert Manlye to the use and profit of the said Mary so long as he shall think good. To Elizabeth Gaylard, daughter of William Gaylard, a yeo shepe. To John my son £20. To Elizabeth my daughter £20. To Mary my daughter £20, to be paid by Edmund my son. Residue to Hugh my son, whom executor. Supervisors: William Palmer and John Ivery. Witnesses: Robert Manley, Robert Baull, Henry Rewe. Proved 31 August, 1572.   (Taunton Wills, Book V, f. 13.)

---

* *Savage*, II, 238.
† Court Rolls, Manor of Taunton Deane, Somst.
‡ *Treat Genealogy*, pp. 9, 18, 26.
§ Recorded in Calendars there, File 1614, No. 110.

Will of GILES ALVYN of Pitmister, (co. Somerset), dated 4 May, 1567. To Edmund Gaylard £5. To John Gaylard £5. To Christopher Gaylard 40s. To Elizabeth Gaylard £8–6–8. To Mary Gaylard £8–6–8. To Hugh Gaylard £3–6–8. To Elizabeth and Mary Gaylard, children of William Gaylard, 4d. each. To John Luddon, Christopher, Roger, Elizabeth and Margerie, children of Hugh Luddon, 4d. each. To Robert White, William, George, Hugh, Johan, Elizabeth and Margaret, children of William White, 4d. each. To the children of Robert Lidden 4d. each. To the children of Thomas Lidden 4d. each. To every of my brothers and sisters 4d. To Andrew Howdon 4d. Residue to Johan my wife, whom executrix. Supervisors: John Iverie and Henry Rewe. Witnesses: John Iverie, Robert Ball, Henry Rewe. Proved 17 August, 1572.
(Taunton Wills, Book V, f. 33.)

Will of HARRIE VILDUE of Henton George (*i. e.* Hinton St. George), (co. Somerset), dated 2 June, 1546, witnessed by Robert Gaylard. (Taunton Wills, Book I, f. 377.)

Will of ALICE HANNINGE of Fourland in the parish of Crewkerne, (co. Somerset), widow, dated 30 Oct., 1559. To Robert Gaylard a yeow and a platter. (Taunton Wills, Book III, f 149.)

Will of ANTONIE GAILERD of Langford Budfield, (co. Somerset), dated 25 Dec., 1565. To my son Nicholas I give my best cote. Residue to Julian my wife and Jone my daughter, whom executors. Witnesses: none. Proved 20 Feb., 1565–6.
(Taunton Wills, Book IV, f. 125.)

Will of JOHN GAILERD of Stocklinch Mawdlen, (co. Somerset), dated 13 August, 7 Eliz. To John my son my best wean and wheles. To Margaret my daughter a cow called Redie, with a white patch in the buttock, and a crock of brass with long leggs. To Agnes my daughter a brazen crock and a potenger. To John Bremell v pounds of wull. Residue to Alice my wife, whom executrix. Witnesses: Nicholas Phillips, parson, Robert Jefferie, John Patterd, John Raynall. Proved 19 April, 1566.
(Taunton Wills, Book IV, f. 142.)

Will of ANTHONY GAYLARD of Dillington in the parish of Ilmister, (co. Somerset), dated 10 May, 1572. Being sick in bodie. To be buried in the churchyard of Ilmister. To Margaret my daughter a cow and a heifer of twelve months old. To everie of of my children, that is to saie, to John Gaylard, Robert, William, Mary and Jone, 20s. apiece at their several ages of twenty years. Poor of Ilmister 12d. Residue to Jone my wife, whom executrix. Witnesses: Robert House, John Gaylard. Proved 18 May, 1573, by the executrix. (Wells Wills, Book 17, f. 106.)

Will of ALICE CHAPLIN of Draiton, (co. Somerset), widow, dated 23 April, 1576. To John Gaylard my son two acres of wheat.

To Jane Gaylard, daughter of said John, a sucking calf. Legacies to Thomas Salwey my son, Jone Salway my daughter, and Margaret my daughter. Residue to Christian my daughter, whom executrix. Overseers: Thomas Hawker, Roger Roceter and William Doleman. Witnesses: Thomas Hawker, Roger Rosseter, William Doleman, Edmund Daw, John Daw, Thomas Ball, John Langedon, curate of Draiton. Proved 8 May, 1576.
(Taunton Wllls, Book V, f. 247.)

Will of JOHN SKRIVEN of Dillington in the parish of Ilmister, (co. Somerset), dated 6 Feb., 1579–80, witnessed by Robert Gaylord. (Wells Wills, Book 19, f. 88.)

Will of WILLIAM JAMES of Furland in the parish of Crewkerne, (co. Somerset), dated 14 April, 1581, witnessed by Geffrye Gallard.
(Taunton Wills, Book VI, f. 25.)

Will of SIR THOMAS STUCKY, clerk, parson of Stocklynch Ottersey, (co. Somerset), dated 27 June, 1581. To Agnes Gaylard a platter. (Taunton Wills, Book VI, f. 43.)

Will of JOHN HANINGE of Crookerne, (co. Somerset), dated 15 Oct., 1581. To my brother in law Jefferie Gailerd 10s.
(Taunton Wills, Book VI, f. 136.)

Will of JOHN GAYLARD of Draiton, (co. Somerset), dated 10 Nov., 1587. Being sick of bodie. To the church 2s. To the poor men's box 6d. To my daughter Anne my great brazen panne and a bandise. To Henry my son my mault mill. To my son John my pair of lumbes with all things thereto belonging. Rest to Mary my wife, whom executrix. Witnesses: Richard Bettie, curate, William Baker. Proved 13 Jan., 1587–8.
(Taunton Wills, Book VII, f. 78.)

The will nuncupative of ROGER GEYLARD late of Drayton, (co. Somerset), made the 1st day of Februarie, 1622–3. I give to my daughter Elizabeth £40, my second best bed, and a malt gurnard; to my daughter Alice 6s. 8d.; to her children 3s. 4d.; and my will is that Samuel Geylard shall have the youse of the heifer I gave to Roger Geylard, son of Samuel Geylard. The rest of my goods I give to my wife and do make her executrix. Witnesses: Thomas Kingdon, Joan England, Edith Gaylard. Proved 24 April, 1623, by the executrix (*not named*). Sureties with the executrix: John Anneley of Curry Rivell, butcher, and Edmund Dawe of Drayton, yeoman. (Taunton Wills, 1623, File 39.)

I JOAN GAYLARD of Barrington, co. Somerset, widow, being sick of body, do make this my last will and testament: I give to the parish church of Barrington 5s.; to the poor of the said parish 5s.; and all other my goods I give to my son John Gaylard, whom I make my executor. Dated 15 August, ¦1630. /Signed:

50

Joan Gaylard./ Seal: A swan. Witnesses: John Drayton, John Berintone. Proved 5 Nov., 1630, by the executor named.
(Taunton Wills, 1630, File 47.)

I JOHN GAILARD of Draiton, co. Somerset, mason, this thirtieth day of September (*no year*) do make this my last will and testament: To be buried in the churchyard of Draiton. To mine eldest son John my great brass pott and my working tools. Item I give to my second son William my middle kettle, my cupboard, and two pewter dishes, all of which goods shall remain in the custody of my wife Alice so long as she live unmarried. All the rest of my goods I give unto my wife, whom I make executrix. Witnesses: William Baker, John Stapel. Proved 2 Dec., 1630, by the executrix. (Taunton Wills, 1630, File 74.)

The 1st day of March, 1632–3, I AGNES GAYLERD of Ile Abbotts, co. Somerset, spinster, do make and ordain this my last will and testament: I give unto my sister Elizabeth Gaylard £5 and all my goods except two bonds, which I give unto my brother Robert Gaylard, whom I make my whole executor. I give four shillings unto the poor of Ile Abbotts, to be distributed by John Gibbs and John Pytts. Witnesses: None. Proved 22 March, 1632–3, by the executor. (Taunton Wills, 1632, File 175.)

14 Nov., 1661, I EDMUND GAYLARD of Pitmister, co. Somerset, yeoman, being in good helth, do make and ordain this my last will and testament in manner and form following: I give to the poor of Pitmister ten shillings. [To my daughter Mary Gaylard £200 to be paid after my surrender of my two farthing-lands in the Tything of South Trendel in the Hundred of Pounsford. To Martha Gaylard my daughter £120. To Agnes Gaylard my daughter £100, to be paid within two years after my surrender of the said lands, which lands I have surrendered unto my son in law Joseph Stoden according to the custom of the Manor of Taunton and Taunton Dean, together with certain overlands, upon condition that he shall pay all my debts and legacies.]* To my daughter Mary the bedstead in the old parlor. To my daughter Martha my side bedstead in the old parlor. To my daughter Agnes Gaylard my little pottage pott. To my daughter Jone Sely one great chest and one coffer which Potter Sely her husband hath in his custody. To my daughter Joan's four children 40s. apiece at one and twenty. To Sarah Stodden, daughter of my son in law Joseph Stodden, 40s. at one and twenty. To Sarah Sely and Sarah Stodden one puter (*pewter*) dish apiece. The residue of my goods I give unto Joseph Stodden, my son in law, whom I appoint executor, and my brother George Gaylard and John Durston to be overseers. /Signed: *Edmund Gaylard./* Witnesses: John Hawkritch, William Poole. Proved 18 April, 1663, by the executor. (Taunton Wills, 1663, File 93.)

---

* The portion in brackets is crossed out of the original.

51

9 September, 1665, I George Gaylard of Pitmister, co. Somerset, yeoman, being in good health, do make and ordain this my last will and testament: I give unto my son John threescore pounds, to be paid by my son George after the land comes into his hand. I make my wife Elizabeth executor. I give unto my son George four pound a year to be paid by my wife Elizabeth during her life out of the whome (*home*) living. I give to my son Joseph the low bed and bedstead in the kitchin chamber. I appoint ten acres that was Babb's, and ten that is Luscombe Hill, to be let out for two years. I desire George Staddier and John Streete to be overseers. /Signed: *Georg Gaylard.*/ Witnesses: Richard Booth, Anthony Cade. Proved 1 June, 1667, by the executrix. (Taunton Wills. 1667, File 82.)

19 August, 1673, I Thomas Gaylard of Chaffcombe, co. Somerset, being sick and weak of body, do make and ordain this my last will and testament in manner and form following: First I bequeath my body to the christian burial in Chaffcombe. I give to my wife Elizabeth my bed and bedstead; to my son Elias 10s.; and to my son John Gaylard, to Thomas Gaylard, and to Edith Jennings 12d. apiece. All the rest of my goods I give to my son Henry Gaylard, whom I make my only executor. And my pleasure is that my wife Elizabeth, while she keeps herself in my name, shall have the use of certain (*specified*) household stuff. /Signed: *Thom: Gaylard.*/ Witnesses: Elias Gyllett, John James, Hananell Palmer. Seal: A talbot or hound courant. No Probate. Inventory taken 23 August, 1675, £63-19-0.
(Taunton Wills, 1675, File 19.)

The last of October, 1689, Samuel Gaylard, whilst he lived of the parish of Drayton, co. Somerset, made his last will nuncupative in these and the like words: I give unto the three children which I had by a former wife tenn pounds apiece, and the residue of his goods he gave unto Grace his relict, whom he made executrix, and this was putt in writing within six days after the testator's death according to the Act in that case provided. Published in presence of John Wines, William Wines, and Susannah Gooden. Proved 23 Nov., 1689, by Grace Gaylard, relict and executrix. Inventory of the goods of Samuel Gailard of Weeck Perham in the parish of Drayton, co. Somerset, deceased, taken 13 Sept., 1689: "Item 11 acres of wheat in house and in mow, £15. Item for Lent corne £7. Item eight cowes, £19, four oxen £16-10, five horses £11-15, fourteen sheep £3, one chattle lease £1-12-6. Total of Inventory, £115-8.
(Taunton Wills, 1689, File 27.*)

Drayton and Burton, Somerset: William Wylmote, in right of Agnes his wife, holdeth by copy dated 16 May, 4 and 5 Philip and Mary, one cottage containing three acres, with pasturage for two beasts, in Southmore, and one acre of wood in Drayton Wood,

---

* Four other Gaylard wills, calendared at Taunton, are now missing.

To hold to the said Agnes and to Roger Gaylard, son of John Gaylard, for the term of their lives, by the rent of 5s. (Rentals and Surveys, Miscellaneous Books [Land Revenue], Vol. 255, f. 32.)

I JOHN THOMPSON of the parish of St. Mary Magdalen, Bermondsey, co Surrey, distiller . . . commit my body to the earth, to be interred in the vault with my late son Robert Thompson in Bermondsey churchyard, and I direct that the expenses of my funerall shall not exceed £40. And touching the disposal of my temporal estate, whereas I have already given unto my son John Thompson £500, and to my daughter Jane, in marriage with Thomas Ford, surgeon, £500, and have settled on her, after the decease of me and my wife, all the freehold messuage situate in Princes Street in the parish of St. Mary Rotherhith, and whereas I have made no provision for my younger son Andrew, now I do hereby dispose of my estate as followeth: To Mr Langdon of Bermondsey, gent, and his wife, and to Capt. Daniel Russell of Bermondsey and his wife, each a ring of one guinea value; to my cousin Alexander Thompson of Rhode Island in New England, distiller, tenn pounds of lawfull money of Great Britain; to my cousin Sarah Garth, widow, daughter of my sister Jane Dix, £5; to my servant Gilbert Williamson £5; to the two daughters of my late uncle Robert Thompson of Montrose in North Britain, deceased, and to the daughter of my late uncle William Thompson of Montrose, deceased, my sixteenth part of the ship *Owners Goodwill* whereof Robert Arbuthnot is master; to my wife Jane Thompson, during the term of her life or widowhood, the rents of my several messuages, whether leasehold or freehold, in St. Mary Magdalen, Bermondsey, and St. Mary Rotherhith, co. Surrey, she paying to my sister Jane Dix, widow, 2s. 6d. by the week from the day of my death, and to my cousin Catherine Garth, widow, the daughter of my said sister Jane Dix, one annuity of £5, and after her (the said Catherine's) decease, to Robert Garth her son during the term of his life. And whereas I am possessed of 40 shares in the Company for Smelting Lead with seacoals, commonly called Lead Shares, I do give unto my wife the dividends of ten shares during her life or widowhood, and after her death or marriage I give the said dividends to my three children John Thompson, Jane Ford and Andrew Thompson equally; and the residue of the said 40 shares I give unto my said three children equally. All the rest of my estate I give unto my wife, except such part as shall hereinafter be given to my son Andrew when he shall attain to full age—my said wife to carry on the trade of a distiller during that time, and then to take my said son as a co-partner with her; and after the decease or marriage of my wife I give to my said son Andrew my dwelling house and stillhouse situate in West Lane in St. Mary Magdalen, Bermondsey, together with six other messuages in said lane, and the messuage in Salisbury Lane in said parish, etc. Other messuages devised in remainder to other children. Executrix: my wife Jane. Dated 6 April, 1740. Witnesses: Patrick

Shea, Abra: Harman, Daniel Stow.   Proved 2 May, 1740, by the
executrix.   (P. C. C.   Browne, 157.)

The Alexander Thompson, legatee in the above will, was
certainly that Alexander Thompson of Newport, Rhode Island,
who was married at Bristol, R. I., to Mrs. Ann Gladding of that
place, 12 Aug., 1702, by the Rev. John Burt.*
The town records of Newport are practically non-extant.
They were carried away by the Tory Sheriff, at the evacuation of
the place by the British in 1779, and sunk, with the transport in
which they were carried, in Hell Gate on the passage to New York.
They were returned in December, 1782, by General Carleton,
then in command of New York, but in a deplorable condition
from their long immersion in salt water and subsequent neglect.†
They are now being subject to expert restoration but it is improbable that much can be saved from the ruin.
An Alexander Thompson who married at Cumberland, R. I.,
4 May, 1794, Joanna Wilkinson, may have been a descendant.‡

I RICHARD JONES, now belonging to the Shipp *Mayflower* of
London, being sicke in body, make my last will and Testament
. . . this twentie nynth daye of September, Anno 1638.   I
give and bequeath to Elizabeth Austin £10, and in case the
said Elizabeth be married or contracted to any man but my selfe
ere the return of the abovesaid Shipp from St. Thoma, I will
that the said sum be equally divided amongst my other legatees.
To the ship's company £5 to drinke.   To my father £20.   To
my brothers Roger, John and Lewis £6 apiece.   To my sisters
Loure and Mary £5 and £4 respectively.   Richard Jones £5.
Thomas Jones £3.   Sister Ellinor's children £10.   John Worcester my rugg and pillow.   John Chester my best hatt.   To my
master Thomas Bratheridge a small runlett of sugar.   Witnesses:
John Worcester, John Chester.   Executor: brother Lewis Jones.
I will that my loving friend Captaine Peter Andrewes be putt in
trust for gathering together my debts, etc.   Witnesses: As above.
Proved 23 January, 1638-9, by the executor named.
                                              (P. C. C.   Harvey, 9.)

While it is by no means certain that this was the celebrated
Pilgrim ship, as she would have been a very old vessel at this
date, the co-incidence of a ship *Mayflower* and the name of Jones,
was so striking that the will seemed worthy of a place in this
collection.
An earlier *Mayflower* was named in the will of one William
Bradstock who died abroad (*in partibus transmarinus*) dated
19 Aug., 1619, and proved in the Prerogative Court of Canterbury
(Soame, 74).‖   This vessel we also fail to identify with the
historic ship.

---

* Arnold's *Vital Records of Rhode Island*, VI, 52.
† *Newport Hist. Magazine*, VI, 117.
‡ Arnold's *Vital Records, op. cit.*
‖ *Abstracts of Wills, Register Soame*, by J. H. Lea, p. 294.

CLUES FROM ENGLISH ARCHIVES
CONTRIBUTORY TO AMERICAN GENEALOGY.

BY J. HENRY LEA AND J. R. HUTCHINSON.

Will of ELIZABETH SALTER of Dedham, co. Essex, widow, dated
1 Dec., 1660. Being aged and weakly in body. I give to Thomas
Salter my son £10, and to John, Elizabeth and Hannah, children
of my said son by Phillippa Rouse his first wife, £30 amongst
them or so many of them as shall attain the age of one and
twenty. To Theophilus Salter my son £5. Item I give and
bequeath unto Abigail Hammond my daughter, of New England,
the sum of tenn pounds to be paid unto her within two years
and six months after my decease, or, if she depart this life, then
to her children equally at their ages of one and twenty. Item I
give and bequeath unto my daughter Hannah Phillipps of
New England the sum of five pounds besides that five pounds
that she have of mine already, to be paid within two years after
my decease, or, if she departs this life, then to her children at
one and twenty. Poor of Dedham 20s. Mr. Robert Astlye,
pastor of the church in Stratford, 20s. The residue of my goods
I give to Samuel Salter my son, and him I ordain executor.
Witnesses: Bezaliel Anger, Stephen How "the eler." Proved
15 June, 1662, by the executor.

(Com. London, Essex and Herts, Alderton, 136.)

Theophilus Salter was resident at Ipswich, Mass., in 1648.
John Hammond of Watertown, Mass., had wife Abigail* and
Nicholas Phillips married 4 December, 1651, Hannah Salter,†
in whom we can recognize with certainty the two daughters of

---

* *Savage*, II, 343.
† *Ibid*, III, 14.

the testatrix. Bezaliel Anger we also recognize as one of the well known family of that name so intimately connected with the Shermans in the Emigration period. Compare also the will which follows.

Will of DANIEL DEACON of Dedham, co. Essex, taylor, dated 22 April, 1668. Being sickly and weak in body. Cousin Samuel Deacon, clerk, £50. Cousin Joseph Deacon of Colchester, shoemaker, £10. Cousin Daniel Deacon of Langham, £15. Cousin Mary Frances of Stratford, £5. Children of my cousin Susan Comball, deceased, £5. Nicholas Prigg, clerk, £5. Mrs Ellen Astye, widow of Mr Robert Astye, clerk, £5, and to that Society of people that he sometimes meet with £5, to be distributed by my executor amongst the meanest of them. Cousin John Deacon's widow £10, and every of her children that she had by my cousin £10 at 21. My executor shall pay into the hands of my cousin Daniel Deacon of Langham that £10 given to John Deacon, son of John Deacon, whom he hath taken for an apprentice, and pay the said £10 to the said John Deacon when he cometh of age. The other two children (under 16) of John Deacon, deceased, and their mother, his widow. Item I give to those ministers that have most frequently preached the gospell to the Natives in New England & have endeavoured to bring them to the knowledge of Christ, the sum of five pounds; (and) if they be dead, then to their children. To Mr Matthew Newcomen, late Minister in Dedham, 30s., and to Mrs Elizabeth Smith, ye widow of Mr George Smith deceased, 30s., and if either of them be dead, then I give it to their children. Poor of Dedham £10 and tenn good Bibles. Poor of Langham £5 and five good Bibles to be distributed by Mr Seaborn. To Elizabeth, wife of John Dowdell, junior, that beadsteadle that she usually lodgeth in. Residue to my cousin William Parker, tayler in Dedham. Executor: my friend Bezaliell Anger, clothier in Dedham. Witnesses: John Dowdell, John Dowdell, junior. Proved 11 July, 1669, by the executor. (Com. London, Essex and Herts, Fish, 374.)

We have probably in the above testator a near relative of the John Deacon, blacksmith, who came with wife Alice in the *Abigail*, in July, 1635, he aged 28 and she 30, settled at Lynn, Mass., where his wife died 27 July, 1657, and he remarried 25 December following, Elizabeth, widow of John Pickering and afterward removed to Boston.

In a deposition taken in 1662* he calls himself five years older than in the passenger list. There seems no connection between this John and that earlier one who died suddenly at Plymouth in 1635–6, and whose property was trusteed, 2 July, 1640, by John Howland to Daniel Salmon of Saugus for Richard Francis *alias* Deacon.

This eight daie of Aprill, 1616, I GEORGE RUGGLE the elder of Sudburie in the Countie of Suff., clothier, dyseased of bodie. . . .

---

give and bequeath vnto Jefferie Ruggle my youngest sonne that tenement howse that I nowe dwell in, and I give out of this howse vnto John and Samuell, sonnes of the said Gefferie Ruggle my youngest sonne, tenne poundes apeece at their severall ages of one and twentie, and vnto Susan, daughter of my said sonne, the like summe at her age of eighteene yeares, Yf Susan, nowe wife to my sonne Gefferie, doe outlive him, I will that she have the said howse during the tearme of her naturall life; but yf she die, then I will that the howse descend to the sonnes of my sonne Gefferie. To Martin Harris, sonne vnto Martin Harris my sonne in lawe, and to John Harris sonne to the same Martin, five poundes apeece at full age; and yf either of them die before said age, I will that it retorne vnto Bridgett Harris their mother. To John Ruggle's children, my eldest sonne, namely, George (under 21), Phillip, now wife of George Hammonde, Elizabeth (under 18) and Susan (under 18), 20s. apeece. To my sonne George Ruggle's children, George, John and Amos (at 21), and Anne Ruggle (at 18), 20s. apeece. To my brother William's sonne Thomas 13s. 4d. Brother Edward Ruggle 15s., and to my sister his wife 5s. to buye her some lynen, and to his children Nicholas, Richard and Mary Ruggle 6s. 8d. apeece. Elizabeth Bushop 10s., and her fower children (minors) 6s. 8 d. apeece. To the childe of Fama Horne lately deceased, 6 s. 8d., to be paid him at his age of one and twentie. Sonne in lawe Robert Allden 13s. 4d. and Robert his sonne the like sum. Thomas Ruggle my brother 20s. and his five children (minors) 6s. 8d. apeece. To George, sonne of my eldest sonne John Ruggle, £50 conditionallie that when he comes to the tyme of enjoying it he shall freelie impart that peece of grounde that belongeth to the howse where John Ruggle my sonne nowe dwell, to that part that George Ruggle my sonne nowe dwell in. I doe give and quitclaim all my right to that howse which my sonne George Ruggle nowe dwelleth in, with the other howse that Nicholas Ruggle did dwell in, vnto my sonne George Ruggle and his heires for ever for a certain summe of money that I have had of him. John Berrie 13s. 4d. Mr Jenkins, preacher of All Saints, 20s. Mr John Harrison, preacher of God's words at St. Peter and Gregorie in Sudburie, (sum not stated.) To that reverent preacher of God's worde in London, Mr Bacheler, 20s. Mr Peachie, preacher of Great Waldingfeilde, 20s. Mr Sephery, preacher, 20s. Mr Greenewood 10s. Mr Sandes, preacher at Boxforde, 20s. Mr James Allen, scholler, 20s. *Mr Rogers of Dedham, preacher, 20s.* Mrs Mills of All Saints, widowe, 13s. 4d. and her sonne John Mills 10s. at full age, or, if he die before said age, the money shalbe equallie parted amongst his fower systers, who shall likewise have 6s. 8d. apeece at eighteene or marriage. Poore of All Saints 20s., of St. Peter's 10s., of St. Gregorie's 13s. 4d., of the hamlet of Balington 6s. 8d. All the rest of my goods I will shalbe parted equallie between my fower children John, George and Jefferie Ruggle and Bridgett Harris, saving that I give to Mr Sallis of Brissett 20s., to Mr Gullsonne of Dedham, schole master, 20s., to Susan Ruggle, nowe my wife £10, and to Mr Bawle 20s. Executors: my sonnes John and George Ruggle. Witnesses: Robert John, John Day, Thomas Tailer. Proved 10 May, 1616, by the executors named.

(P. C. C.   Cope, 52.)

Jeffrey Ruggles of Boston, Mass., came over in the fleet with Gov. Winthrop in 1630. He was from Sudbury in Suffolk, and died before the end of the year. It is interesting to note that he had help from the Rev. John Rogers, also a legatee in the above will, during the famine of that period.*

Jeffery, George and John Ruggles, Sr., of Boston, may have been and probably were, brothers or very near kin, but it seems unlikely that they were the three sons of these names mentioned in the testator's will. They were far more likely to have been grandsons of this George who died in 1616 or, possibly, sons of one of his three brothers, Thomas, William or Edward.

Will of TOBIAS BOXE "being bound to go a voyage to St. Christopher's in the good ship called the *Hopewell* of London, Cooper," Dated 25. December, 1628. I give to Annis Bar*k*er [*sic*] of London, spinster, 46 pounds of tobacco in the hands of Leanard Huitt, quartermaster of the good ship the *Indeavor* of London, bound from Virginia, which she received of George Ayres, planter of Virginia; also all my clothes and pay which shall be found due to me. Sole legattee and executrix: the said Agnes Bar*b*er [*sic*]. Signed: [*Tobias Box*.] Witnesses: James Man: Josias Man. Proved: 15 Dec., 1629, by Agnes Bar*b*er [*sic*] the executrix named.   (P. C. C.   110, Ridley.)

I EDWARD WATERS of Elizabeth Cittie in Virginia, gent, being sicke . . . bequeath my body to be decently buried in the church or churchyard where I shall depart this life. . . . All my lands in Virginia I give vnto William Waters my sonne, and for all my other goods in England, Virginia, Ireland or els where, I appoint sale to be made of them by my executor, by the advice of my brother John Waters of Midleham in Yorkshire and Mr Lionell Rowlston of Elizabeth Cittie, gentleman, and (*the proceeds*) to bee equallie divided betweene Mrs Grace Waters my nowe wife, William Waters my sonne, and Margaret Waters my daughter, their portions to be vsed by mine Overseers while my said children shall come to the age of one and twentie years or bee married. Executor: William Waters my sonne. Dated 20 August, 1630, at Great Hornemead in Hartfordshire. I will that Mr Pennington my good friend at the redd lyon in Cheapside, London, bee first paid fowerscore and eight pounds which I have had of him . . . to cleare my tobacco nowe beinge in his Sellar in paine therefor. Witnesses: Daniel Cage, Phil: Cage, Solomon Cole. 18 Sept., 1630, commission to John Waters, brother of deceased, to administer during the minority of William Waters, son of deceased, the executor named.

(P. C. C.   Scroope, 81.)

---

* Pope's *Pioneers*, 394; *Savage*, III, 586.

58

A *very defective* abstract of this will was printed by Emmerton and Waters in the Essex Institute Historical Collections* with a valuable note outlining the whole of Waters' most romantic career.†

JOHN and CHARLES STUART:—Test. Dative of HENRETA BURNET, residenter in Edinburgh and relict of John Stuart, merchant in Carolina, who deceased in Edinburgh in January, 1718, given up by Mr Robert Cheyne, minister of the gospel and residenter in Edinburgh and executor dative as creditor to defunct, for that he on 23 April, 1718, obtained decreet of cognition against John and Charles Stuarts, merchants in Carolina, and sons to the said Henreta Burnet. Confirmed 1 May, 1718.

(Com. Edinbr.)

COLNE, 12 Oct., 1775: Be it remembered that on 2 June, 1775, JOHN RUSHTON of Manchester in the county of Colleton and province of South Carolina, gent, in consideration of £356 to him paid by Richard Sagar of Southfield in Great Marsden in the chapelry of Colne and county of Lancaster, merchant, surrendered one messuage lying at Grindlestone Hurst in Great Marsden, with divers lands there, To the use and behoof of the said Richard Sagar and his heirs for ever.

(Court Rolls, Honor of Clitheroe, co. Lanc.)

Will of JOAN WHITE of West Quantoxhead (co. Somerset), Nuncupative "declared a little before her death." To Richard White, her eldest son, she gave 20 shillings. To her son GAWEN WHITE "if he were living" 12 pence. To her daughter Agnes her best petticoat. Her daughter Alice Residuary Legatee and Executrix. Witnesses: John Cambear, Alexander Wither. Proved 2 May, 1637. Inventory 4 January, 12 Charles I, by Richard Edments, Richard Lukas, John Slococke, Hugh Downe & Samuel Cooksley. (Archdeacon Taunton, File 1637, No. 14.§)

Gawen, Goyen, Gowen or Going White, as his name was variously written in the records, was a planter at Scituate, and proprietor and town officer there 1644. He married 15 October, 1638, Elizabeth Ward, servant to Mr. Hatherley, and died before 8 December, 1664, when his inventory was taken by Timothy and Joseph White, who are conjectured by Savage to have been his sons. Elizabeth White, who married 18 September, 1662, Thomas Pinson, was probably his daughter.§

Will of WILLIAM GYLLETT of Chaffcombe, co. Somerset, dated 1641.* My daughters Habiah and Mary. Land which my son Nathan made over to me by letter of Attorney. My son William, the next reversioner of said land, shall surrender his estate (*therein*) unto Thomas when requested thereunto. I give and

* Op. cit., XVII, No. 1.
† Cf. also *N. E. Hist.-Gen. Register*, XXXI, 393.
‡ Permission to print this will, found during researches in his behalf, we owe to the courtesy of Mr. J. B. White.
§ *Savage*, IV, 509; Pope's *Pioneers of Mass.*, p. 492.

bequeath unto my son Jeremiah my chattle (*lease*) of court ground. To all my children in England I give two silver spoones apiece. I give and bequeath unto my son William and his heirs my land called Bomers lease, on condition that he do pay out of the same one annuity of twelve pounds, vizt., to my daughter Habiah £4, to my daughter Mary £6, and to my son Jeremiah 40s. To Thomas, Jeremiah, Mary and Habiah each of them one chayre and one frame stool. The rest of my goods I give to my son William, whom I make executor, and Mr Joseph Greenfield, Mr Luffe, my brother Richard, and my kinsman Henry Hutchins overseers. Signed: [*William Gyllett*]. Witnesses: None. Proved 16 April, 1641, by the executor.

(Taunton Wills, 1641, File 13.)

The Christian names in this will give unmistakable evidence that we are here dealing with a member of the family of that JONATHAN GILLETT who came, with his brother NATHAN or NATHANIEL, to Dorchester, Mass., where he was freeman 6 May, 1635, Nathan having been admitted the preceeding year, and both of whom removed later to Windsor, Conn.

Jonathan had a son Jeremiah, born 12 and baptised 20 February, 1647, at Windsor, and Nathan a daughter Abia, born 22 August, 1641, a coincedence of unusual names which can hardly have been accidental.†

It seems highly probable that in the testator, WILLIAM GILLETT, we have the father of the two emigrant brothers, bequests to whom were omitted because they had received their portions before leaving England, and the casual mention of Nathan having made over land by Power of Attorney probably refers to an act performed at the time of his departure. In this connection the bequest "*to all my children in England*" is noteworthy.

I WILLIAM RANDALL of Lincoln's Inn, co. Middlesex, Esq., being sick and weake in bodie. To my brothers John and Thomas Randall £200 each; to my brother Robert Randall £100 and all such lands and tenements as I have at Knowle, co. Warwick; to my sister Knight's children 100 marks at 21; to my mother Elizabeth Randall, if she recover from that distemper which she is now under and become able to manage her own estate, 100 marks, but if she doe not recover I give the said sum to my brother Robert's children; to my sister Margery if she become a true Protestant within seven years, 100 marks; if not, then to her children at 21; Item I doe devise will and appoint that there shalbe paide to Richard Bellingham Esq., now in New England, upon his sealing and delivering a general release to my executors, the sum of fourscore pounds; To Lady Smith late wife of Sir Francis Smith deceased £40; to William Sprigg late of Babburie now of London gent £20; to Mr Slader of Broughton £10; to Mr Burroughs preacher at Ulborough £10; to Mr John Burroughs his brother my late servant 20 nobles; to my sister in

---

* The top of this will is defective, a large V-shaped piece being eaten out of it by damp.

† Stiles' *Hist. Windsor*, II, 289, 297; *Savage*, II, 255; Pope's *Pioneers*, 187.

law Mrs Mary Knightly £10 to buy her a nagg; to old Mr Dod 20 nobles; to Mr Hartford minister of Banbury £5; to Mr Wells minister living now in Banbury £5; to Mr Henry Halhead the debt he oweth me and £30; to Mr Crosse of Clements Inn and Mr Francis Lawrence of London all debts they owe me; to Mr Gilpin minister of Knowles £10; to Mr. Wheatley of Banbury apothecary £5; further legacies to old Mr Halhead, Benjamin Lovell of Preston, Thomas Hands of Lutterworth, Andrew Broughton of Maidston, Mr Thomas Fish of Wedgnock, Hugh Hopkins of Wedgnock Park, father in law Richard Knightly, Esq., uncle and aunt Gunter, Katherine Wood with them, Mr William Allen and wife of Banbury, old Mrs Wheatley, and Atalanta Moore. £1200 of mine yet in the hands of Lord Say and Seale. Rent charge of £100 out of lands in the tenure of Captain Gunter for the maintenance of the school of Preston, Northants, the poor of Banbury, and the poor of Henley in Arden. Residuary legatees and executors: my brothers John, Thomas and Robert Randall. Overseers: my father in law Mr Richard Knightley and Mr William Sprigg. Signed and sealed 11 April, 1642. Witnesses: Fran: Croke, William Bruce, Thomas Trapham. Proved 1 Aug., 1642, by John and Thomas Randoll, power being reserved to Robert the other executor.

(P. C. C. Cambell, 100.)

Mr. Richard Bellingham, named in the above will, was one of the most important of the early settlers in Massachusetts Bay. He was descended from an ancient Lincolnshire family* and was himself the son of William Bellingham of Manton and Bromley in that County, whose estate he administered 11 July, 1620.† He had been recorder of the City of Boston in Lincoln for eight years (1625–1633) and came with wife Elizabeth (daughter of Samuel Backhouse of Swallowfield, co. Berks., M. P. for Windsor in that county), and son Samuel (Harv. Univ., 1642) to America in 1634. He at once assumed a leading position in the Colony, was chosen a Selectman immediately after his joining with the Church here, representative in 1635, Deputy-Governor thirteen times, and Governor in 1641, and ten years in all afterwards. He died 7 December, 1672,‡ aged 80, being the last surviving patentee of the charter.§

On the 2 November, 1646, John ffish and Jonathan ffish, his brother, then of Boston in New England, drew a bill of exchange on their father Thomas Fish of Wedgnock Park at Good Rest House or els in Warwick, in Warwickshire, England,‖ and later, a letter of Attorney dated 28 February (12th month), 1647, was issued by John Fish of Wroxall in the county of Warwick to Edmund Leach of London, merchant, to sue for debts due to him " by any persons in New England or els where in America " with

---

* See his pedigree in Harl. Soc., vol. L, p. 117.
† P. C. C. Admon Act Books.
‡ See his will in *N. E. Hist.-Gen. Register*, XIV, 237.
§ *Savage*, I, 161; *Pope*, 44; *Register*, XXXVI, 381.
‖ Aspinwall's Note Book, 261.

especial reference to two bonds of £80 and £60 each from Thomas Dexter dated in November and December, 1640.*
The pedigree of the Knightly family, here mentioned, was recorded in the Visitation of the county of Warwick taken in the year 1619.†

8 July, 1675, I, WILLIAM FISH, citizen and leatherseller of London, do give unto my daughter Susanna, after the death of my mother Isabella Fish, widow, all that my messuage or tenement situate in or near Barking in the county of Essex, adjoining unto Firnehill, in the present possesion of my said mother; and for default of heirs of the body of the said Susanna, I give the same unto my wife Susanna, and after her death unto my brother Thomas Fish and the heirs of his body, I give and devise unto my wife Susanna all that parcel of ground at Milend Green which I hold by lease from Sir William Smith. I give unto my daughter Susanna £150 at 21 or marriage. To my said brother Thomas Fish £5, if he be then living and *shall return home again from beyond the seas* and demand it. To my friend Mr Randall Roper, salemaker, and to Mr Henry Wicks, armourer, 40s. apiece. The residue I give to my wife Susanna, whom executrix, and my friends Mr Randall Roper and Mr Henry Wicks Overseers. Witnesses: Thomas Ilot, Tobyah Winne, scr.
Codicil, dated 8 July, 1675. If when my daughter Susanna comes to full age, she be minded to sell the premises to her devised, I will that she shall have power to do so, if her mother be dead. Witnesses: Thomas Ilott, Tobyah Winn, scr. Proved 14 October, 1675, by Susanna Fish, relict and executrix.
(P. C. C. Dycer, 99.*)

Compare also the will of Augustine Fish of Bowden Magna, co. Leicester, proved 23 September, 1647 (P. C. C. Fines, 186), who names "William Fish in New England, if he return, etc.," which has already been published.‡

12 June, 1683, I, JOSEPH SMITH the elder of Thaxsted, co. Essex, grocer, do make my last will and testament in manner and form following, that is to say, I give unto Judith my wife some household goods of all sorts, and to my son Joseph that house and land which I bought of the widow Leader and Newman her son, lying near Cutler's Green in Thaxted, the rent thereof, after my wife's decease, to be for my grandchild Joseph Smith, to bring him up well in learning until his age of fifteen years, when he shall be put out apprentice, and at his age of twenty-four years he shall have the full estate, or, if he die, his brother Thomas shall have it. I give unto my son Joseph the threee crofts I bought of Henry Leader, lying near Cutler's Green, on condition

* *Ibid*, pp. 234, 235.
† Harl. Soc., XII, 399.
‡ For permission to print the above interesting will we are indebted to Mr. John D. Fish, from whose collection it has been taken.
§ *Water's Gleanings*, vol. I, page 141.

that he pay to his sister Hannah, wife of John Day, £2–10, and
so from one quarter to another so long as she shall continue in
this nacon of England; and if it happen that my son in law John
Day should come over into England, and should leave his
daughter Hannah, (*then I give to her*), after her mother's decease, the sum of fifty pounds; and if the said John Day should
happen to come over in this nacon and shall take his wife
and child away with him and carry ym out of this nacon, then I
give unto him fifty pounds, desiring him to be quiet withal and
not to be contentious; but if he will not be quiet then I give him
but one shilling and no more; and if my daughter Hannah Day
shall go over sea and come again into England and be in want,
then my mind is she shall have the aforesaid rent paid as aforesaid. I give unto my ten grandchildren, Judith Level, Mary
Level, Hannah Level, Sarah Level, Robert Level, Mary Smith,
Isaac Smith, Joseph Smith, Thomas Smith and John Smith 20s.
apiece. To Robert Smith of High Rothing, husbandman, son of
William Smith, 20s. To my poor friends called by ye name of
Quakers £5. To Abraham Pledger 40s. Thomas Potts 20s.
Residuary legatees and executors: Joseph Smith my son and
Robert Level my son in law. Witnesses: John Freeman, George
Mills, John Wright, Robert Pomfret. Proved 22 Oct., 1688, by
the executors.

(Com. London, Essex and Herts, Reg. Hamor, f. 243.)

The Quaker reference made in this will is interesting and
would seem to show a probable connection with Pennsylvania
of some of the legatees.

I Capt. Robert Smallay of the Bermoda hundred doe make
my last will, that is to say, I give to my man Christopher Hardyn
three barrells of Indean corne; to my man Thomas Chapman
fifty waight of the best Tobacko; to my man Richard Kyes
five yards of kersey and twoe barrells & halfe of corne Indean;
to my man Thomas Oge three barrells of Corne Indean; to my
wife Elizabeth Smallay my house and ground at the Bermoda
hundred, twoe cowes and other livestock there, and all my goods.
There are certayne notes in my truncke to receive Tobacco for
other men. More, there are notes of Mr Peers, with Ensigne
Chaplyn and Mr Proctor their names specified. Proctor is
to pay me xxli of the best Tobacco for corne wch he had of
Leivetenent Bartlet. Sir Thomas Dale oweth me for threescore
and three pounds of Tobacco at iijs. iiijd. the pound. All my
own Tobacco is in my house at the Bermoda hundred. I am to
have of Thomas Chapman fower hundred pounds of Tobacco at
Henrico. I doe give to Capt: Samuell Argall, Esqr., nowe
Gov'nor of Virginea, two yoke of oxen when my Tobacco hath
payd for them, whome I doe entreate to be my executor. Yeoven
the 19th day of December, 1617. Witnesses: Henry Richardson,
John Downeman. 15 Nov., 1621, commission to Elizabeth Smalley,
relict of deceased, to administer, Samuel Argall, the executor,
renouncing. (P. C. C. Dale, 19.)

CLUES FROM ENGLISH ARCHIVES
Contributory to American Genealogy.

By J. Henry Lea and J. R. Hutchinson.

Nash v. Elbridge: Bill of Complaint of Thomas Nash of Claynes, co. Worcester, gent., executor of the will of Richard Guy late of Ashton upon Tarrent, co. Gloucester, gent., deceased, and Susan late wife of said Richard, dated 16 April, 1646. One Giles Elbridge of the City of Bristol, merchant, deceased, was in his lifetime seized of lands known as Watton farm, lying in Watton, co. Gloucester, and being so seized, he did, about five years since, demise the said lands to the said Richard Guy for a term of years yet enduring, by the yearly rent of £105. About two years since the said Richard Guy made his last will, appointing plaintiff and one Edward Guy his executors, but owing to the troubles of the times the said will is not yet proved in due form of law. About two years since the said Giles Elbridge also died, after whose decease the said premises ought to descend and come to John Elbridge, son and heir of said Giles, but for the delinquency of the said Giles Elbridge the Committee for Gloucester long since seized upon the said farm and rent, and the said John Elbridge, having as executor gotten the said lease into his possession, doth sue plaintiff for the aforesaid rent and for great sums of money, alleged to be due and unpaid unto his said father in his lifetime, and doth further pretend that the said Richard Guy stood indebted unto his said father in a bond for £100. The witnesses who could prove the truth of these statements are all either dead or beyond the seas.

ANSWER of John Elbridge, defendant, sworn 1 June, 1646: It is true that Gyles Elbridge did grant, 1 May, 17 Charles I., to Richard Guy the said messuage called Wattons farm for seven years for £105 per annum, but the said Richard Guy failed in his payments. Giles Elbridge made his will 24 Feb., 1643-4, and thereby devised the premises to this defendant, and shortly after died. (Chan: Pro., Chas. 1., N. 5: 21.)

The place of origin and parentage of Giles Elbridge, the Pemaquid Patentee of 1632, had been abandoned as an insoluble problem by Col. Chester and other early workers,* but it was reserved to be the good fortune of one of the writers to find this clue in the Bristol Town Records, too late indeed for incorporation into Prof Salisbury's monumental work† but early enough, happily, to give the talented author the satisfaction of knowing the truth before he passed away.

The following brief sketch embodies several facts, beside his affiliation, not heretofore known.‡

Giles Elbridge, son of William Elbridge, apothecary, of the City of Gloucester, was bound apprentice to Robert Aldworth and Martha his wife, of Bristol, 13 June, 1608,§ and was admitted a Burgess 1 Oct., 1615,‖ in virtue of this service, Robert Aldworth being then an Alderman of the City, and whose partner he subsequently became.

His first wife was Elizabeth Aldworth, daughter of John Aldworth, the brother of his former master, to whom he was married before 1624. He married, secondly, at St. Stephen's, Bristol, 30 April, 1635, ¶Mrs. Mary Hooke, daughter of Humphrey Hooke, merchant and Alderman of Bristol. She was buried 30 Nov., 1637, in the Aldworth Family vault in the Church of St. Peters, Bristol.**

Giles Elbridge's sons Robert, John and Thomas Elbridge were also admitted to the freedom of the City in right of their father,†† the last named having been a joint grantee with him of Pemaquid.‡‡ Capt. Giles Elbridge died in 1643 and was buried, 25

---

* *Family Memorials*, 1885, by Prof. E. E. Salisbury, pt. i, p. 118.
† Op. Cit. See account of *Aldworth & Elbridge Families*, pt. i, pp. 103-143.
‡ See also Aldworth and Elbridge wills in *Waters' Gleanings*, i, 632-6, and 734-5.
§ *Bristol Apprentice Books*.
‖ *Bristol Burgess Books*, 12 Dec., 1630.
¶ St. Stephens Parish Register.
** *Family Memorials*, op. cit., pt. i, p. 132, but there called *daughter* of her husband.
†† *Burgess Books*.
‡‡ *Savage*, ii, 106.

Feb., of that year, in the same vault with his wife. * His will
was probated in the Prerogative Court at London, 19 March,
1643-4.† (Oxford Will filed.)

Will of JOHN TROWBRIDGE of Exeter, co. Devon. There is
oweinge vnto me from my uncle Mr. James Marshall of Exon,
merchant, £49, and from my father Mr Thomas Trowbridge £10
which I lent him, and I have sent for Muclinx (*sic*) eight peeces
of Sarges, cost twentie pounds And twentie fowre pounds Mr
Jno: Manninge of New England, merchant, owes me, and twentie one pounds Mr William Davis of Muskeeta in Newfoundland
owes, which I have ordered George Pardon, master of the Will-
inge Minde, to receive of him this yeare there and carry it with
him for St. Lukas and bring home returnes with him, All which
summes amounts vnto £129, of which if it please God to take me
hence £20 shalbe disbursed for my buriall, and of the other £109
I give vnto my honored father fortie pounds, to my brothers
Thomas, William and James Trowbridge betweene them £50, to
my aunt Mace £5, and to my cozen James Marshall £14. Dated
at Taunton, 20 Oct., 1653. Witnesses to the identity of the handwriting: James Marshall, senior, Christo: Clarke, junior, Chr:
Dore. 26 June, 1654, commission to Thomas Trowbridge, father
and principal legetary named in the will of John Trowbridge, late
of the city of Exeter, deceased, to administer.

(P. C. C. Alchin, 492.)

The legatee in the preceeding will was certainly the Captain
John Manning of Boston, Mass., merchant, who was of that place
as early as 1640, of the Ancient and Honorable Artillery Co. in
1641, later an Ensign of same and called *"Captain"* in town
records after 1655, probably from his having commanded a vessel, as he does not appear to have held that office in the Artillery
Co. He died after 1664. He is not to be confused with the Capt.
John Manning of New York (1664–1685) Sheriff there 1667–72,
and whose unjust punishment for the surrender of Fort James to
the Dutch in 1673 is a matter of history. His residence, on an
island in the East River, was carried by the marriage of a step
daughter (failing his own issue) to Robert Blackwell who gave
his name to the now well known Blackwell's Island.‡

Will of JOHN SHEPARD of Towcester, co. Northampton, mercer, dated 16 July, 1643. I give and bequeath unto my eldest son
WILLIAM SHEPPARD now in New England all the goods which I
sent over unto him in May or June, 1643, in a ship called the
Concord, which are expressed in a book and amount to £72; and
also all other goods which he carried over at his first going thither,
if it please God that they come safe to him and that he live to
enjoy and possess them in a married estate, either in New England or in Old England ; but if it should please God that he

* *Family Memorials*, pt. i, p. 119.
† *Ibid.* loc. cit.
‡ *Manning Genealogy*, by W. H. Manning (1902), pp. 780 and 803 ; Savage
Gen. Dict., iii, 147, Pope's Pioneers, 209.

should die before the said goods come to him, or he be marrried, then my will is that they be returned for the use of my executrix and surviving children, provided that my son WILLIAM shall have power to dispose of five pounds as he seeth good; and for this part of my will in particular I desire my brother THOMAS SHEPARD of Cambridge in New England, and Mr. Collins now of the same town, to be overseers to see it performed; and I do further give and bequeath unto my said son WILLIAM SHEPPARD my house in Northbarrstreet in Banbury, if so be it please God he live to come over again to Old England and be married there, or live in Old England unmarried, or if he should be disposed to sell it (upon good advise) and be desirous to live in any other land or place, then my will is that my son JOHN, my son SAMUEL, and son DANIEL shall have 20 marks apiece out of the sale of it, if they live; but if my son WILLIAM die before he return to Old England again, and be not married, nor have anie heir of his body lawfully begotten, then the said house, shall go to my other three sons and my daughter ELIZABETH, or if all die, then to my wife for life, and thereafter to my right heirs. Son JOHN the house I purchased of Thomas and John Winfield, in the high street in Towcester, at 21. Son SAMUEL the house purchased of John Hayle of Hechencoate in the parish of Towcester, at 22. Daughter ELIZABETH £100 at marriage, provided she do not marry until she be 18, unless with consent of her mother. Youngest son DANIEL, at 21, four acres of land purchased of my father in law William Kingston lying in Towcester Fields and Spittlefields, two acres purchased of Michael West, two acres purchased of Anne Jennings, and the meadow purchased of Robert Marriott of Caldecott. Daughter Anne Hartly 40s. to buy her a ring, and to her son Francis Hartly two silver spoons. My adventure of £150 for lands in Ireland, in which my cousin Richard Farmer hath £100, and my brother George Waple £50, shall be divided amongst my sons. Residue to wife Frances, whom executrix. Overseers: brother Georgo Waples, cousin Richard Farmer, friend John Linnill, and my son WILLIAM SHEPPARD if he live to retnrn home again. The house in Towcester which my father WILLIAM SHEPPARD did give unto me his eldest son and to my heirs after the decease of his wife, my mother in law Amy Sheppard, I give to my wife for life, in accordance with my father's will, after the death or my said mother Amy. Witnesses: William Pitchford, Andrew Paine, Peter Deakin. Proved 6 June, 1646, by the executrix. (P. C. C. Twisse, 88)

Rev. Thomas Shepherd, first pastor of the church at Cambridge, Mass., born at Towcester, co. Northants, 5 Nov., 1605, graduated at Emanuel College, Cambridge, England,* came to Boston, 1635. He married (1) in England, 1632, Margaret Toutiville, who died in 1636 and he married (2) 1637, Joanna Hooker, daughter of Rev. Thomas Hooker and (3) 1647, Margaret Boradile who remarried to Mr. Jonathan Mitchell. He died 28 Aug.,

---

* *History of First Church of Cambridge.*

1648.* He was evidently identical with the brother of the testator and was uncle of Samuel Shepherd of Cambridge, Mass., freeman there 13 March, 1635-6, proprietor and town officer 1638-9, and Major. He was living with his wife Hannah in Ireland in 1658† but at that time still retaining membership of the Cambridge Church.

It seems more than doubtful whether the William Shepherd, eldest son and principal legatee in the above will could have been that William of Dorchester whose unsavory record in the Massachusetts Courts in 1636 is so well known‡ or that later William of Taunton, Mass., in 1650, who is tentatively suggested as being identical with the last named.§ Nor is the identification with that William of Connecticut who, in 1677, was divorced from his wife, more satisfactory.

Much more probable is it that William, the legatee, returned promptly to England after his father's death in 1646, took possession of his estate and left his bones in English soil. An examination of the Parish Registers of Towcester will probably prove this to have been the case. They date from 1561 and furnish valuable information regarding the family.

The fourteenth day of August, 1656, I WILLIAM BOYS of Cranbrooke in the county of Kent, clothier, being in some good measure of health, doe make and ordaine this my last will. My bodie I will to be decently buried at the discretion of Joan my wife, whom I make sole executrix of this my will. I give and bequeath unto Sibylla Boys my eldest daughter £200 when she shall attaine the age of eighteene years; to Mary Boys my daughter the like summe at her said age; and to my four sonnes John, Thomas, William and Joseph Boys £200 apiece of good English money at their severall ages of one and twentie years. As for my house and land in Cranbrooke, which now I inabite and which I lately purchased, viz., seven parts of eight parts thereof, I give the same unto Joan my wife during her naturall life and after her decease unto my four sonnes before named equally and to their heirs for ever. And if it shall happen that the other part should be desired to be sold, which now belongs unto John Slow sonne of Thomas Slow in New England, then my mind and will is that my wife shall purchase the same in behalf of my four sonnes, paying for it out of the portions before given them. If my said wife happen to marry again she shall give sufficient suritie to my brother Edmund Colvill of Maidstone for payment of my children's portions. Witnesses: none. Proved 24 Feb., 1656-7, by Joan Boys the relict and executrix. (P. C. C. Ruthen, 72.)

Thomas Slow, was of Providence, R. I., and admitted freeman there in 1655.‖ There was a joseph Boyes, tanner, in Salem,

---

* *Pope's Pioneers of Mass.*, p. 412.
† Cf. the mention of "adventure of £150 in Ireland, to be divided amongst my sons" in the will.
‡ *Savage*, iv, 77.
§ *Pope's Pioneers*, p. 412.
‖ *Savage*, iv, 108.

Mass., and proprietor there in 1638, who died in 1684, but it is improbable that he was the son Joseph of the testator, who would have been already eighteen years in America at the making of the will, while the children of the testator were evidently very young at that time.*

THIS third daie of September, 1657, I THOMAS ENSIGNE of Cranbrooke in the countie of Kent, yeoman, being sicke and weake in body, do make this my last will and testament: I give and bequeath unto my uncle William Austen 20s.; to my aunt his wife 20s.; to my cousin Hannah Miller, William Austen, Sarah Austen, and Mary Austen, being the son and daughters of my said uncle William Austen, 20s. apiece; to my cousin Sarah Johnson, widow, relict of Ambrose Johnson late of Biddenden, co. Kent, clothworker, deceased, 6s. 8d.; and to my cousins Martha Woolball and (*blank*) Woolball, the two daughters of Richard Woolball of Biddenden, clothier, 6s. 8d. apiece. I ordain and make my cousin John Austen, son of my uncle William Austen, sole executor of this my last will, unto whom I give full power to take up the yearly rents of my lands situate in Stapleherst and Cranbrooke, now in the occupation of Lawrence Tyler, for and during the term of five years, to pay my legacies aforesaid, and also to pay to Christopher Bourne of Biddenden, yeoman, £7-7 when the same shall become due. I give and bequeath unto my dearly beloved father Thomas Ensigne in Nue England all the rents and profits of my messuage, barn, garden, orchard, close and six pieces of land, containing 26 acres, being the same before mentioned, now in the occupation of Lawrence Tyler, to the use and behoof only of my said father and his assigns during his natural life, after the end of five years next after my decease; and as for the fee simple of my said messuage and land, as expressed in one deed of division bearing the date 20 Feb., 1632–3, I give the same to my brother John Ensigne his heirs and assigns for ever, provided always that he my said brother do pay unto my two sisters, Hannah and Sarah, ten pounds apiece at their several days of marriage or ages of twenty years, which shall first accede. And further it is my mind and will that what goods shall be sent to me from Neu England, which I shortly expect, my executor and my loving friend Mr Harman Sheaf, whom I make overseer of this my will, shall have and sell the same to the best advantage and make return thereof to the use of my brother and sisters in Neu England. Signed: [*Thomas Ensigne,*] in presence of Henry Greene, Peter Master. Proved 24 March, 1657-8, by John Austen, (*cousin and*) sole executor.†   (P. C. C. Wootton, 198.)

Thomas Ensigne, planter, of Scituate in 1638, freeman there 6 March, 1638–9, deacon in 1653. He married, 17 Jan., 1638, Eliza Wilder. His will dated 16 July, 1663, and proved 9 June, 1664, by its mention of his surviving children, John, Hannah and

---

* Pope's *Pioneers*, p. 62.
† The words *"cousin and"* are from the Probate Act Book.

Sarah, completes his identification as the father of the testator in in "Neu England."

The Registers of Cranbrook, Biddenden and Staplehurst, all dating from an early period, make this clue an easy one to follow for any persons interested.

I MARY LANGHORNE *alias* INGLESBY, being sensible of appraoching death, make this my last will: My body I leave to be disposed of by my executor as becometh his father's wife and his mother, not pompeously. There is money to defray the charges in Mr John Cooke's hands. I appoint my son Sir William Langhorne my executor and give him £100 to buy him a ring, though his kindness to me deserveth great part of what I have, and though I have nothing worthy of his acceptance I give him the new suit of hangings I brought to Charlton; and if my son Die I desire Mr Cooke to see my will fulfilled. I give to my son Thomas Langhorne £300 and my silver tankard, my diamond ring, my gold watch, and his father's seal ring; to my daughter Katherine James £20 and my gold bodkin, and to her two sons £5 apiece; to my daughter Dorcas Pordage £30, and to her two daughters £5 apiece; to my grandson John Conyers, Esq. £10, and to his three sons 40s. apiece; to my daughter Conyers my pearl necklace; to my brother Clement Oxenbridge and his wife £4, and to his daughter Katherine 40s.; to my dear friend Mrs Petchell my silver cawdle cupp; to her husband 20s.; and to her three children 20s. apiece; to poor prisoners that are honest people £5; and to poor widows which fear God £5. There is owing to my brother Oxenbridge's children £40 borrowed by Captain Ingoldsby and never paid, and they are all dead but one in Jamaica and one in New England, which never came to demand it, but if they should I would have it paid though they are very rich, yet it may be they may in time come over, but I fear they are dead. Dated 24 Nov., 1686. Witnesses: Christopher Jeakins, Edward Rolt, Anne Keey. Proved 16 Dec., 1686, by Sir William Langhorne, Bart.. the excutor.   (P. C. C. Lloyd, 167.)

The above testatrix was daughter of Daniel Oxenbridge, Doctor of Physick, of St. Stephens, Coleman St., London, from Warkwirth, Northumberland. (Will dated 21 Dec., 1641, proved 12 Sept., 1642, P. C. C. Campbell, 110)* and his wife Katherine, daughter of Thomas Harby Esq.,† and was the wife successively, of William Langhorne of London and Putney, and of Hitchin, Herts., merchant, and of Capt. —— Ingoldsby, who was probably deceased at the making of her will.

Clement Oxenbridge, her brother, was of Wimbledon, co. Surrey was still living in 1686, and John Oxenbridge, the other brother, pastor of the First Church of Boston, Mass., until his death in 1674. (Will dated 12 March, (1st mo.) 1673–4, proved 9

---

* *Waters' Gleanings*, i, 419.

† *N. E. Register*, xliv, 195. Called there in error by Waters, *daughter* of Clement Throgmorton.

Jan., 1674 (5),* Suff. Prob. Lib. vi, 75) His daughters Bathshuah, wife of Richard Scott, and Theodora, were undoubtedly the two children surviving "one in Jamaica and one in New England" of their aunts will.

Sir William Langhorne, Bart., the son and Executor, born about 1634, was an East India merchant, of Gray's Inn, 7 July, 1652, and of the Inner Temple, London. He was created a Baronet 28 Aug., 1668, purchased the estate of Charlton, near Greenwich, Kent, in 1680. He was twice married but had no issue and at his death, 26 Feb., 1714–15 the title became extinct.†

20 May, 1686, I NATHANIEL MICKELTHWAITE the elder of London, Merchant, give unto my wife Joanna £1250; to my son Nathaniel £1250, including the lease of the messuage in Coleman Street wherein I now dwell, or if he die I give the said messuage to my son Jonathan, or in default to my friends Mr Thomas Cubben and Joseph Sibley and my brother in law Mr Francis Crane in trust for my daughter Sarah Benson, wife of Joseph Benson. To my son Jonathan £1100 over and above what I have given with him in placing him apprentice to Mr Archer, my messuage in Pye Ally in Fanchurch Street to be reckoned part of the same. My sisters Anne Knight *alias* Whiteman of New England, Elizabeth Tue *alias* Coleman (*elsewhere "Cole"*) of London, widow, and Hester Crane, wife of the said Francis Crane. My nephew William Tutty of Cheshunt, co. Hertford, baker. Nathaniel Benson my grandson, son of my daughter Sarah Benson. My estate of inheritance in certain lands in Ireland, in the Barony of Rathcouroth, co. Westmeath, let by lease unto Lewes Moares of Colgony. Executors: wife Joanna and sons Nathanil and Jonathan. Witnesses: William Naylor, James French, Phillip Constable, John Wheatley, scr. Proved 6 Dec., 1686, by the executors.

(P. C. C. Lloyd, 168.)

Robert Whitman or Whiteman of Ipswich, Mass., came in the *Abigail* from London, 19 June, 1635, aged 20,‡ he married in 1648 Susanna —— , who died in 1664 and in Nov. of that year he remarried Hannah Knight and was still living in 1679.§ Thus far on the authority of that eminent historian, James Savage, but in the will of William Tutty of St. Stephens, Coleman Street, London, gent., dated 10 Oct., 1640, and proved 9 Jan. following (Com. Lond XXVIII, fo. 234)‖ we have mention of "my eldest daughter Anne, lately married with Alexander Knight of Ipswich in New England beyond the seas," while the will of John Tuttie, citizen and fruiterer of London (son of Wm. Tuttie, gent. dec'd, dated 3 and 5 Sept., and proved 3 Oct., 1657, (P. C. C. Ruthen, 372)

---

* *Waters Glean.*, i, 420. The Oxenbridge wills and valuable notes in Waters should be carefully read by all interested.
† *Complete Baronetage*, by G. E. C., iv, 45.
‡ *Hotton's Lists*, p. 88.
§ *Savage Gen. Dict.*, iv, 524.
‖ *Waters' Gleanings*, i, 842–843.

names his "sister Hannah Knight of New England, and her children" and also his "sister Elizabeth Tew" and her son Nicholas Tew and "brother Micklethwaight."

William Tutty, in the will above cited mentions "Nathaniel Micklethwaite, my wife's son, executor of Paul Micklethwaite late Doctor of Divinity, deceased" which Nathaniel was evidently the testator of the above will, the sisters Anne and Elizabeth being evidently uterine only and the actuall daughters of William Tutty.

11 March, 17 James I., I WILLIAM SHAWE of Wapping in the countye of Middlesix, maryner, being in good and perfect health. This my present intended voyage to Virginia. I give to my six children John, Martha, Mary, Joan, Elizabeth and Sarah Shawe, and to such child or children as my wife now goeth withall £800 equallye amongst them, John and the said child or children unborn to have their portions at one and twenty, and my daughters at one and twenty or marriage; and if all my said children die before their portions come due, then I give the said £800 amongst all the children of my brother Thomas Shawe of Haslington, co. Chester, yeoman, equally. My wife shall have the said money, and the education and bringing up of my said children, untill they come of age. I forgive my brother Thomas all such debts as he oweth me. To my sister Margaret Browne, wife of Hugh Browne of Sandbiche, co. Chester, husbandman, 40s. Sister Cicely Abram of Haslington, co. Chester, widow 40s. Poor of Wapping 40s. To my wife's brother Joseph Chapman 30s. To her brother Jonathan Chapman all my books and sea instruments. To her brother Samuel Chapman 20s. Mr Sedgwick, preacher, of Wapping, 20s. Mr Mekin of London, preacher, £3. Cousin John Shawe of London, goldsmith, £3. Friend Robert Papworth of London, chandler, £3. Residuary legatee and executrix: wife Martha. Overseers: friends Robert Mekyn and Robert Papworth, and cousin John Shawe. I will that my lands in the realm of England or elsewhere shall descend to my son John Shawe as my right and next heir. Witnesses: Richard Greene, scr., Jo: Dearslye. Proved 11 Oct., 1620, by the executrix.

(P. C. C.   Soame, 36.)

1606, Nov. 10, William Shawe of the Tower p'ish & Martha Chapman daughter of William Chapman of Lymehous deceased, License, (*married.*)   (Psh. Reg.   Stepney, Mx.)

I, RICHARD DAVYES now of the parish of St. Leonard's Shoroditch, co. Middlesex, and late of Peankatanke River in Virginia, planter. Dated 26 Aug., 1660. To my wife, Joan Davyes 220 acres of land, being my whole plantation in Peaukatauke River, in Virginia. Also my stock of tobacco, and said wife Executrix. Witnesses: Edward Boswall, Edward Tudman, William Davis, Adam Eve, scrivenor. Proved 5 July, 1661, by the Executrix named.   (P. C. C.   May, 107.)

CLUES FROM ENGLISH ARCHIVES
CONTRIBUTORY TO AMERICAN GENEALOGY.

BY J. HENRY LEA AND J. R. HUTCHINSON.

PRIMO die Januarij, 24 Charles I., I TOBIAS PAYNE of Kingscaple, co. Hereford, gent., make and declare my testament and
and last will in manner and forme following:—I will my body to
be buried in the church of Kingscaple. I give to the poor of
Kingscaple 40s., to the poor of Sellecke and Foye 20s., to the poor
of Howcaple 10s., to the poor of Fownehope 20s., to the poor of
Hentland 20s., to the poor of Ballingham 20s., and to the poor of
Little Burche, Acornburye and Little Dewchurche 30s. To William Payne my eldest son my capital messuage with the lands
thereto pertaining lying in Brodston and Slymbridge, co. Gloucester, for the term of his life, with remainder after his decease
to Tobias Payne his son and the heirs of the said Tobias for ever.
To Thomas Payne my second son all my messuages, lands and
tenements lying in Kingscaple called Lankes Lease, which I late
had on the grant of Thomas Smith of Huntleys, co. Hereford. To

Joan my wife £50. William Morgan my tenant 40s. Tobias Payne, son of the aforesaid William Payne, £20. To Thomas Payne my son and John Payne my son and their heirs all that my messuage called Ruckston, with all lands thereto pertaining, lying in Kingscaple and Fownehope, formerly in the tenure of David Ketherowe deceased; also one other messuage in Kingscaple, within the town there, called Pennalle, in the tenure of John Hyett; and one capital messuage called Daston in the Parish of Hentland. To John Payne my son and his heirs one parcel of meadow (½ acre) lying in Fownehope, called Blackfield, adjoining a parcel of meadow there which I hold in right of Joan my wife and which is part of a tenement in Fownehope called Haverds Farme, purchased to me and my heirs of Thomas Scudamore, gent., deceased, and others. All other my lands and tenements in Fownehope I leave to William my eldest son for life, with remainder to the aforesaid Tobias Paine his son and his heirs for ever. To Joan my wife for life all my messuages, lands and tenements in Rosse Burg and Rosse For, with remainder to my son John and the heirs of his body, or in default to my own right heirs for ever. To Thomas Paine my son and his heirs one messuage in Kingscaple in the tenure of Thomas Lawrence, late conveyed to me and my heirs by Edmund Orchard, deceased, they paying to the Guardians of the parish of Kingscaple 26s. 8d. yearly. Sons Thomas, William and John £50 each. Thomas Puckmore my servant 40s. Anne Paine, John Paine, Richard Paine and Jaine Paine, sons and daughters of William my son, £5 each. To Alice Paine, Margaret Paine, Mary Paine and John Paine, sons and daughters of Thomas my son, £5 each. To William Paine, son of my son William £60. John Baglie my cousin 40s. George Lawrence my servant 20s. Executors: William Paine, Thomas Paine and John Paine my sons, whom Residuary Legatees. Supervisor: Richard Prichard, clerk, vicar of Selecke, to whom £3. Wit: Richard Prichard, Joseph Underwood Thomas Meredith, William Paine, Thomas Paine, John Paine, John Paine, Tobias Paine, junior. Proved 8 Feb., 1649-50, by the executors named.* (P. C. C. Pembroke, 27.)

Tobias Paine came from Jamaica to Boston, probably shortly before 1665, when he married Sarah, daughter of John Winslow (brother of Governor Edward Winslow) and widow of Miles Standish, Jr. His nuncupative will, dated 11 Sept., 1669, was admitted and administration granted 21 Sept. of same year, to his relict Sarah for herself and infant son William, born the same year. (Suff. Mass. Wills.)†

This Tobias Paine of Boston, with son William, is beyond doubt the Tobias, son of William, named in the will of his grandfather Tobias Payne of Kingscaple, co. Hereford, the testator of 1649.

---

* Translated from the original Latin.

† *Paine Fam. Record*, i, 46; *Savages Gen. Dict.*, iii, 337; *N. E. Register*, xix, 310.

WILL of SARAH BRINLEY, wife of Lawrence Brinley of London, merchant, dated 21 July, 1642: Whereas by agreement made before marriage with my said husband it was covenanted between us that it should be lawful for me to dispose and give by my last will or other writing all such goods as then belonged to me except the sum of £1000 agreed to be paid to my said husband in marriage with me. Now by this my last will I do give and bequeath unto Samuel, Lawrence, Richard and Nathaniel Brinley, sons of my said husband, £6–13–4 apiece at 21; to Mary and Anne, the two daughters of my said hasband, the like sum each at said age; to Francis Bickley and John Bickley, sons of John Bickley my late husband deceased, the like sum each at said age; to Samuel son of John Symonds late of Stamford deceased, £5 at said age; to my brother in law Mr Thomas Brinley and his wife 40s. apiece to buy them rings; to my brother in law Nicholas Brinley and wife 40s. apiece to buy them rings; to Susan Gregory, widow, 40s.; to Nicholas Barnett and Susan his wife 30s. each; to my brother in law Thomas Cooke and my sister Jane his wife £5 apiece; to William Powell and Frances his wife £5 apiece; to my sister Anne Love, wife of Thomas Love, 30s.; to Mr Charles Yeoman, Esq., £5; to my cousin Francis Bickley, Esq. 30s.; to my cousin Elizabeth Hopkins, wife of Edward Hopkins, 30s.; to my sister Bridget Barker, wife of Henry Barker £5; to Mr Marmaduke Tenant and wife 30s. apiece; to William Whitworth and Sarah his wife 30s. apiece; to my brother in law Henry Haselwood and Katherine his wife 20s. each; to Dorothy Conn, wife of Thomas Conn, 30s.; to Widow Greene 20s.; to Joan Burte, wife of William Burte, 30s.; to Joseph Brinley, son of my said husband and of me the said Sarah, £50 at 21 with the £50 subscribed by my husband amongst the Irish Adventurers; to Sarah Bickley my daughter £300 at 21 or marriage; to my mother Margaret Beale £10 a year for life; to my sister in law Alice Bolter £3 a year for life: and to Thomas Ball my servant 20s. Residuary Legatee and Executor: my husband Lawrence Brinley, who shall have the guardianship of my daughter Sarah during her minority. Witnesses: Thomas Conn, scr., Thomas Bull. Proved 10 Nov., 1642, by the executor named.

(P. C. C. Cambell, 121.)

Lawrence Brinley of London, merchant, son of Richard Brinley of Wittenhall, co. Stafford, was living in London with wife Mary, daughter of John Minifie of Honiton, co. Devon, and children Samuel, Lawrence, Richard, Mary and Anne in 1634, when his pedigree was registered in the Visitation of that year.* The will shows that another son, Nathaniel, was subsequently born of this marriage, that the first wife died, and, before 1642, Lawrence Brinley had married the above testatrix, Sarah, widow of John Bickley.

The wills of Lawrence himself in 1662 (P. C. C. Laud, 151) and his brother Thos. Brinley of Datchett, co. Bucks, in 1661 (P. C. C. May, 193,) Auditor to Kings Chas. I & II, have already

---

* *Harl. Soc.*, xv, 101.

been printed* with valuable note by the late John Ward Dean in H. F. G. Waters' Collections. Although registered in the Visitation as from Staffordshire, the monument of Thomas Brinley at Datchett, states that he was born at Exeter in Devon.†

2 February, 1659–60, I THOMAS HARPER of London, gent . . . give and devise all that my messuage wherein I dwell, situate in Fetter Layne, and all those lands I lately yurchased of Mr Thomas Willsheim, lying in Great Bowden, co. Leic., and the three pieces of meadow I purchased of John Johnson, together with the four acres of land since purchased of him, and the four acres of meadow purchased of my brother William Harper, situate in Great Bowden, with the house which was part of my grandfather's (sic,) that I bought of Mr Holford after the death of Mary Bent, to my nephew Richard Mowse and heirs, upon trust to discharge all such legacies as are charged upon my house in Fetter Layne by the will of John Ball deceased, and likewise £50 more which Sarah, wife of the said John Ball, hath charged it with by her will, and to pay the yearly rent of £30 in manner following namely, to my sister Hellen Russell and her husband, during the life of said Hellen, £15 a year, and after my said sister's death then to my brother Russell, my brother Peabodie, my brother Mowse and his wife, and my brother Presgrave and wife, £5 a year for life; and if my sister Presgrave outlive her husband, she shall have 50s. a year for life, by reason she was a loving kind mother in law to the two children my sister left behind her. Sister Mowse's two daughters £50 each. Brother Peabody's children by my sister Isabel £50 each. Brother Presgrave's two daughters by my sister Anne £50 each. To the children of my sister Mowse's daughters, of my sister Isabel's daughters and of my sister Anne's daughters, £10 each, the latter at 20. I forgive my brother William Harper the £16 he oweth me, on condition that he pay to his sister Joan 20s. I forgive my brother Richard Harper £5 he oweth me, he paying to his brother John 10s. "if it be demanded." Elizabeth Howlett, my first mother in law's daughter's daughter, £20 in satisfaction of what was given to me for her at her age of 21. Her brother Nevett Howlett £15 at 21. I forgive John Wenniffe and wife the money they owe me, for their care of me in my sickness. Cousins Mary and Elizabeth Mowse all my linen, and to one of them my Perkinson's Herball and to the other my Gerard's Herball. Cousin Hannah Shipley's son £10 at 21, and my executor shall pay for his schooling until he can write and read. Brother Mowse my watch and seal ring; sister Mowse my silver bowle and guilt spoone. Cousin John Harper's sons now in the Blewcoate Hospitall £5 at 21. Sister Hellen the £20 I am engaged to pay her with £20 more. Cousin Richard Harper formerly living in Hounditch at the Signe of the Harpe £5. And whereas I have in my hands twentie shillings belonging to a youth in Barbadoes or Virginny whose mother's name is Rebecca Lever, living in Brandford, I dew give to the

---

* *Waters' Gleanings*, i, 13–14.
† *Lipscomb's Bucks*, vol. iv, p. 441.

said youth in lew and satisfacon thereof fortie shillings to be paid him within halfe a year after my death. I give to Nicholas Dancas and Joan his wife living in Chisique the 40s. they owe me. Mr James Fletcher's wife all my chaney, being one and twentie pieces. Parish of Bowden in Leicestershire where I was borne £5, my brother Russell to have the distributing thereof. To my brother Harris the shepherd and various friends rings with this posie written in them all, viz., "You will follow T. H." Residuary Legatee and Executor: nephew Richard Mowse. Overseers: my brother Mowse and my brother Russell. Witnesses: Thomas Pawley, George Hilton, Samuel Mather. Proved 26 March, 1660, by the executor named.   (P. C. C.   Nabbs, 8.)

I KATHERINE WANNEL of the parish of Christchurch, London, widow, being at this present in health . . . committ my body to be buried in the grave of my father and mother, or soe nere to them as may bee, in the north Ile of the new or upper church of the parish of Christchurch, close by my pewe doore where I nowe vse to sitt, by the steppes that goe to the Chauncell; and my worldly goods I dispose of as followeth:—£5 to bee laid out about my funerall, and my will is that noe banquetting shal-be vsed thereat, but only Naples Biskett and wyne. To my worthy Mistress Mrs Dorathy Lackford, widowe, six silver spoones worth three pounds. To my grandchild Elizabeth Jackson all my child bedd lynnen and all other my fine lynnen. To my grandchild Arthur Jackson my fetherbedd in the Garrett. Money legacies to my said grandchildren, including £5 apeece out of the lease of my dwelling house in the parish of Christchurch. If both my said grandchildren depart this life before their said legacies of money be paid, then the same shall remain vnto my daughter Elizabeth Hallam, to whom I give my great Bible. To my grandchild Elizabeth Jackson I give Dr. Prestons workes, and Master Dodd vppon the Commanndments, and Mr. Dike's works vppon the Sacraments, and the Annothamy of a Christian with Master Cooper's workes in itt, and all other my bookes I give unto my daughter Elizabeth Hallam and to my said two grandchildren, except only my pocket bible and six of my other bookes, which I give to and amongst my grandchildren in Virginia, and my desire is that my said daughter shall send and convey the same over vnto my said grandchildren in Virginia soe soone as conveniently may bee after my decease. Item I give and Bequeath vnto my grandchildren in Virginia theise parcells of goods and legacies following, that is to saie, vnto my grandchild Elizabeth Sheeres my redd and blew mowheire peticote and my three peticotes that I weare every day, one of my two gownes, two smocks, two aprons, two coyves, two handkerchers and two paire of cuffs; vnto my grandchild Martha Sheers two shifts of my lynnen cloathes; and vnto my grandchild Susanna two shifts of lynnen for a child of eight yeares of age; and I give to every of my said three grandchildren in Virginia, Elizabeth, Martha and Susanna Sheeres, twentie shillings apeece to be paid them at their severall ages of twenty and one yeares. To my daughter Elizabeth Hallam and her nowe husband James Hallam my tenement called the Three Pigeons, situate in Newgate Markett, during their lives and the life of the longer lyver of them, with remainder to my two grandchildren Elizabeth and Arthur Jackson equally. Cousin John Hobson 10s. John Heard my late husband's sonne in lawe 10s. Anne and Judith Whitfield 20s. apeece at one and twenty. Residuary Legatee and Executrix:—my daughter Elizabeth Hallam. Dated 28 May, 1653. Witnesses: Joseph Yelverton, John Gooder, Richard Gill, scr., Thomas Gill. Proved 29 Aug., 1653, by the executrix. (P. C. C. Brent, 161.)

I JOHN ATKINS of Verginia beinge weake and sicke in bodie doe make my last will and testament as followeth Imprimis I doe bequeath my body to be buried in the vsuall buryinge place by James Citty. Item whereas I stand indebted to di'vers p'sons aswell heere in Verginia as in England and there is owinge me in this country about six thousand waight of tobacco due this Cropp Nowe I doe earnestly desire Mr Luke Boyse of the neck of land that he would take uppon him the administration of all my goods and chattells here and first to satisfie all such debts as I doe owe in this Country and to send into England so much to paie my debts there as by my booke of Accompts will appeare And for the rest of my estate I doe bequeath it as followeth vizt I doe remitt vnto Mr Luke Boyse whatsoeu' he is indebted to me, to Peter Stafferton all the moveables and househould stuffe in the howse where I dwell (except one wainscott Chaire wch I give Mr Davison); to Mr. Christopher Davison one hundred waight of tobacco and remitt vnto him whatsoeu' he is indebted to me. Item I am covenant to pay Peter Stafferton a thousand waight of Tobacco this Cropp as also he is to enjoy one third of my Cropp of Corne whom I earnestly desire to have justly satisfied and whatsoeu' shall remaine I doe bequeath to my brother William Atkins dwellinge neare the Beare in Bassinghall in London. September 3, 1623, subscript per John Atkins in the presence of Chr: Davison Peeter Stafferton.

2 Oct., 1624, commission to William Atkins, brother of deceased, he having named no executor.

28 Aug., 1626, commission to Richard Atkins, brother of said deceased, to administer (during the minority of Elizabeth, William, George, Anne and Lee Atkins, children of William Atkins) goods non-administered by the said William Atkins now deceased.

1 June, 1627, commission to Humfrey Atkins, brother of John Atkins, late in parts beyond the seas deceased, to administer goods non-administered by William and Richard Atkins also deceased. (P. C. C. Byrde, 84.)

Luke Boyse of Charles City, Va., came in the *Edwine* in May, 1619, aged 44, and Alice his wife arrived in the *Bona Nova* in April, 1622, both were living, with two servants, 24 Jan., 1624.*

---

* *Muster of Virginia Inhabitants*, Hotton, p. 202.

Peter Stafferton, probably identical with the *Mr.* Stafferton and his wife living "*in the maine*" in James City, 16 Feb., 1623.*

Christopher Davison, perhaps son of Alice Davison, widow, of James City, 16 Feb., 1623.*

Reference may be made to the will of William Boys of Cranbrook, co. Kent, 1656-7, (P. C. C. Ruthen, 72) already printed in these collections.† A Francis Boyce of London, button hole maker, aged 25 years, who was bound for St. Cristophers from Dartmouth and took the oath of allegiance before the mayor of that place 20 Feb., 1634,‡ may have been of the same family.

Will of ROBERT REEVE of Caldercote in the parish of Towcester, yeoman, dated 21 April, 1638. To my son George Reeve threescore pounds. I give unto my son Thomas Reeve five pounds if ever he come over into England to demand it, and if he never come to demand it, it shall never be paid him. I give unto my son William Reeve £5 if ever he come into England to demand it, and if he never come to demand it, it shall never be paid him. To my son John Reeve £5. To my daughter Jane Reeve £30. To my daughter Anne Reeve £35 at 18. Son Robert Reeve £40 at 20. To all my wife's children each a ewe and a lamb, all but John Garner, and he shall have the bauld colt. William Harris a ewe and a lamb. Poor of Towcester. Rest to my wife, whom Executrix, and William Shepard the elder and Richard Winkles of Field Barcoote Overseers. Witnesses: William Sheppard the elder, Thomas Shepard. Proved 12 July, 1638, by Agnes the relict.

(Northants Wills, S. 2., 1638-40, f. 47.)

A William Reeve, aged 22, came in the *Elizabeth & Ann* 29 April, 1635,§ from London to New England and was of Salem, Mass., in 1668, but if, as conjectured by Savage, he was brother of John of Salem,‖ he could not have been the William of the will, as his brother John had already sailed in the *Christian* for Boston in 1635, (aged 19) three years before the date of the will which evidently refers to him as then still in England. Thos. Reeve, aged 24, who came in the *Mathew*, 21 May, 1635, to St. Christopher's¶ may have been the other brother.

I RICHARD JOHNSON the elder of Bugbrook, being weak in body, do make my last will: To my four grandchildren 10s. apiece at 16. To my son Tho: Johnson, who is now beyond sea, twentie pounds. To all my children that are married five shillings apiece. To my daughter Mary fortie pounds at marriage. To my daughter Alice fortie pounds at marriage. Poor of Bugbrood 6s. 8d. To my three servants one shilling each. Richard Curtisse one shilling. Nicholas Middleton my sister's (*son*) one shilling. Rest to my wife, whom Executrix, and my friends

---

* *Hotten*, p. 176.
† *Record*, vol. xlii, p. 96—Jan., 1911.
‡ *Hotten's Lists*, p. 151.
§ *Ibid.*, p. 72.
‖ *Savage*, iii, 523.
¶ *Hotten*, p. 81.

Edward Pickering and Robert Savage Overseers. Undated will. Witness: George Jay. Proved 21 May, 1642, (*by whom not decipherable.*) (Northants Wills, S. 2., 1630–42, f. 183.)

There are several of the not uncommon name of Thomas Johnson in New England in the first half of the 17th Century.

Thomas Johnson of Hartford, Conn., cobbler, was admitted 1640.

Thomas Johnson of Hingham, Mass., 1635, came in the *Hopewell*, Capt. Babb, from London (aged 25) and was drowned in Boston Harbor 29 May, 1656, leaving widow Margaret but no children.

Thomas Johnson of Dover, N. H., 1648–1657, died about 1661 leaving an only daughter who soon followed him.

Thomas Johnson of Sandwich, Mass., 1643, Deputy to the Plymouth Court 1637–38, served in the Narraganset War 1645. His daughter Priscilla born 20 Nov., 1657. He was perhaps identical with Thomas of Dover *ut Supra.**

Will of ANNIS SMITH (of Halcote), dated 1 Dec., 1643. I give and bequeath all my goods, chattels and lease unto my cousin William Blackmoore and his sister Annis Blackmoore equally, if my son William be dead; provided always that if my son William be alive, my will is that he shall enjoy all my said goods, etc., paying to the said William and Annis £14. Poor of this parish 2s. 6d. William Hurst 20s. and his sister Margaret Hurst 20s. John Whitacres 20s. Michael Bagley 10s. Anne Edin 20s. Brother George Blackmore £4. Sister Paine 20s. I desire that my executors receive but £6 of Richard Burges, who oweth me £7 upon bond. My will is that these legacies be not paid these six years, unless my son william return. Witnesses: Richard Prideaux, Richard Marriatt, Martin Glense. Proved 28 Nov., 1644. (Northants Wills, S. 3., 1645–60, f. 106.)

24 June, 1650, I JAMES DOXIE of Moulton, co. Northampton, husbandman, being weak in body, do ordain this my last will: I give and bequeath to my wife Sarah Doxie the use of my house for life, if she continue widow. I give and bequeath to every child the sum of five pounds, that is to say to Thomas Doxie my son five pounds, and to James, John and Humfrey my sons, and to Alice Tebbot my daughter and Anne and Isabell Doxie my daughters five pounds apiece, but to my daughter Margaret Doxie seven pounds; and I ordain that every one shall have the yearly annuitie of five shillings out of the rent of the said house until the above sums be fully paid, unless my sons James and John, whom I constitute feoffees in trust and executors, shall sell and alienate the same, as I hereby give them power to do, and shall thereby pay the sums above mentioned so much the sooner. To my wife Sarah and my children above named I bequeath my goods and chattels not yet bequeathed, to be divided equally amongst them. I bequeath to my grandchild Margaret Tebbott

---

* *Savage's Gen. Dict.*, ii, 557–558. *Pope's Pioneers of Mass.*, 261. *N. E. Gen. Register*, x, 84.

20s. I will the part and portion above mentioned, given to my son Thomas (now in New England), to rest in the hands of my son James Doxie till my said son Thomas come to demand it, and if he never come, it shall belong to my son James. Witnesses : Richard Hooke, clerk, William Jones. Proved 19 August, 1650, by James Doxie, power reserved to the other executors.

(Northants Wills, S. 3., 1645-60, f. 232.)

Thomas Doxy applied for a house lot in New London, Conn., 25 Feb., 1650. By his wife Catherine he had Thomas and possibly other children. He died about the middle of March, 1651-2, his wife being called "widow" 9 April, 1652, she remarried Daniel Lane the same year and they removed to Long Island about 1662, Daniel Lane becoming one of the patentees of Brookhaven in 1666. Thomas Doxy, the son, sold the homestead in New London, with his mother's consent, in 1673 or earlier, to Christoper Christopher. Thomas Doxy the father was a sailor and owned a coasting vessel sailing from New London.*

20 August, 1638, I ROBERT BOOTH of Rothwell, clerk, do make and ordain, etc.: To Thomas Wilson my son in law 12d. To Susanna his wife 12d. To their children John, Dorothy and Susanna Wilson each 12d. I give to John Booth my son, if he be living and ever come to demand it, 40s. To Robert Garrett my son in law 40s. Rest to Judith my wife for life, to bring up my children Elizabeth and Marie Booth, and after her decease I leave my country house to the elder of my daughters and the cottage to the younger. Executrix: my wife. If my wife die before my daughters be brought up, then I appoint Joseph Shortland and Marie his wife to be possessed of my said houses until my children come to years. If my daughters die, I give my said houses to Thomas Shortland and Elizabeth Shortland his sister after the decease of my wife. Dated 24 (*Sic*) August, 1638. Witnesses: John Elkin, Richard Chapman. Proved 15 Sept., 1638.

(Northants Wills, S. 2., 1638-40, f. 40.)

Will of RICHARD WRIGHT, clerk, late rector of Everden, co˙ Northampton, dated 1 April, 1633. My house and land in Wargrove, co. Berks, I give to Frances my wife during her life and after her decease to my son Richard if he be then in England, to have during his life; and after his decease I give the same unto Richard, son of my son Theodore Wright and to his heirs for ever. Son John 1s. Poor of Everdon 40s. My chest of vyolls and all my books to my son Francis. To my three daughters Jone, Rebecca and Joyce each £10. Son Samuel £5. Grandchildren Elizabeth Wright and Rebecca Beane each 20s. Rest to Frances my wife. Executors, my wife Frances and my son Francis. Witnesses: John Stannard, Will: Hedge, Will: Osborne. No probate. Inventory taken 21 June, 1638.

(Northants Wills, S. 2, 1638-42, f. 127.)

---

* *Savage Gen. Dict.* ii, 69 ; *Caulkin's Hist. New London*, pp. 68, 82, 157, 232, 269.

81

CLUES FROM ENGLISH ARCHIVES
CONTRIBUTORY TO AMERICAN GENEALOGY.

BY J. HENRY LEA AND J. R. HUTCHINSON.

Will Nuncupative of THOMAS MAYO of Evenly, co. Northampton, shepherd, declared 28 Sept., 1638. Son William 50s. Daughter Alice 50s. Daughter Mary the elder 50s. Daughter Judith 50s. Daughter Mary the younger £10. To my son John, who hath been gone I know not whither these three or four years, if he return within three years after my death, 20s.; otherwise I give it to my daughter Judith. Rest to Alice my wife, whom Executrix, and I desire Mr Holbrooke to be a friend to my wife and children. Proved 5 Oct., 1638, by Alice the executrix.
(Northants Wills, S. 2, 1638–42. fol. 21.)

This could not have been the John Mayo of Barnstable, Mass., minister, who came in 1638, was ordained 15 April, 1641, and brought from England children Hannah, Samuel, John, Nathaniel and perhaps Elizabeth; removed to Eastham 1646, and to Boston 1655; returned to Barnstable in 1673, and died at Yarmouth in 1676, leaving widow Thomasine, nor the John Mayo of Roxbury, who was brought over by Robert Gamblin, Jr., in 1633, as son of his then wife by a former husband.*

Will of JOHN DUNCKLEY of Daventry, laborer, dated 13 Dec., 1640. Legacies to daughter Agnes Rose, wife of John Rose, my grandchild Anne Rose her daughter, and to my grandchildren William Rose, Thomas Rose, Margaret Rose, and John Rose the younger; and to my daughter Elizabeth Jackson. I give unto my grandchild Alexander Lovell one joined bed in case he shall come to demand it; if not, then to his mother Elizabeth Jackson aforesaid. I give to my grandchild Thomas Lovell 20s. if he come to demand it. Legacies to my grandchildren Nathaniel Lovell, Elizabeth Jackson, Agnes Jackson, Mary Jackson and Richard Jackson. Executor, John Lovell. Witnesses: Richard Allen, Richard Jackson, Edward Wilson. Proved 16 March, 1640–41. (Northants Wills, S. 2, 1631–7, f. 122.)

Alexander Lovell of Westfield, Mass., in 1649, married 30 October, 1658, Lydia, danghter of Benjamin Albee of the same place, identical with the Alexander *Lovett* whose house was burned by the Indians in 1676. He died in 1709, his will, made in 1701, states that he was, at that time, eighty-two years of age.†
He left sons Alexander and Nathaniel besides other children by two wives.

---

* *Savage* iii, 187; *Pope's Pioneers*, pp. 308–9.
† *Savage*, iii, 123. *Tilden's Hist. Medfield*, p. 424.

4 February, 1686–7, I WILLIAM TAYLOR of Revells within the parish of Buckland Newton, co. Dorset, gent., being weake of body . . . devise and bequeath unto my kinsman Oliver Lawrence, sonne of Rawleigh Lawrence of Revells, gent., all my messuages, burgages and dwelling houses in Somerton, co. Somerset, to have and to hold unto the said Oliver and the heirs males of his body, with successive contingent remainders in tail male to Rawleigh Lawrence, second sonne of the said Rawleigh, to every other sonne or sonnes of the said Rawleigh the father and Elizabeth his nowe wife, to my kinsman John Cole late of Chiselborough, co. Somerset, clerk, to my cozen Walter Frampton of Buckland Newton, gent., and to my own right heirs for ever. I give and devise unto the said Rawleigh Lawrence the father and Elizabeth his wife my kinswoman, all my lands and tenements lying in Revells and known by the name of Revells, which descended to me from my father, as also all my lands and tenements at Naps-hill in Buckland Newton, called Vincents, which I purchased of Daniel Proctor, Esq., to have and to hold to them the said Raw-leigh and Elizabeth for the term of their naturall lives and for the life of the longer liver of them, with remainder to the said Oliver Lawrence and his heirs males, charged with one yearly rent of £8 payable to my kinsman John Cole, clerk, during his life. Poor of Buckland Newton 40s. Cozen Mr William Lyde one shilling and my little house clock. Kinsman Mr. John Myhill (having heretofore had a small portion belonging to him, in lieu whereof I bred him up) £50. Kinsman Mr Walter Frampton, his wife, sons and daughters, each 12d. Cozen Mrs Anna Somers of Froome St. Quintin, widow, 2s., and her son (my godson) Mr William Somers 2s. Kinswoman Elizabeth Lawrence all my sheepe at Revells. Oliver Lawrence all my books and household furniture. Cozen Elizabeth Bartlett of Sturton Candle widow, and her sons and daughters, 12d. each. Cozen Mr Thomas Lang-don of the City of Exon 40s. Godson Mr Robert Somerton of Yeovile five pence and noe more. And whereas I have in my hands £40, the money of my kinsman Mr John Cole, heretofore of Dublin in Ireland and nowe in one of the Western Islands in America (as is supposed), my desire is that my executor pay the said sum to the said John Cole upon demand. Residuary Legatee and Executor: Rawleigh Lawrence, husband of my kinswoman Elizabeth Lawrence. Overseers: my friend Mr John Fisher of Sherburne and my kinsman Mr Robert Somerton. Witnesses: Robert Coker, Will: Frampton, Rob: Oxenbrigge, John Blud-worth, Samuell Dunninge, Nathaniel Ryall. Proved 6 Aug., 1688, by the executor named. (P. C. C. Exton, 112.)

27 Nov., 1679, I RICHARD WHITE of the Cliffe near Lewis in Sussex, brasier, being aged and weak in body, do make this my last will: Whereas I have already given to my daughter Rebecca Gumfield in New England the sum of fourteen pounds which I have sent her in goods, I do hereby give her £10 more; and whereas I have already given to my daughter Hannah Glover £75 in money and goods, I do hereby give her £45 more to make

her portion equal to my daughter Harman's. I give to my son in law Robert Dormer 10s.; to my grandson Richard Dormer, son of the said Richard, £5; to my grandson William White, son of my son Samuel White deceased, 20s.; to my grandson Richard Tyler 1s.; to my grandchild John Tyler 1s.; to my granddaughter Mary More and her husband John More 10s. apiece; to my grandson Samuel Tyler £30, and if I die before he hath learned his trade of me, my executrix shall put him out apprentice; to my grandson Samuel Glover £30; to my grandchildren Benjamin, Susanna, Richard, Hannah and Elizabeth Harman, and to my daughter Harman's last child not yet baptized, £25 between them; to such children of my daughter Rebecca Gumfield as shall be living at the time of my decease 20s. apiece; to my son in law John Plawe and Elizabeth his wife 12d. apiece; to poor widows in the parish of St Thomas in the Cliffe 20s.; to the poor of Brighthelmstone 20s.; and to my brother in law Overy Page 20s. The rest of my goods I give to my daughters Hannah Glover and Susannah Harman. Executors: my daughter Hannah Glover and my friend John Homard of the Cliffe. Overseers: Mr William Russell of Lewes, apothecary, and my brother in law Overy Page. Witnesses: John Prior, Richard Paine, John Crouch. Proved 13 July, 1680, by Hannah Glover, power reserved to John Homard.   (P. C. C.   Bath, 101.)

I MARY MARTIN of Hargrave, co. Northampton, widow, being infirm in body, do make this my last will: I give unto my son Halton Easton £50, to Halton his son £6, to Mary his daughter 20s.; and to my daughter in law Anne his wife 10s. I give unto the five children of my son Oliver, viz., to John Easton £9; to Oliver the son of my son Oliver (who is beyond the seas) five shillings if ever he come into England; to Peter son of my son Oliver, £9; to Mary Eston, daughter of my son Oliver, £27; and to Philadelphia, daughter of my son Oliver, £9. I give unto Philadelphia my daughter in law, mother of these five children, £9; and to the five children of my son John Cotchett, viz., to Thomas Cotchett £9, to Oliver and Richard Cotchett £9 apiece, to John Cotchett, £18, and to Mary Cotchett £22-10-0. The residue of all my goods I give to my son in law John Cotchett, whom executor. Dated 17 Jan., 1680–81. Witnesses: Tho: Thorowgood, Isaac Quick, Jonathan Heacock, Proved 20 June, 1681, by the executor.   (P. C. C.   North, 96.)

I JOSEPH INGRAM being now bound for Virginia. My father and mother each of them mourning. Mourning to my sister Anne Smith, my brother Thomas Ingram, my brother Robert Ingram and Mary his wife, my brother John Ingram, my sister Hester Ingram, and my brother William Ingram. Poor of my native town of St. Ives 40s. Residuary legatee: Anne Smith, daughter of my sister Anne Smith, at 18 or marriage; but if she die "before either of them," I give two-thirds to my sister Anne Smith, and the other third to my brothers and sisters. Executor: my father Robert Ingram. Dated 6 October, 1651. Witnesses:

Robert Ingram, junior, John Ingram, John Blyhton. Proved 22 Sept., 1653, by the executor named.   (P. C. C. Brent, 367.)

Edw. Ingram, aged 18, came in the *Blessing* from London, 1635.*

We have interesting information regarding Richard Ingram who came over in July, 1634, and who founded a New York family to the direct descendants of whom *only* we should be pleased to communicate the facts which are strictly of a confidential nature.

22 Februarie, 1627-8, I SYMON BRADSTREETE, Cittizin and Grocer of London, beinge weake in bodie . . . First to declare to the world howe largely and bountifullie I have dealt with my daughter Margaret the nowe wief of Edmund Slater, Cittizen and Mercer of London, I hereby assuredlie affirme that the said Margaret (notwithstanding she married the said Edmond Slater without my love leave or consent) hath hadd and received at sundrie times out of my owne proper estate . . . in freehold land coppihould land, lease land, plate, rings, jewells, household stuffe, choice childbedd lynnen and other lynnen to the value of ffive hundred poundes as is menconed in one deede of guift made unto my nephewe Samuell Bradstreete bearing date the one and twentith daie of this instant month Nevertheless I give unto my my said daughter one little white silver cupp and one great silver and guilt salt. All the rest of my estate I give unto my said nephew Samuell Baadstreete whom I make sole Executor. Witnesses: James Beckett, Robert Weston, Mathew Tarlton, John Leaves sr., Robert Hanson his servant, Henry Dugard, Thomas Allan. Proved 28 Feb., 1627-8, by the executor named.

(P. C. C. Barrington, 14.)

1625, May 23, Edmund Slater of St. Magnus, London, Mercer, and Margaret Bredstreete, of Bishop Stortford, Herts., spinster, dau. of Simon Bredstreete of Brainford, co. Middlesex, Brewer: at Lamborne or Birchanger, co. Essex.

(Licence in Court of Bishop of London.)†

26th July, 1598, I WILLIAM BURROUGHE Esquier being at this present sicke in body . . .   And wheresoever it shall please God to call me . . . yf it be at Lymehouse or neare London and not far dostant of it or at the seas I will that my bodie shalbe buried in the parishe churche of Stebenhethe neare unto the place where my first wief Judith lyeth or in the Chauncell Whereas I covenaunted before marriage betweene me and the Lady Jane Wentworthe nowe my wiefe to assure to her for terme of her liefe as for her ioyneture & in leuve of her dower somuche lande as should be of the yearelie value of fourescore poundes And whereas I have by my deede conveyed to my said wiefe my farme at Mileende in the parishe of Stebunheth called Mewes otherwise the White Horse with the lands to the same belonging nowe in the occupacon of John Robinson and Stephen Howton

---

* *Hotten*, p. 108.
† Harl. Soc., xxvi, 153.

And also my howse in London neare unto Roodchurche at the upperend of Tower streete nowe in the tenure of Martin Archdale My will is that my wiefe shall have and enioye all the said landes and tenements dureinge her lief Also I give unto my said wiefe all such plate jewells leases etc. as was hers before I married her £200 in money one of my standinge cupps silver and guilt the chaine of gould she usuallie weareth one ring with a mount Turkes and one other ring with a blewe saphire in it And whereas I have entered into bond (by the perswason of my said wiefe before I married her) unto Jane Wentworthe neece and goddaughter to my said wiefe (which Jane is nowe in my howse) (*to give her*) the somme of two hundred pounds at her marriage my will is that it shalbe performed according to my said bond To my wiefe the two coache horses and the coache Yf my daughter Mary be not preferred by me in marriage dureinge my liefe then I give unto her £1000 and if she doe marry with the likeinge of my executors then I give unto her £1000 more and my will is that she have yearely towards her maintenaunce vntill she be married threescore poundes. To my sonne Walter Borroughe £200. To my three sisters Agnes, Margery and Jane to everie of them £20. To my sister Borroughe, widdowe of my brother Stephen, deceased, £20 and to her three daughters vnmarried viz Mary, Anne and Elizabeth to everie of them £30. To Judith wief of John Bassall and Susan wief of William Kinge, being my said brother's daughters £20 apeece. To George Laryman £10. To the Companie at the Trynity Howse for a dynner £10. To the widdowe of Preator late bot (*swain*) of H. M. shippe the Swallowe £10. Poore of Stepney £20. Poore of Northam, co. Devon £20 to be ymployed as my cosen Thomas Leighe and some others of the said parishe shall thinke best Executors: Sir Henry Palmer Knighte, my cosen Mr Thomas Leighe and my nephewe John Bassall who shall dispose of the rest of my goods according to my wrightinge indented committed to the custody of the overseers of my will and others. Overseers my wiefe the Lady Elizabeth Countess Dowgar of Rutlande and Mr John Brewster to everie of whom twentie marks Witnesses: William Jones, Joseph Pett, William Bygatt, Richard Nottingham. Proved 28 Nov., 1598, by Thomas Browne, Not. Pub., proctor for Sir Henry Palmer, Knt., Thomas Leighe and John Vassall (*sic*), the executors named.   (P. C. C. Lewyn, 89.)

Will of HENRY MANIFORD of Long Burton in the county of Dorset, gentleman, dated 23 April, 1642. My farm, capital messuage and lands called Woodbridge, my lands purchased of Raynold Hutchins, and all other my lands in Woodbridge and Hollwall, co. Somerset, I give to my executrix and overseers, they paying to my son John Maniford £35 yearly until he attain the age of 26 years, and to his wife, if he marry after the age of 21 years with the consent of my executrix and overseers, £60 by the year from the death of my said son. Daughters Elizabeth, Hannah and Marie £400 each. Sons Samuel and Henry. Brother William Dunning, clerk. Friends Mr William Derby and Mr James Mewe. Lands in Brockhampton in the parish of Buckland, called Chaston. Wife Johan the rent of the leasehold ground which I bought of Mr Chafyn and Mr Ralph FitzJames. Sister Johan Maniford, widow, £5, and her daughter Johan £5. Henry and Josiah Maniford, sons of my brother William Maniford, deceased, £10 apiece. Item I doe give my parte of all such cattle and other things as I and others with whome I have adventured have or shall have by our said adventure in Newe England in America to my said sonne Samuel, and I desire my said overseers and such other of my friends that joyned in that adventure with mee to have a care that the same be preserved for his vse untill my said sonne Samuell shall come to years of discretion to manage those affaires himselfe. Samuel, son of my brother William Dunning, a silver bowle. God-daughter Elizabeth Derby a silver bowle when she is married. Residuary Legatee and Executrix: Johan my wife. John and Hannah Luffe, my daughter Luffe's children, £50 apiece, and her two other children a silver bowl apiece. Overseers: my brother Mr William Dunning, clerk, William Derby, and my son in law William Luffe. Witnesses: Benjamin Walter, William Luffe, William Derbie, Joan Luffe, Joseph Derbie. Proved 20 Nov., 1647, by the executrix.   (P. C. C.   Fines, 240.)

A Captain John Maniford who occurs 1647 to 1651 as of Barbodoes trading to Boston, Mass., having dealings in tobacco and other commodities,* and probably a shipmaster, is no doubt the son John of the will, but the son Samuel seems to have left no trace here and probably he either died without issue or returned to England.

8 September, 1653, I Nicholas Sellecke of Clatworthy in the Countye of Sommersett, yeoman, being sicke of body . . . doe give to the poore of Clatworthye 2s.; to my sonne John Sellecke £5 and £3 I must pay his brother William for his debte; to my daughter Charity Upton 50s. which she oweth me; to my sonne Robert Sellecke 3s. 4d.; to my sonne David Sellecke 3s. 4d.; to my daughter Merab Eames 3s. 4d.; to my sonne Simon Sellecke 3s. 4d.; to my sonne William Sellecke the beddstedd which was brought from Clatworthye to his howse; and all the rest of my goodes to my sonne Nicholas Sellecke, whome I make my whole Executor. Witnesses: Sarah Blinman, John Venson, John Welsh. Proved 17 Feb., 1653–4, by the executor named.
(P. C. C.   Alchin, 383.)

Daniel Sellick of Boston, Mass., soapboiler, had wife Susan, daughter of Henry Kebby,† and sons David, born 1638, Jonathan 1641, John 1643, Nathaniel 1645, and daughters, Joanna 1647, Elizabeth 1652, and Susanna 1653. He died at Accomac in Virginia 1654.‡

---

* Aspenwall's Note Book, pp. 120, 260. Suff., Mass., Deeds, Lib. i, 293.
† See will of John Kebby, brother of Henry Kebby, in *Waters' Gleanings*, i, 406.
‡ *Savage*, iv, 50; *N. E. Register*, xliv, 194; *Waters' Gleanings*, i, 442.

Will of WILLIAM CURTYS of Towcester, gent, dated 17 Nov., 1637. I give to my son William 12d. To my son Thomas (yf he be living) 12d. To my daughter Locksmith 12d. To my daughter Howse 12d. To my wife's children 12d. apiece. Rest to Audry my wife, whom Executrix, and Robert Roote and Richard Bridges the elder Overseers. Proved 17 March, 1637–8, by the executrix. (Northants Wills, S. 2., 1636–40, f, 69.)

Thomas Curtis, aged 24, (in 1624) of Wariscoyack, Va., servant of Mr. Daniel Gookine, came in the *Flyinge Harte* to Virginia in 1621 and in 1623 was living at Elizabeth City.*

As Daniel Gookin left Virginia to take up his final residence in New England, it is quite possible that this Thomas Curtis of Virginia was identical with Thomas Curtis of Wethersfield, Conn., in 1639† or earlier and who died at Hartford‡ in 1681, aged 83, making his birth accord very closely with the above. But the Thomas of Wethersfield had a brother not named in the will.

Will of FRANCIS FOSTER of Grafton Regis, co. Northampton, dated 10 Jan., 1640–41. Being very sick and weak in body. To be buried in Grafton churchyard. To the poor of the parish 10s. To Mr. Stilton of Potterspury 10s. for a sermon. To my mother Anne Foster and my sister Margaret Foster my wine licence belonging to Grafton Regis. To my sister Margaret Foster £20 at marriage or one and twenty. I give unto my loving brother William Foster§ ten pounds when he returns from beyond sea; but if in case he should not return, then it is my will that the ten pounds be equally divided betwixt my brother Edward Foster and my sister Margaret Foster. To my brother Edward Foster all my tools and timber, sawed or unsawed. To Christopher Rawlin my father's servant 10s. William Brayfield 5s. Joan Clarke 2s. 6d. Elizabeth Chambers 2s. 6d. Executor and Residuary Legatee: my father Edward Foster. Witnesses: Richard Lee, Francis Wright, Peter Browne. Proved 13 Feb., 1640–41, Inventory taken 1 Feb., 1640–41, by Francis Butler, Francis Wright and Richard Lee. Sum total, £89–10–0.
(Northants Wills, S. 2., 1636–40, f. 285.)

I WILLIAM DEANE of Great Missenden in the county of Bucks, yeoman, being sick and weak in body, do make and ordain this my last will and testament: Whereas I have surrendered into the hands of Thomas Ives the elder, gent, and John Judge, now lords of the part of the Manor of Peterly, Stone, Netherbury and Great Missenden, all that messuage or tenement wherein I now dwell, situate in great Missenden, together with 15 acres of land, to the use of my last will, now I do hereby bequeath the said messuage and lands to my brother Thomas Deane of Great Missenden, yeoman, and his heirs. I give and bequeath unto my

---

* *Hotten*, pp. 184, 243, 254.
† *Stile's Wethersfield*, ii, 262; *Savage*, i, 487.
‡ Savage states erroneously that he died in Wallingford. *loc., cit. supra.*
§ William, son of William Foster baptized 15 Oct., 1678, at St. Jas, Barbadoes. *Hotten*, p. 497.

said brother Thomas and his heirs all that close of arable land called Boddy Croft, situate in Great Missenden, containing 4 acres. I do give and bequeath unto my loving brother Mathew Deane the sum of twenty pounds, to be paid to him within one month after his arrival in England, but in case he never come into England again, then his legacy to be void; and in case he shall come into England again, and my executor shall not pay him his legacy, then my will is that my brother Mathew Deane shall enter into the close called Boddy Croft and enjoy the same. The rest of my goods I give to my brother Thomas Deane, whom Executor. Dated 26 March, 1684–5. Witnesses: Thomas Ives, John Judge, Wm Hakewell, junior, John Hoare, Henry Harris. Proved 8 July, 1704, by the executor named in the will.

(Arch: Bucks, 1704–5, No. 41.)

Matthew Deane, with wife and two children, two servants and two slaves, were living at St. Michaels, Barbadoes, in 1680.*

CLUES FROM ENGLISH ARCHIVES
Contributory to American Genealogy.

By J. Henry Lea and J. R. Hutchinson.

Will of John Cheesman of the parish of St. Mary Magdalen in Bermondsey, Co. Surry, gent., dated (*blank*) December, 1663, 15 Charles II. Lands in Heese or Hessen, Norwood, Norcourt or Norcote, Southall, Eling *als* Zeling, old Brentford and new Brentford, Co. Middx., both free & copyhold, to my wife Margarett for life to educate my granchild Anna Cheesman till 24 June 1670 or her marriage & to her remainder of lands after wife's decease, with remainder to my brother Edmond Cheesman, with remainder to my nephews Edmond and Thomas, sons of said brother, they to pay £200 to each of the daughters of my said brother. All lands in Braban, co. Kent, (*Brabourne*) to heirs of my deceased nephew Thomas Cheesman who was my eldest brother's sonne. To said grandchild Anna Cheesman all lands, plantations etc. in County of Gloucester in continent of Virginia, remainder to said nephews Edmond and Thomas Cheesman, sons of said brother Edmond but to be to my wife during her widowhood with remainder to my said brother Edmond for his life. My lease of now dwelling to said wife, remainder to Thomas, my said deceased nephew Thomas Cheesman's sonne, or £40. To Elisabeth

---

* *Hotten*, p. 445.

Bynn, widow, 20s. yearly. To servant Ellinor Harvill £10 & to Elizabeth Harvill her sister 20s. yeerley for six years. To poor of St. Mary Magdalen aforesaid where I dwell £10. To poor widows of Redriffe, co. Surrey, £5. My 2 negroes Misce & Mary his wife, now in Virginia, to be free on my wife's death. My wife Margarett Res: Leg. & Extrx: or, if she marry, my friends Mr. James Betts of London, grocer, Mr. Robert Skrine, Cittizen & Iremonger of London, Mr. John Harrison of the parish of Stepney, co. Middx., marriner, & Mr. William Turner of London, merchant, Exors: in trust till 24 June 1670 & then account to said nephews at their ages of 21. [*John Chesman*]. Witnesses: Richard Childe, Jonathan Monday, Lewis Andrewes, Scr. Proved at London, 2 May, 1665, by relict and Extrx: named.

(P. C C. Hyde, 46.)

We have here the will of Lieut. John Chisman of Elizabeth City, Virginia, who came out in the *Flying Hart* in 1621, with his brother, called in the ship's list *Edward*, but undoubtedly identical with the *Edmond* of the will. The will of his widow, Margaret Cheeseman (proved 21 July, 1680, P. C. C. Bath, 92) has already been printed by Mr. Waters with annotations by the writer* calling attention to its value in throwing light on the MASON family of Virginia and others.

Will of OBADIAH INGRAM, Citizen and Merchant Adventurer of London (*Citizen and Merchant Tailor but died abroad†*) Draper, in good health, dated 20 January, 1632, 8 Charles, to mother Martha Harvey, first wife of Edward Ingram in London, two thirds of my estate. Uncle Thomas Lee, armorour of London, to be Exor: with my mother & to bestow her said share on her in time of need, soe long as it shall please god her husband Symon Harvey liveth with her. Sister Martha Harvey £10 which her father Symon Harvey oweth by bond due in January 1623. Uncle Lee's children each a bible of 20 shillings. Cosin Thomas Lee, said uncle's eldest son, to be Exor: if he die. [*Obadiah Ingram*]. Witnesses: John Alsop, Thos: Middleton. Pro. at London, 24 April, 1635, by Martha Harvey, mother and Extrx:, Thomas Lee, the other Exor: being deceased.

(P. C. C. Sadler, 32.)

Reference may be made to will of JOSEPH INGRAM of Virginia in the preceeding number‡ and the Edward Ingram named in note thereto, who came out in the *Blessing* from London in 1635. The wills of the uncle and Exor:, Thomas Lee of London and *his* son, Capt. Thomas Lee, follow and may be useful in the identification of these people.

Will of THOMAS LEE, Citizen and Armorer of London (*of St. Bride's Parish§*), dated 29 December, 1632. Six children now

---

* *N. E. Register*, xlvii, 250, and *Water's Gleanings*, i, 691–2.
† In Probate Act Book.
‡ *July, 1911*, vol. xlii., p. 296.
§ Probate Act Book.

living wch are vnprefferred, viz. Thomas, Jonathan, Nathaniell, Barbara, Sarah and Rebecca Lee each £100. Daughter Mary, now wife of Tristram Stephens, Mariner, £5 over and above her portion already given. The Armorers Company of London £5 for a peece of plate. Poor of St. Brides, London, where I now dwell £5. To wife Barbara all lands at Padnell als Padnall Corners in parish of Barking, co. Essex, also two new houses in Lambe Alley, near Bishopsgate Street in parish of St. Buttolph, with reversion to son Thomas, also one thirty second part of shipp Raynbow of London and she Extrx. Proved 9 December, 1634, by relict Barbara. (P. C. C. Seager, 113.)

Will of Captain THOMAS LEE of shipp *Crispine*, uppon the Coast of Chormandell, dated 4 October, 1636,. To brothers Jonathan and Nathaniel Lee and 5 sisters, Sara, Martha, Rebecca, Marie and Barbery, each one ninth of estate. Uncle, Captain William Reignsbery, dwelling in Wapping, one ninth estate. To poor of East India Company's Hospital £3. Poor of St. Brides parish, London, £3. To mother, Barbery Lee, dwelling in St. Brides parish, one ninth of estate and she Extrx: or, if she be dead, my Vncle Reignsbury Exor. Witnesses: Aar° Baker, Humphrey Weston, Richard ffitch. Died abroad, will pro. 30 July, 1638, by mother Barbara Lee *als* Buckeridge.*
(P. C. C. Lee, 87.)

Will of JOHN HOWETT of Elizabeth City in Virginia in the parts beyond the seas, planter, dated 6 September, 1654. To wife Elizabeth if living at my death and be unmarried, contrary to the now report from Virginia, one third of my whole estate. To my brothers and all my kindred one shilling each. Residuary Legatee and Exor: friend Mr. Thomas Howett, citizen and cooper of London. Witnesses: Rob't Earle of Prior, Hy. Fancon. Proved 28 July, 1659, by the Exor: named in the will.
(P. C. C. Pell, 524.)

Will of WILLIAM LANGTON of Citty of Bristol, merchant, sick and weake, dated 17 June, 1654. To brother John Langton all lands given me by will of my uncle William Burrowes of Bristoll, Gent., with remainder to my brother Joseph Langton. Sister Elizabeth Langton, wife of brother John, 40 shillings. Mrs. Katherine Bridge same. Mrs. Anna Symes same. Brother Thomas Langton all goods I have in the providence and all money due me for freight in last voyage & as for such goods as I haue lately Come home from the barbadoes & goods I expect daily from said Barbadoes I give to my brothers Joseph and Ezekaell Langton & to my two sisters Mary Vaughan & Joane Langton. To Mr. William Callis & his wife each 40 shillings. Ralph Hayens for service in my sickness 40 shillings. Brother John Langton Res: Leg: and Exor: [*Willm. Langton*]. Witnesses: William Atwood, Ralph Haines. Proved at London, 20 May, 1656, by Exor: named. (P. C. C. Berkeley, 141.)

---

* Probate Act Book.

Nuncupative will of JOHN PARRY, whilst he lived inhabiting in Virginia, dated 24 March, 1637. To Samuel Minifrey,* his servant, all coopers tooles, suit of clothes & a shirt. To John Martin certain clothing. To Stephen Pendle same. To Raph Hunter, groome, Bedd and Rugg. To brother William Parry his wages & all debts due him. Witnesses: Josua James & Raph Hunter, groome. Proved 30 July, 1638, and admon. with will annexed granted to brother William Parry. (P. C. C. Lee, 87.)

Will of JOHN DIGGS, dated at Rotterdam, 5 March, 1656. Body to be embalmed, wrapped in lead and sent to Feaversham, thence to Chilhang (sic.) there to be layed in the vault of my fathers. Brother Edward Diggs sole Exor: and to him £2000. Sister Anne Hammond £200, half of which I was once tould by her husband was a sufficient Legacie. To poor of Chilham parish £50. Overseers: friends Mr. George Smith and Mr. Mathew Bulwer, marchants, and to each £100. [Mark] Signatum John Diggs et sigillatum cum sigillo in cœrâ rubrâ sub Impresso Vlterius est subscriptum. Witnesses: Cuthbert Morley, mark, John Webb, meig. Jacobi Astell, N. P., August, 1656. Proved 30 September, 1656, and Letters of Admon. granted to George Smith and Mathew Bulwer, Trustees to administer for sole use and during absence of Edward Diggs the brother and sole Exor:, for that he is now governor of the Jsland of virginia and residing there and cannot speedilie doe the same.
(P. C. C. Berkeley, 455.)

The above testator was second son of the well known Sir Dudley Diggs, Knt., of Chilham, co. Kent, Ambassador to Russia, etc., who took so prominent a part in the discoveries of his time and in the settlement of Virginia. His mother was Mary, younger daughter and co-heir of Sir Thomas Kempe, Knt., of Olantigh, co. Kent, who brought Chilham Castle to her husband as her dower.†

The brother and executor, Edward Diggs, was Governor of Virginia, 1655 to 1658, and died 15 March, 1675, in Virginia, his holograph will being admitted to probate in the General Court of Virginia and commission issued to Elizabeth Diggs, his relict and Executrix.‡ Captain (afterward Colonel) William Diggs, one of the witnesses, (probably another of the eight sons of Sir Dudley,) married a daughter of Henry Sewell of Pautuxent, Maryland, and became a prominent citizen of that state.§

The sister, Anne Hammond, was the wife of Anthony Hammond of Nonington, co Kent, gentleman, son of Sir William Hammond, of St. Albons in same place Knt.,‖ by his wife Eliza-

---

* Cf. will of Thomas Mathewes of Va., surgeon, (pro. 3 July, 1645, Com. Lond. xxx, 50) ptd. in *Record* (Oct. 1909, xl, 239) with note *re* George Menefie.
† *Visit. Kent in Harl. Soc.*, xlii, 64–5, and Alex. Brown's *Genesis of U. S.*, ii, 878–9.
‡ Neill's *Va. Carolorum*, 383.
§ *Loc. cit.*
‖ *Visit. Kent. in Harl. Soc.*, xlii, 47.

beth, daughter of Anthony Aucher, gentleman.* Her name is shown by the will reference and the Visitation pedigree to have been Anne, but she is called *"Mary"* by a clerical error in her marriage license.†

The will of Richard Kempe, which follows, is interesting in this connection as probably concerning some member of the family of the mother of the Governor and the preceeding testator.

Will of RICHARD KEMPE of Kich-neck in the Collonie of virginia, Esquire, sick and weake, dated 4 Jan., 1649. My wife Elizabeth and daughter Elizabeth my Executrycs of whole estate in Virginia and all moneys due in England by Accompte and all proceeds of Tob: shiped this yeare. My vnckle Ralph wormeley to be Exor: during minority of my child. Kich-neck and all lands belonging to be sold and to make good a sale of 300 acres on the other side of the creeke I have made, hee putting in security to pay 10000 weight of Tob: in cash. My will is that my Exors: grant vnto George Keado 50 acres in barren necke where he liveth, for my plantation at Kappalianocke I leave it to discretion of my Exors: and the servants also. My wife and child to depart this Cuntry. My part of the house Att Towne to be sould, Mr. Richard Bennett to make good the sale. To vncle Ralph wormeley £10 for a ring. To brother Edward Kempe £5. To nephew Edmund Kempe one new servant, 2 cowes, 500 lbs of Tobaccoe towards his buildings. To my beloved friend Richard Lee 40 shillings for a ring. I pray god to bless this Collony. To Sir William Berkeley £10 desiring his favour to my poore wife and child and not to be of any Jnterruption to their departure out of the Collonie. Signed [*Rich: Kempe*]. Witnesses: Richard lee, Edmunde Kempe. Proved at London, 6 December, 1656, by Elizabeth Lunsford *als* Kempe, relict and one of the Executrices named, Elizabeth Kempe, the daughter and Ralfe wormley the other Exors: being both deceased.

(P. C. C. Berkley, 455.)

Richard Bennett was one of the associates with Edward Benett, merchant of London, and others, 21 November, 1621, in a Patent for the old grant of the Isle of Wight plantation, also called Warrosquoyak and Lawne's Creek, in Isle of Wight county, which had been granted to Christopher Lawne and his associates, but had lapsed from the death of the said Lawne in 1620.‡

---

* *Visit. Kent in Harl. Soc.*, xlii, 47.

† The license reads "Anthony Hammon of Nonington, *armiger*, and Mary Digges, daughter of Dulei (*i. e.*, *Dudley*) Digges of Chilham, *miles*, at Chilham, June 21, 1633." *Cant. Marr. Licences*, Cowper's edition, ii, 447.

‡ Neill's Va. Company of London, 194. See also will of Christopher Lawne (pro. 17 June, 1620, P. C. C. Soame 56) printed in RECORD (April, 1909, xl, 84) with notes by the writer.

CLUES FROM ENGLISH ARCHIVES
Contributory to American Genealogy.

By J. Henry Lea and J. R. Hutchinson.

Will of Sergant Major JOHN JOHNSON of the Jsland of Barba-does, dated 16 June, 1655. To three of my sisters Zonaberiah, Francis and Jane 8000 lbs of sugar each. Son in law Edward Crofts and his sister Elizabeth Crofts same. To his daughters Mary Crofts and Thomazine Crofts same. Son in law William Crofts same. Daughter Jane £1000 in ten years. To wife Elizabeth one third of estate and if with child £500 more to it at 18. Son John Res: Leg: and Exor: and wife Elizabeth Extrx: in trust till he is of age. [*John Johnson*]. Witnesses: And: Walmesley, Robert Handforth, S: Peyton. By the Governor:—Captain Andrew Walmesley & Mr. Robert Handforth appeared before me this 4 of ffebruary 1655 and made oath to signature [*Davy elldearle*]. Recorded in the Secretary's office 16 July, 1656, attested by me John Pocock, Dep[ty] Secry. Proved at London, 27 November, 1656, by Elizabeth Johnson relict & Extrx:
(P. C. C. Berkeley, 247.)

Compare will of LUKE JOHNSON of Virginia already printed in these collections.*

WILLIAM COLLCUTT late a seaman in the ship *Planter*, in Virginia beyond sea, widower. Dated about 28 or 29 March, 1659. In case my wife is dead I give to my sister Anne West £5. To John Noseiter 40/. To Thos. Prinderges, one of the mates of this ship 50/. To Edward Reddish 15/. To John Frost, boson, 15/. To David Man 5/. Res: Leg: Patience Dandy my wife's kinswoman. Wits: Thos. Prinderges, David Man. Admon with will granted 5 August, 1659, to Anne West, the aunt and curatrix to Patience Dandie, a minor, the cozen & Res: Leg: named in will. (P. C. C. Pell, 446.)

Will of WILLIAM BESSE, citizen & girdler of London. Dated 19 April, 1641. To be buried in the parish of St. Buttolphes without Bishopsgate, London, whereof I am now a parishoner, near my former wife. To my brother Mr. Richard Bragge 40/ &

---

* *Record*, vol. xli, p. 77.

to my sister his wife £5. To my sister Joane Hardwick 40/. To friend Mr. George Goulden of Paternoster Rowe, silkman, 40/. To my godson William Bragge £5. To Elizabeth, Marie & Sara Bragge, children of the said Richard, £4 each. To my cousins Francis & Stephen Totthill each 40/. To kinswoman Anne Penn, widow, 40/ & to her three children 20/ each. To kinswomen Sara & Rebecca Tothill 40/ each. To kinsman John Tothill 40/. To cousin Francis Tothill's child 20/. To friend Mr. John Greenhill, cordwainer, 20/. To friend Mr. Richard White 20/. To my brother Phillip Williams £5. To kinsman John Besse, my brother's son £20. I give all the rest of my goods & all my plantation, etc., which I have in Virginia & which are now coming home from there, to my wife Elizth: Besse, whom I make Extrx: Overseers: my said brother Richard Bragge & the said Mr. Geo: Goulden. Wits: Hy Collett, George Turner, Jo: Underwood, Not: Pub: Proved 12 May, 1641, by Elizth: Besse, relict & extrix.
(P. C. C.   Evelyn, 64.)

Will of JANE COLLIER of St. Mary Rotherhithe, co. Surrey, widow. Dated 18 April, 1722. To my daughter Mary Read, now wife of Richard Read, mariner, late of Rotherhithe, but now of Merry Land in Virginia, all my wearing apparrel if she be living; if not, then to my grandchildren Richard Read and Joseph Moore. Residuary legatee, the said Joseph Moore. Executors, my son in law Richard Read, my brother in law Richard Taylor of St. Martin's in the Fields, co. Middlesex, cordwainer, and Anthony Bayles of Rotherhithe, barber. Witnesses: Thomas Coattam, John Kidder, Not. Pub. Proved 6 Nov., 1723, by Anthony Bayles, power being reserved to the other executors.
(Arch. Surrey, 1722–25, fol. 199.)

Will of JOSEPH TORKINGTON of Virginia in parts beyond the seas, planter, dated 28 January, 1652-3. I bequeath all such temporal estate as I have in Virginia or England to my brother Samuel Torkinton, Citizen and Grocer of London, and appoint him executor. Witnesses: Zach: Cropton, John Hothersall, Richard Hopkins, Harbert Akehurst, Edward Bridgman. Proved 26 April, 1653, by the executor named. (P. C. C.   Brent, 320.)

I, WILLIAM LITTELL of Chelmsford in the county of Essex, carpenter, being aged, do make and ordain this my last will and testament. I give to my son John 5s. The copyhold estate which was my late wife's. I give to my grandson William Littell, now living in Georgia in America, the like sum of five shillings, to be paid to him when demanded. I devise my freehold messuage in the hamlet of Moulsham, in the parish of Chelmsford, now in the occupation of Edward Moody, to my son in law James Hawkes, the same being mortgaged to him. To my daughter Mary, wife of the said James Hawkes, my freehold messuage and farm lying in St. Giles in Colchester and East Donyland, now in the occupation of John Esty; also my messuage wherein I lately lived, lying in Moulsham. To my granddaughters Martha, Love and Elizabeth Pavett, daughters of John and Love Pavett, £10 apiece at 21. Elizabeth Tedder of Springfield, widow of Henry Tedder deceased, £10. The rest to my daughter Mary Hawkes, whom Executrix. Dated 8 August, 1752. Witnesses: Tho: Lawrence, Thos: Bones, William Smart. Proved 20 Oct., 1757, by Mary Hawkes, widow, relict of deceased (*sic*), sole Executrix.

(Commissary of London, Essex and Herts, Bawtree, 433.)

The last day of June, 1646, I RICHARD WILLIAMSON, Cittizen and Merchantaylor of London, being sickly and weake in body . . . give and bequeath vnto my brother Roger Williamson residinge in Virginia the summe of twenty shillings, and doe forgive vnto him all the money which he owes me. Item I give and bequeath vnto all the children of my said brother living at the time of my decease five poundes equally amongst them, to be paid vnto their father for their vse within two years after my decease. To my cousin Thomas Williamson £3, and to my cousin Alice Williamson his sister other £3. To my cousin Anne Nightingale, to whom I have given a porcon in marriage, 5s. Cozen Sarah Williamson £20 at one and twentie or marriage, or, if she die before said time, then to the children of my brother Roger Williamson equally. The lease of my nowe dwelling house, and all the rest of my goods, I give vnto my wife Mary, whom I appoint my Executrix. Witnesses: Edward Boldston, William Tuder, Ralph Dawson, Chr: Flavell, scr. Proved 5 Dec., 1646, by the Executrix.

19 Nov., 1651, commission to Martha Osboston, sister to Mary Williamson, whilst she lived relict and executrix of said deceased, to administer goods left unadministered by said Mary, during the minority of Sarah Williamson, brother's child to the said testator deceased, and legatee named in the will. (P. C. C. Twisse, 189.)

February the Six and Twentyth, 1672–3, ELIZABETH FOSTER, widdow, late wife of Henry Foster in Virginia, late deceased, did make her last will, that is to say, shee did nominate and appoint her mother Elizabeth Higginson, widow, late wife of Humfrey Higginson, to be her only Executrix, and did give and bequeath vnto her all her whole estate. Witnesses: Thomas Hasellwood, Mary Higginson, John Betts. Proved 14 March, 1673–4, by the executrix. (P. C. C. Bunce, 35.)

Humphrey Higginson, aged 28, sailed August, 1635, in the ship *George* for Virginia. Member of the Council, 1642–1655, and Colonel of militia. He lived in 1655 at Harop (*now Williamsburg*), returned to England and lived at Ratcliff, died March, 1665–66 (his will in Waters' *Gleanings*).* He had a brother CHRISTOPHER who lived in Virginia. A letter from Virginia, of Richard Kempe, dated 24 April, 1640, describes him as a "kinsman of the Bishop of Ely" (*Wrenn*). They were probably brothers of Captain Robert Higginson.† (W. G. Stannard.)

I, WILTSHIRE REEVE the elder, of Hubbard's Hall in the parish of Harlow, co. Essex, gent., being indisposed in my health, doe

---

* Waters' *Gleanings*, i, 644.
† *William & Mary Quarterly*, v, 186.

make and ordain my last will and testament in manner and form following, that is to say: First I direct that all my debts, for which my capital messuage called Hubbard's Hall and the land thereto belonging now stand mortgaged, shall be paid. I give unto my wife Joan Reeve all my capital messuage and Manor of Hubbard's Hall wherein I now dwell, with all the lands thereto belonging, and also the messuage called Brooke House, with a shop, situate in Churchgate Street in Harlow and in the occupation of George Speede, William Alefounder and William Sharpe, during the term of eight years, upon trust, and towards the maintaining and educating of my eldest son and the other children I have by my said wife; and from and after the expiration of the said term I give and devise all my said capital messuage and Manor, together with the said Brooke House, unto Wiltshire Reeve my eldest son and his heirs for ever, except the north end of my said mansion, which I give unto my wife during the term of her natural life. I give unto my son Wiltshire Reeve £100; unto John Reeve my second son and heirs my messuages, being nine in number, situate in Harlow, at his age of 21 years; to Joan my wife my farm called Hills and certain lands late in the tenure of Robert Nightingale, lying in Epping, during the term of her natural life, with remainder unto Francis Reeve my third son and his heirs; to Judith Reeve my eldest daughter £300 at 21 or marriage; to Anne Reeve my second daughter £300 at 21 or marriage; to Jane Reeve my youngest daughter and her heirs my two messuages in Shoo Lane in Foster Street in Harlow, late in the occupation of John Edden and Henry Colling; to my said daughter Jane £200 at 21 or marriage; to my sisters Letitia Wickstead and Anne Spademan each a ring of 20s. value; also I doe give and devise all my plantations, lands, tenements, etc. at or neer James River or elsewhere in Virginia in the parts beyond the seas, unto my sister Susan, now Susan Mareen, now or late residing in Virginia, and to her heirs for ever. I make Joan my wife guardian of my sons and daughters and their estates during their minority. Residue to my wife, whom Executrix. I do confirm a certain Indenture bearing date 27 Aug., last past, made between me the said Wiltshire Reeve and Joan my wife of the one part, and Richard Day and John Smith of the other part, whereby I and my said wife have made some provision for our said children. Mention of an obligation bearing date 21 Sept., 1704, in which I stand bound unto Thomas Spademan of London, apothecary, and Anne his wife, my sister, conditioned for the payment of £20 yearly unto them. Dated 13 Sept., 1707. Witnesses: John Taylor, Samuel Harrison, Ri: Harrison. Proved 1 Dec., 1707, by the Executrix.

(Arch: Middlesex, Essex and Herts, Sanney, 267.)

Will of WILLIAM WALL of Standon, co. Hertford. I give and bequeath unto my brother John Wall of the parish of Goshen in Chester County and Province of Pensilvania in America the sum of thirty pounds, and if he should happen to be dead before me then I will and order the same to be paid to his children. I give to my nephew Richard Wall £20 over and above the £20 I gave him in my lifetime, or, if he die before me, to his children; to John Barler who married Anne, daughter of my brother Thomas Wall, £20, or if they be dead before me, then to their children; to my kinsman Richard Deane £20, or to his children; to my kinsman Richard Holford £10, or to his children; to my nephew Thomas Wall £10, or to his children; to Henry Madder £5, or to his daughter Elizabeth; to my sister Elizabeth Wall, widow of my brother Walter Wall, £5; to Edmond Rowley who married my niece Sarah Wall, £10; to Catherine Begford, daughter of my niece Mary, wife of John Hollis, £5; to John, son of said John and Mary Hollis, £5; to my sister in law Mary, widow of Thomas Wall, £5, or to the children of her daughter Anne, wife of John Barler; to Joseph Sollam who married Elizabeth my sister in law, £5; to the poor of Tixall, co Stafford, 20s.; to my nephew William Wall and heirs all my free and copyhold lands at Latchford in Standon, co. Herts; to Catherine Dale of Standon one guinea; to Edward Moore of Standon, gardiner, 20s.; to the poor of Standon 40s.; to Joseph Mitchell of Standon 20s.; to Edward Odell of Puckridge, carpenter, 20s.; to my nephew William Wall and John Bridges of Standon, my friend, £180-2 in trust for the payment of the foregoing legacies. I order my body to be buried in the upper part of the South Isle of Standon Church, near to the body of Hannah Edwards, deceased. All my wearing apparel I give to my three nephews Richard Wall, Thomas Wall and William Wall. Executors: my nephew William Wall and my friend John Bridges. Dated 13 Sept., 1754. Witnesses: John Goodwin the elder, John Goodwin the younger, Henry Roberts. Proved 2 Oct., 1754, by the Executors.

(Arch. Middlesex, Essex and Herts, Amis, 43.)

Will of WILLIAM HAYWARD of Belton, co Suffolk, labourer. Dated 24 December, 1638. To Mary Catter, "which I keeps," 40s. to be paid into the hands of John Catter her father. To Francis Hayward, son of Simon Hayward my brother, 40s. to be paid into the hands of his uncle Burn "for the child's use." To Mary Hauknit my prentice 40s. To Gregory Holt's children, Abigail and Lydia, 10s. apiece. "I do ordain & make William Hayward my son my sole Executor, but if it be apparently proved that he be dead & have no issue then my will is that the remainder of my goods and chattles shalbe (*sold*) by my supervisor whom I put in trust to be put into the hands of the Churchwardens & overseers for the poor of the town of Belton to be paid unto them by my supervisor within one whole year next after it be aparently proved that my son William be dead without issue." I ordain and make Edward Watson my supervisor. Witnesses: Wm. Pope, Joseph Falk. 13 February, 1638-9, administration of the goods of the said William Hayward deceased, with this will annexed (William Hayward the executor being in parts beyond the seas), was granted Edward Watson, supervisor under the said will, until such time as the said William Hayward should return. (Ipswich Wills: Register 1638-40: fol. 78.)

13 February, 1638-9, administration of the goods of William Hayward of Belton, deceased, granted to Edward Watson, super-

visor under the will of said deceased, for so long as William Hayward, the executor under said will, remains in part beyond the seas. (Ipswich Act Book, 1638–9, fol. 46.)

Will of HUMFREY LEY in Partibus Transmarinus. My Deare Harte & Loving Sister my unfeined love remembered vnto thee with my love vnto my Aunt & Sister Mary and her children trusting in God that these few lines will find you all in good health as J am att present (Thanks be to God for it) Loueing sister these few lines are to certify you of my now being in the Downes & had our Merchant beene aboard wee had set saile presently the winde being now faire for us J did xpect yor answere of a letter that J sent yo^u that J might haue disposed of my selfe to you in that which J gaue yo^u a hinte of in my laste & in whose hand it is But your not writing did cause mee to stop my hand of not writing. My brother James Ewde is very well & in good health & desires to be remembered to his wife & children & to my Aunt & to yor selfe J was this day sennitt with him att Chattam & parted from him the Evening their shipp was paid of the Thursday before that J was there. My deare sister this is the laste for this boute to thee but know not but that windes and wether may giue us a sight of each other J could wish it if it might stand with the will of God But if God haue otherwise disposed wee must waite till God giue us that opportunity which J hope in his good tyme will And soe leaue thee to the alseeing God who is the keeper of all those that truly ffeare God J leaue thee to God & rest Thy euer Loueing brother till Death. [*Humphrie Ley*.] ffrom the Downes the Twenetith of September One Thousand Six Hundred ffifty Eight. Our shipps name is the Phinicks (*Phoenix*) Captain Robert Church Commander bound for virginia to James River & vp the Bay to Mereland & soe for Holland, it will be some Eight moneths. William Ganger is one of our Company and doth desire to haue his Duty remembered to his mother & his love to my sister (*sic*) and yourselfe. That which J gaue you a hinte of is in the hande of Elizabeth ffosse The ffifty if J never see thee againe J give that and all other meterialls that J haue in the world to thee my sister Judeth Ley. [*Huuphrie Ley*]. Proved 19 March, 1662, and commission issued to Judith Skiner *als* Leigh, sister and universal legatee of H. Leigh, late in pts a bachelor deceased. (P. C. C. Juxon, 38.)

At a Court of Vice Admiralty held for the Province of New York, Friday, the 7th of October, 31 Geo. II, 1757, before Hon. Lewis Morris, Esq., Commissioner of said Court.

Capt. William Dobbs Lybellant
                    agt
            Brigantine Mentor &^{c}.

On Wednesday, 5 October, anno pr'dt. said Capt. Dobbs of Sloop *Goldfinch*, Capt. John Cren of sloop *Fox*, Capt. Peter Haley of sloop *George*, Capt. Thomas Holins of sloop *Thomas*, Capt. Geo. Stephen of sloop *Stanwix* and Capt. Edw. Bishon of sloop *Thurloe*.

Exhibited before said Court lybell against French Brigantine *Le Mentor* reciting His Majesty's commissions to aforesaid vessels, as private vessels of war, that said vessels about 23 August last past on the High Seas about Lat. 21° 35′ North and Lon. 72° 31′ West, then took the said French brigantine of 120 tons and 22 men, commanded by one Jacque Millyon and having aboard also a Bill of Ransom for the shipp *Happy Return* of Londonderry, executed by Alexander Steward of said shipp, drawn on Messrs Mosson, Gamble, Wm. Hambleton and James Mitchell, merchants in London, for £1000, pray sentence. Condemned 17 October, 1757.

Power of Atty for owners to Thomas Greg of Belfast to receive prize money, Certf. by Jno. Conger, Mayor of New York, signed by owners.
       Evart Byvanck
       Lawrence Kortright
       Waddell Cunningham
       David van horne
       And^w Barclay
       Saml Van Horne
Rec. in Peculiar of St. Katherine by the Tower, London.

CLUES FROM ENGLISH ARCHIVES

Contributory to American Genealogy.

By J. Henry Lea and J. R. Hutchinson.

The fourteenth day of August, 1656, I William Boys of Cranbrooke in the county of Kent, clothier, being in some good measure of health, doe make and ordain this my last will. My bodie I will to be decently buried at the discretion of Joan my wife, whom I make sole executrix of this my will. I give and bequeath unto Sibylla Boys my eldest daughter £200 when she shall attain the age of eighteen years; to Mary Boys my daughter the like summe at her said age; and to my four sonnes John, Thomas, William and Joseph Boys £200 apiece of good English money at their severall ages of one and twenty years. As for my house and land in Cranbrooke, which now I inabite and which I lately purchased, viz., seven parts of eight parts thereof, I give the same unto Joan my wife during her naturall life and after her decease unto my four sonnes before named equally and to their heirs for ever. And if it shall happen that the other part should be desired to be sold, which now belongs unto John *Slow* sonne of Thomas *Slow* in New England, then my mind and will is that my wife shall purchase the same in behalf of my four sonnes, paying for it out of the portions before given them. If my said wife happen to marry again she shall give sufficient suritie to my brother Edmund Colvill of Maidstone for payment of my children's portions. Witnesses: none. Proved 24 Feb., 1656-7, by Joan Boys the relict and executrix. (P. C. C. Ruthen, 72.)

The above will was printed by us in the Record of January, 1911, but is repeated here as it contains an evident error in the reference to *John Slow* son of *Thomas Slow* of New England, for attention to which we have to thank our esteemed correspondent Mr. Henry Wykoff Belknap of Salem, Mass., whose notes on the subject we have pleasure in printing herewith and whose contention that the name should be Stow is undoubtedly correct, as his reference to a note on this will in the New England Register made by the careful hand of Mr. William S. Appleton*, goes to confirm his argument as well as the suspicion of Savage† that an error might exist in the American Records in these names.

A very careful rereading of the will at Somerset House has developed the fact that *the names are exactly as heretofore printed*, so that the error was evidently that of the registering clerk of the period, as is too often the case. Mr. Belknap's letter follows:

"The will refers to a house and land in Cranbrooke of which one eighth part belonged to *John Slow* sonne of *Thomas Slow* in

---

* *Vide infra.*
† *Savage* iv, 108, *but says "if not Stowe?"*

New England. In a note the contributors state that Thomas Slow was of Providence, R. I., and was admitted Freeman there in 1655, with a reference to Savage as authority.

Savage does make this statement but qualifies it by adding *"if not Stowe."* That his doubt was justified there can be little question and, so far as this will is concerned, a reference to it will be found in the New England Register, Vol. 53, page 301, in which the name is given as STOW.*

John Stow, according to the Rev. John Elliott's Record of Church Members, arrived in New England the 17th of the 3rd month anno 1634. He brought with him his wife and six children : Thomas, Elizabeth, John, Nathaniel, Samuel and Thankful. Elizabeth Stow, the wife of John Stow, she was a very godly matron, a blessing not only to her family but to all the church & when she had lead a christian conversation a few years among us she dyed & left a good savor behind her.

Through the publication in the New England Register, page 58, January, 1912, we have the records of the Parish of All Saints Church, Biddenden, Co. Kent, between 1558 and 1638, so far as they relate to the family of BIGGE and among them is that of the marriage 1608 of John Stowe and Elizabeth Bigge 13 September.

In the ship Elizabeth which sailed 9 April and arrived in New England 17 May, 1634, bringing John Stow and his family, we also find his mother-in-law Rachel Biggs and, despite the fact that Mr. Waters in his GLEANINGS has given as much relating to the Bigge or Biggs family†, no light has ever been thrown upon the maiden name of Rachel, so that it was with much satisfaction that, among the Bigge entries of marriages in St. Mildred's Church, Tenterden, Co. Kent, published in the same number of the Register, was found 1583—John Bigge of Cranbrooke and Rachel Martin of Lidde, 14 September. In the McDonough-Hackstaff Genealogy it is stated that Rachel Bigg was born in or before 1579 and in view of the date of her marriage, it would appear that it was certainly before but, because of a mistake in the list of passengers on the *Elizabeth*, we cannot tell her age when she landed. In this list it is given as 6 , which may have been meant for 69 perhaps if she was about 17 when married.

Rachel Bigg made her will 17 November, 1646 and it was attested by Richard Peacocke, one of the witnesses, 30 June, 1647, her "sonne in law" John Stowe being Executor, so that Savage is in error in stating that John died in 1643. It would appear that he sold his land in Roxbury in 1648 and removed to Concord probably late in the year, as he made an Inventory of the estate of John Levins of Roxbury 30 August, 1648. He probably later removed to Middleton, Conn., and died there. His son Thomas went to Middleton in 1659 and Samuel removed there in 1652.

HENRY W. BELKNAP."

Salem, Mass., Feb., 1912."

---

* It would be curious to know whence Mr. Appleton derived his authority for this statement as the names are most clearly written Slow in the will.

† *Waters' Gleanings*, i, 21, ii, 1365-72.

Our apologies are due alike to our correspondent and to our readers for the delay of over a year from the receipt of his letter and the laying of it, and the above corrections, before the public, a delay which has been in no manner the fault of the writers but due to matters entirely beyond their control.

Will of RICHARD ODELL of Newport Pagnell, (*Bucks.*) miller, dated 21 November, 1636. To William Oddell my eldest son, my freehold land in Cranfield, co. Beds. Mary Oddell my daughter £20 at marriage or 21. Elizabeth Oddell, daughter of John Oddell my brother, 10 shillings. Residue to Martha my wife, whom Extrx. and John Oddell and Robert Markes of Newport Pagnell, blacksmith, Overseers. Witnesses: — Richard Hull, Thomas King, Robert Bitchnoe. Proved 10 January, 1636-7, by the Extrx. named. (Arch: Bucks:, Bk. 36, fo. 80.)

Archdeacon's Visitation holden in the Church of Newport (*Pagnell*) Co. Bucks., 17 April, 1637.

NEWPORT: EDWARD HARTLEY (*cited*) for quarrelling by words with WILLIAM ODELL in the churchyard and stabbinge the seyd William through the arme. (Here follows a list of petty fines imposed for non-appearance in answer to various citations before the Archdeacons' Court.) He was questioned for this at the Assizes and punished. In the margin appear the words: 17 October, 1639. *Absunt Nova Anglia.* Beneath are the words WILLIAM ODELL *ut supra.* (Visitation Books, 1635-8, no folio.)

We note in the above that the Latin verb is in the *plural*, thus clearly indicating that *they* are absent or abroad in New England, which is fully confirmed by the line below relating to William Odell and showing that *both* of the parties to the combat were then in New England.

William Odell (also written Wodell, Odle, Woddle, Woodhull, etc.,) was of Concord, Mass., as early as 1639 where his children James and Rebecca were born. He died at Fairfield, Conn., in 1676, his will proved 6 June of that year, names his sons William and John Odell and daughter Rebecca Moorehouse. His son James had predeceased him in 1641. An Ursula Wodell or Odle, who married Christopher Woolly or Wollie at Concord in 1646, may have been his sister.

He had been suspected to have come from Cranfield, co. Beds., where the Parish Registers show a flourishing family of the name* but the above documents refute this and clearly prove the place of his origin and his paternity. Bedfordshire is an adjoining county to Bucks. Cranfield lies about five miles East by South from Newport-Pagnell while Odell, no doubt the cradle of the race, is about ten miles to the North of both in Bedfordshire. The Parish Register of Newport Pagnell exists from 1558.

Edward Hartley, the aggressor in the fray, seems to have left no record of his presence in New England. It is very improb-

---

* *N. E. Register,* Jan., 1906, lx, 91, see also *ibid.* xlv, 99, 7-8.

able that he was connected with the Richard Hartley of New London, 1656-1662, who was from Yorkshire.*

17 February, 1639-40, I RICHARD WARD of Faxton in the county of Northampton, yeoman, being sick in body, do now make my last will : I give to Mr Francis Nickolls 20s. To Mr Edward Nickolls 20s. To Mr Edward Bagshew 20s. and to his wife 20s. To Mr Francis Bagshew and to Mr John Bagshew 20s. each. I dow give and bequeath to Mr Thomas Dudley, governor of New ingland, three pound. To Mr Clark, minister, 20s. of the 40s. he oweth me. To my brother Philip Ward £5 and to his four children 20s. apiece. To my brother Ambrose Ward £5. To my brother Andrew Ward £5. To my brother James Ward £5. To my sister Margaret £5. To my sister Margery £5. To Thomas Goosy 20s. To Grace Goosy 20s. To Susan Goosy 30s. To Henry Ward £3. To Richard Ward, son of Henry Ward, £3. To Richard, son of Andrew Ward, £3. To Grace Ward and Alice Ward 40s. apiece, and 40s. to be divided between Henry Ward, Richard Ward, Grace Ward and Alice Ward. To my maid Catering King £4. To Grace Fouthery 10s. To Elizabeth Coper 5s. To Joan Fathery 5s. To John Godfrey 5s. To Thomas Rems of Broughton 5s. William Holt of Cransley 5s. Poor of Foxton 40s., whereof ten shillings is to be raised of Richard Browne of Draughton. Executors: Ambrose Ward, Andrew Ward, James Ward and Henry Ward, and Robert Goosy Overseer. Witnesses: Robert Goosy, James Ward, Henry Ward. Proved 20 March, 1639-40.   (Northants Wills, S. 2., 1636-40, f. 296.)

Andrew Ward of Watertown, Mass., freeman there, 14 May, 1634,[†] removed the following year to Wethersfield, Conn., to aid in the foundation of the new town (then called "Connecticut Watertown") he being one of the five dismissed from the parent town for that purpose. He was a prominent and influential citizen, member of the first Court in the Connecticut Colony in April, 1636; member of the upper house in 1637 when war was declared with the Pequots; twice member of the lower house, 1637 and 1638; deputy from Wethersfield for four sessions after the confederation of the three river towns in 1639, and frequently a member of the General Court and a Magistrate. In 1640, he, with others, bought the land comprising the present town of Stamford for the New Haven Company, he afterward removed, with Rev. Mr. Denton, to Hempstead, L. I., but, about 1650, returned to Connecticut and settled at Fairfield. He was a representative to the upper house of New Haven Colony 1646 and 1653 and died at Fairfield in 1659, his will dated 8 June of that year.[‡]

He has been said to have been the son or grandson of Richard Ward of Homersfield, co. Suffolk, and descended of an ancient family long seated there,[§] but this statement rests upon the

* *Savage*, ii. 368.
† *Pope's Pioneers*, 477. *Savage's Gen. Dict.*, iv, 406.
‡ *Stiles' Anc. Wethersfield*, ii, 726; *Bond's Watertown*, p. 619.
§ *New York Mail and Express*, 27 March, 1897. *Andrew Ward and His Descendents*. (1597-1910) pub. New York, 1910.

unsupported conjecture of an early Anglo-American genealogist most of whose work, subjected to the light of the clearer criticism of to-day which demands facts instead of fancy, is found to be untrustworthy and misleading.

In the above will, however, we have certainly the clue to the true ancestry of this distinguished colonist. The connection shown with Gov. Thomas Dudley, already known to be of Northamptonshire stock, first attracted the writers' attention and careful study of the will makes it certain that the testator was a member of the Visitation family of WARD who were of Braffield and Little Houghton, in Northants, and whose pedigree was recorded in 1618-19.* Nor does the will leave us in much, if any, doubt that the testator and his brother Andrew (the probable Emigrant,) were the sons of Stephen and Joice (Traford) Ward of Northampton town and younger brothers of the Ambrose Ward named in the pedigree.

The JOYCE WARD, widow, of Wethersfield, Conn., was most probably NOT identical with JOYCE the wife of Stephen Ward of Northampton town in England, the mother of the testator according to the Visitation pedigree already cited, as the children named by her in her will do not at all agree with those of Joyce (Trafford) Ward of Northampton who was almost certainly the mother of the Emigrant and his brother Ambrose, mentioned in the above will of Richard of Faxton. Yet it is noteworthy that it is stated by Judge Adams in his manuscript that "The late ex. Governor Marcus L. Ward of New Jersey said that he was a descendant of the widow Joyce Ward of Wethersfield and that her husband's name was Stephen and that he died in England. It seems incredible that there could have been two Stephens each with a wife Joyce at the same period and this part of the pedigree will demand the strictest scrutiny.

If further confirmatory evidence were needed of the derivation of the Wethersfield people from the Braffield stock, we find it in the constant recurrence, among the American descendants, of the Christian names of the last mentioned English family, as shown in the will, every one of which is repeated and notably the very unusual ones of *Ambrose, Andrew, Richard, Alice, Grace* and *Margery*, while those of *Stephen, Robert, Daniel* and *Isabell* of the recorded pedigree also appear. All of them but *Richard* and *Andrew* being conspicuous by their absence from the Homersfield pedigree.

It is also noteworthy, in further contravertion of that errorious derivation, that we find in the Parish Registers of St. Mildred's Cornhill, London, the burial of a Mr. Andrew Warde, gent., 23 January, 1615,† who was probably the son of that Richard Ward of Homersfield and Gorleston, Suffolk, who was so lightly accepted as the American Emigrant without a scintilla of evidence beyond the Christian name.

---

* *Metcalfe's Visit. of Northants.*, p. 151, also *Bridge's Hist. of Northants.*, by Whalley, Vol. i, p. 339.

† *Harl. Soc., Psh. Reg. Series*, vii, 219.

Research along the lines indicated will undoubtedly confirm the derivation as here promulgated.

Reference may also be made, in this connection, to a series of notes on the Ward Family which appeared in the amateur genealogical page of the Boston Transcript some years ago and which, while proving nothing, treated the matter with unusual perspicacity and clearness. They are 8 March, 1902, and No. 438, 15 July, 1903, (disproving the Grenville connection,) No. 6951, 15 March, 1905, and No. 708, 29 May, 5 June, and 21 June, 1905, the first of these relating to the Capel connection and the last three to the Joice Ward problem which, while well treated, is left unsolved.

Archelaus Woodman, mercer, was of Newbury, Mass., in 1637, freeman 17 May of that year, town officer and lieutenant 1670, representative to the General Court 1674 and 75. He came over in the *James* of London from Southampton, embarking 6 April and arrived 3 June, 1635. In passenger list of same is called Hercules and as of Malford (*i. e. Christian Malford*, Wilts.,) mercer. He brought wife Elizabeth who died 17 December, 1677 and he married second Dorothy Chapman, 13 November, 1678. He died 7 October, 1702. Edward Woodman, brother of above, also of Newbury, came with wife and sons Edward and John and had four or more children born here. Freeman 25 May, 1636, representative September, 1636 and several times later. He died before 9 November, 1653, when his widow is mentioned.*

In spite of the clear reference in the passenger lists it has found impossible to trace the pedigree of these two brothers in England, largely owing to the fact that the early parish registers of Christian Malford, previous to 1650, were destroyed by fire. In view of this fact the wills and extracts of neighboring registers which follow are of special interest, as throwing a side light on persons who were certainly members of the same family although their exact relationship may never be known.

Will of PETER SMITH *als.* WOODMAN of the parish of Christen Malford in Diocese of Sar: (i. e. *Sarum*), dated xv ffebruary 1566. To mother Church of Sarum 4d. To parish Church of Cristen Malford 3s. 4d. To the Church waye 3s. 4d. To the poor 5s. To daughters Joane and Alice Woodman each £20. Res: Legatees and Exors: sonn Hughe Woodman and wief Alice. To Thomas Chester a pair of Bellowes and a Bike Horne and the Sledge of the streighte beame. To brother in lawe Nicholas Rimell a hose cloth. To Johanne, daughter of said Nicholas, a grey mare. To sister Mawde, weif of said Nicholas Rimell, a grey mare colte. Thomas Leyceter a Coote and pair of Hose. John Compton pair Hose. John partrege of Sutton, Hose, Jerkin and Boots. William partredge frese Jerkin and pair Boates. To brother in law william Wellstede nighte gowne. Elizabeth Creye a Redd petticott. John wellstede 10s. he oweth. To all godchildren 12d. each. Overseers: Thomas Rede & George Collman. Proved at London xxii May 1566 by Justinian Kidd, Atty for Agnes Smith *als.* Woodman, Extrx:, power reserved to other Exor:

(P. C. C. Crymes, 14.)

* *Savage* iv, 640; *Pope's Pioneers of Mass.*, 513.

Will of JUNE ARCHARD of Standley,* widow, sick, dated 24 April, 1614. To be buried in the parish Church of Chippenham. To Bridget and Margaret Byreymon, daughters of Bridget Atkyns each £50. Elizabeth (an infant) and Johane, daughters of Mr. Richard Attkyns. William sonn of John Mereyweather and June and John, daughter and sonne of same. John Attkyns. June Bereyman. To poor of Chippenham and Cossam (*Corsham*) each parish 20s. To Agnes wif of Thomas Wodman. Overseers: William Geale and Phillip Cogeswell. Daughter Bridget Attkyns Extrx: Robert sonn of Richard Atkyns, Thomas Younge. Signs by mark. Witnesses: William Geale, Richard Atkyns & Phillip Cogswell. Proved at London, 10 May, 1621, by daughter and extrx: named in the will. (P. C. C. Hale 41.)

ASHTON KEYNES, WILTSHIRE.

1615—olyver Carter & Elizabeth woodman were married xvi november.

1597—Johana Woodman, vidua, sepulta fuit 3 June.

1615—Leonard Woodman buried xi Martij.

1601—Elenora Woodman filia Leonardi Woodman baptizata fuit 20 Dec.

1625—Margareta Woodman vid: sepulta Decembris 13

LEIGH-DE-LA-MERE, WILTSHIRE.

Bishops' Transcripts:

1620—Baptized 9th. April 1620 Jacob Woodman the sonne of Thomas Woodman.

1622—Baptized the 31st. of M . . . Zacharias woodman the sonne . . . Thomas woodman.

1666—Baptized likewise Jsaacke the sonn of Jacob Woodman.

1668—Rebecca the Daughter of Jacob Woodman & Mary his wife were baptized 11 March 1668.

1673—Jacob sonn of Jacob Woodman baptized September 1st.

1677—Priscilla ye daughter of Jacob Woodman baptized 21 day of January.

BRISTOL PARISH REGISTERS.

TEMPLE CHURCH.

1622—Leonard Hancock and Edith Woodman married 25 February.

ST. THOMAS CHURCH.

1646—Thomas Brookes *als*. Witherley and Susan Woodman married 30 May.

In this connection may be appended a few stray entries from various parish registers which contain interesting names and references, which may prove to be of value.

ST. MARY KEY, IPSWICH.

Churchwardens Accounts:

Account of Edward Hedge and John Blomefeild the younger, churchwardens: Easter 1634 to Easter 1635:—

* A hamlet two miles east of and in Chippenham and four miles south of Christian Malford (*co. Wilts.*).

Items: Given with the widow Parker's son to bynd him forth an apprentice to Newe England 15s. 3d.

Perhaps the Walter Parker aet. 18 who came in the *Love* in July 1635.

STEPNEY, MIDDX.

1641-2—John and Daniell, sonnes of Hugh Browne of Ratcliffe, maryner, and Elizabeth his wife, both born at Salam in New England, the said John being ten years old the tenth of March next, and the said Daniell being seaven years old about the fourth of August next, baptized 9 February 1641-2.

1687—Charles Ashcom of Pensilvania in America and Martha Earle of Ratcliffe, spinster, married 18 July.

ST. NICHOLAS, DUBLIN, IRELAND.

1693—Mary daughter of Henry Coursey, junior, (of the province of Maryland in America,) and of his wife Elizabeth Coursey *alias* Desminieres, was baptized here 3d. August 1693.

A Thomas Causey had Patent of 150 acres of land in Charles City, Virginia, in 1635 and 300 acres at the mouth of the Appomattucks River, on six head rights in 1636, who may have been of the same family as the above.

CHELMSFORD, ESSEX.

1610—Thomas son of Thomas Withers of Chelmsford baptized 3 June.

1617—John son of Robert Ogdon baptized 30 June.

LITTLEPORT, CAMBRIDGESHIRE.

Transcripts (Registers before 1753 have perished).

1605—John Tylne and Joan Neale married 16 August.

1606—John Tylne baptized 11 November.

1609—Joan Tylne, daughter of John, baptized 3 September.

1615—John Tilny buried 6 June.

1616—Richard Dunkin and Joan Tilny married 22 April.

The above interesting bit of Tilney family history may relate to a John Tilney of Virginia in the early part of the 17th Century, who is believed to be of the gentle family of that name of Boston in Lincolnshire and whose descendants are numerous in Suffolk and the surrounding counties.

ROWLEY, YORKSHIRE.

1620-21—February 21—Institution of Ezekiel Rogers, clerk, A. M., to the rectory of Rowley, vacant by the death of Henry Pickard, clerk, last incumbent, at the presentation of Sir Francis Barrington, Bart., patron of the living.
(Reg. of Insts., York, 1619-30.)

1638—June 6—Institution of Thomas White, clerk, M. A., to the rectory of Rowley, vacant by the resignation of Ezekiel

Rogers, the last incumbent, at the presentation of Sir Thomas Barrington, Bart.

(Reg. of Insts., York, 1632-68.)

In the above we have the record of the Rev. Ezekiel Rogers who led a large band of his parishioners from Rowley to found the town of Rowley in Massachusetts.

Here we conclude this series of contributions to the tracing of Anglo-American family history in which it has been our privilege and pleasure to aid amateur seekers for the truth, but these were designed for such seekers alone, and have been so far perverted by certain readers of the RECORD from their original object that it has seemed wiser to discontinue them. We will gladly respond to queries as to unpublished CLUES.

NEW YORK GLEANINGS IN ENGLAND.

CONTRIBUTED BY LOTHROP WITHINGTON, LONDON.

Andrew Nicoll of the City of New York, gent., Captain-Lieutenant of the Independent Company commanded by Captain Hubert Marshall. Will, 28 Jan., 1746–7; proved 9 Feb., 1748–9. I direct my executors to sell all that my tract of one thousand acres of land in Orange County near the high lands in the province of New York and now in the tenture of William Pestles and out of the money arising, I give £200 to be put out at interest and applied towards the maintenance and education of Susannah Nicoll, daughter of George Nicoll, late of the City of New York, deceased, till she come of age or is married; but if she die, then to Elizabeth Nicoll, widow of the said George Nicoll and mother of the said Susannah Nicoll. To Richard Nicholls of the City of New York, Attorney at Law, £60. To Hellegonda Bayard of the City of New York, widow, £30. To George Burnet of the City of New York, shopkeeper, £20. To Helen Nicoll, widow of my brother James, late of Aberdeen in North Britain, £20, but if she die before me, then I give the said £20 to the Rev. James Orem, Chaplain to the Forces in this province. Residuary legatees: the said James Orem and Richard Nicholls. Executors: James Orem, Richard Nicholls, and George Burnet. Witnesses: John Burnet, James Emott, John McEvers. Proved by Rev. James Orem, clerk, with power reserved, &c. Lisle, 50.

John Stone of London, merchant. Will, 22 May, 1693; proved 14 Aug., 1693. To be buried in Bunhill Fields. Cozen Vickers of Jamaica and his daughter at present with her grandfather, Mr. Gerard Douw in New York. Hannah (Johanna?) Vickers, widow of late uncle Vickers. Cozen Hollister of Colchester. Cozen John Daniell and John Daniell, junior. Cozen Samuel Dawes. Cozen Susan Bateman and her sister Mary Turner. Nephew John Stone of Cheapside. Nephew John Scarlett of Brickellsea. Sister Durrell's two children she had by John Story. Poor of Leonard's, Colchester. Cozen Frances Boucher, wife of Mr. ——— Boucher, clerk. Friends Mr. Samuel Stone and Mr. Jonathan Stone. Cozen Thomas Hollister and his wife. Friend Dr. Isaac Chauncy.   Coker, 131.

James Battersbye, late of Flushing, Province of New York, bachelor, deceased. Administration, 23 Feb., 1716–17. To Thomas Prickman, guardian of Hester Prickman, a minor, niece (ex sorore) and next of kin to defunct. Admon. Act Book, 1717.

Henry Benson, late of the City of New York in America, but deceased in H. M. Ship *Princess Mary*. Administration, 2 March, 1746–7, to William Bryant, Attorney for the relict Judith Benson, widow, now residing at New York.   Ditto, 1747.

Thomas Biles, late of New Yorke in America, widower, deceased. Administration, 26 Feb., 1701–2, to his son Thomas Biles.   Ditto, 1702, folio 27.

Philip Boyles, late of the City of New York in America, but in H. M. Ship *Ludlow Castle*, deceased. Administration, 25 Feb., 1743–4, to William Bryant, Attorney for Catherine Boyles, widow, the relict now residing at New York.   Ditto, 1744.

Anne Clinton, late of New York in New England, spinster, deceased. Administration, 26 June, 1751, to John Catherwood, Esq., Attorney of the Honorable George Glinton, Esq., now residing at New York, father of the defunct. A former grant in Feb., 1745–6, to Maynard Cuerin, Esq., having ceased at his death.   Ditto, 1751.

John Comer, late of New York in America, bachelor, deceased. Administration, 2 April, 1736, to his brother Walter Comer.
                                              Admon Act Book, 1736.

Stephen Crego, late of New York, but on the ship *Archangel*, deceased. Administration to John Corbett, Attorney for Margery Crego now at New York relict of the defunct, 13 May, 1692.
                                                 Ditto, 1692, folio 91.

James Depont, late of New York, bachelor, deceased. Administration, 26 July, 1706, to Robert Myre, principal creditor, Ester Bernon, mother and next of kin in England, first renouncing.
                                                Ditto, 1706, folio 139.

Richard Gatehouse, late of New York in North America, bachelor, deceased. Administration, 1 April, 1761, to his father John Gatehouse.   Ditto, 1761.

John Goven, late of New York in New England, afterwards of H. M. Ship *Launceston* and *Assistance.* Administration, 3 Jan., 1746–7, to his relict Elizabeth Goven. Ditto, 1747.

Thomas Grimditch, late of New York, deceased. Administration, 8 March, 1683–4, to his relict Eshew Grimditch. Ditto, 1684.

William Heathcote, late of the province of New York in America, bachelor, deceased. Administration, 8 Jan., 1722–3, to his mother Martha Heathcote, widow. Administration, 6 Feb., 1735–6, to Samuel Baker, one of the Attorneys of Martha Heathcote, widow, now residing at New York, mother of the defunct.

Elizabeth Heathcote, late of the City of New, spinster, deceased. Administration, 6 Feb., 1735–6, to Samuel Parker (as above) for her mother Martha Heathcote. Ditto, 1723, folio 11, and ditto, 1736.

William Hooker, late of New York in America, and formerly of H. M. Service, deceased. Administration, 4 Feb., 1748–9 to William Bryant, Attorney for Cloe Hooker the relict, now residing at New York. Ditto, 1749.

James Larkin, late of New York in New England. Administration, 26 March, 1697, to Lancaster Symms, husband of Catharine Symms als. Larkins, late wife of said James Larkins.
Ditto, 1697, folio 41.

John Lindesay, late of New York in North America, deceased. Administration, 18 April, 1753, to his relict Penelope Lindesay.
Ditto, 1753.

Edward Man, late of New York, bachelor, deceased. Administration, 19 March, 1706–7, to his sister Martha Man.
Ditto, 1707, folio 42.

Benjamin Mitchell, late of Niagara in North America, bachelor, deceased. Administration, 12 Dec., 1761, to his father William Mitchell. Ditto, 1761.

The Hon. John Montgomerie, Esq., late Governor of New York in America, widower, deceased. Administration, 31 March, 1732, to Robert Dalrymple, Esq., Attorney for Sir John Anstruther, Bart., principal creditor, Elizabeth Ogilvy als. Montgomerie, wife of Patrick Ogilvy and sister of the defunct, first renouncing Ditto, 1732.

Edmund Mott of New York in parts beyond the seas, bachelor, deceased. Administration, 27 Feb., 1704–5, to Joseph Bentham, S. T. P., principal creditor, Bridgett Mott and Elizabeth Mott, sisters, first renouncing. Ditto, 1705, folio 30.

John Newman, late of the City and Province of New York in America, bachelor, deceased. Administration, 15 Dec., 1744, to his brother Thomas Newman, John Newman the father first renouncing. Ditto, 1744.

Mary Pinhorne, late of the City of New York in America, widow, deceased. Administration, 19 May, 1740, to George Streatfield, Attorney for John Pinhorne, son of the defunct.
Ditto, 1740.

Lucy Roddam, late of the New York in America, deceased. Administration, 11 Nov., 1751, to her husband Robert Roddam, Esq. Ditto, 1751.

111

John Stevens, Esq., late of the City of New York in America, and Captain of a Company of Foot in the American Regiment commanded by the Hon. Colonel William Gooch in the Island of Cuba, deceased. Administration, 2 April, 1743, to Richard Jenneway, Attorney of Blandina otherwise Belinda Stephen the relict, now residing in New York.   Ditto, 1743.

Owseel Van Sweeten, late of New York in America, bachelor, deceased. Administration, 13 July, 1705, to sister Beatrice Owzeel, with will annexed, Jan., 1702, of whom Jacob Minor (*sic* Gacomina) Crugar, widow and administrator of Valentine Crugar, is named sole legatee and executrix.

Ditto, 1705, folio, 153.

Ann Waghorne, late of New York in New England, widow, deceased at sea. Administration, 13 Feb., 1750-1, to William Nourse, Attorney of Richard Brough, now residing in Co. Nottingham, brother of the defunct.   Ditto, 1751.

Joseph Woodrow, late of New York in America, bachelor, deceased. Administration, 14 Jan., 1705-6, to his aunt by the mother's side (Amitae ex materna latere) Sarah Taunton, widow, the said Mary (*sic*) Taunton having first made a declaration in presence of Almighty God to well and truly administer.

Ditto, 1706, folio 8.

NEW YORK GLEANINGS IN ENGLAND.

CONTRIBUTED BY LOTHROP WITHINGTON, LONDON.

It is with much pleasure that I hope to contribute from time to time to the RECORD these Gleanings from the English archives concerning New York families. They are partly suggested by the unpublished collections of Mr. Henry Fitzgilbert Waters, now in my care, and partly from my own gatherings in the past, and to these skeleton references which I fill in for publication I hope also to add much quite new notes in the future as I come across New York matter in my searches. This work is on similar lines to my contributions to various other historical publications of our original Colonies. For a particular account of the work of Mr. Waters and myself here in England see the *Virginia Historical Magazine* for January, 1903, page 291. The notes of Mr. Waters, not elsewhere printed, are being edited by me for the *Genealogical Quarterly Magazine.* It has seemed to me however, most appropriate for the notes of Mr. Waters specially referring to our early Colonies to be issued where they are of most interest. This plan enables me to add as much as possible from our own work.

30 Little Russell Street, W. C.,   LOTHROP WITHINGTON.
    London.

Robert Macky of Budge Row in the City of London, now of London Field, parish of Hackney, Middlesex, merchant. Will, 14 Nov., 1771; proved 3 Dec., 1771. To nephew Robert Macky of Mile End Stepney, otherwise Stebenheath, Madeira Merch[t], son of brother John Macky, deceased, Freehold Estate in London Field aforesaid with messuage, Brewhouse, Coachhouse, Stable, &c., also all freehold in the city of Exeter, and all other Real estate. Executors to lay out £20,000 in public stocks, as a fund to pay my debts, annuities, and legacies. To Niece Elizabeth Macky, sister to Robert, annuity of £200. To Iphigene Armstrong, daughter of my niece Jane, the wife of Captain Edmund Armstrong of Greenwich, Kent, at 21 an annuity of £200. To

John Macky, only son of my nephew Patrick Macky, late of Cole-raine, Ireland, deceased, now at the age of 10 years, if living at 21, £5000 and interest thereon, and meanwhile not more than £150 nor less than £50 per annum for education. To Anne Whitford of Edmonton, Middlesex, annuity of £50 and unto her son aged 13 years commonly known by the name of Robert Whitford, now residing with her and educating at the school kept there by Mr. James Ware, if living at 21, £2000, £500 to be used as apprenticeship fee and interest for education, &c., &c. To Edward Scanlan, late of Stockholm in Sweden, meɪchant, £40 yearly for life. To friends Robert Allen of Ironmonger Lane, London, Linnen Merchant, and William Semple of Charles Street, St. James, Westminster, Middlesex, England, two of my executors £500 apiece. To Honorable George Macky and Hon-orable General Alexander Mackay 100 guineas each to purchase diamond rings for their respective wives and to kinsman William Patterson, Esquire, governor of the Island of St. John in North America, 100 guineas to purchase ditto for himself and wife and to his brother John Patterson of New York in America 50 guineas ditto. To Anthony Askew, physician to Saint Bartholomew's Hospital and Ebenezer Forrest of York Buildings in County Middlesex, Gentlemen, 50 guineas each. To St. Bartholomew's Hospital £1000. To Bethlehem Hospital ditto. To London Hospital £500. To St. Thomas Hospital ditto. To faithfull ser-vant Daniel Brookes my apparel, woolen and lynnen and 30 guineas beside wages. To women servants Mary Pasfeild, Mary Nicholls, Mary Eaton, and other Maid Servant at House in Budge Row, 10 guineas each. To bookkeeper John Motier above his salary £100 on condition he settle my books. To my clerk Mat-thew Chorley £80 ditto for assisting ditto. To my other clerk Angus Macky £200 above his salary on condition of his closing all my accounts particularly the Insurances. I discharge William Patterson of Letterkenny, county Donegal in the Kingdom of Ireland, gentleman, and Walter Patterson, Daniel Patterson, and John Patterson, his sons, from all claims on bond. Residue to Nephew Robert Macky. Executors: Said Robert Macky, Robert Allen, William Semple. Witnesses: Theo. Forrest, William Watson, Thomas Bourn. " The Sundry Special Injunctions which I charge my Nephew Robert Macky to see executed though not mentioned in my Will vizt.: Five Hundred Pounds to John Wilkes, Esqr. if it appears to my Execrs. that he will have occasion for that money to discharge all the dutyes and Expences of his Office of Sheriff but from what I know I should think he would not have Occasion for it. I give to the Irish Prostestant Charter Schools One Hundred Pounds payable in Six Months. I believe it is mentioned in my Will all the Linnen to my Man Daniel but that neither is or was intended only my own Body Linnen then in use; there is a New Piece of Linnen cut in Budge Row I give that to my niece Eliza. Macky and to my Nephew Robert Macky all my wrought Ruffles; there is a great Number of Old Shirts in Budge Row useless to Daniel which I think should be equally divided among the Maids in Budge and Hackney. A Gold Ring Value Two Guineas to be given to each member of the Beef Stake Society and the Motto about which Mr. Forrest will give Directions; there is a poor Woman that lives a little below in the Town called Sarah Banks that I have given for some years past fifty pounds a year to and she is paid up to the first of May next. Now I desire that said pension may not only be continued but Increased Ten or Twenty Pounds a year if she behaves decently and quietly after my decease and this at the discretion of my nephew Robert Macky. Hackney 17 November seventeen hundred and Seventy five."   Trevor, 492.

[This interesting and important will may serve to connect the scattered branches of the romantic wandering Macky or Mackay family, especially between Scotland and Ireland. Many descendants of the Irish branch are found in New York and Pennsylvania. The Hon. George Macky was a younger son of the 3d Baron Reay and father of the 8th Baron, ancestor of the present Lord Reay. General Alexander Mackay or Macky was a younger brother of George. Ebenezer Forrest, the jovial Beefstaker, was author of a well known book illustrated by Hogarth.—L. W.]

Jacob Beaumon late of New York, mariner, late belonging to the Launcester, since to the Chester and after to the Marmaid. Will 24 April 1747; proved 8 December 1748. Sole legatee and executor, friend Richard Creek of Milton next Gravesend, county Kent, victualler. Witnesses; Richard Cook, Thomas Natt.
Strahan, 353.

Barbara Blangdone, late of City of Bristol, now of London, widow. Will 6 January 1701-2; proved 13 December 1702. To child or children of my grand daughter Ann Ginn which she shall have born or be with child of at my death £100 at 21 &c. Remit to William Ginn husband of Ann Ginn £100 due on bond. To Brother Richard Brock of Bristoll £5 for life annually. To Thomas Callowhill of Bristoll merchant and James Freeman ditto, apothecary, £15. Item I give to the child or children of John Sheepard at New Yorke, if he hath any liveing at my Decease Fifty one pounds of lawfull English money, &c, &c. To George Whitehead and Thomas Lever of London £5 apiece. To William Walker, son in law of John Obee of London, 50s at expiration of his apprenticeshipp, and to his brother Benjamin 50s at 21 or marriage. To Ruth Obee ditto, all to be paid to John Obee the father. To my neece Susannah Nevet of Parke place near Westminster £50, giving to her daughter Pawley widow, £10, to her daughter Ann Nevet £10 and to her daughter Elizabeth Nevet £10. To Jane Edwards daughter of my friend Thomas Edwards of Bristoll a Guinea. To James Freeman, Nathaniel Marks of London, and Thomas Callowhill, overseers, ditto each. Residue to granddaughter Ann Ginn wife of William Ginn of London, executrix. Witnesses: William Martin clerk to Mr. Springett, Thomas Cooper, Benjamin Browne.   Ash 248.

William Giles, St. Giles in the Fields, county Middlesex, at present of the City of New Yorke in America, Merchant. Will 9 September 1702; proved 26 January, 1702-3. To my Father and mother and to the Rest of my brothers, viz.: Thomas, George,

John and Joseph Giles an equall share, lott, and proportion of my personal estate. If father and mother die, their shares to Brothers Thomas and George Giles, reserving £20 for nephew John Giles (son of brother George Giles) at 21. To sister Anne Underhill £5. I desire £5 to be given that my Soule bee prayed for at discretion of my executors. Executors: Peter Rogers, Gent, Charles Rhodes, Chirurgeon, brother George Giles, staymaker, and John Burroughes of City of New York, merchant. Witnesses: William Bisell, Christina Veenves, Richard Harris. Sworn before Jo. Bridges, Surrogate. Degg, 6.

Thomas De Lavall, Citty of New Yorke in America. Will 9 June 1682; proved 7 February 1682-3. "I give and bequeath vnto my sonne in law William Darvall All my land lyeing and being in the bounds of Harlem vpon the Island of New Yorke As also All that Island called or knowne by the name of greate Barnes Island being neere Harlem aforesaid. Item I give and bequeath vnto my said sonne William Darvall my mill at the Esopus. Item I give and bequeath vnto my son John De Lavall All my houses and Lands at the Esopus except the Mill before bequeathed." To sonne John all debts due me contracted before 1664; to sonne in law William Darvall all ditto after 1664. To daughter Margaret Coddrington £50. To sister Anne Cornewell £5 per annum for life and ditto to her daughter Anne, to be paid by sonne John De Lavall, and he also to provide my brother in law Edward Dyer competent meate, drinke, and Apparell for life. If it please God any of my daughters come to want, sonne John to relieve them, and he to pay out of first moneys from Esopus any dues to my sonne Coddrington for his wives porcion or other accompts. Sonne John De Lavall, executor. Witnesses: Cousscan (?), John Tuder. Codicil 10 June 1682 "I give and bequeath vnto my sonne John de Lavall All that my part of the Mill called the Younkers Mill Lying in Hudsons River. Item I give and bequeath vnto my sonne in law Thomas Coddrington all my Land and houses lyeing and being at Gravesend vpon Long Island." Whereas land at Harlem and greate Barnes Island is given to sonne in law William Darvall, he to pay money due to Mr. Samuel Swinock of London, Merchant. "I give and bequeath vnto my Granddaughter Frances Darvall my peece of Land or ground lyeing beyond the Smiths Fly in New Yorke called by the name of the Cherry garden. Witnesses: Edward Dyer, John Tuder. A true coppy of originall in office of Records for the Province of Newyorke, John West, clerk. Administration to Thomas Landon attorney for John De Lavall now over seas, son and executor of Thomas De Lavall late of Citty of New York deceased over seas. Drax. 17.

John Ashton late of New Yorke in America, widower, deceased. Administration 7 November 1704 to his son George Ashton. Admon Act Book 1704, folio 224.

Benjamin Applebee late of the City of New York in America, but deceased in county Dorset. Administration 1 March 1743-4 to William Bryant, Attorney of the relict Frances Applebee now residing in New York. Admon Act Book 1744.

Including "Gleanings," by Henry F. Waters, not before printed.

CONTRIBUTED BY LOTHROP WITHINGTON,
30 Little Russell St., W. C., London.

Mary Ann Peloquin, City of Bristol, Spinster. Will 7 April 1768; proved 13 August, 1778. Whereas I am seized in fee of one undivided moiety of the Manor or Landship of Churchill, county Somerset, and certain messuages &c. in the parish of Churchill, I bequeath said moiety to James Laroche, Esqr., one of the aldermen of the City of Bristol, Isaac Piguinet, Esquire, one of the Common Council of said city, Mr. Christopher Willoughby, chamberlayne of ditto, and Mr. Richard Arding of ditto, Gentleman, in trust for Mr. Nathaniel Elias Cosserat of the City of Exeter, Merchant (son of the late Mr. Nathaniel Cosserat ditto deceased) and to his issue male and then female, and in default to Mr. Bernard Lewis Zieglier of Exeter, Gentleman (son of Mrs. Esther Zieglier, ditto, widow) and his heirs. To Mayor and Aldermen of Bristoll £19000 in trust to put in Government Securities at three per cent, to employ annually on St. Stephen's Day (December 26) in St. Stephen's Bristoll, interest on £500 for Rector, Curate, Clerk, and Sexton for their pains taken, and income on £15000 for distribution to 38 poor men and 38 poor women free of City of Bristoll &c., also interest of £2500 on poor Lying-in women (wives of freemen) as nominated by wife of Mayor if married or of senior married alderman, and interest of residue of £1000 to 20 poor widows and single women and 10 poor men inhabiting St. Stephen's &c. For reparation of church of St. Stephen's £300. To Bristoll Infirmary £5000 to be invested in Government Securities, but if the laws of the land had permitted, then I should have directed £5000 to be invested in Lands of Inheritance in Bristol or counties of Gloucester, Somerset, or Wilts for said Infirmary. To the General Hospital at Bath £500. To the Society for promoting Christian Knowledge in London £500. To the Society for propagating the Gospell in foreign parts £1000. To Mr. Barnard Lewis Zieglier £3000. Executors in trust: said James Laroche, Isaac Piguinet, Christopher Willoughby, and Richard Arding, and to such £500 as recompense. Whereas by will of my late brother David Peloquin, Esquire, I am possessed of messuages in my occupation and Lofts, warehouse, &c in Queen Square in said city of Bristol for remainder of term from Mayor, Burgesses, and Commonalty, I bequeath the same to Mrs. Ann Casamajor of Queen Square Bristol. Residue of estate to said Mr. Nathaniel Elias Cosserat, or if he die, to any child of his, or in default to Mr. John Peter Yvonnet of London, son of John Paul Yvonnet of Isleworth, Esquire, deceased, and his children in default to before named Mr. Bernard Lewis Zieglier &c. Witnesses: Robt. Hale, Geo. Rogers, Edwd Carter. Codicil 7 April 1768. To Mrs. Esther Ziegler of City of Exter, widow £500. To Mr. John Cosserat, Exeter, Tallow Chandler, £500. To Mrs. Hannah Cosserat and Mrs. Bernice Cosserat, ditto, spinsters, £500 each. To Peter Jay Esquire of Rye near New York in America £1000. To Sir James Jay, Knight, son of said Peter Jay, now resident in England £500. To Mrs. Frances Courtland of New York aforesaid widow £1000 and to Mr. James Courtland her eldest son £500. To Mr. —— Vanhorn (son of Mrs. Judith Vanhorn late of New York aforesaid widow deceased) £500. To Mr. John Peter Yvonnet of London (named in my will son of John Paul Yvonnet late of Isleworth, Esquire, deceased) £3000. To Mrs. —— Dagge, wife —— Dagge, of —— (eldest daughter of said John Paul Yvonnet deceased) £200. To Miss Susannah Yvonnet (the other daughter) £2000. To Master —— Guinand and Miss —— Guinand, son and daughter of Mr. —— Guinand of —— (grandchildren) of said John Paul Yvonnet £500 a piece. To Mrs. Clementia Laroche (wife of James Laroche, Esq., Alderman of Bristol and one of my executors) £1000. To Mrs. Mary, Mrs. Elizabeth, and Mrs. Ann Casamajor, all of Bristol, spinsters, £1000 a piece. To Mrs. Maria Casamajor (Grand Daughter of Mrs. Casamajor, late of Clinton, county Gloucester, widow deceased) £2000. To Mrs. Clutterbuck, widow of —— Clutterbuck, Esq. late Alderman of Bristol £500. To Mrs. Esther Carew, wife of Reverend Mr. Carew of Pillaton near Callington in Cornwall £500. To Mrs. Rebecca Hooker, wife of Mr. —— Hooker, one of the clerks of the Bank of England £500. To Mrs. Ann Thomas (Daughter of Mr. Moses Thomas of Landulph in Cornwall) £400. To Mr. Frank Thomas at Plymouth Dock £200. To Mrs. Cook, widow of —— Cook late of Biddeford, Devon, Barber, deceased £500, and to each of her five daughters £300. To Mr. Richard Arding, one of my executors, £1000 more and to each of his children £200. To Mrs. Oriana, Mrs. Susannah, and Mrs. Mary Clements, all of Bristol, Spinsters £100 apiece as tokens of Regard. To Mrs. Rachell Deverell of Bristoll widow £100 ditto. To Mrs. Sarah and Mrs. Mary Gwatkin both of Bristol, spinsters ditto. To Mrs. —— Hobhouse (wife of John Hobhouse of Bristol, Esq) ditto. To Mrs. Martha Hopkins wife of Mr. William Hopkins of Bristol Linnen Draper £500. To Mrs. Thruppe late of City of Bath, but now of Bristol, Spinster, £100. To Miss Maryann Smith daughter of Jennison Smith late of Barbadoes, Esq. deceased £500. To Mrs. —— Allen wife of —— of Bristol Merchant £500. To Mrs. Ann Collet of Bristol widow £500. To Mrs. Esther Eagles of Bristol Spinster £500. To Mrs. Allen of Bristol (widow of Mr. Richard Allen) £100, and unto Master and Miss Allen her son and daughter £50 apiece. To Mr. James Daltera of Bristol Merchant £300. To Mrs. —— Gundy of Bristol widow £100. To Elizabeth Lawrence Spinster (daughter of Mr. —— Lawrence of Bristol, Engraver) £300. To Mr. Elias Melchisedic Francis of the City of London £500, and to each of his three daughters £400. All said legacies to be paid by executors within a year of decease to legatees or in case of minors to parents or guardians &c. To the following persons annuities, viz: Mrs. Maryann, Mrs. Mary, and Mrs. Susannah Goizin of Bristol Spinsters £100 between them; to Mrs. —— King of Bristol widow (mother of Mrs. Brownet, ditto, milliner, deceased) £20; Mrs. Maryann Pineau of Island of Guernsey £10; Mrs. Mary Williams of Bristol (Granddaughter of late Mrs. —— Latouche) £10; Mrs. —— Hemmings of Bristol widow of Richard Hemmings Cordwainer £20; Ann Bennocke, Bristol widow £10; Mrs. —— Backle, Bristol, widow of—— Backle Barber £5; Isaac Piguenet Esquire and Mr. Richard Arding executors £30 for Mrs. —— Herring who lives with me, widow of Mr. Richard Herring of Bristol sadler; to said executors also £15 for late servant Elizabeth James Spinster. Executors to invest £8000 in one of the Parliamentary Funds for these annuities. Witnesses: Robt. Hale, Geo. Rogers, Edwd Carter. Second codicil 1 June 1768. To Mr. Nathaniel Elias Cosserat, son of Mr. Nathaniel Cosserat of Exeter deceased my Silver Tea Kettle and Lamp, my silver waiters and my large coffee pot, my Desert knives and Desert Spoons. To Mrs. Mary, Mrs. Elizabeth, and Mrs. Ann Casamajor all furniture of Fore Parlour in my house in Queen Square, Bristol, and Furniture of my Bed Chamber in the Foreroom one story High, also all my Books and coloured china. To Mr. Richard Arding the Furniture of the back Parlour, high chest of Drawers in the back Room one story high, my cotton Bed and Bedding and Window curtains in the fore Room two story high, also all my blue and white china, and Table Linnen. To Miss Frances Caroline Arding my new Silver coffee pot. To Miss Ann Maria Arding my Gold watch and chain. To Mrs. Herring, widow to Mr. Richard Herring sadler, my Yellow Bed and Bedding and Window Curtains in the Back Room one story high and high chest of Drawers in the best of the fore Rooms two story high. Rest of Household Furniture not mentioned to Mrs. Herring widow, Mrs. Hemmings widow, late servant Elizabeth James, and Betty Lawrence equally. To Mrs. Mary, Mrs. Eliza, and Mrs. Anna Casamajors my silver Bread Basket and all my laces and personal wearing Linnen. To Mrs. Laroche, wife to Alderman Laroche, my Silver Chamber as a keepsake, Candlesticks and Snuffers, likewise my Tea Chest and silver cannister and sugar Dish. To the daughters of Mr. Richard Arding all my Brocaded and Tisua Night Gowns. To Miss Maria Casamajor all my Brocaded Negligees. To Mrs. Herring widow and to Mrs. Hermitage widow all other wearing apparel. To Mrs. Herrings [sic], Mrs. Hemmings, Betty Lawrence, and Elizabeth James all my Silver Table Spoons and Tea Spoons. To Mrs. Atwood wife of Mr. Atwood in Orchard street, Bath £20. Desire the Gentlemen my executors that my Funerall may be the same as my late sisters but the under Bearers to be drest. I give mourning to all my servants. Signed Mary Ann Peloquin. Witness: Robt Hale. 3d Codicil 27 April 1768. To the Rector for time being of St. Stephens, Bristol £100. To

Mrs. Leah, Miss Elizabeth, and Miss Jane Thomas, all three daughters of Mr. Moses Thomas of Landulph, Cornwall £200. To Mr. John Peter Yvronet £2000 more. To Mrs. Fido wife of Mr. —— Fido Plummer in Bristol £100. To Mrs. Eliza Hatfield, Preston, Milliner £50. To Mrs. Mary Williams, Grand Daughter to the late Mrs. Latouche, £100 more. To Miss Maria Casamajor, before mentioned Daughter to Mr. Henry Casamajor of Bristol my Edistone Light House in memory of her good Friend A. P. Signed Maryann Peloquin. Witness: Robt Hale. 4th codicil 6 January 1769. To Mr. John Peter Yvronet £3000 more. To Mr. Joseph Daltera, Junior, Merchant in Liverpool £100. To the children of Mrs. Rebecca Hooker wife of Mr. Samuel Hooker, One of the Clerks of the Bank of England, £200 each to be paid to parents or Guardians. To Mrs. Caroline Arding, wife of Mr. Richard Arding, my new pair of large Silver Candlesticks. To Mrs. —— Roach, Widow and Sister to the worthy Doctor Drummond, Physician in Bristol £300. To Mr. Willoughby, son of Mr. Christopher Willoughby, chamberlain of the City of Bristol, £300. Signed Maryann Peloquin. Witness: Robt Hale. 5th codicil, 19 November 1769. To Mr. Augustus Jay, eldest son of Peter Jay, Esq. of Rye near New York £100. To Mrs. Eve Monroe wife of the Reverend Mr. Monroe of Albany in America £500. To Miss Ann Jay her sister £500. To Messrs. Peter, John, and Frederick Jay, her Brothers £500 each. To my Housekeeper Mrs. Herring £60 more. To Ann Ashbee, formerly our servant at Bath £50. To Mr. Andrews, Purveyor of Plymouth Dock £100. To Mr. James Daltera, merchant, £400 more. Signed Maryann Peloquin. Witness: Francis Downey. 6th codicil. 4 March 1771, Mr. James Laroche, Esq. and Mr. Richard Arding, two of trustees for manor Churchill, Somerset, and executors, and Ann Bennocke widow, one of annuitants being all dead, her annuity to be appropriated to others, and Reverend Dr. Josiah Tucker, Dean of Gloucester, and Mr. Robert Hale of Redland, parish of Westbury upon Trym, county Gloucester, appointed as trustees with Isaac Piguenet [sic], and Christopher Willoughby, and £500 to each, &c. To Mrs. Francis Payne of Bristol spinster annuity of £10 as in case of Ann Bennocke, deceased. Signed Maryann Peloquin. Witnesses: Sam¹ Newman, T. Griffiths, Geo. Rogers. 7th codicil, 5 December 1772. Isaac Piguenet having been afflicted by Providence with illness depriving him of use of his Limbs and rendered unfit person for Management of my affairs, said Christopher Willoughby, Josiah Tucker, and Robert Hale with Doctor Archibald Drummond of Ridgway, county Gloucester, appointed Trustees and Executors, and to Dr. Drummond £500 etc. Signed Maryann Peloquin. Witnesses: Saml Newman, Thos. Griffiths, Geo. Rogers. 8th codicil (undated, unsigned and unwitnessed). Revokes £3000 to Mr. Bernard Lewis Ziegler and £60 annuity instead, and Dr. Josiah Tucker, Mr. Robert Hale, and Dr. Archibald Drummond (the now executors of my will) to invest £2000 in 3 per cent Consolidated Bank Annuities for same. To Mr. Frank Thomas, Organist, son of Mr. Moses Thomas of Plymouth

Dock £1000. 9th codicil (ditto). To Master Robert Bound Arding £200. To Mrs. Bonbonons wife of Mr. Bonbonons of Bristol £100, and all my chairs, Tables, Carpets, and Pier Glasses in my Back Parlour, the high chest of Drawers in back Parlour one pair of stairs, and the Cotton Bed and Cotton Window Curtains in the fore Room two story high. To Mrs. Esther Cosserat £100. To Miss Betty Casamajor, daughter of Mr. Henry Casamajor, £500. To James Laroche Esq., Nephew to the late Alderman Laroche, £300. To Mrs. Eleanor Laroche £100 as a token of regard. To Mr. Henry Casamajor, son of the late Mr. Casamajor of Clifton £500. To Mrs. Manon Piguenet £100. To Mrs. Mary, Mrs. Elizabeth, and Mrs. Ann Casamajors [sic] all Table Linnen. To Mrs. Mary Herring and Mrs. Susannah Herring spinster £10 each. To Miss Bartlett, daughter of the late Alderman Bartlett £100. To Mrs. Wells, widow, and Miss Bloom, Daughters to the late Mrs. Collet £50 each. To all servants with me £10 each. To Frances Down in Trinity Alms House £10. To Joseph Daniel, my coachman, if in services at decease £40. To Mrs. Sarah Bane, Mantuamaker £20. To Mrs. Lawrence wife to Mr, Lawrence, Engraver, £20. To Mr. Peter Wells, senior Surgeon in Bristol, £100. 10th codicil. 14 April 1778. To Mr. James Daltera, of Bristol, merchant £500 more. The mark A. P. of Mary Anne Peloquin. Witness: Robt Hale. 8 August 1778. Attestations of Robert Hale of Atford in parish of Bradford, Wilts, Esquire, James Daltera of city of Bristol, merchant, and George Rogers of ditto, Gentleman, that said Robert Hale did in year 1776 by instructions from Mary Ann Peloquin, late of Bristol, spinster, deceaeed, prepare codicil no. 8 and witnesses believe she added legacies to Mr. Frank Thomas with her own hand afterwards &c. Also as to codicil No. 10 signed A. P. Same date. Affidavit of said Robert Hale, and George Rogers, and of Frances Downe of Bristol, spinster, as to codicils nos. 2, 3, 4, 5, and 9, being all in handwriting of deceased. Will and ten codicils proved by Rev. Josiah Tucker, Doctor of Divinity, Robert Hale, Esquire, and Archibald Drummond, Doctor of Physick, surviving executors named in 7th codicil.   Hay, 331.

David Peloquin, City of Bristol, Esq. Will 1 October 1765, proved 14 May 1766. Whereas I am seised in fee and inheritance of moiety of the Manor of Churchill, county Somerset, and of certain lands there, I bequeath same to my sister of the half blood Mrs. Mary Ann Peloquin, also to said sister certain messuages and dwelling House in my occupation and Lofts, Warehouses, and Cellars in Queen Square, Bristol, for remainder of term of forty years from Mayor, Burgesses &c. but request of said sister to give reversion of same to Rector of St. Stephens in Bristol &c. To Treasury of Bristol Infirmary £200. To said sister for life my Silver Chandelier to make as little use as may be and with caution that it may be a more respectful legacy to Mayor, Burgesses, and Commonality of Bristol after her decease. To my three cousins Marianne, Mary, and Sarah Gorzen £20 apiece. To my cousin Esther Ziegler of Exeter, widow £20. To my friend Mr. James Daltera of Bristol, Merchant £15. To Margaret Hemmings widow of Richard Hemmings late of Bristol, Shoemaker, £10, 10s. To Elizabeth James, spinster, now living in my house and a servant to my sister and self, £10, 10s. and mourning. Rest to said sister Mary Ann Peloquin, executrix. Witnesses: Robt Hale, Geo. Rogers, Edward Carter.

Tyndall, 192.

Frances Peloquin, late of City of Bristol, spinster, deceased. Administration 13 June 1764, to David Peloquin Esquire, natural and lawful brother and next of kin. Administration 21 June 1766 of ditto left unadministered by David Peloquin, Esq. the Brother now also deceased, to Mary Ann Peloquin, spinster, natural and lawful sister and next of kin.

Admon Act Books (Torriano Section), 1764 and 1766.

[David Peloquin was mayor of Bristol in 1751 and the remarkable will of his surviving sister, Mary Ann Peloquin, sufficiently indicates their connection with a whole network or French Huguenot families in England and the American colonies.—L. W.]

NEW YORK GLEANINGS IN ENGLAND,

Including "Gleanings," by Henry F. Waters, not before printed.

CONTRIBUTED BY LOTHROP WITHINGTON,
30 Little Russell St., W. C., London.

Thomas C[harles] Williams, merchant, City of New York. Will 17 December, 1780; proved 14 October 1784. On board ship *Parker.* To wife Sarah Williams all Household Furniture and all Real Estate in City of Philadelphia, that is our house or store between Chestnut and Walnut Street, fronting Water and Front Street, also one third of all other real and personal estate. To brother John Williams in New York, £1000 currency. Rest to father Samuel Williams for life, then to brothers William Williams, Samuel Williams and John Williams and sisters Jane, Hanah, Esther, and Susan. Executors: Samuel Shomaker, Esquire, now of New York, my wife Sarah Williams and brother John Williams, New York. Witnesses: Eben^r. Putnam, Ab^m. L. Smith, Robert Rolls. "New York, Octob^r. 14, 1781. As I am now about going again to Virginia and the Term of Life is uncertain do make this Codicil to my last will and Testament as I have great property at Risque on the Seige at York Town and may be lost do make this further provision for my beloved wife Sarah Williams." She to have her home in Philadelphia and £1000 before any division, etc. Witness: Bartlee Smith, City and Province of New York, 26 August, 1782, Before Cory Ludlow, Surrogate, attestation of Robert Rollo, Captain of his Majesty's American Legion as to himself and other two witnesses Abraham L. Smith and Ebenezer Putnam. Also attestation of Bartlee Smith of New York, gentleman, as to codicil. True copies, Sam. Bayard, Junr., Secretary. Proved in prerogative court of Canterbury by widow Samuel Williams and brother John Williams, reserving to Samuel Shomaker, Esq.

Rockingham, 581.

Cornelius Thompson of the Town of New York in the Province of Jersey [sic] in America, Seaman, now of H. M. S. Dolphin. Will 30 May, 1772; proved 8 July, 1775. All to Friends Philip Nicolson of Whitehaven in the County of Cumberland and John Healy of the parish of Bury in the Suburbs of the City of Cork, executors. Witnesses: Da. Dalzell, Jno. Colpoys, Act^g. Captn. Joseph Milburn Master.

Alexander, 291.

Henry Cruger the Elder late of the City of New York in North America, but now residing in the City of Bristol in Great Britain. Will 11 June, 1779; proved 2 March, 1780. To eldest son John Harris Cruger all estate in Island of Jamaica or elsewhere in West Indies. To daughter Mary Walton, wife of Jacob Walton of the City of New York, Merchant, £1000. To three

Grandchildren, Henry Cruger Van Schaack, Cornelius Van Schaack, and Elizabeth Van Schaack, children of Peter Van Schaack and my daughter Elizabeth Van Schaack, deceased, £2000. To my youngest son Nicholas Cruger of the Island of St. Croix in the West Indies, Merchant, £500. Also £500 to be put out at interest to pay Sister Mary Cruger £25 annually. Discharge son Henry Cruger, junior, of debt of £1270, 7s, 10½, and also balance due on obligations for him and John Mallard. As to residue of estate, one fourth to son Henry Cruger, junior, one fourth to daughter Mary Walton, one fourth to son Nicholas Cruger, and one fourth to said Grandchildren, issue of late daughter Elizabeth Van Schaack; sons-in-law Peter Van Schaack and Jacob Walton to be trustees for same, &c., &c., manumit and make free my negro man servant, Piro. Executors in North America: said sons-in-law Jacob Walton and Peter Van Schaack, and son Nicholas Cruger. Executor in West Indies: son John Harris Cruger. Executors in Great Britain: Friends Thomas Hayes and Jeremiah Osborne. Will signed and attested in duplicate. Witnesses: Willm. Battenby, Mary Spencer, Martha Hopkins. Proved by Thomas Hayes and Jeremiah Osborne, executors as to effects in Great Britain.   Collins, 125.

Barnaby Bryn of the Township of Jamaica on Long or Nassau Island in the Province of New York in North America, gent. Will 6 May, 1771; proved 18 May, 1776. Executors to sell all estate and pay £1000 current money of New York to wife Jane Bryn, or if she does not approve, then one third of my fortune to her. Also to wife one Horse, Horse Chaise and Harness, one Desk and Book Case, one Clock, Beds and Bed Cloaths in my Dwelling House and my Negro Boy Othello. To Captain Robert McGennis of the City of New York, £5. Rest to my two brothers and four sisters, to wit: Christopher Bryn and James Bryn, Judith Bryn otherwise Carey, Ann Bryn, Bridget Bryn otherwise Dunn, and Elizabeth Bryn. Executors: William Byard and Robert Byard, both of City of New York, Esquires, and Terence Kerin of ditto, attorney at Law. Witnesses: Sampson Simpson, Geo. Burns, Jonathan Hampton. Proved by James Rivington, attorney for executors William Bayard and Terence Kerin residing in City of New York, and of Robert Bayard, residing in Province of New York.   Bellas, 213.

John Van Driessen, Junior, Physician on H. M. Ship *Squirrel.* Will 12 September, 1740; proved 23 January 1741-2. To my loving mother Eva Van Driessen of the City of Albany in America, all estate, viz: my right in my Father's estate, being one fourth part of certain Houses and Lands in the County of Albany and my share in his personal estate as by his will dated 29 January, 1737-8, with all my wages, dues, &c. To brothers Petrus and Henry Van Driessen, cloathes and apparell. To sister Ann Van Driessen, ten guineas. Executor: Mother Eva Van Driessen. Witnesses: John Cruger, Hen. Cruger, John Cruger, Junr. Proved by Peter Warren, Esq., attorney for mother and executrix Eva Van Driessen, Widow, residing in the City of Albany in the Province of New York.   Trenley, 36.

Peter Jay. The State of New York by the Grace of God Free and Independent. Dutchess County, 27 and 28 of May before Thomas Tredwell, Esq., Judge of Our Courts of Probate, the last Will and Testament of Peter Jay, deceased (a copy whereof is annexed) was proved and administration granted to Frederick Jay and Egbert Benson, two of the executors, &c. At Rundout, county of Dutchess, 3 June, 1782, Joseph Hazard, C^{lk}.

Peter Jay, late of Rye, County of Westchester, but now of Rambout Precinct in county of Dutches, State of New York, Esq. Will 28 January, 1778–9; proved 27 May, 1785 [in the Prerogative Court Canterbury]. To my executors £500 money of New York for maintenance of my son Augustus during his life, and after his death said £500 to my four sons James, Peter, John, and Frederick, &c. To executors £1800 in trust for support of my daughter Eve Munro for life, and if majority of executors think fit for education of my grandson Peter Jay Munro, and after death of daughter said money to him at 21, &c., and if he die to my said four sons, &c. To daughter Ann Maricha Jay, £1800. Rest of estate to four sons James, Peter, John and Frederick, son Peter if he choose to have my farme at Rye with all Islands, Marshes, &c., at a valuation, &c., and son John to have choice of Farms in Bedford county, Westchester, son Frederick the Water Lot on which he has lately built a Stone house in Dock Ward, city of New York, bounded Northerly by the street called Dockward warf and opposite to the House and Stonehouse lately in occupation of Everet Bancker, Easterly by Lot of Augustus and Frederick Van Cortlandt, Westerly by the Lot of John William Vandanbergh and runs Southerly into the River as far as the Right of the Mayor Aldermen and Commonalty extends, lately granted to me by said mayor, &c., and to be assigned to Frederick at a valuation, my other children who with Frederick become proprietors of house lately occupied by Everet Bancker not to avail themselves of covenant that no buildings be erected on the Water Lot opposite to the rear thereof, &c., and whereas it is probable that the Reverend Harry Munro will refuse to join his wife the said Eve Munro in making the release whereby it may not be in her power to comply, I therefore exempt her from the penalty but no payment to be made to grandson Peter Jay Munro till release is made by his mother Eve, &c. If Frederick shall not incline to take the Water Lot, he is to be paid for his improvements, &c. All children to be released from any sums charged in my Ledger, but son James to pay Balance particularly specified in a small book, &c. My two Negro Women, Zilpha and the elder Mary in consideration of long and faithful service to be indulged in choice of future masters, and if with sons, then sons to pay not exceeding £30 for each. If daughter Ann Maricha or sons James, John, or Frederick die, then to others, &c. Executors: James, John and Frederick. Witnesses: William Van Wyck, Theodorus Van Wyck, jun'r, John Van Wyck. Codicil, 22 June, 1780. The £500 and £1800 in trust for and the £1800 bequeathed to daughter Anna Maricha to be paid in Spanish Milled Dollars at 8 shillings a Dollar, and trust of executors revoked in this case and sons John and Frederick, and friend Egbert Benson made the trustees and Egbert Benson made additional executor. Witnesses: Wm. Van Wyck, Theod. Van Wyck, George Way. Attested 27 May, 1782, in Dutchess county before Thomas Tredwell, Judge of Probate of state of New York, by William Van Wyck, Esquire, Theodorus Van Wyck, junior. Esquire, and John Van Wyck, miller, all of Rumbout, Dutchess county, ditto, attestation of said William Van Wyck, and George Way of Rumbout precinct, yeoman, as to codicil. Second codicil 11 September, 1781, Peter Jay, late of Rye, county of Westchester, now residing at Poughkeepsie, county of Dutchess. Having purchased messuage and Lot of land in Poughkeepsie where I now reside, said messuage to be part of residuary estate. Witnesses: Egbert Benson, Aug^n. Lawrence, James M. Hughes. Attested 28 May, 1782, by Egbert Benson of Poughkeepsie, Esquire. Third codicil 18 December, 1781, Peter Jay, late of Rye, county of Westchester, now residing at Poughkeepsie, county of Dutchess, make this codicil to my will now deposited with my papers at Kent in Connecticut. Whereas my son John is now absent beyond Seas, and some time may elapse before he can authorize consent to division, &c., and circumstances of other divisees requiring immediate division, and not being sure as to provisions in will, major part of executors now authorized to divide estate, &c. To son James all family portrait paintings. To son John my Negro Slave Plato, and till said son declare acceptance of this Legacy, said slave to reside with such other of children as he elect. Negro slave Mary to be given to such child as she elect, but being infirm and like to become a Burthen, executors to pay to said child for the risque, &c. Witnesses: Theodorus Bailey, James Kent, Anthony Hoffman. Attested copy of will and three codicils and the several certificates by Thomas Tredwell, Judge of Probate, in absence of the Clerk Sealee in presence of Matthew Cowper, Henry Cowper, and Sam. Brackford, witnesses. Administration in Prerogative Court of Canterbury (with will and three codicils annexed) of Peter Jay, formerly of Rye, county of West Chester, but at Poughkeepsie in county of Dutchess, State of New York in North America, Esquire, deceased, to James Daltera, lawful attorney of Sir James Jay, knight, John Jay and Frederick Jay, Esquires, sons and executors.   Ducarel, 256.

Henry Long, Esquire, St. Andrew Holborn, Middlesex. Will 5 February, 1722-3; proved 17 December, 1723. Whereas by articles of 27 February, 1719, before marriage with now dear wife Margaret Webb, I agree to lay out £12000 in purchase of land, &c. I give to said wife my messuage in Red Lyon Square, St. Andrew Holborn, for rest of term, and all her jewells, Rings, plate, pictures, Household goods, &c., my coach chariott, coach Horses and Harness, my living stock of cattle, £200 to put herself and family in mourning and to maintain her till interest on the £12000 accrues, &c. To my daughter Ann Long messuage and farme in Baford, Herts, bought of —— Clarke in occupation of George Nash at £15 per year, also farm in Bayford purchased of —— Gardner in occupation of widow Bassell at £1, 10s, 0d, per year, and also £3000 at 21 or marriage. If daughter Ann die, then £1000 to my wife, £1000 to son Richard Long, and other £1000 to my mother Margaret Long and my sisters Margaret Harvey, Sarah Long, and Jane Long. "Item I give unto Charles Long, natural son of Elizabeth Plumley, late of New York, deceased, the sum of three hundred pounds, which Charles Long was lately in the service of Mr. Wilson of New York, merchant." To Henry Philip of Ware, Herts, Carpenter, and his children, £200. To my two Aunts, Sarah Haggard and Catherine Haggard, and my three Nieces, Mary, Margaret and Anne Harvey, children of my sister Margaret Harvey, widow, £100 apiece. To my brother Thomas Long £1500, owing by my Father Barker on bond. To my three sisters, Margaret Harvey, Sarah Long and Jane Long £400 apiece. Whereas by my marriage articles, 28 January, 1713, with Jane Cary, one of the daughters of Richard Cary, the mannors of Bayford and Bay, &c., are settled on my issue male and in default to my heirs, &c., and whereas I have no issue male by late wife Jane Cary, but one only Daughter Jane Long who is seized of said mannors of Bayford and Bay, now if Jane die before 21, I give said mannors to my son Richard Long, with remainder to my daughter Ann Long (paying £1000 to my brother Thomas Long and £500 each to my sisters Margaret Harvey, Sarah Long, and Jane Long) and then to my brother Thomas Long, &c. Whereas daughter Jane is amply provided for by settlement on my marriage with my (her) mother, to Jane only £20 for mourning, her Grandfather Richard Cary, Esquire, to be her Guardian till 21 or marriage. That my dear mother may not be unprovided for in her old age, executors to pay £50 a year for life. Executors: wife Margaret and brother Thomas Long. Wife to be guardian to son Richard and daughter Ann till 21. Witnesses: Wm. Proby, Sam. Diggle, Wm. Plumpton. Proved by brother Thomas Long, reserving to widow Margaret other executrix. Proved 11 February, 1723-4, by widow Margaret.   Richmond, 262.

John Bary, late sailmaker on board the Phenix Man of War, out now going to New York (deceased at parish of St. George-in-the-East, Middlesex). Will 1 September, 1778; proved 15 January, 1778-9. All to Hannah Randall of St. John's Wapping, Middlesex, wife of James Randall, mariner. Witnesses: Samuel Wozener, Ann Smith.   Collins, 3.

James Larkins, late of New York in New England, deceased. Administration 26 March, 1697, to Lancaster Symms, lawful husband of Catherine Symms, alias Larkins, lately the wife of defunct.   Admon Act Book, 1697, folio 41.

Anthony Rogers, late of New Yorke in America, deceased. Administration 13 June, 1704, to Thomas Parry, guardian of Catherine Rogers, junior, a minor, daughter of the defunct, Catherine Rogers the relict first renouncing.
                                    Ditto, 1704, folio 123.

Joseph Billopp, late of New York in America, widower, deceased. Administration 10 November, 1712, to his brother

127

Christopher Billopp, Middleton Billopp, son and only issue of the said defunct having been cited and not appearing.

Ditto, 1712, folio 207.

John Bridges, LL.D., late of New York beyond seas, deceased. Administration 15 July, 1712, to Godfrey Lee, principal creditor, Jane Bridges the relict, and Eliza Bridges the daughter being cited and not appearing.

Ditto, 1712, folio 139.

John Lord Lovelace, Baron of Hurly, Berks, late Governor of New York, deceased. Administration 1 February, 1713–14, to his relict Charlotte dowager Baroness of Hurly.

Ditto, 1714, folio 25.

Thomas Gorstich, late of New Yorke beyond seas, bachelor, deceased. Administration 4 August, 1714, to his mother Jane Gorstich.

Ditto, 1714, folio 162.

Christopher Cock, late of New Yorke, widower, deceased. Administration 23 October, 1714, to his brother John Cock.

Ditto, 1714, folio 202.

Robert Drummond of New York, deceased. Administration 11 February, 1717–8, to Charles Drummond, Esq., attorney of John Drummond the father dwelling at Keldiese, Scotland. Died ten years ago, (warrant), of the King's Ship *Scorling*.

Ditto, 1718.

Robert Drummond, late of New York in America, deceased. Administration 22 February, 1717–8, to his relict Elizabeth Drummond.

Ditto, 1718, folio 28.

Gilbert Heathcote, late of the Province of New York in America, bachelor, deceased. Administration 10 July, 1731, to his mother Martha Heathcote, widow.

Ditto, 1731.

Mary Heathcote, late of the Province of New York, spinster, deceased. Administration 10 July, 1731, to her mother —— Heathcote, widow.

Ditto, 1731.

Robert Elliston, late Comptroller of H. M. Customs in the province of New York in America, Esq., deceased. Administration 21 April, 1759, to the Rev. Abraham Maddock, clerk, attorney of Mary Elliston the relict, now residing in New York.

Ditto, 1759.

Thomas Biles, senior, late of New Yorke in America, widower, deceased. Administration 26 February, 1701–2, to Thomas Biles, natural and lawful son.

Ditto, 1702, folio 27.

John Royse, London, merchant, bound out on voyoge to New Yorke. Will 18 June, 1683; proved 8 November, 1686. To deare and honoured Father, Mr. Daniell Royse and Friend Mr. James Wancklen 40s. each for rings. To my wife £200. Residue in three parts, one third to brother Daniell Royse, and other two thirds again in three parts, two thirds to children of Sister Winne, and one third to children of Sister Weeks. Executors: Father Mr. Daniell Royse and Mr. James Wancklen. Witnesses: Tobijah Winne, scrivenor, Dan[l]. Chandler, George Copping his serv[ts]. Proved by Father Daniell Royse, other executor renouncing.

Lloyd, 154.

NEW YORK GLEANINGS IN ENGLAND,

Including "Gleanings," by Henry F. Waters, not before printed.

———

CONTRIBUTED BY LOTHROP WITHINGTON,
30 Little Russell St., W. C., London.

———

Richard Annely. Will 25 March, 1736; proved 24 October,
1750. If it should please God I should die before my arrival at
New York, or any time after my arrival, brother Thomas Annely
to take on executorship, paying debts, and giving overplus to
sister Elizabeth Annely. Have had management of all goods
sold in partnership before 26 December, 1735, and at departure
from New York left with Mrs. Judith Bourdett, wife of Mr. Samuel Bourdett, Junior, accounts of money owing, &c., and in case
of any miscarriage, said Samuel Bourdett or his wife (or whom

129

else) to deliver some accounts to executor, &c. Deposition 17 October, 1750, of Walter Jenkins of parish of St. Michaell in city of Bristol, Gentleman, and Susannah Annely of St. Nicholas, Bristol, widow, that they knew Richard Annely, late of New York, merchant, deceased, for a period of upward of ten years, and that he died about September, 1743, &c. Greenly, 313.

Abraham Huisman, City of New York, Merchant. Will proved in 1748. To Hendrick Garret, the son born in Wedlock of Abraham Blancks and Maria Van Bulderen of Croningen in the united provinces, all wearing Linnen and my Diamond Ring. To Benwjna Helena, daughter born ditto, household Linnen and plate. To Joseph Murray of City of New York, Esq., and Richard Nicholls, ditto, gent., £70 current money of New York each for troubles as executors, and £20 ditto, each for mourning. To servant Joseph Crane, £300 current money of New York and one of my negroes he shall choose, for faithful services, &c. All real estate in America to said executors in trust for said Hannah Garret and Benwjna Helena, &c. Executors in America: Joseph Murray and Richard Nicholls. Executor in London: Joseph Mico of London, merchant. Witnesses: George Harrison, John Burnet, Joseph Webb, junior. Codicil, 12 June, 1748. To Josiah Crane, £125 more and my silver mugg. To Mr. Simeon Sonmaine, £25. Witnesses: Peter Evetse, William Conihan. A true copy, Geo. Bangor. D. Sec'y. Proved by Joseph Mico as to effects in Great Britain. Strahan, 368.

Stephen Kibble of City of New York, Merchant. Will 7 August, 1779; proved 1782. To beloved mother, Mrs. Martha Kibble, now of City of London, 100 Guineas and to my Niece, Dorothy Wallace, 50 Guineas. To said niece one-third of dwelling house and lott in Wall Street in City of New York, now in possession of Thomas Leonard. Rest of estate to executors for wife and daughter Catherine at 21 or marriage, &c. Executors: wife Catherine Kibble and friends William Butler Esq., James Doyle and Benjamin James. Witnesses: Richard Bayley, Surgeon, John L. C. Roome, pub. Not., Tho. Wright. Attested 14 December, 1779, before Cary Ludlow, Surrogate for City and County of New York, by Richard Bayles, Surgeon, and John Le Roome, Publick Notary. Proved by executors, certified copy to Sam. Bayard, Junr., D. Sec'y. Proved in Prerogative court of Canterbury by William Butler, Esq., reserving to other executors. Gostling, 32.

Martha Arnold of Newgate Street, London, widow. Will 26 August, 1780; proved 27 March, 1786. To Mary Nott, wife of Randolph Nott of Newgate Street, London, hosier, for her life the yearly interest of £500 for her sole use, and after her decease I give the said capital sum to John Stephenson, now resident with Henry White Esq., of New York in North America, if he be living, if not I give the same to my brother William Baker of Abingdon in Berkshire and my nephews William, John, Thomas, and Francis Baker and my nieces, Elizabeth Baker and Martha Baker, six of the children of brother William, and to the said Mary Nott, and Thomas Nott and Mary Nott, the said son and daughter of the said Randolph, or to such as are living. To said Mary Nott, wife of said Randolph Nott, all wearing apparel, sheets, &c. To brother William Baker £10. To Randolph Nott £10. Residuary legatee: the said John Stephenson, now resident with Henry White in New York in North America, Esq., but if he be not living, then to said brother William Baker and nephews William, John, Thomas, and Francis Baker and nieces Elizabeth and Martha Baker, said Mary Nott, wife of Randolph Nott, and Thomas and Mary Nott. Executor: John Stephenson of Brentford Butts, County Middlesex, Esq. Witnesses: Jane Marsh, Jane Ardin, Spring Gardens, Charing Cross, John Townshend, opposite St. Georges Church, Southwark. Administration of Martha Arnold, late of Christ Church, London, to John Stephenson the younger, residuary legatee, John Stephenson Esq., the sole executor, renouncing. 13 June, 1795, administration of goods left unadministered by John Stephenson, the younger, the residuary legatee since also deceased, to Mary Nott, wife of Randolph Nott, John Stephenson Esq., executor, renouncing, John Blackburn and Edward Biley, the executors of the will of the said John Stephenson the younger, having renounced. 24 August, 1829, administration of goods not administered as well by John Stephenson as also by Mary Nott, to Thomas Baker, a legatee. Norfolk, 134.

Benjamin Watkins* of Covrt Colman, Glamorgan. Will 20 December, 1701; proved 13 December, 1703. To daughter Mary Watkins, £60 out of messuage in Langan as empowered by deed of enfeofment, 1 November, 10 William 111, between me and David Bennett, then of Lalleston, since deceased. To son John Watkins, free and copy lands "Penglan" in parish of Cogchurch and manor of Cogty [sic] Wallen purchased of William Howell, Gweullian his wife, Morris David and Elizabeth his wife, alsoe "Tir Leyson" in ditto purchased of Edward Sant, William Thomas, David Phillip and William Phillip, also "Cannʳ rwfach als Sychbant" in ditto purchased of William Thomas, also customary lands at "Peny prisge" in ditto purchased of Kewelin Griffith and Mary Griffith, also tenement purchased of William Nicholls in parish of Coyty and Mannor of Coyty Anglia and ditto purchased of Evan John in said parish of Cogty [sic] and Mannor of Cogty [sic] Anglia, after term of settlement on my now wife, &c., paying to daughter Mary £40 which with the £60 to fulfiill bond of £200 to brother in law David Bennett for payment of £100 to Mary, &c. To grandson Benjamin Bassett, £10. To granddaughter Alice Bassett, £5. To daughter Alice Watkins, £100 out of leasehold in Newcastle, Glamorgan, purchased of Thomas Richards Llewelin, after which the tenement to eldest son William Watkins and other tenement to son Thomas Watkins. To daughter Anne Watkins, £100 out of tenement in Coyty purchased of William Nicholls, then said tenement to my

---

* Mr. Waters has marked on his bare reference to this will, which I have taken the abstract of at Somerset House: "N. Y. (says Mr. Jones)." This doubtless refers to David Jones, Esq., whose acute criticism and special knowledge of Welsh matters came so handy in settling the hotly contested parentage of Roger Williams. Doubtless Mr. Jones has good grounds for connecting this Watkins' will with early Welsh Families in New York.—L. W.

second son, John Watkins. To wife, all household stuff, paying to my three daughters in case she married, 40s. apiece. Rest of personal estate to wife and three daughters. Executors and Guardians: Brother John Watkins, brother in law Thomas Bennett, and my Allisemen John Bennett, Esq., Gervase Powell, Rees Powell his son, and Thomas Powell of Toudy. Witnesses: Mary Bennett, Michael Williams, Da. Pugh, Evan Powell, Joseph Watkins. Proved by Mary Watkins, relict, reserving to daughters Mary, Alice, and Anne Watkins, other executrices.   Degg, 242.

Ouzeel Van Swietan, inhabitant of New York in America, at at present in city of London. Will 23 January, 1693–4; proved 2 January, 1702–3. All estate, leases, lands, tenements, goods, and chattels to my particular and much esteemed friend Mr. Valentine Cruger of London, merchant, executor. Witnesses: Edward King, Edward Holmes, Benjamin Ashe, Robt. Sinclair. Administration to Jacob Myna Cruger, relict and administratrix of Abraham Cruger, executor, also deceased. [3 July, 1705, administration of said Ouzeel Van Swieten late of New York in America, bachelor, deceased, granted to natural and legitimate sister Beatrice Ouzeel, revoking administration with will annexed in January, 1702, to Jacob Minor Cruger, relict and administratrix of Valentine Cruger, executor and universal legatee, by reason that the said Valentine Cruger died during the lifetime of said Ouzeel Van Swieten. Admon Act Book, 1705, folio 153.]
Degg, 14.

Mary Slater, widow and relict of Collonell Henry Slater, formerly Governor of the Province of New Yorke. Will 14 September, 1704; proved 13 March, 1704–5. All estate to Mrs. Mary Leaver of the Citty of New York, executrix. Witnesses: Margarett Magregory, Mary Harris, Rich. Harris. Administration to Charles Loewick, attorney for Mary Leaver, now in New York, executrix of Mary Slater, late of New York, deceased.
Gee, 63.

Richard Sharwin als Sherwin, late of City of New York in North America. Administration 18 November, 1783, to John McTaggart, attorney for relict Ann Sherwin, now resident in New York.   Admon Act Book, 1783.

William Hooker, late of City of New York in America, formerly belonging to H. M. S. Ships the *Advice*, *Lynn*, and *Suffolk*, but on hoard H. M. Ship *St. George*, a mariner on H. M.'s service, deceased. Administration granted 4 February, 1748–9, to William Bryant, attorney for Cloe Hooker, relict of deceased, residing in New York.   Admon Act Book, 1749 (Register's Seat).

Samuel Ward, late of Staten Island in State of New York in North America, but now of Parish of St. Pancras, Middlesex. Will 22 April, 1797; proved 2 May, 1797. To beloved brother Joseph Ward of Essex County in State of New Jersey in America, in Township of Newark, one-third of estate. To my brother Caleb Ward of Staten Island in the County of Richmond and State of New York, one-third. To Joseph Moor of Hopewell in State of New Jersey, one-third. Executor: friend Thomas Courtney, woolen draper and tailor of Finch Lane, Cornhill,

132

London, in County of Middlesex. Witnesses: Thos. Courtney, James McAtee, Castle, Kentish Town. Resealed 28 April, 1797. Witnesses: James McAtee, John Lambert, Mary Jaffey, Ann Bull.

Exeter, 381.

John Cortland Schuyler, Town of Water Vliet, County of Albany. Will 27 December, 1793; proved 2 August, 1797. Exeautors authorized to sell real estate. To wife Angelica, daughter of Henry Van Renssalaer Esq., £1400 money of State of New York in Bar of dower. To wife Angelica all household furniture and negro slaves. To mother Barbara Schuyler £500 ditto in bar of dower of estate from my Father Cortlandt Schuyler, deceased. Residue of estate in Europe as well as in United States of America to my brothers and sisters, children of aforesaid Cortlandt Schuyler, deceased. Executrix in Europe : Mother Barbara Schuyler. Executrix in United States of America: father in law Henry Van Rensaelaer and Uncle Stephen Schuyler, Esq. Witnesses: Francis Nicoll, Osisa M. Huntington, County of Albany. 13 January, 1794, attestation of Philip Schuyler and Francis Nicoll that they saw the testator and Osias M. Huntington sign. Abraham G. Lansing, Surrogate. Administration of John Cortland Schuyler, Esq., late of Bethlehem in County of Albany in America, and a Lieutenant on half pay in H. M. Marine Force, &c., granted to Francis William Schuyler, brother and one of the residuary legatees, Barbara Schuyler, mother and executrix, dying in lifetime of testator.

Exeter, 567.

Phebe Tolmie of the City of New York. Will 4 January 1791. and 15 of our independence; proved 27 August 1795. To sister Philena Barnes the lots of ground on Cherry Street of 50 feet with Buildings etc. also one silver guilt pott and £50. for life, then to my niece Pheba Cumins. To nephew David Harris after sister Philena's decease lots and buildings on Water street, apparell, jewels, except gold watch with two seals set in gold, my deceased husband's portrait, and Bracelet to said Niece Pheba Cumins and Isabella Rose daughter of Dr. Rose. Residue of estate in America to be sold for funeral and other charges and remainder after to nephew David Harris. To Capt. John Bolderson Jr. and Capt. Joseph Dillain 30 guineas each. To John Tresidor 15 guineas of money in Bank of England. Rest of money in banks to be paid to the mother of my deceased husband Normand Tolmie and his nephew Thomas McKinsy, elder son of deceased Husband's youngest sister. Executors: George Douglas Jr. and William Beekman Jr., of this city. Witnesses: Charles Titus, Roswell Graves, Francis Titus, City and County of New York. Certificate of David Gelston Surrogate, of proof of will 27 August 1795 by witnesses Charles Titus of Bushwick, Kings county Esq., Francis Titus of ditto, yeoman, and Roswell Graves of New York grocer. Certificate of Richard Varick, Mayor of New York 17 November 1775. Will of Phebe Tolmie, formerly of Chelsea, Middlesex, but late of New York in North America deceased. Proved by Samuel Douglas one of executors and attorney for George Douglas Jr. and William Beekman Jr. Harris, 433.

NEW YORK GLEANINGS IN ENGLAND,

Including "Gleanings," by Henry F. Waters, not before printed.

CONTRIBUTED BY LOTHROP WITHINGTON,
30 Little Russell St., W. C., London.

Norman Tolmie of city of New York, Mariner. Will 29 Oct. 1765 in the sixth year of the reign of our sovereign lord George the Third; proved 1 April 1788. All to wife Phebe Tolmie, executrix. Witnesses: Rudolphus Rittzema, Robert R. Livingston Jr., Michael Jeffrey. Proved by executrix. Calvert, 217.

The people of the state of New York by the grace of God Free and Independant send greeting.

Abraham Mortier Citizen of New York in His Majesty's dominions in North America and deputy Pay-master of his Majesty's troops there. Will 28 March 1769; proved 13 January 1785. To each of my executors £100. To my wife Martha all money owing to me and land outward of New York granted to me by the Rector and people of the city after her to Elizabeth Banyer the wife of Goldstron Banyer, New York, Anne Maden sister of the same, Elizabeth Banyer and Elizabeth Appy daughter of the same. My wife Martha and my brother David Mortier of London and the said Goldstron Banyer executors. Witnesses Samuel Jones, Francis Stephens, William Newton. Cadwallader Golden His Majesty's Lieutenant Governor at the time this will was proved in New York. Proved in Prerogative Court of Canterbury by David Mortier. Ducarel, 33.

James Leadbetter late of the city of New York in America but now of Dean street in the Co. of Middlessex, Gentleman. Will 14 January 1799; proved 28 January 1799. To my son Hugh Percy Leadbetter of London and to my daughter Mary Leadbetter now in America all my real and personal estate in Great Britian, America or elsewhere. I appoint Rev. John Wardill A. M., and Daniel Coxe Esq of Hill Street, Berkley Square excutors. Witnesses, Honora Flamand, Joseph Perry, Ann Perry. Proved in Prerogative Court of Canterbury by Rev. John Wardill Clerk.

Howe, 50.

Nicholas Cullen of town and port of Dover, Merchant. Will 27 June 1696; proved 14 June 1697. To twenty poore widows of Parish of St. Mary the Virgin £13 yearly forever to be distributed weekly every Sunday evening, 3d. each widow, by churchwardens and overseers of the poor, for which I charge my now dwelling house, storehouse, &c. in Dover £6 clear of all taxes and abatements and £7 on 43 acres of Marshland in Parish of Promehill als Bromhill near Lid in Romney Marsh. To chnrchwardens &c. of St. Mary's small messuage in occupation of George Smith Tayler neer the fishmarket to spend issues in bread for poore on first sunday in December every year. "Item, I doe give and bequeath unto the poor of New York in America the sume of fifty pounds to be paid out of my effects there to be distributed at the discretion of Mr. Abraham Depister, Mr. Jacob Lister of New York Merchant and the elders and Deacons of the Parish church of New York aforesaid. Item, I give and bequeath to the poor of Albiana in America the sume of Twenty five pounds to distributed at the discretion of the said Mr. Abraham Depister and Mr. Jacob Lister and the elders and Deacons of the Parish church of Albania aforesaid." To William Cullen, sonn of my Uncle William Cullen of Dover deceased, at 21 dwelling house, store houses, &c. (my mother Katherin Cullen to have convenient dwelling for life), also Stone house near lime kilns adjoyning widow Elvins, also £500, provided Isaac Lamb, brother in law of William Cullen, be not concerned in intermeddilng. To Elizabeth Cullen daugter of said Uncle Luke Cullen £50. To Nicholas Terry and Michael Terry, sonns of Michael Terry of Canterbury, gent, £100 a peece. To Thomas Terry, son of ditto, £100 at 21. To Mildred, daughter of ditto, £100 at age or marriage, Michael Terry the father not to intermeddle in any legacy. To Katherine and Mary, daughters of Peter Favet and Katherine £5 apeece and all debts due from them. To Elizabeth Crookes, daughter of John Crookes, £400 at 21 or marriage. To my mother Katherine Cullen one small tenement and 18 acres in Cheriton, Kent, also £200. "Item, all my estate in Virginia both real and personal I give and divise and bequeath unto the daughters of my late Uncle Thomas Cullen of Carolina deceased to equally divided amongst them, share and share alike." If any legatees prefer leases or mortgages in place of money, execpt for poor, then executors to deliver, &c. Overseers: William Brookman of Birchbough, Kent, Esq. William Turner of Canterbury, Esq. and John Millard of Dover, Gentleman. Executors: James Atkinson of Rotherhith, Surrey, Gentleman. Rest to legatees porpotionately. Witnesses: Stephen Bull, William Limbery, Jr. Stephens. Pyne, 113.

John Watts late of the colony of New York, but now of Jermyn Street in the parish of St. James, county Middlesex, Esq. Will 3 July 1789; proved 12 September 1789. To son Robert Watts now in New York £1350 consolidated 3 per cent Bank Annuities which I have directed my Bankers Messrs. Coutts and Company to hold for him, also all sums owing to him as in acount lately remitted by him which I have marked on the back with letter A, as equivalant for £6000 New York currency I promised to leave him, also I confirm the gift of my Lot on which my Mansion house in New York stood. Also I confirm to my son John Watts the gift of my farm in New York called Rose Hill valued at £6000 New York currency. To Thomas Coutts, Edmund Antrobus, and John Antrobus of the Strand, Middlesex, Esqs., my executors, £3000 to invest in 3 per cent fund for my Daughter Anne Kenedy, wife of Archibald Kennedy independent of her said husband, and at her death for her children. To son Stephen Watts £3000. To said executors £3000 in trust for daughter Susannah Kearney, independent of her husband, and after her death to her children. To trustees £3000 in said stock for daughter Mary wife of Sir John Johnson, independent of her husband and at her death to her children, at 21. To Trustees £3000 for daughter Margaret Lake, widow for life, then to her children at 21 &c. To Trustees £2000 for grandson Thomas William Lake son of daughter Margaret Lake at 21 &c. Residue to children Robert, John, Anne, Stephen, Susannah, Mary and Margaret. Executors: said Thomas Coutts, Edmund Antrobus, and John Antrobus. Witnesses: Andrew Dickie, clerk to Messrs. Thomas Coutts and Company, Archibald Lindsey, Parish of St. Mary Lebon Peruke maker, William Baxter, Baker, of Charlotte Street in parish of St. Pancras. 1787 May 1788 June, Robert Watts, Esq. with John Watts Esq., Debtor Ballance £78 7s 4d cash of Fred. Jay on bond £157, ditto of John Stevens January 30. 1776 £176 (which reduced what he called his third to £1320 10s 0d and the deduction of 7 years 5 months Interest, then £20 on 100, reduced whole to) £1380 13s 9d. Ditto on Harrison's bond £890-11s, on Byrd's bond £47-6s advance 6 percent makes £1000 7s 4d, John Watts's direction to T. Coutts and Co. to transfer £1000 sterling to Robert Watts's account, £1778 15s 6d Balance Due on Rutherford Stevens & Parker's joint bond ℱ2072. Total £641 3s 11d. Credit Cash paid into Treasury to secure Rutherford Stevens & Parker's bond of £2072 at 4s per £, £440 6s 0d ditto paid to Lewis and Cox Lawyers for extra trouble in recovering Harrison and Boyd's debts £28 4s 4d, ditto paid William Patterson in the Jersey suit £8. Total £476 10s 4d Ballance £5984 13s 7d. Codicil 18 July 1789 Executors to lay out £50 in a testimonial for daughter Ann Kennedy for Tenderness and Friendship during my illness. 8 September 1789 Attestation of Andrew Dickie of George's Court, St. John, Clerkenwell, Middlesex, gentleman, one of witnesses of will of John Watts formerly of the colony of New York, late of St. James, Westminster, said county Middlesex deceased with accounts and codicils and that he was present in house of Captain Archibald Kennedy in Percy Street, Rathbone Place said county 3rd of July last with Archibald Lindsay and William Baxter and that the name Jno Watts to codicil is that of Testator. Before John Nicholl, Surrogate, James Townley Notary Public. Proved by Edmund Antrobus and John Antrobus, executors, reserving to other executor Thomas Coutts, Esq. Affidavit 11 September 1789 of Richard Lamb of Strand, parish of st. Martins in the Fields, Middlesex, gentleman attesting account current with Robert Watts marked "A" and dated 3 July 1789 and signature of John Watts to account and codicil Before George Harris, Surrogate, Thomas Adderley, Junior Notary Public. Macham, 477.

William Davis of Newe Yorke, Marriner now belonging to the Alborer Ketch, Captaine Vincent Commander. Will 10 May 1694; proved 25 August 1694. Wife Ellen Davis executrix and attorney to demand of Honorable Treasurer, or paymaster of Navy all dues as by His Majesty's decree of 23 May 1689.

Box, 191.

Gerrit Onckelbag, St. Mary, Newington Butts, Distiller. Will 9 January 1724-5; proved 15 December 1732. To daughters Nellie, wife of John Vangelder of the City of New York on the Continent of America, Turner and Rebecca, wife of John Breesleda of the City of New York on the Continent of America, Turner, all goods and lands. To friend Nicholas Swan and Ann his wife of St. Mary, Newington Butts, Surrey, Chandler, Gold rings with a heart and hand in a cypher. Executor: said Nicholas Swan. Witnesses: John Webb, Gos. Conen, Wm. Hill, Matth. Bancks. Bedford, 291.

Magdalen Debrosses of the City of New York single woman. Will 12 July 1781; proved 1 June 1796. To sister Elizabeth Desbrosses use of all estate, executors to apply same for her life, but if she do not want or demand the same, then to apply to better schooling of the Under Aged children of my Nephew James Desbrosses of the City of New York, Merchant, and Elizabeth his wife, already born or to be born. To William Desbrosses, son of said James Desbrosses and Elizabeth £500 New York currency on death of sister Elizabeth if of age, or at 21; if he die to Elias son of said James Desbrosses and Elizabeth ditto. To daughters of said James Desbrosses and Elizabeth all Household goods, apparel, etc., at death of aforesaid sister Elizabeth. Rest to sons and daughters of said James Desbrosses and Elizabeth his wife born or to be born as tenants in common at 21, after decease of my sister Elizabeth, etc. Executors: said James Desbrosses and his son James Desbrosses Junior, and David Clarkson of Flat Bush in Kings county, Gentleman, and Samuel Jones of the Township of Oyster Bay in Queens county, Attorney at Law. Witnesses: Rich. Hamar, Samll Pell, Robt Auclemuty, City and County of New York Ss. Before David Gelston, Surrogate, Oath of Richard Harrison of said City, Esquire, that he and other witnesses Samuel Pell and Robert N. Auclemuty signed will etc. True copy attest David Gelson. Proved in prerogative court of Canterbury by William Thwaytes attorney for James Desbrosses the elder, one of surviving executors, James Desbrosses Junior and David Clarkson dying in lifetime of testatrix and Samuel Jones renouncing. Harris, 302.

Mary Slater, Widdow and Relict of Collonell Henry Slater, formerly Governor of the Province of New Yorke. Will 14 September 1704; proved 13 March 1704-5. To Mrs. Mary Leaver of the Citty of New Yorke, executrix and her Heires all estate. Witnesses: Margarett Magregory, Mary Harris, Rich. Harris. Administration to Charles Lodwick, attorney for Mary Leaver, nowe at New Yorke, executrix of will of Mary Slater at Newe Yorke deceased. Gee, 63.

NEW YORK GLEANINGS IN ENGLAND,

Including "Gleanings," by Henry F. Waters, not before printed.

Contributed by Lothrop Withington,
30 Little Russell St., W. C., London.

James King, sometime of New York, now of Port Glasgow, County Renfrew. Will 30 April, 1788; proved 18 November, 1788. Being eldest lawful son of James King of Drum, County Renfrew. To James King and Elizabath Hynemanals King my father and mother, all my property. To Nancy alias Agnes Turnbull, daughter of Robert Turnbull, £100. To Charlotte Smith Duncan, £100. Executors: James King and Elizabeth Hynemanals King. Robert Turnbull of Petersburgh in Virginia and Charles Duncan at present of Glasgow, but shortly going out to Virginia. These last to be executors of my property in Virginia or other parts of the United States of North America or in the British Colonies. Witnesses: Alex. Watson, John Gillies. Calvert, 544.

Cuthbert Heathcote, late of New York, batchelor. Administration 10 July, 1731, to mother Martha Heathcote.
Admon Act Book, 1731.

Mary Heathcote of New York, spinster. Administration 10 July, 1731, to mother Martha Heathcote.

Admon. Act Book, 1731.

William Smith, City of New York. Will 16 November, 1783; proved 15 February, 1796. To John Phenderheath, Esq., who married my daughter Janet, all lands in Moore Town whereof I am legally seized, having been only his Trustee since Lady Moore gave the order to transfer the title to him. I remitted to Mr. Phenderheath out of the funds he left with me in 1776 when he sailed from this country, £1,000 to pay Lady Moore; and in favour to my daughter Jennet I intend the loss on Bonds and Continental Paper Money to be born by my whole estate as I intended giving her £3,000. To my wife £3,000. To each of my other children, £3,000. All my estate to be divided among my children except my son William who is to have a share and a half. My children to be executors as they attain their majority, including my wife, with power to partition lands and dispose of estate, and this power I give to my wife alone while she remains my widow and has not a majority of my children of age with her in the colony of New York, etc. Witnesses: Thomas Smith, Robert Whyte, Jas. Smith.

Harris, 97.

Rev. Winwood Serjeant, late of New York, North America, now of Bath, County Somerset. Will 1 Dec., 1779; proved 19 October, 1780. All my estate to my wife Mary Serjeant for life, then to my three children, Marmaduke Thomas Serjeant, Mary Brown Serjeant, and Elizabeth Serjeant, equally divided among them. Executor: my wife Mary Serjeant. Witnesses: Mary Pember, Alex. Hay, W. Percival, all of Bath.

Collins, 491.

John Peckharness of City of New York, Merchant. Will 1 September, 1795; proved 28 November, 1796. To Richard and Deborah Peckharness of Great Britain, my brother and sister, all my estate, real and personal in Great Britain, subject to a payment of £20 to George Smith of City of New York, Tavern Keeper, to whom I leave all my estate in America, real and personal. Executors: Richard and Deborah Peckharness. Witnesses: Richard Corner, William Pitt Short, Abraham Cadmas.

Harris, 574.

John Griffiths of City of New York, Merchant. Will 13 March, 1764; proved 7 Dec., 1799. To my son John £4 New York money as a bar to any claim he may have on my estate, being my eldest son. All my estate, real and personal, to my wife for life. If she marry, one third to go to her, the interest of other two thirds to support my children. If she continue a widow till my youngest child reach 21, as follows: my wife to have so much as will keep her in comfort, the remainder to be shared amongst my children equally. Executors: wife Jane and sons John and Anthony. Witnesses: Thomas Vardill, Mark Valentine, James Ernott. Oaths of Thomas Randall, Gent, of New York, and John Teneych of New York, Merchant, to the genuineness of two of the witness's signatures.

Howe, 841.

William Cunningham, Surgeon of H. M. S. *Windsor*. Will 30 January, 1789; proved 8 May, 1789. All to my wife Mrs. Margaret Cunninghame, whom I make my executrix. Witnesses: Catherine Rhodes, Mary Hyne. City and County of New York. On the 17 February, 1789. Appeared William Maxwell and George Turnbull of said County, Gents, and swore to the handwriting of William Cunningham. Administration 8 May, 1789, to Thomas Maude, Esqre., lawful surviving Attorney of Margaret Cunningham, of the will of William Cunningham, formerly Surgeon ot H. M. S. *Windsor*, but late of the city of New York.

Macham, 241.

Anne Bolton, widow, of Bridport, County Dorset. Will 8 September, 1799; proved 11 December, 1799. To my friend Reverend Thomas Howe, five guineas. To my cousin Anne Herinsole my gold watch. To my friend Elizabeth Herinsole my silver teapot. To Mrs. Rebecca Arnold all the rest of my plate, household stuff, and books. To my niece Catherine Brown my clothes, to be sent her in three months after my decease, directed to care of Aaron Burr, Esq., of New York, America. All the rest to my brother Joseph Brown. Executor: my cousin Thomas Collins Colfox. Witnesses: Ann Burr and Edward Dally.

Howe, 823.

Thomas Hart of the City of New York, Mariner. Will 25 August, 1761; proved 11 January, 1774. After all my debts and funeral expenses are discharged all my estate to go to my wife Ester Hart whom I make and ordain my whole and sole executrix. Witnesses: John Harrison, Simon Fleet, Hugh Gaine.

Bargrave, 16.

William Brownejohn, Senior, of the City of New York, Druggist. Will 14 June, 1783; proved 14 June, 1785. The People of the State of New York by the Grace of God Free and Independent Know that in the Registry of our Court of Probates are registers containing letters testimonial in words following, etc. My wife Mary to have the direction of my funeral. To my eldest son William Brownjohn or my heir in full barr of their claim on my estate £5 New York currency. To my wife the house I now live in, in Hanover Square, New York, Ground in Tews Alley, New York, £700 per annum New York Currency, 200 guineas to purchase a carriage and horses if she think fit to call upon my executors for it, and to have the use of all my household stuff, slaves, plate, etc., for life. To the Rector and the Inhabitants of New York, in Communion with the Church of England as by Law Established, £100 for the Charity School. All my servants to have decent mourning at my expense. My executors to have £100. The rest as follows: one equal seventh part to each of my children, William Brownjohn, Samuel Brownjohn, Elizabeth the wife of Joseph Bartow, Mary the wife of Timothy Hurst, Catherine the wife of Oliver Templeton, and Rachel the wife of John Price, the remaining seventh part to the children of my son Thomas Brownjohn, deceased, that is to say, William, Elizabeth, Mary, and Catherine, share and share alike, to be placed in the British National funds or in good land security. The rest of my real estate as follows: The said £200 to be paid quarterly to my wife, and, after necessary expenses, the residue to my children, one seventh each and one seventh to my said grandchildren. After my wife's death, one seventh my personal estate that has been in her use to be sold and one seventh of each to my children, one seventh to the aforesaid grandchildren. Elizabeth Brownjohn, widow of my said son Thomas, to receive one half of all the said grandchildren's share. If any of my children die, the bequests to go to their issue. On bond with the said Timothy Hurst and his brother Charles Hurst to George Folliott of New York, Esquire, being chiefly for debt of said Charles, to be recovered of estate of Charles Hurst, etc. Executors: my wife Mary Brownjohn and friends Gabriel William Ludlow, Cornelius Clopper, James Bechman, Henry Bemsen. Codicil to above will dated 14 June, 1783. If any dispute arise over loans, advancements, or payments and dispositions specified above, the major part of my executors to appoint an arbitrator, the other parties to choose another, and the major part of my executors to have full power to administer the award. Witnesses to will and codicil: Hugh Gaine, Eleazer Miller, junior, Daniel McCormick.

Ducarel, 291.

4 August, 1783. Appeared personally before me Carew Ludlow Surr. for City and Province of New York; Hugh Paine, Printer and Bookseller, and Eleazer Miller, Junr., of said City, Merchant, who swear to said Will and Codicil of William Brownejohn, deceased, and likewise that they saw Daniel McCormick the other witness subscribe his name thereto.

Attestation of the Probate granted on 4th August last to Mary Brownejohn, the widow and executrix, by George Clinton, Esquire, governor of our State, General and Commander in chief of the Militia and Admiral of the Navy of the same at the City of New York, 18 May, 1784.

Ducarel, 291.

Daniel Squier now in the City of New York in America. Will 24 November, 1778; proved 14 December, 1786. To Jane Moor, daughter of George Moor of the Parish of Rotherhithe, London, and to her heirs all my real and personal estate, it being my desire that she shall be my sole heir. Executrix: Jane Moor. Witnesses: Francis Levett. J. Greg, Robert Canning.

Norfolk, 635.

Stephen Mesnard, late of City of New York in America, but now of parish of St. Johns in Southwark, County Surrey, Mariner. Will 23 January, 1748-9; proved 21 February, 1775. To my mother Elizabeth Mesnard of New York, widow, my house, etc., in Duke Street, New York, in the tenure of my said mother, after her death to go to my wife Lucy Mesnard with the remainder of my goods after my debts have been paid. Executrix: my wife Lucy Mesnard. Witnesses: Robert Vincent, Thos. Brapple, Abraham Harman, Notary Public.

Alexander, 60.

Richard Ayscough of City of New York, Practitioner of Physick and Chirurgery. Will 22 May, 1760; proved 22 November, 1760. To my daughter Sarah Ayscough, £500 of New York money. To my brother John Ayscough, Junior, £100 of Great Britain currency. To my brother Thomas Ayscough £50 of Great Britain currency. To my wife Anne Ayscough my house in Hanover Square in the East of said Citie of New York, after her death to be sold and the money bestowed as follows: To my mother in law Ann Langdon, widow of Richard Langdon, deceased, £500 New York currency; one third of all the rest of my property real or personal to my wife Anne; the rest and remainder to my son Richard Ayscough and to such child or children my wife Anne shall bear by me hereafter. Executors: my wife Anne, my uncle the Rev. Doctor Francis Ayscough, my friend Charles Williams of New York. Witnesses: John Barnet, Com. C. V. Horne, Isaac Goelet, City of New York.

Lynch, 412.

Waldron Blau of City of New York, New York. Will 23 June, 1783; proved 19 November, 1787. To my son Richard Blau my house and block opposite the Exchange in Broad Street, New York, in tenure of Jonathan Clarke. All the rest to my wife Eleanor Blau, and at her death to be sold and divided amongst my children, share and share alike, except that as my eldest son Uriah has had £100 from me, all my other children to receive £100 before the division be made. If my wife re-marry, the estate be sold and she to have £1,000 of New York currency, the rest to be divided as above. Executors: my wife Eleanor and my son Uriah. Witnesses: Nat. Chandler, Fras. Groome, John Knapp.

Major, 485.

Richard Nicholas of City of New York. Will 26 September, 1772; proved 3 October, 1783. To be buried in my vault in Trinity Churchyard. To Joseph Wilson of New York City, £7 per annum, and to be buried at my expense when he dies. To the Corporation for the relief of Widows and Children of Clergymen of the Church of England in America, £25. To Peter Middleton, Doctor of Physicke my gold watch for his tenderness to my two grandchildren, Margaret and Ann Burgess. To my daughter Mary Auchmuty, wife of Samuel Auchmuty, D. D., the silver ring given to my late son William Robert by his godfather Robert Ellison, deceased. To my daughter Mary Auchmuty and granddaughter Frances Montresor one fourth of my estate. To my daughter Jane Harrison one fourth. To my daughter Elizabeth Colden one fourth. To my three granddaughters Susanna and Anne Burgess and Susanna Margaret Middleton one fourth. If my negroes Leeds, Quash, and Doll are too feeble to provide for themselves, my executors to do so. Executors: Samuel Auchmuty, George Harrison of New York, Alexander Colden of Kings County, and Peter Middleton. Witnesses: John Charlton, John Rice, Jos. Hildreth. Codicil 15 March, 1774; £800 to be put out at interest as follows: Interest on £600 for the relief of my wife's sisters. Interest on £300 for the relief of my negroes Leeds, Quash, and Doll, and I manumit them. Whereas one of the executors of my will has departed this life, I appoint his son Richard executor in his place. Witnesses: James Auchmuty, John Burt Lyng, Yellis Mandeville.

Cornwallis, 527.

142

NEW YORK GLEANINGS IN ENGLAND,

Including "Gleanings," by Henry F. Waters, not before printed.

CONTRIBUTED BY LOTHROP WITHINGTON,
30 Little Russell St., W. C., London.

Hugh Montgomery of London, merchant, now bound for New York. Will 12 November, 1698; proved 24 January, 1699–1700. To Mr. Alexander Lind of St. Ann. Blackfryars, London, merchant, all my whole estate, both real and personal, and I appoint him full and sole executor of this will and testament. Witnesses: Edmund Willcocks, Robert Terry, William Walker.

St. Chrsitofhers, September 10, 1699.

I, Hugh Montgomerie on New York, but now in the Island of St. Christofhers, Gent. "I desire that Captain John Finch should take that money and lay it out at the best advantage in Sugars and consign it to John Ellison owes me himselfe to the value of £24 more or less, and that John Ellison should receive of John Cable the sum of £5. 10s. in heavy pieces of eight @ 4s. 6d apiece and to receive of Thomas Taylor the sum of one pound, fourteen shillings, and I desire you to write, to one Daniel Bitts in Norwark to send the money £1.14s. and to receive of William Wesser £2.2s and to sell my part of the sloop. The said John Ellison lo lay out the money to the best advantage and consign it to Alexander Lind to be found at William Gordons next door to the sign of the Goat in Lothbury in London. All my cloaths to Edward Parminter." Witnesses: Geo. Grawes, Edward Parmitor. Noel, 11.

Robert Codenham, late of Shadwell, England, now of New York, mariner. Will 23 November, 1688; proved 26 February, 1699-1700. To my wife now living at Shackley's Walk in Shadwell, all my estate for her use and my children. Richard Jones of New York, merchant, executor. Witnesses: George Heathcott, Thomas Clarke, Edward Buckmaster, George Brewerton.

New York, January 28th, 1688-9.

Inventory of the Estate of Robert Codenham, late Mr. of the slupp *Charles* as it was taken by us undermenconed according to the order of the Mayers Court beareing date.

	£	S.	D.
In Cash	14.	14.	7½
Two suits of Cloathes much worne, one great coat, three old coats all at	3.	10.	o
One Tobacco Stopper, one knife, one snuff Box, one Tinder box, one prospective glasse, one Comb Case		5.	o
16 pair of Old Stockens	2.	5.	o
8 pair of Wollen Socks		6.	3
One boy named Edward Puckford Apprentice to the said Codingham	5.	o.	o
Various other Articles amounting in all to	59.	3.	9
Ballance of Accompt due from Richard Jones	89.	10.	11
Due from Jacobus V. Courtlandt being money received from Jamaica	23.	13.	o

One Bill signed and sealed due from Jos. Edloe of Calvert County in Maryland for the sume of twenty three pounds, six shillings and 4d Sterling money of England payable 10th of October, 1688.

One Bill signed and sealed due from Jos. Edloe abovesaid for two thousand and four hundred and twenty pounds of good sound and merchantable Leafe Tobacco in Caske payable 10 October, 1688. Tho. Clarke.

Chr. Gore. Noel, 21.

Anthony Elsworth, late of New York, now residing in the parish of Abchurch, London. Will 30 March, 1784; proved 10 April, 1784. To my friend Jacob Hart, formerly of New York, but now of St. Michael, Crooked Lane, London, £100, if he die first, then to his wife Easter Hart, if she be dead to Moses Hart their son. To Hettie Blackwell, daughter of Montague and Miriam Blackwell and Grand-daughter of said Jacob Hart, £50. To my nephew Francis Elsworth, son of my brother Joseph Elsworth of New York City, £50. After the decease of my wife Elizabeth Elsworth, my estate to be divided between Sarah Penny, daughter of Archibald and Catherine Penny, and to Sarah and Jacob Elsworth, son and daughter of Francis Elsworth and to the three daughters of Joseph Elsworth. Executors: Montague Blackwell and Thomas Hayward of London. Witnesses:

James Niven, Abm. Hart. Codicil dated March 30, 1784. My estate to be put under the control of the Lord High Chancellor of England for him to administer except the £100 to my friend Jacob Hart.
Rockingham, 198.

William Brownjohn, Senior, Druggist of New York City. Will 14 June, 1782; proved 14 June, 1785. To my eldest son William Brownjohn, £5 current money of New York in full barr of his claim or if he be dead, to my heir at law. To my wife Mary Brownjohn the Lot I now live on in Hanover Square for life, also £700 current money of New York per annum, also 200 guineas for the purchase of a carriage. To the Church of England of New York, £100. My servants to have suitable mourning given them. To each of my executors, £100. My estate in equal parts that is 1-7 each to each of my children, William Brownjohn, Samuel Brownjohn, Elizabeth, wife of Joseph Barton, Mary, wife of Timothy Hurst, Catherine, wife of Oliver Templeton, and Rachel, wife of John Price, the remaining 1-7 to children of my son Thomas Brownjohn, deceased, that is to say, William, Elizabeth, Mary and Catherine. The rest in trust to my executors in trust, they to pay my wife the said £700. To Elizabeth Brownjohn, widow of my said son Thomas during her widowhood one moiety of the share bequeathed to her children. Whereas, I became bond with the said Timothy Hurst and his brother Charles Hurst, for a considerable sum of money to one George Folliott of City of New York Esq., my executors to take all lawful measures for the recovery of any money which I or they pay in consequence of the same. Executors: my wife Mary Brownjohn, my friends Gabriel William Ludlow, Cornelius Clopper, James Bickman and Henry Benson, all now or formerly of New York City, merchants. Witnesses: Hugh Gaim, Eleazer Miller, Junior, Daniel McCormick. Codicil 14 June, 1783, to the effect that if any dispute arise to be settled by Arbitrators. Witnesses: Hugh Gaine, Eleazer Miller, Junior, Daniel McCormick.
Ducarel, 291.

Daniel Horsemanden of City of New York, New York Province, Esquire, Chief Justice of the same Province. Will 5 February, 1777; proved 8 April, 1786. As my late dear sister Ursula Horsemanden, Spinster, did by her last will and testament bequeath to me £2,500 invested in an annuity in the South Sea Stock, she having also appointed Lucretia Horsemanden relict of my late Brother Reverend Samuel Horsemanden, executrix of said will, said will having been proved in Prerogative Court of Canterbury. I give out of the said £2,500, £1,000 to the Rector of St. Giles, Cripplegate in London for the time being a standing trustee of the late Bishop Andrew's Charity for the said Charity, and I give Mr. Olive, now or late of Goudhurst, County Kent, England, yeoman, who agreed with me for the purchase of my farm at Goudhurst, £600 out of said stock. The remaining £900 to the said Lucretia Horsemanden. My Chariot and horses to Elizabeth, wife of my worthy friend Miles Sherbrooke of City of New York, merchant. To my goddaughter Maria Horsemanden Byrd, daughter of Colonel William Byrd of Virginia, £500 and

145

the sum of £1,500 New York money. To the Rector and inhabitants of New York City, Church of England Communion £100 to be laid out in building their Rector's house lately destroyed by fire and rebuilding the Charity school house, a pulpit and desk in Trinity Church. To Kings College, New York City, £500. The residue to my executors, Miles Sherbrooke and my worthy friend Thomas Hayes of Bristol in England, Merchant. Witnesses: James Desbrosses, junir, Samuel Jones, Jacob Rhinelander.   Norfolk, 223.

Henry White, formerly of New York but now of London. Will 19 May, 1786; proved 27 January, 1787. To my son Henry White all my real estate in North America and all my property there. To my wife all my plate and household furniture. To my friends, Henry Thorton now M. P., for Southwark, Brooke Watson, Esq., Alderman of London, and David Gordon of Lime Street, London, all my estate on trust to convert into money and to pay my wife an annual sum of £500 clear, while she shall continue my widow, but upon her marriage she to have an annual sum of £200 for life. My trustees also to divide my estate amongst my children, namely Henry White, Frederick Corland White, John Chambers White, William Tyron White, Anne and Margaret and Frances White, in equal shares, £2,000 to be deducted from Frederick Corland White's share for the expenses I have been at in making purchases for him in the Army, said £2,000 to be divided amongst the others and to be paid when 21 years old or in the case of the girls when married. My wife to be guardian of my daughters. Son Henry White, executor in America. Henry Thornton, Brooke Watson, David Gordon, executors and trustees in England. Witnesses: Jno Francklin, junior, Bedford Square, Arthur Anstey, Lincolns Inn, Charles Wilson, Inner Temple. Codicil dated 23 May, 1786. Whereas, I have learnt that my son Henry White was lately in treaty for the purchase of my late dwelling house in Queen Street in New York City, which was seized and confiscated by that State, the money I advance him to be deducted from his share and to be divided amongst my other children. My wife joint executrix with him for America. All compensation for losses in America to be reckoned in English property. Witnesses: Jno Francklin, junior, Bedford Square, Arthur Anstey, Lincolns Inn, Charles Wilson, Inner Temple.   Major, 49.

NEW YORK GLEANINGS IN ENGLAND,

Including "Gleanings," by Henry F. Waters, not before printed.

CONTRIBUTED BY LOTHROP WITHINGTON,
30 Little Russell St., W. C., London.

John Buxton of City of New York, Baker. Will 12 December, 1782; proved 24 April, 1795. To my wife Ann Buxton all my estate real and personal in England and America during the time she remains my real widow, in case of marriage with any other man she is only to have ⅓. To my son Charles Buxton and his heirs for ever all my Real estate in the Parish of Church Broton in Derbyshire also the Corner house I now live in situate in William and Fair streets, City of New York. To my daughter Sarah

Buxton the house next to the said corner house. In case my children die without issue I give all to my Brother Will: Buxton and his children. Executors: Ann Buxton, wife, friends: Thomas Pearsall, watchmaker and John Lawrence, merchant both of said city. Witnesses: Joseph Delaplaine, Thomas Steele, William Hale. Newcastle, 241.

Jacob Beaumon, late of New York, Mariner, late belonging to the *Launceston* since to the *Chester* and after to the *Mermaid*. Will 24 April, 1747; proved 8 December, 1748. All my goods and estate to my friend and executor Richard Creek of Milton next Gravesend, County Kent, victualler. Witnesses: Richd. Cork, Thos. Nott. Strahan, 353.

Cornelius Thompson of the Town of New York in the Province of Jersey in America, Seaman, now of his Majesty's Ship *Dolphin*. Will 13 May 1772; proved 8 July 1775. All wages, prize money etc. which I may have due or entitled at my death to my loving friends Philip Nicholson of Whitehaven, County Cumberland and John Healy of the Parish of Bury in the suburbs of the City of Cork and appoint said two, executors of my will. Witnesses: Da: Dalzell, Jno. Colpoys Actg. Captn. Joseph Milburn, master. Alexander, 291.

Charles Mackintosh, City of New York. Will 2 February, 1747–8; proved 3 February, 1749–50. My son Phineas and my daughter Susanna shall be maintained out of profits of my estate till they are 21. All my estate to my wife Susanna Mackintosh and to my son Phineas and my daughter Susanna to wit, one fourth to my wife, one half to my son Phineas, one fourth to my daughter Susanna. If Phineas die his share to be divided between my said wife and daughter, if my daughter die her share to my son Phineas. Executors: wife Susanna and my friends Stephen Bayard of the City of New York and Richard Alsop of New Town upon Long Island. Witnesses: Elisha Parker, Par. Parmyter, Dno. Crofts. Greenly, 51.

Charles Crommelin of Province of New York in America, but now in London. Will 27 May, 1732; proved 22 April, 1740. Having by various Losses and misfortunes in trade been thrown into many and great debts which have driven me from home to seek for succour among my relations in Europe. To the end I might not be obliged to part with my Patrimonial lands in order to satisfy for the said debts and having by the Blessing of God obtained partly by Gift from some Relations in France and partly by Easy purchase from others in London in full right and title for my Self and my heirs to three fourths of Certain Bond debts (Particularly Specified in certain documents and powers now in my hands for the recovery of the same) due from the estate of James Smith of the Island of St. Thomas in America deceased which Bonds are in the hands of Mr. Jerome Joseph Le Jeune of the Island of Martinque in America and dwelling at the Salines in that Island and the said Estate of the said James Smith deceased having partly by Seizure on the part of the Danish Government in the said Island of St. Thomas under certain pretended Colours and partly by Embezzlement I have caused application to be made to Denmark for the same and am now sailing for Martinque to receive the said bonds thence to St. Thomas and thence to New York to return to my family. My creditors to be satisfied with the principal of my debts. My estate to be divided amongst my wife and children £100 to my son Daniel above his share. My debts to Mr. Samuel Baker, Mr. Francis Gourdon merchants and Mr. ——— Jeuvrein of City of London, making £260 to be paid first. Executors: Mr. Samuel Baker of London, Messrs. John and Joseph Read merchants in New York, my son Daniel at present at Rotterdam. Witnesses; George Schutz, Not. Pub. 1732, Anth: Frost, James Fleming.   Browne, 103.

Hugh Wallace, late of New York Esqr. now residing in Norfolk Street, Strand. Will 15 March, 1785; proved 26 June, 1788. To my wife Sarah Wallace £1000 New York Currency, one annuity of £400 per annum New York currency. All my estate real and personal to my three brothers, William Wallace, Magill Wallace and Alexander Wallace upon trust for purposes hereinafter mentioned, that is to the children of my said brothers, William, Magill and Alexander and my sister Elizabeth Watson, when 21 or day of marriage. My Trustees to retain the share of My Neice Lucy, daughter of my Brother William now wife of Doctor James Currie, to pay the interest from time to time to the personal use of my said neice. Executors: Wife Sarah, Brothers William, Magill and Alexander Wallace. Witnesses: Wm. Sleigh, Jno. Knight, Thomas Dunn. Hugh Wallace formerly of New York now of Waterford, Ireland. To my wife Sarah all my watches, wearing apparell. Robert Paul, City of Waterford, Trustee and Joint Executor 40 guineas. Dated 2 February, 1787. Witnesses: John Allen, Simon Preston, Not. Publ. Hugh Wallace, city of Waterford 28th March, 1787. Whereas I have made over all my estate to the children of my Brothers William, Magill and Alexander and my sister Ann Elizabeth Watson. I charge the said estate with the payment of legacy to my wife and the £400 American Currency per annum. My trustee to use a part of said children's share not exceeding £500 to place him or her in a trade or in promoting them in the Army or Navy. Witnesses: Humy. May, Simon Preston, Not. Pub. Ann Lloyd. A true Copy which I attest Hen. Upton, D. Regt. [Extracted from the Registry of His Majesty's Court of Prerogative, Ireland.]

Calvert, 334.

Colonel John Cavalier, late of Kingston, Jamaica, now of St. Andrews, Holborn, County Middlesex. Will 16 August, 1735; proved 24 October, 1735. To my Nephew John Cavalier of the City of New York in America £200 current money of Jamaica. To my nephew Henry Cavalier of the said City £200 current money of Jamaica. To my nephew John Mellish of the City of London £200 money of Jamaica. To Mr. John Cavalier Goodin, Son of Mr. George Goodin of parish of Westmoreland in Jamaica

£200 Jamaica currency. To Mr. Samuel Kermer Main, of St. Andrews parish in Jamaica, £100 Jamaica currency. To Mr. William Goodwin of the Parish of Kingston, Jamaica £100 Jamaica Currency. To Mr. Anthony White of Yellows parish in Jamaica £50 current money. To Mrs. Anne Vallette, wife to Mr. Peter Vallette and her daughter Jane Vallette both of Port Royal in Jamaica £50 Current money. To Mr. John Craford of the parish of Kingston Jamaica £50 current money. To Mrs. Rachel Beach of Kingston, Jamaica £25 current money. To Mrs. Mary Lee, wife of Benjamin Lee of Kingston, Jamaica £25 current money. To my neice Helena Barrow of Barbadoes £500 current money. To my wife Elizabeth Mellish of the City of London £40 per annum. To my nephew Daniel Jouet late of New York but now resident in Jamaica all my wearing apparrell and an emerald ring set with four Diamonds. To my nephew Daniel Jouet and George Goddin of Westmoreland aforesaid all my fire arms, swords, scimetars and walking Canes between them. To Doctor Nicholas Harris my gold watch. To Colonel William Goodon a pair of gold Knee Buckles. To my cousen Catherine Goodin, daughter to my neice Mary Goddin a gold purse Spring. To Mr. Daniel Dickens a pair of gold Knee Buckles. To Mrs. Mary Dickens, a plain Gold ring, that was my wife's wedding ring. To Mr. Michael Atkins a silver cup. To my negro woman Parthenia her freedom. My Plantation called New River Plantation in St. Andrews, Jamaica to my sister Mary Jouet of New York in America. Daniel Jouet and his sister Mary Jouet and my neice Mary Goodin, wife to Mr. Mr. George Goodin between them. Executors: Mr. Michael Atkins of Bristol, merchant, Mr. Samuel Dickens of Kingston, Jamaica, Mr. Samuel Kermer Main, of St. Andrews, Jamaica and my nephew Daniel Jouet. Witnesses: Wm. Wood at Whitehall, Jno. Dickens, Ann Izard, Geo. Masters. Ducie, 202.

John Watts late of the Colony of New York but now of Jermyn Street of St. James, Esquire. Will 3 July, 1789; proved 12 September, 1789. To my son Robert Watts now in New York £1350 I have directed my bankers Messrs. Coutts and Sons to pay him and all moneys mentioned in an account lately sent him by me. To my son John Watts the gift I made to him of my farm called Rose Hill in New York. To Thomas Coutts, Edmund Antrobus, and John Antrobus £3000 in trust for my daughter Ann Kennedy wife of Archibald Kennedy Esqre. To my son Stephen Watts £3000. To the aforesaid trustees £3000 for my daughter Susannah Kearney, also £3000 for my daughter Mary, wife of Sir John Johnson, also £3000 for my daughter Margaret Lake, widow, also £2000 for my grandson Robert William Lake, son of my daughter Margaret Lake. All the rest of my estate to my children Robert, John, Ann, Stephen, Susannah, Mary and Margaret to be equally divided amongst them. Executors: Said Thomas Coutts, Edmund and John Antrobus as trustees and executors in Great Britain. Executors in America: Sons Robert and John. Witnesses: Andrew Dickie, clerk to Messrs. Thomas Coutts and Company Archibald Lindsay of the parish of St. Mary,

Lebon peruke maker. William Baxter, Baker, of Charlotte Street in the parish of St. Pancras.

Dr. Robert Watts Esq.   with John Watts Esq. Cred.

		£	s.	d.
1787 May	To Ballance due upon Account	78.	7.	4.
	To Cash recd. of Fred Jay on his Bond in full	151.	0.	0.
1788 June	To Cash recd. of John Stevens, Jan. 30, 1776 £168 which reduced what he called his third to £1320, 16s. 6d. and the deduction of 7 years 5 mo. Interest, then £20 on every hundred reduced the whole to	1380.	13.	9.
	To Cash received on Harrison's Bond, Pens. Curry	890.	0.	0.
	On Byrd's Bond £47. 6s advance 6⅔ p. cent makes in all	1000.	7.	4.
	To John Watt's directions to T. Coutts and Co. to transfer £1000 Stg. to Robert Watts Acct.	1778.	15.	6.
	To Ballance due on Rutherford Stevens and Parkes Joint Bond	2072.	0.	0.
		£6461.	3.	11.
	By Cash he paid into the Treasury to secure Rutherford Stevens & Parkers joint Bond of £2072 at 4/3 P. £.	440.	6.	0.
	By Cash paid to Lewis Cox Lawyers for their extra trouble in recovering Harrisons & Boyds Debts	28.	4.	4.
	By Cash paid Wm. Patterson on the Jersey Suit	8.	0.	0.
		476.	10.	4.
	By Balaunce	5984.	13.	7.
		£6461.	3.	11.

It is my will that my executors pay to my Daughter Ann Kennedy £50 to be laid out in some Testimonial of regard and gratitude for the tenderness and Friendship she has shewn me during my illness. Jno. Watts, London. 18 July, 1789.

Macham, 477.

NEW YORK GLEANINGS IN ENGLAND,

Including "Gleanings," by Henry F. Waters, not before printed.

CONTRIBUTED BY LOTHROP WITHINGTON,
30 Little Russell St., W. C., London.

Joseph Smith of the City of New York in the State of New York, Merchant. Will 11 May, 1792; proved 19 September, 1795. To wife Dorothy, Household Furniture, Books, Plate, etc. (except hereafter given to daughter Elizabeth), also moiety of 3 per cent English funds at Bank of England for life, and if daughter Elizabeth die without issue said moiety, etc., etc. To daughter Elizabeth other moiety, etc., also my Family Quarto Bible, Silver Watch, half pint silver mug, and Gold Sleave Buttons, Desk or Bureau, best case of Drawing Instrumsnts, Mahogany Tent Bedstead with Bedding, Mahogany Square Table and 30 volumes of Books she may choose. Stock in trade to be sold and one third to wife, rest to daughter Elizabeth. If daughter die without issue her share to wife for life then to Martha Roberts, daughter of Joseph Roberts of Harlow, county of Essex, Kingdom of Great Britain, etc., etc. Executors; William Kenyon and Frederick Rhinelander of City of New York, Merchants, and Robert Carter of ditto, Cabinet Maker. Witnesses; Daniell Parcutt, Francis Child, junior, Francis Child, City and County of New York. s.s. 28 October, 1794, before David Gelston, Surrogate, Oath of Francis Child of said city, gentleman, that he saw testator and other witnesses subscribe a True coyy of original. Attest. David Gelston. Surrogate.

Administration in Prerogative Court of Canterbury to Keene Stables Esquire, attorney, for Dorotha Smith, the widow, and Elizabeth Smith, the daughter, William Kenyon, Frederick Rhinelander and Robert Carter the executors having renounced.

6 February, 1822, administration to John Stables Esq. attorney for Elizabeth Nelson, hertofore Smith, the daughter surviving legatee, now residing at New York. Keene Stables Esq. being deceased. Newcastle, 569.

Lewis Graham of Town of West Chester in the county of West Chester. Will 15 October, 1793; proved 19 December, 1800. All to daughter Margaret at 18 or marriage, except to friend Mrs. Margaret Skinner 100$. My faithful Negro Man Slave named George to be manumitted and estate charged with his support if he pecomes necessitous. Executors: Friends Egbert Benson, John Parkinson, and Thomas Hunt. Witnesses: Samuel Finley, John Burroughs, Peter Bloome. Westchester County Ss 13 December, 1793. Before Peter Bell, Surrogate. Oath of Samuel Finley of town of Westchester Physician. True Copy attest

Peter Bell. At town of Pelham, same day, proved by Thomas Hunt and Egbert Benson. Proved in Prerogative Court of Canterbury, as will of Lewis Graham, late of Pelham in the county of Westchester in North America, by Effingham Lawrence, Attorney for Egbert Benson and Thomas Hunt, two of the executors, living in New York in North America, John Parkinson, the other executor being first summoned and not appearing.

Adderley, 560.

Thomas Crowell, late of the Province of New York in North America, but now resident in the county of Middlesex in the Kingdom of Great Britain. Will 4 April, 1798; proved 24 May, 1800. Executors to sell all goods except cloakes, Lynen, and wearing apparell, pay debts, prove will, and to procure two neat mourning rings of two guineas value, and residue to my son and daughters and children of son Joseph Crowell, deceased, viz., one fifth to son Thomas Crowell of Elizabeth Town in the State of New Jersey in North America, one fifth to daughter Sarah Tayler of Midleton in New Jersey aforesaid, one fifth to daughter Agness Wright of Woodbridge in New Jersey, one fifth to daughter Catherine of Staten Island in New York, and other fifth to Edward Crowell and Catherine Crowell, children of son Joseph Crowell, deceased, etc., etc. Executors to send to son Thomas Crowell full account etc. and cloakes, apparells mourning rings, and all securities except necessary for execution of will, to be packed up for son Thomas Crowell. Executors: Friend Anthony Van Dam of Guilford Street near the Foundling Hospital, Witnesses: Robt. Smith, Edw. Lawrence, No. 26 Princess Street, Cavendish Square. (Probate Act says late a Captain of Kings Militia in City of New York, but of St. James Westminster, Middlesex.

Adderley, 353.

Thomas Bealey of City of New York, Mariner. Will 16 December, 1780; proved 11 October, 1791. All to wife Sarah Bealy executrix. Witnesses: Wm. Ducie, Charles Hart. Bevor, 450.

James Jauncey, late of the City of New York in America, but now of London. Will 24 October, 1787; proved 5 July, 1790. Desire wife Mary Jauncey to receive Bills of Exchange I have by me, vizt; Hibbert & Stevenson 2 bills of Exchange £2211:4s:7d. and Alexander Lindon 3 bills £3163:5s:2d., the whole of 5 bills £5374:9s:9d. as also £7594: 19s:5d. in cash in hands of Messrs. Sergeant Chambers & Co, whole amount £12,969:9s:2d. sterling. To son William, son John Jauncey, and daughter Mary Jauncey, all monies in public funds in this Kingdom in 5 per cent put in by Messrs. Thos. Coutts & Co., Messrs. Drummonds & Co., Messrs. Sargeant Chambers and Co., and Messrs Davies Newman & Comp'y, amounting to sum of £23,608: 5s:1d. as also £8470: 16s:7d. in 3 p cents, cons^d. put in by Messrs. Thos. Coutts & Co., Mr. John Blackburn & Messrs. Drummonds, these 5 p cents and 3 p cents in my own name, and receive dividends, also £3,500 Bank Stock put in by Messrs Drummond for which they receive dividends, also £3,299: 7s:11d. in 3 p cents put in by Messrs. Thos.

Coutts & Co., who receive dividends, all amounting to £38,874: 9s:7d. equally to three children. Out of large claim I expect to receive from Govermen for Bonds and Mortgages, £1000, to son William, £1000 to son John Jauncey and rest to son William and son John, and daughter Mary Jauncey, reason for difference between John and William is that William has saved some of his estate in New York and son John lost his. Executors: Thomas Coutts, Esq. of the Strand, Sons William Jauncey, and John Jauncey and daughter Mary Jauncey. Witnesses: John Relph, Leadenhall Street, John Warren, Sandys Street, John Todhunter, Leadenhall Street. [Proved by son William Jauncey one of the executors, reserving to Thomas Coutts, John Jauncey, Esq. and Mary Jauncey, Spinster, other executors.] Bishop, 339.

William Hughes, formerly belonging to his Majesty's ships *Augusta*, Liverpool, and despatch boat, late Quarter Master of his Majesty's ship *Delaware*, but at the Hospital at New York, in the pay of his Majesty's Navy, a Batchelor, deceased. Administration 25 May, 1781, to John Hughes lawful attorney of Mary Byrne, formerly Hughes (wife of John Byrne) mother of deceased, now residing at Parkgate in the county of Chester.
Admon Act Book, 1781 (Register's Seat.)

*Edmund Winslow, late of New York and Chaplain in his Majesty's ship *Thames*, Clerk. Administration 22 December, 1781, to Gilbert Deblois attorney for widow Jane Isabel Winslow, now residing at New York. Ditto.

David Currie otherwise Curry, late belonging to his Majesty's ship *Vulture*, but at Sandy Hook, a Seaman in Pay of his Majesty's Navy, a Batchelor deceased. Administration 3 March, 1781, to John Currie, lawful Attorney of Isobel Currie, formerly Findlay, widow, mother and next of kin of deceased, now residing at Leith in North Britain. Ditto.

Malcolm Mac Isaac, late of New York in North America' Batchelor deceased. Administration 24 March, 1781, to Father Archibald Mac Isaac. Ditto.

Peter Derisme late of City of New York in North America, Batchelor, deceased. Administration 7 April, 1781, to sister Elizabeth Beaufile Duval (wife of John Duval), Anne Derisme, widow, mother and next of kin, being cited and not appearing. Ditto.

John Clyff, late belonging to his Majesty's Sloop *Vulture* at Long Island in North America, seaman in the Pay of his Majesty's Navy and Batchelor, deceased. Administration 22 February, 1781, to sister Elizabeth Dawkins, wife of Thomas Dawkins, next of kin. Ditto.

John Waller, Esq, late Major of Brigade in the Provincial Forces under the command of General Oliver De Lancey at Jamaica in Long Island, Esquire, Batchelor, deceased. Administration 19 February, 1781, to father Jacob Waller. Ditto.

* Edward, not Edmund.

William Rolfe, late of New York in America and belonging to the Merchant ship *Achilles*, Batchelor, deceased. Administration 23 January, 1781, to Brother Thomas Rolfe next of kin.

Ditto.

Joseph Troheir, formerly of Liverpool, county Lancashire, but late of New York in America, a bachelor, deceased. Administration 24 October, 1781, to sister Hannah Scotte (wife of James Scott).

Ditto.

Edmund Herbert, late of Minchinhampton, County Gloucester, but at New York, deceased. Administration 18 August, 1781, to Anna Maria Herbert his widow.

Ditto (Stubb-Seal.

NEW YORK GLEANINGS IN ENGLAND,

Including "Gleanings," by Henry F. Waters, not before printed.

CONTRIBUTED BY LOTHROP WITHINGTON,
30 Little Russell St., W. C., London.

Charles Mackintosh of the City of New York. Will, February 1747/8; proved 3 February 1749/50. My son Phineas and Daughter Susanna to be maintained out of my estate till they are 21 or married. Estate between my wife Susanna, son Phineas, and daughter Susanna, one quarter to wife and daughter each, one half to son. Executors: Wife and Friends Stephen Bayard of New York and Richard Alsop of New Town, Long Island. Witnesses: Elisha Parker, Par. Parmynter, Dud. Crofts. Administration of goods of Charles Mackintosh, formerly of New York, late of St. Martins in Fields, deceased on High Seas, to John Fell, husband of Susanna Fell als Mackintosh, relict of deceased, now residing in New York, former letters granted in June last to Alexander Mackintosh, as dying intestate, being revoked.

Greenley, 51.

George Shipley, City of New York, State of New York, Cabinet maker. Will 21 December 1796; proved 16 May 1804. All goods to Hannah my wife, late the wife of William Lee, deceased. Executrix: Wife Hannah Shipley. Witnesses: Francis Child, Senior, Dennis Heely, Francis Child. Proved in City of New York 12 October 1803, oath taken of witnesses. Administration in Preprogative Court of Canterbury granted to William Remington Esq, attorney of Hannah Shipley, now resident in New York.

Haseltine, 359.

William Burnett, Governor of New York and New Jersey. Will 6 December 1727; proved 9 July 1730. To be buried at the Chapel of the Fort at New York near my wife Mary and one of my children, if I die in New York Province My Brother in Law David Mitchell and my sister Mary his wife to sell my property in Holland and England and my share in the produce of my Father's History, and to satisfy all that remains due to the estate of my late Brother Gilbert from me; also my executors to send over to England all my books and pamphlets to be sold and applied in like manner.   My son Gilbert Burnett to be sent over to them, and the residue of above estate to him.   Gold and Silver Medals bearing images of King George the First, Princess Sophia, and King George, II, and the gilt Tea Table given to my father by Princess Sophia, to son Gilbert and heirs male as a memorial that my father's faithfull services to the protestant succession in that Illustrious House were well accepted before their accession to Throne of Great Britain.   Property in America to children, William, Mary, and Thomas by my late wife Mary Vanhorn.   Executors and guardians of three youngest children: Abraham Vanhorn and Mary his wife. Witnesses: Jo: Bovin, John Hasholt, Stephen Debtors.   Auber, 183.

NEW YORK GLEANINGS IN ENGLAND,

Including "Gleanings," by Henry F. Waters, not before printed.

CONTRIBUTED BY LOTHROP WITHINGTON,

30 Little Russell St., W. C., London.

George Forrester of the City of New York, Mariner. Will 4 August 1748; proved 14 February 1750/51. To William Holt of New York, Vintner, my friend and executor, all shares in the *Sunderland*, man of war, and the *Antelope*, privateer of New York. Witnesses: Charles Gilmore, Peter van Vechter, John Bryant.

Busby, 45.

John Rush of New York in America, Hatter, and by God's grace shall return thither again. Will 13 May 1743; proved 1 June, 1743. To my wife, now at New York, all my wearing Apparell and Utensils and Stock in Trade that is now in my possession in London, except the hatboxes, they to be sold and the money to be sent her with £10 value in copper halfpence. To Edward Daniel of Redmaid Lane, County Middlesex, Cooper, £20. Rest to my son John and daughter Sarah when 21. Executor: said Edward Daniel. Witnesses: Ann Way, James Burn, John Perry.

Boycott, 208.

Margaret White of East Greenwich, county Kent, Spinster. Will 5 June 1766; proved 12 January 1767. All my copyhold lands and Estate in Manor of Ealing otherwise Zeling, county Middlesex, to my nephew Thomas White, son of my late deceased Brother, Thomas White of Serjeants Inn, Esq. If he dies without any issue, I give the said estate to my Nephew and two Nieces, children of my late deceased Brother Francis White, who are now living in New York in North America. To my servant Martha Hopton, all my clothes, and £20. To my nephew Thomas White, and Joseph Blisset £500 Old South Sea Annuity, part of £800 standing in my name, in trust for my said servant Martha Hopton. Residue and all reversions to said nephew Thomas White, now living in Southampton. Executors: Nephew Thomas White and Mr. Joseph Blisset of Six Clerks Office, London, gentleman. Witnesses: A. Mole, Andw. Hatt, Walter Vincent.

Legard, 31.

158

Enoch Stephenson, City of New York, Province of New York in America. Will 3 Febuary 1735/6; proved 1 December 1753. To my wife Catharine Stephenson, all my jewels, household goods, Negro Slaves, namely Maria and her son and daughter, Quaco and Sarah, Qua a negro Boy and Cato a negro girl. All the rest and residue of my estate real and personal to my wife Catherine Stephenson, and my children, viz: Enoch, Catherin, Isabella, John, and Richard, and to such child or children as may hereafter be born to me, share and share alike. If I die in New York, my executors to call in all my estates and to sell the house I bought of John Price, situated on Port Royal, Jamaica, and also two Lots of land I bought of David Jemison in King Street in Eastward part of New York. Executors and Guardians to my children: my wife Catherine, my brother Pennington Stephenson, at present residing in England, Peter Valet and Joseph Robinson, both of New York, merchants, and if my children should go to Jamaica during their minority, I appoint my friend Colln. Edwin Sandys their guardian there. Witnesses: Gul^n Verplanck, Abraham Van Horne, Junr., Willm. Hewtin.   Searle, 325.

Susannah Thurnam, widow and relict of Francis Thurnam, late of the City of New York, America, Merchant, deceased. Will 23 August 1758; proved 26 January 1760. To my daughter Elizabeth Thurnam all my wearing apparrell; if she die in infancy, between my two sisters in law, Elizabeth, wife of Nicholas Roosevelt, and Gertrug Thurnam, that is the silks and Linen, the calico and stuffs, to my Aunts Agnis Lockwood, wife of Joseph Lockwood, half, Grace Williams, wife of William Williams, one quarter, and Sarah Brown, wife of Isaac Brown, one quarter. My fee simple estates in England or America as follows: one half to my son Richardson Thurnam, and one half to my daughter Elizabeth. In case of death of both children without issue, I give four equal fifth parts to Brothers and sisters in law, Ralph Thurnam, John Thurnam, Elizabeth Roosevelt, and Gertrug Thurnam, and the remaining one fifth to my Uncle and Aunts, Joseph Lockwood, Grace Williams, and Sarah Brown. My leases in the City of London or elsewhere in England to my executors in trust for my son and daughter. Executors: Brother in law John Thurnam, of City of New York, Merchant. Nicholas Roosevelt, of the said City, Goldsmith, and Dirck Schuyler, of said City, Merchant. Witnesses: Thomas Pettit, Abraham Bussing, John McKesson. Proved by John Thurnam, reserving to the other executors.   Lynch, 40.

Mary Boudinot, living in parish of St. Giles in the fields, Middlesex, Spinster. Will 9 July 1712; proved 26 May 1716. To poor of the French Church called Greek Church one guinea. To my nephew Elias Boudinot, living in New York, one guinea, and to all his brothers and sisters one guinea each. To John Belin my nephew and to his daughter who is at Rotterdam one guinea. To James Belin, son of Allard Belin, my nephew, deceased, one guinea. To Mary Belin, my grandniece, daughter of Mr. James Belin and Jane Montague, the rent of 38 livres Tournois French money upon a house at Marons Boat in the Province of Xaintonge in France. To my grandnephew Allard Belin, merchant in London, and to his sister Jane Mary Belin, £60 each. Residuary Legatee and Executrix: My grandniece and goddaughter Mary Belin, daughter of Mr. James Belin. Witnesses: Stephen Brigand, Anthony Sion, Isaac Delpech, Not. Pub. 1712. This is truly Translated out of French by me Isaac Delpech, Notary Public.   Fox, 92.

Gilbert Burnet, Esquire, now in London, Eldest son of William Burnet, late Governor of New York, deceased. Will 17 June 1762; proved 21 June 1762. To my friend, Mrs. Jane Walton of Scotland Yard, Westminster, Spinster, all Interest Money now due to me in Holland and America, or elsewhere, and all my personal estate. To my son Thomas Burnet, now Apprentice to Mr. ——, Apothecary, all the rest and residue of my real estate. Executrix: said Jane Walton. Witnesses: Manuel Ielees, Richard Lovett, Tolson Banting.   St. Eloy, 234.

Peter Wraxall, at present residing in City of New York. Will 10 September 1759; proved 13 February 1762. To my honoured father and friend Mr. John Wraxall of Bristol in England £20. To my sister Mrs. Ann Wraxall, by my father's first wife and my own mother, £400. To my sister Mrs. Mary Wraxall of Bristol £50. If Ann die before my decease, £300 of the above £400 to my niece Elizabeth Wraxall, daughter of my Brother Richard Wraxall, £100 to my said sister Mary. To my friend Sir William Johnson, Baronet, £20. Life and Death are the indubitable appointments of a Wise Righteous, and Benevolent God. To his Mercy through the intercession and merits of my Lord and Saviour Jesus Christ, I comitt my soul and my most beloved wife and friend. I desire I may be buried without any kind of Expense which may border upon Ostentation. Executrix and Residuary Legatee: Wife Elizabeth Wraxall. Secretary's Office New York, 10 September, 1759. Anne Devisme, John Watts, and Beverley Robinson, make oath to truth of depositions and Elizabeth Wraxall is granted execution. [Signed] Geo: Banyar. Anne Devisme, wife of Peter Devisme being a sister of Elizabeth Wraxall, relict of Peter Wraxall.   St. Eloy, 86.

Sir Henry Moore of the Island of Jamaica, Bart, at this time his Majesty's Governor in Chief of the Province of New York in North America. Will 11 April 1769; proved 7 June 1770. All my estates, real and personal in Jamaica and Great Britain, to Henry Dawkins, Esquire, of Standlinch, County Wilts, Edward Morant, Esquire, of Pilewell, County Hants, Edward Long, Esquire, of Jamaica, sole Judge of the Court of Vice-Admiralty in that Island, and John Gordon, Senior, of St. Mary's parish, Jamaica, practitioner in Physic, in trust to pay my debts, and then to my wife Catharina Maria Moore £600 per annum out of my estate of Moore Hall, parish of St. Mary, as by marriage indenture of 11 January 1750/51, and at her decease to my child, John Henry ·Moore, and his heirs. To my daughter Susanna

Jane, now wife of Captain Alexander Dickson of H. M. 16th
Regiment of Foot, £3000. Residue to my said son, whose guardian I appoint my wife Catharina Maria Moore. Witnesses:
Fransis Child, Robt. Hull, Phil. Livingston, Junior.

Jenner, 237.

Christopher Billop, prisoner in the Fleet prison in the parish
of St. Brides in the City of London, gentleman. Will 25 April
1724; proved 24 April 1725. My plantation in Bentley and Manor
of Bentley and Mansion house, etc, in province of New York,
upon Stratton Island I give to my daughter Mary, now wife of
the Reverend William Skinner, Clerk, for life, and then to her
heirs Male, in default to Christopher Farmar, second son of my
son in law Thomas Farmar, he to pay £200 New York money to
every daughter of said Mary Skinner, daughter Mary to leave
to Christopher or whoever inherits, five good Feather beds,
sheets, etc, curtains, and Vallences, pewter and woden ware for
six people, Table linen, 5 pair Iron Dogs, five shovells and Tongs,
five Chambers, Table in each romms. Seats used in that Country,
Utensills for Dairy of ten Cows, Casks in Cellar for Cyder, four
horses, six oxen fit for ploughs, ploughs, harness, etc, ten Milch
Cows and Calves, three steers of three years old, four of two
years, four Heifers of two years, ten yearlings a Bull of two years,
ten Hogs of 12 months, two Sows and a Boar, 100 ewes and a
Ram, Ten weathers of two years, and   , whoever inherits
to take the surname [sic] of Billop without the mixture or addition of any other Surname whatever. If Christopher dies, to
Thomas Farmar, third son; if he dies, to Brook Farmar, fourth
son; if he die, to Robert Farmar, fifth son; if he die, to Samuel
Farmar, sixth son; if he die, to William Farmar, seventh son.
My plantation near Rareton River, known as Junions Land in
province of New York to my daughter Anne Farmar, wife of
said Thomas Farmar, and her heirs male excepting Jaspar Farmar, eldest son of said son in law Thomas Farmar, to whom I
give only £20. Out of money due to me from Sr Alexander
Rigby's, Knt, estate late deceased, amounting by this time to
£5200, I give to Mr. James Fittar of London, Merchant, £200,
and to my Nephew Thomas Billop of Deptford, county Kent,
£500. To said William Skinner, clerk, £500. The residue after
payment of my debts to the younger children of Thomas Farmar.
To my Neice Hannah Booth, £50. Executors: James Fittar and
Nephew Thomas Billop. Trustee: William Skinner. Witnesses:
Tho. Frank, Wm Abell, Wm Abbott, John Baker, Edward Games.
Memorandum 16 May 1724, Whereas but £20 given at first to
Hannah, made £50 by testator. Witnesses, ditto.

Romney, 80.

Thomas Cooper of the parish of Matfellon als. White Chapel,
county Middlesex, also Citizen and Merchant taylor of London.
Will 1 February 1714/15; proved 1 February 1715/16. To my
Brother Robert Cooper £125, a silver cup and silver poringer,
also 15 shares in the Company for Smelting [written "selling"
in first entries] down Lead with Pit Coal and Sea Coal, and after

161

his decease 5 of the shares to Thomas Prigg, son of Robert and Anne Prigg, and 5 to Mary Payne his sister, wife of John Payne; also I give to him all money owing to me from John Fisher, Doctor in Colchester. To Thomas, son of Robert and Anne Prigg, deceased, 10 shares in aforenamed Company. To George Whitehead £5. To Thomas Pistow, Esquire, Hatter, £30. To Martha Collier, Wife of William Collier, Butcher, £10. To Elizabeth Bowing, wife of Edward Bowing of Boram, £5. To Ann Wilkinson, my servant, £5. To Thomas Pitstow, Esquire, and Mary Payne £40. To John Knight £10, all my shares in the said Company for Smelting down Lead and all my interest in the New Pensilvania Company, and all the rest and residue of my estate in England and New Yorke and East and West Jersey in America to Thomas Pitstow and John Knight, in trust for Mary Payne, wife of said John Payne. Executors: Thomas Pitstow and Mary Payne. Witnesses: Tho. Butler, Daniel White, Susanna Butler. Proved by the affirmation of the executors.

Fox, 22.

Ann Crookston, of the parish of Saint George in the East in the County of Middlesex, widow. Will 10 September 1750; proved 23 February 1753. To Eldest Son, Samuel Crookston of East Ham, Essex, Shipwright, 1s. To youngest son, John Crookston, now at Eastchester beyond the Seas, 1s. Rest to Granddaughter, Mary Ann Goadby, of St. George's, Spinster, executrix. Witnesses: Jane Armin, Jas Bennett.

Commissary of London,
Register No. 77 (1753–1754.)

William Mountgomery, late of New York. Will 1 September 1799; proved 16 July 1782. To loving friend, Margaret Mountgomery, daughter of Samuel Mountgomery, Merchant in Armagh, £50., if Mr. Andrew Thompson of Newry in Ireland has not paid the same, but if paid [not written above, sic] to trustees, etc. To Cousin, William Mountgomery, son to Mr. John Mountgomery, my silver watch, and after my brother Joseph, and James 2 bonds given up remaining part of rent and personal estate (except moities are in Mr. Lightbodys) to four brothers, John and Joseph, James and Robert Montgomery. If I die in Mr. Lightbodys' house, to Elizabeth Lgihtbody best bed etc. To Mrs. Agnes Lightbody 100 dollars, looking glass, candlestick, etc. To Margaret Mountgomery, daughter to Samuel Mountgomery, merchant in Armagh, my chinen bowel, not tricked, and diamond ring. Executors: Brothers, James and Robert Mountgomery. Witnesses: William Edmondson, Gabriel Lightbody. Will of said William Mountgomery, formerly of New York, but late of Newingdon Precinct in America. Proved by brother James of Armagh, executor, reserving to Robert.

Prerogative Court of Ireland,
Will Book No. 98 (1782), folio 68.

162

NEW YORK GLEANINGS IN ENGLAND,

Including "Gleanings," by Henry F. Waters, not before printed.

CONTRIBUTED BY LOTHROP WITHINGTON,
30 Little Russell St., W. C., London.

Edward Amhurst of Annapolis Royal in America, Esquire, but now residing in Cecil Street in the Strand in the County of Middlesex. Will 5 June, 1754; proved 25 June, 1754. All to my wife Mary Amhurst of Annapolis Royal. Executors: my wife Mary Amhurst and my friends Phillip Bromfield and Thomas Blanure of Lombard Street, London. Testator being seized with a paralytic stroke put his mark. Witnesses: E. Winniett, J. Morgan, F. Monson.
Penfold, 157.

William Cosby, Esq., Governor of New York and New Jersey in America. Will 9 March 1735-6; proved 3 July, 1739. The tract of land purchased of the Germans called the Manor of Cosby on both sides of the Mohaeke River in Albany County to my two sons William and Henry. One third part of my lands in Rochester in Ulster County and the mines there to my wife Grace Cosby and the other two parts to my said two sons. My House and ground in Soho Square, London to my wife. My house at St. Leonards Hills and lands adjoining to my wife for life and at her decease to my son William. Residuary Legatee and Executrix: My wife Grace Cosby. Witnesses: James De Lancey, John Felton, Charles Williams, Will Cosby, Joseph Murray.   Henchman, 145.

Abraham Duane, Commander of his Majesty's Sloop, the *Beaver*. Will 3 January 1767; proved 28 August 1767. Sole Legatee and Executor: my Brother Cornelius Duane of the City of New York in North America. Witnesses: Richard Wells, David Hunter, George Dawford. Proved by William Neate, attorney for Cornelius Duane now residing at New York in North America.   Legard, 303.

Augustine Gordon of St. Johns Wappen, county of Middlesex, Chyrurgeon being now bound out in a voyage to sea. Will 2 November 1705; proved 8 December 1712. All my lands and estate in America I give to my wife Margarett for life and then at her decease to my son William Gordon. Residuary Legatee and Executrix: my wife Margaret. Witnesses: Joseph Haden in Wapping, Margaret Mearillon in Wapping near the Hermitage, Ephraim Bromwich, Scrivener in Virginia Street.
                                   Barnes, 235.

Hector Mackenzie, late of the Town of Bath on the Cohorton River in the County of Steuben and state of New York in the United States of North America, but now living at No. 63 Hatton Garden, county Middlessex, Esq. Will 16 October 1802; proved 5 August 1807. To William MacCra of Cree Bridge in County of Kirkubright, Galloway, Esq., and Daniel Wilson Davison of Clements Inn, Gentleman, all lands in the County of Steuben, opposite Mud Creek, formerly surveyed for Benjamin Patterson, two lots in Township No. 4, formerly surveyed by William Kersey, land in Township No. 5, surveyed by William Kersey for Hector Mackenzie which were confirmed by indentures made in September 1800 between Charles Williamson of Bath and me, also tract of land in Township No. 6 abutting on Crooked Lake, by an indenture made by Peter Faulkener of East Town in Pennsilvania, also land from William Dunn of Bath and land from Charles Cameron, also a messuage in Morris street in Bath, land from Finlay McClure, and all my money and goods in trust for my wife Diana, during her lifetime, and then after her decease for my children, to be equally divided among them when 21. Executors in trust of my will and guardians to my children: the said William McCra and Daniel Wilson Davison. Witnesses: F. Gogerly 2 Mount Roe, Lambeth, Elizabeth Mackenzie, Wandsworth Road, H. M. O. Mackenzie, same place.
                                   Lushington, 685.

William Smith. Will March 5 1755; proved 3 May, 1756. To James Skinner Esq. Sir, immediately after my decease its my desire that you and Mr. Adrian Philips become possessors of my shallop *Charming Peggy* of Bonacord. I charge my estate with the payment of two hundredweight of refined wax to Doctor Robert Jeffreys, ditto to Mr. Tobias Lisle. What Mr. Lewis Voss is indebted to me I forgive him. To "Crony 12 cans of such money as he chooses." My slave Angella I make free and give her for her sole use my slave man Thomas and my slave woman Domingo. I give my slave woman Tombang to Leestia, Rest of my goods to be remitted to Johnson and Fothergill, Merchants of London for the benefit of my friends. Executors: Governor Mr. Skinner and Mr. Adrian Phillips and all accounts depending between you (Mr. Skinner) Mr. Louree and my self I refer to you settling. At Bracoe Port in presence of Robert Jefferys, Daniel Crony. Glazier, 150.

GENEALOGICAL NOTES FROM THE HIGH COURT OF ADMIRALTY EXAMINATIONS.

By J. R. HUTCHINSON.

Richard Hooper, of Wapping, sailor, deposes 15 Sept., 1621, on behalf of Francis and Thomas Challoner, creditors of David Middleton, that when in March, 1619, the *Jonathan*, of London, lay in the Downs bound for Virginia, David Middleton and his two sons, Lewknor and Arthur Middleton, were, by order of the Virginia Company, put on board her to be transported to that plantation. On the voyage out David Middleton died.

Samuel Moll, of Rochell, in France, *sed moram trahens in Virginia*, chirurgeon, aged 41, deposes 11 June, 1623, that he does not know Hester Hamor, but in January last there was a coffin made to bury the dead corps of one Thomas Hamor, which departed this life at James Town in Virginia, by one Nathaniel Jeffreyes, a joyner dwelling there, who carried the coffin to the house where Hamor lay dead and put his dead corps into the same, and that afternoon the coffin, with the dead corps in it, was carried to the common burying ground and there interred. This he knows because he was then one of the surgeons of James Town and lived in the house with the joyner. Denis Davies of St. Giles Cripplegate, barber-surgeon, aged 55, who lay sick at James Town when Hamor died, corroborates; and Thomas Edwards of St. Mary Aldermary, salter, aged 34, deposes 19 June, 1623, that Thomas Hamor died in the house of his brother, Capt. Ralph Hamor.

Stephen Bolton of Wapping, sailor, aged 40, deposes 12 May, 1625, that William Edwards and James Boydon went sailors to New England in the *Unity*, and remained there. Tobias White of Ratcliffe, master of the *Unity*, aged 35, deposes 13 May, 1625, that the *Unity* arrived at New England 25 June, 1624. In Boydon's room he brought home to England one Gregory Castle, a lusty young man.

Thomas Piddock of London, merchant, aged 27, deposes 2 May, 1628, that in June and July, 1624, this examinate was at Menhegen in New England, with Edmund Dockett and William Pomfrett, as factors for Abraham Jennings of Plymouth, and Ambrose Jennings and William Crosse of London, merchants.

Robert Penn, of Virginia, planter, aged 25, deposes 6 May, 1629. concerning the ship *George*, consigned to William Ewens, at his plantation in Virginia.

Agnes Kempton, of St. George's, Southwark, widow, deposes 6 Nov., 1629, that the 46 hogsheads of tobacco laden at Virginia in the *Anne* of London, Peter Andrewes master, and consigned unto the examinate by William Perrye, overseer of the last will of her son John Rilye, deceased, did belong to and were laden for the account of her son and his partners, and that this examinate has no interest therein but as executrix of her son's will. Isabell, wife of William Perry, merchant of Virginia, aged 40, deposes 26 August, 1629, that about Christmas last one John Rily of London, merchant, died in the house of examinate's husband in Virginia. Amongst his effects was found a writing of copartnership, dated 25 July, 1627, and signed by William Crowther, Charles Whichcot and John Rily.

Isaac Manstridge, of London, grocer, deposes 6 August, 1629, that about a year since he went purser in the *Truelove*, Thomas Gibbs captain, on a voyage to Virginia. There went in the same ship one Christopher Young, who had bound himself apprentice to Gibbs. Desiring to stay in Virginia, Young entreated Gibbs to turn him over to Thomas Burbage, an English merchant who went out in the same ship as factor for some London merchants, which Gibbs did.

George Preston of St. Botolph's, Aldgate, cooper, aged 45, deposes 16 Nov., 1622, that the letter beginning "Uncle Preston, my best love," was brought from Virginia by a passenger, one Goodwife Moyses, who came home in (Edmund) Gardiner's ship the *Seaflower*, which letter was sent to this examinate, from Virginia by one Maurice Thompson and is all written in his own hand. Thompson did write other letters at the same time to his father, dwelling in Hartfordshire. Richard Grove of St. Olave's, Southwark, navigator, aged 38, deposes 10 Dec. 1633, that Mr. George Thompson and his brother Maurice Thompson have traded to Virginia for many years.

Willian Tucker of Redriffe co. Surrey, Esq., aged 44, deposes 17 June, 1634, that he hath used to trade and send goods and passengers to Virginia these three and twenty years, and within that time hath lived in Virginia and is one of the Council there. He and his father before him were (Customs) searchers at Gravesend.

William Pearse of Boston in New England, sailor, aged 43, deposes 14 June, 1635, that, having known Sir Richard Saltinstall these six years, he was requested by Mr. John Humphreys, one of Sir Richard's partners. to look out for and buy a ship for a voyage to New England. With the advice of John Taylor, shipwright, he bought the *Thomas* afterwards the *Richard* of London, Nicholas Trerise, master. There went in her 20 passengers, who were to pay for their passage five pounds a head.

John Gibbs, dwelling at Floure de Hundred in Virginia, planter, aged 35, deposes 16 June, 1635, that on the 26th of December last, he being then at a place called Waynoke in Virginia, at the house of William Emmerson a planter there, the said Emmerson did deliver unto him a schedule of tobaccoes to be shipped on board the *Robert Bonadventure* of London, Richard Gilson master, then lying at Point Comfort, for the account of Mr. Lewis Evans of Woodstreet, London, merchant. The schedule was written by Arthur Harwood, a kinsman of Emmerson, and a duplicate thereof was sent into England by one Courtney, who returned passenger in the said ship, this examinate returning in the *Defence.**

Hugh Bullocke of All Saints Barking, Esq., aged 59, deposes 23 Jan., 1635-6, that he came passenger in the *John and Dorothy* from Virginia, where he is one of the Council of State.

Ambrose Calthorp of St. Dunstan's in the West, gent, aged 33, deposes 4 March, 1635-6, that he came passenger from Virginia in the *John and Dorothy.* He further deposes 16 May, 1636, that on the 11th of January last he had in the ship *Constance,* then and now delayed at Ilfracombe in her voyage to Virginia, four servants, namely, William Gillam, John Elwoode, Thomas Hudson and William Hulett, of whom Hulett and Hudson have since run.

William Fitter of Mariland in the West Indies, gent, aged 38, deposes 7 April, 1636, that in June or July last was three years, the *Dove* pinnace was set out from London on a voyage to Maryland by Cecil, Lord Baltimore. Leonard Calvert, governor of Maryland, and Jeremy Hawley and Thomas Cornwallis, two of the commissioners for that plantation, went out in the *Ark,* which accompanied the pinnace. Examinate was formerly servant to the Lady Stafford at Stafford Castle in Staffordshire, then servant to Capt. Thomas Cornwallis, and is now lodging with Mistress Cornwallis at the captain's house in Holborn.

Sir John Harvye, Knt., governor of the colony of Virginia, deposes 9 May, 1836, aged 54.

Richard Preice of St. Mary Bowe, scrivenor, aged 29, deposes 6 May, 1636, that about October last, at the request of John Smyth, citizen and draper of London, dwelling in the parish of St. Botolph without Aldgate, he did pay unto John Thierrye of London, merchant, at his house in Turne Wheele Lane, the sum of twelve pounds for the passage of John Cooke and Henry Johnson, covenant servants of Smyth, to Virginia.

Charles Dawson of Flushing in Zealand, Esq., aged 42, deposes 16 May, 1636, that he is sending to Virginia in the *Constance* a servant called Henry Morrell.

Richard Rudderford of Virginia, planter, deposes 16 May, 1636, aged 40.

Thomas Palmer of St. Giles Cripplegate, merchant-tailor, aged 35, deposes 17 May, 1636, that he is sending two servants to Virginia in the *Constance,* (whose names are Griffith Mamer and John Palmer, son of this examinate.)

John Digby of St. Andrew Hubberd, citizen and pewterer of London, aged 44, deposes 17 May, 1636, that he has hired a passage in the *Constance,* to Virginia, for one Sampson Alkin.†

---

* Tobacco was at this time worth tenpence a pound in London, " cleere of all charges."

† In the same vessel Digby shipped to Virginia a quantity of goods, consisting of leather drawers, leather stockings, and Spanish leather caps, pur chased of Praise (God) Barbone of St. Bride's, Fleet-street, leatherseller.

Jerome (Jeremy) Hawley of St. Dunstan's in the West, Esq., aged 45, deposes 17 May, 1636, that he was at St. Maries in Maryland with Leonard Calvert and Thomas Cornwallis.

Maurice Thompson of St. Andrew Hubberd, merchant, deposes 3 Jan., 1636-7, aged 32.

Anthony Jones of Warwick Squiocke in Virginia, merchant, deposes 21 March, 1636-7, aged 32.

Capt. Richard Bradshaw, of St. Margaret's, Westminster, deposes 5 May, 1637, aged 41.

John Rosier, inhabiting at Waricsquoyacke in Virginia, clerk, aged 34, deposes 26 June, 1637, that about three or four years since one William Hutchinson, dying in Virginia, made his will and appointed his father, Henry Hutchinson, living in England, to be his executor, and Richard Bennett, Anthony Jones and Robert Sabine overseers. Examinate buried Hutchinson. Henry Hutchinson came over to Virginia to take possession of his son's goods, and likewise died there, whereupon the court appointed Thomas Burbage administrator. James Stone, dwelling in the house of Thomas Freer in Tower-street, merchant, aged 26, deposes 5 July, 1637, that he came into Virginia about a month after the death of Hutchinson the younger, was there when the father died, which was about eleven months later, and has seen the will of William Hutchinson on record in the court of Virginia. Robert Sabyn of Wades Mill, co. Hertford, tallow chandler, aged 45, deposes 25 August, 1638, as to a commission having been sent into Virginia in August, 1637, for the examination of witnesses there in a suit between Hutchinson, plaintiff, and Richard Bennett, Anthony Jones and this examinate, defendants.

George Menefie, an inhabitant of James Town in Virginia, but now resident in the parish of St. Hellen's, London, merchant, aged 40, deposes 3 August, 1637, that he has traded to and dwelt in Virginia these sixteen years.

Capt. Samuel Mathew of Denby in Virginia deposes 29 Jan., 1637-8, on behalf of Joshua Mullard, gent, and Elizabeth his wife, relict and executrix of Capt. William Holmes, gent, late of Virginia, deceased.

John Lillie of Yorke in Virginia, planter, deposes 4 June, 1638, aged 30.

Jenkyn Williams of Yorke in Virginia, planter, deposes 8 June, 1638, aged 23.

Stephen Webb of James City in Virginia, planter, deposes 23 June, 1638, aged 39.

Thomas Browne of Kingsman Necke in Virginia, planter, deposes 3 July, 1638, aged 33.

Richard Perrin of All Saints Barking, late planter in Virginia, aged 26, deposes 10 July, 1638, that he still has land in Virginia.

Oliver Downe of Cheese Cake in Virginia, planter, deposes 17 July, 1638, aged 46.

GENEALOGICAL NOTES FROM THE HIGH COURT OF ADMIRALTY EXAMINATIONS.

By J. R. Hutchinson.

The evidence of witnesses taken before the High Court of Admiralty, between the years 1620 and 1700, is preserved in forty registers, of large folio size and great thickness, containing, on a rough estimate, 20,000 examinations and *ex parte* depositions. The deponents are drawn from practically every class of society and every part of the commercial world, though seafaring men largely predominate. When litigation touched a particular colony, as, for instance, New England or Virginia, witnesses from that colony were heard as a matter of course. Every deposition thus taken is signed, nearly all state the deponent's name, occupation, place of residence and age, while many disclose that most vital of all clues—where the deponent was born. The genealogical value of the following extracts, relating exclusively to the American "plantations," is therefore obvious, but it should not be forgotten that numerous personal allusions to deponents appear in the examinations which cannot be given here owing to restrictions of space.

William Webb of London, merchant, deposes 17 July, 1620, aged 55. He has been "husband" to the Virginia Company for these seven years.

Ferdinando Sheppard of Great Rowleright, co. Oxon, gent, deposes 6 March, 1620-21, aged 22. He is brother to (?Thomas) Shepherd* and brother-in-law to John Farrer, Deputy of the Virginia Company.

Ralph Greene of East Smithfield, smith, deposes 22 Sept., 1622.†

William Johnson of Langford, Wilts, gent, deposes 13 Feb., 1622-3, aged 32. He is servant to Edward, Lord Gorges, owner of the *Prophet Daniel,* now at Poole on a voyage to New England.

---

* The Christian name is omitted here, but a Thomas Shepherd was a member of the Virginia Company.
† Perhaps that Ralph Greene who was later of Boston, N. E.

Samuel Moll of Rochell in France, *sed moram trahens in Virginia,* chirurgeon, deposes 11 June, 1623, aged 41.

Henry Tawney of Winchcum, co. Gloucester, barber-surgeon, deposes 11 July, 1623, aged 29. He went to Virginia in the *Neptune* with Earl De la Warre, to whom he was surgeon.

Anthony Stodderd of St. Michael le Querne, linen-draper, deposes 12 Sept., 1623, aged 53.*

William Peirce of Ratcliffe, sailor, deposes 17 Nov., 1624, aged 33. He was recently at New England, as master of the *Anne* of London.

Benedict Morgan of Plymouth in New England, sailor, deposes 17 Nov., 1624, aged 27.

Robert Cushman of Rosemary Lane, London, yeoman, deposes 18 Nov., 1624, aged 45. He is "husband" for the Company of Planters in New England.

James Shirley of the City of London, goldsmith, deposes 20 Nov., 1624, aged 33. He is treasurer of the New England Company.

Stephen Bolton of Wapping, sailor, deposes 12 May, 1625, that William Edwards went sailor to New England in the *Unity,* Tobias White master, in March, 1623-4, and remained there.

Clement Campion of Limehouse, mariner, deposes 18 May, 1632, aged 34.†

Edward Collins of Chilworth, co. Surrey, gent, deposes 6 Dec., 1632, aged 34.‡

Thomas Gwynn of St. Peter's, Paul's Wharf, citizen and dyer of London, deposes 9 April, 1633, aged 32.§

George Richardson of Wapping, sailor, deposes 6 June, 1633, aged 26.‖

Theophilus Eaton of St. Stephen's, Coleman Street, merchant, deposes 28 June, 1633, aged 43.¶

Benjamin Gillam of Wapping, shipwright, deposes 29 Jan., 1643-4, aged 26.**

---

* He was perhaps father to Anthony Stoddard of Boston, N. E., linen-draper, 1639.

† A Clement Campion sold house and lands in Charlestown, N. E., 1647.

‡ Probably Edward Collins, of Cambridge, N. E., gent, 1636. In his 'prentice days, when at Amboyna at the time of the massacre by the Dutch, he had a unique experience. Three "lotts were putt into a hatt" by the Dutch officials, and deponent, Samuel Colson and Emanuel Thompson, who were prisoners, were compelled to draw them. "They that drew twoe of those lotts were to suffer death, and hee that drew the third lott was to escape." Deponent drew the third.

§ Perhaps that Thomas Gwynn of Boston, N. E., who married Elizabeth, daughter of Benjamin Gillam.

‖ He bought land at Salem, N. E., 1639.

¶ He was of Boston, N. E., 1637.

** He was of Boston, N. E., in the latter part of the same year.

Nicholas Trerise of Wapping Wall, sailor, deposes 5 March, 1633-4, aged 36.*

Christopher Vennard deposes 17 Feb., 1636-7, that Richard Girling of Ipswich, master of the *Hope* of that port, went a voyage from Ipswich to New England in June, 1634, and died beyond the seas 14 May, 1636.†

Thomas Nye of the City of Bristol, joyner, deposes 7 Jan., 1638-9, aged 40, that he came passenger from New England in the *Providence* of London, Thomas Newman, master.

Thomas Davis of Chuckatucke in Virginia, merchant, deposes 11 July, 1639, aged 26.

Allen Kennistone of Warwicke Squeake in Virginia, planter, deposes 13 Nov., 1639, aged 40. He has lived in Virginia for 17 years.

Nicholas Spackman, late of Warwick Squeake *alias* Warrasqueake in Virginia, now of London, vintner, deposes 13 Nov., 1639, aged 49.

Edward Maior of Nants Mumm *alias* the Upper County of New Norfolk (in Virginia), gent, deposes, 13 Nov., 1639, aged 26. He has been a Burgess in the Assembly there.

Robert Davis of Warwick Squeake in Virginia, planter, deposes 13 Nov., 1639, aged 36. He has lived in Virginia 20 years.

Samuel Liverhurte of the Isle of Providence, planter, deposes 10 Dec., 1639, aged 30.

George Faulkner of York in Virginia, merchant, deposes 3 Oct., 1640, aged 24.

Robert Throgmorten of Virginia, planter, deposes 20 Oct., 1640, aged 35. He is brother to Thomas Throgmorton of London, merchant.

Maurice Thompson of St. Andrew Hubberd, London, merchant, deposes 29 Oct., 1640, aged 36.‡

Tobias Smith, a planter in Virginia, deposes 20 Nov., 1640, aged 25.

Thomas Cornwallis of Maryland in Virginia, Esq., deposes 4 Oct., 1641, aged 36.

---

* He was a well known ship-master, who settled at Charlestown, N. E.

† Richard Girling was of Cambridge, N. E., 1635. There is reason to believe him to have been a son of John Girling of Debenham, co. Suffolk. Apprenticed to Robert Cason of Ipswich, mariner, and Abigail his wife, 16 Feb., 1614-15, for eight years, he became a freeman of Ipswich 12 Feb., 21 James I. In 1624 he had his first ship, the *Patient Endeavour*, and in the same year he married Abigail Cason, daughter of his late master. She survived him and had administration of his estate 22 Aug., 1636.

‡ See previous references to him and his brother George. He died in 1675, leaving a will by which he devised his estates in England, Ireland, the Barbadoes, Antigua, St, Christopher's and Virginia to his grandson Arthur, son of his eldest son Sir John Thompson, Bart. His will describes him as of Haversham, Bucks, Esq.

Capt. John Stansby of Michall Leaver, co. Southampton, deposes 3 May, 1642, aged 28.*

Hugh Peters of London, minister, deposes 12 March, 1643-4, aged 41.†

John Bishopp of Newberrye in New England, shipwright, deposes 12 April, 1645, aged 24.

John Gallopp of Boston in New England, sailor, deposes 17 April, 1645, aged 27.

John Maverick of Dorchester in New England, sailor, deposes 24 April, 1645, aged 24. His brother "liveth hard by Boston."

Nicholas Shapleigh of Pescattaqua in New England, merchant, *ubi moram fecit per spacium duorum annorum, antea apud Dartmouth in Com: Devon a nativitate sua, ortus ibidem*, deposes 22 May, 1645, aged 37.‡

Robert Popelye of Virginia, surgeon, deposes 26 June, 1645, aged 30.

John Lewger of the Province of Maryland deposes 6 August, 1645, aged 45.

Giles Brent of Kent in Maryland, Esq., deposes 7 August, 1645, aged 37.

Thomas Cornwallis of Maryland, Esq., deposes 8 August, 1645, aged 40.

Ralph Beane of Maryland, planter, deposes 16 August, 1645, aged 30.

William Taylor of Accamacke in Virginia, gent, deposes 19 August, 1645, aged 23.

Thomas Graves of Boston in New England, mariner, deposes 11 April, 1646, aged 41.

Richard Bartholomew of Boston in New England, merchant, deposes 11 April, 1646, aged 28.

Edward Bendall of Boston in New England, merchant, deposes 14 May, 1646, aged 38. He has lived at Boston for 17 years.

Thomas Hawkins of Boston in New England, shipwright, deposes 14 May, 1646, aged 37. He has lived at Boston for 6 years.

Samuel Sheppard of Cambridge in New England, gent, deposes 16 May, 1646, aged 31. He has lived in New England, for the most part, these 10 years.

---

* Perhaps the Capt. John Stanesby who was of Cambridge, N. E., 1638.

† Deponent is unusually wide of the mark in stating his age. As a matter of fact he was baptised at the parish church of Fowey, in Cornwall, under his father's *alias* of Dickwood, on the 11th of June, 1598.

‡ His statement that he had lived at Dartmouth "from his birth" is not strictly correct. For some few years prior to his emigration he was resident in the city of Bristol, where two sons were born to him—Nicholas, baptised 22 Feb., 1630-31, and Jeffrey, baptised and buried in the following year.

Richard Leader of Boston in New England, merchant, deposes 8 August, 1650, aged 41. He has a brother, George Leader.

Capt. Thomas Willoughby of Willoughby's Hope, Norfolk county, Virginia, gent, deposes 26 Nov., 1650, aged 52. He has lived in Virginia 39 years, is one of the Council there, and Lieutenant of the county of Nether Norfolk.

Robert Henfield of Boston in New England, mariner, deposes 3 Feb., 1650-51, aged 28, that the *Diligence* of Boston, owned by this deponent, Joseph Grafton of Salem, and William Andrews of Cambridge, was captured by the French whilst on a trading voyage on the New England coast, between Cape Cod and Cape Sable, and carried into St. John's in the Bay of Funda.

Roland Bevan of Boston in New England, mariner, aged 26, deposes 3 Feb., 1650-51, that the *Diligence,* whereof Robert Henfield was master, was taken by the French "in March last was four yeares."

Henry Parke of St. Matthew's, Friday Street, London, mariner, deposes 3 Feb., 1650-51, aged 25, that he has lived at Boston in New England for the space of 6 years ended in October last.

John Trewerghey of Dartmouth, co. Devon, merchant, aged 33, deposes 19 March, 1650-51, that he well knew the *Prosperous,* whereof Nicholas Trewerghey went master to New England in or about 1640. He (deponent) had lived in New England about 5 years before her coming thither. He has seen a bill of sale of the ship, made by Alexander Shapleigh, this deponent's grandfather, dated 10 July, 1639.

Nicholas Trewergey of Puscatoqua in New England, sailor, deposes 3 Feb., 1650-51, aged 22, that Robert Henfield and his ship's company were turned ashore by the French on an uninhabited island to the westward of Cape Sable and there left to shift for themselves.

Thomas Kemble of Charlestown in New England, merchant, deposes 26 March, 1651, aged 30.

Edward Winslowe of Marshfeild in the Government of New Plymouth, N. E., Esq., deposes 7 May, 1651, aged 56. He was formerly Governor of New Plymouth.

John Richards of Boston in New England, merchant, deposes 7 May, 1651, aged 26. He has lived in New England about 19 years.

Thomas Mason, late of Virginia, now living upon Tower Hill, London, merchant, aged 52, deposes 24 July, 1652, that Samuel Hart has lived in Virginia these twelve months past, is a citizen of London, and served his apprenticeship at the lower end of Cheapside. John Bishop has lived in Virginia these 22 years past, but on the reduction of that province he removed from thence to Providence, with his wife and family, his said wife being this deponent's daughter.

John Thurmer of St. Catherine's near the Tower, planter, aged 55, deposes 3 August, 1652, that he has lived in Virginia.

John Byrom of Virginia, planter, deposes 16 Sept., 1652, aged 38.

William Ingleton of Wayne Oake upon Charles River in Virginia, planter, deposes 16 Sept., 1652, aged 31.

Giles Webb of Upper Northfolk in Virginia, planter, deposes 16 Sept., 1652, aged 38. He has been an inhabitant of Virginia for above 20 years.

Thomas Stegge of St. Katherine near the Tower, merchant, deposes 17 Sept., 1652, aged 21, that he has lived in Virginia.

William Cleyborne of Virginia, son of William Cleyborne, merchant, deposes 16 Nov., 1652, aged 16. His father has lived in Virginia for 31 years and is now Lieut.-Governor there.

James Heyden, living at this present in St. Dunstan's in the East, London, planter in New England, deposes 5 April, 1653, aged 44.

Peter Butler of Boston in New England, mariner, master of the *Mayflower,* deposes 17 August, 1653, aged 37.

Edmond Scarburgh of Accamack in Virginia, where he has lived these 22 years, deposes 26 Oct., 1653, aged 34.

John Norborne of Bristol, merchant, aged 33, deposes 7 Feb., 1653-4, that in July or August, 1653, he was in New England about his merchandizing occasions.

Thomas Forty of James Town in Virginia, where he has lived above 4 years, now resident in Fetter Lane, London, deposes 8 Sept., 1654, aged 35.

William May, now residing in Fetter Lane, London, but of James Town in Virginia, merchant, where he has lived 4 years and upwards, deposes 8 Sept., 1654, aged 35.

William Morris of Charlestown in New England, mariner, late carpenter of the *Unity* of New England, deposes 21 Nov., 1654, aged 36.

Robert Martin of New Haven in New England, mariner, deposes 2 Feb., 1654-5, aged 39.

Thomas Jenner of Charles Town in New England, mariner, deposes 29 March, 1656, aged 28.*

Emanuel Springfield, draper, aged 21, deposes 25 March, 1656, that he came passenger from Boston, N. E., in December last, in the *John's Adventure,* John Cutting master.

---

* Son of the Rev. Thomas Jenner of Roxbury and Weymouth, N. E. The father returned and died in Ireland, leaving a will (Dublin Wills, 1672-8, f. 120) of which the following is an abstract:—Will of Thomas Jenner, senior, clerk, of Dublin, dated 4 June, 1672, proved 26 May, 1676:— In body infirm and weak. Unto Thomas Jenner my eldest son I give that whole studd of horses and maires which I left behind me in New England, and whatsoever else of mine I left there. To my three grandchildren by my son Thomas, viz. Thomas, David and Rebecca, £5 each. Son David my whole library of books, and if he die without issue, then it shall remain to my son Jonathan, to whom I give also £5 and to my two granddaughters, his children, namely, Mary and Rebecca, which he had by his first wife, £40. Son Jonathan my book called Gerard's Herball. Daughter Rachel, wife of Samuel Blackshaw, £5, and to my three grandchildren by her,

Mary Springfield, wife of Emanuel Springfield, deposes 25 March, 1656, aged 19, that she was in New England from the time of her birth till the *John's Adventure* departed thence. She can read written hand, and write a little.*

John Cutting of Newbery in New England, mariner, master of the *John's Adventure,* deposes 1 April, 1656, aged 63, that Robert Hubberd, and Emanuel Springfield and his wife, came passengers in his ship to England.

Susanna Tillman, at present of St. Botolph without Bishopsgate, wife of Robert Tillman of the same, merchant, aged 34, deposes 12 Sept., 1656, that in May, 1654, she was at Achamack in Virginia with her late husband, David Sellick, since deceased.†

Richard Bennett, Esq., an inhabitant of Virginia, but at present living in London, deposes 12 Feb., 1656-7, aged 49, that he has lived in Virginia these 8 or 9 years and been Governor there.

William Whittington of Northampton county in Virginia, mariner, master of the ship formerly called the *Shepherd,* now the *Northampton,* deposes 19 Aug., 1657, aged 40.

Robert Oldfield of Spalding, co. Lincoln, gent, aged 22, deposes 19 Nov., 1657, that he went a voyage to Virginia in the *Unity,* in 1654. One of the servant passengers, an old woman who was vehemently suspected to be a witch, was set ashore at Dublin, the company fearing she might prove dangerous to the voyage. She had previously been turned ashore from the *Negro,* Locker master, bound for the Barbadoes, on the like suspicion.

Capt. John Aylett, now of London, mariner, formerly living in New England, deposes 22 March, 1657-8, aged 30. He was master and part owner of a ketch called the *Providence,* which, in a voyage from New England to Jamaica, was taken by the Spaniards and carried into San Domingo, where deponent was held prisoner for twelve months and better.

Hezekiah Usher of Boston in New England, stationer, deposes 8 April, 1658, aged 42.

Stephen Talby of Boston in New England, late commander of the *Adventure* of that port, deposes 17 May, 1658, aged 25. His ship was taken by an Ostend man-of-war, off the Start, in January last.

Richard Price of Boston in New England, merchant, deposes 20 May, 1659, aged 23.

---

namely, Samuel, David and Rachel Blackshaw, £3 apiece. Son in law Blackshaw all my goods left behind at Carlow. Son Thomas my great Bible in folio with Baeza his notes thereon. Daughter Rebecca Bean £10. Son in law Bean two guineas. Cousin Anthony Hollingworth and his daughter Mary. Wife Ellen Jenner the rest of my estate so long as she liveth. Executors, my wife and son David.

* She was a daughter of Thomas Makepeace of Dorchester, N. E., gent.

† David Sellick, soapboiler, was of Dorchester, N. E., 1642. He died in Virginia.

Robert Gibbs of Boston in New England, merchant, deposes 20 May, 1659, aged 25.

William Whittington of Ackamack in Virginia, merchant, aged 40, William Melling of the same, merchant, aged 49, and James Cade of London, merchant, aged 52, depose 1 Sept., 1659, that in July last, at Amsterdam, they bought the ship called the *Christina Regina,* now the *Northampton,* on behalf of the aforesaid William Whittington, Lieut.-Col. William Randall and John Michell of Ackamack.

John Clarke of New England, mariner, now belonging to the ship the *Exchange* of London, deposes 9 April, 1660, aged 19.

John Frost of New England, mariner, now belonging to the *Exchange* of London, deposes 9 April, 1660, aged 22.

Thomas Beale of Yorke in Virginia, planter, aged 50, deposes 25 July, 1660, concerning Francis Wheeler, son and executor of the will of Francis Wheeler, senior, deceased in Virginia, and Elianor his wife, also deceased there.

Robert Clements of Wapping, mariner, master of the *Honor,* aged 37, deposes 26 July, 1660, that Elianor, wife of Francis Wheeler the elder, both deceased in Virginia, was mother in law (i. e. step-mother) to Francis Wheeler the younger. The tobacco now claimed was consigned to Perryn Trot of London, brother to Mr. Nicholas Trot of Jamestown, Virginia.

Elizabeth Webb, wife of Thomas Webb of Ratcliff, and late wife of John Thompson, late master of the *Guift of God* of New England, deposes 13 Aug., 1660, aged 34.

John Jacob of Wapping, *ubi habitavit per biennium, mercator, annos agens 23, natus in Ipswich in Nova Anglia,* deposes 5 Sept., 1657.

William Pardon of New Jersey in America, where he has lived for 7 years, planter, deposes 15 May, 1674, aged 51.

Richard Ashall of St. Gregory, London, where he has lived for 7 months, theretofore of Virginia from his birth, deposes 6 July, 1674, aged 25.

John Conyers of Virginia in America, but now living in the parish of St. Sepulchre, London, deposes 31 May, 1675, aged 33.

Nathaniel Greenwood of Boston in New England, shipwright, aged 45, deposes 10 March, 1676-7, that he has lived in New England for 20 years.

Thomas Clerke of the city of New York, merchant, deposes 7 Dec., 1681, aged 31.

John Balstone of New England, sailor, master of the *Adventure* of New England, deposes 31 Jan., 1684-5, aged 38.

Gersham Bownd of Stepney, sailor, aged 39, deposes 14 March, 1684-5, that the *Unity* was built at Salem near Boston at the charge of this deponent, who commanded her.

William Condy of Boston in New England, sailor, aged 47, deposes 18 March, 1684-5, that some four years ago he was for eleven months a prisoner in Algiers.

Samuel Johnson, sailor, of Boston in New England, where he was born and has lived from his birth, deposes 8 Nov., 1690, aged 23.

Aaron Dupuy of New York, sailor, where he was born and has lived from his birth, deposes 1 April, 1691, aged 26.

William Egar of Shadwell, where he has lived for 4 months, born in New England, where he has lived the greater part of his life, deposes 11 Jan., 1691-2, aged 23.

John Edwards of Salem in New England, where he has lived for 20 years, sailor, deposes 20 Feb., 1691-2.

Jacob Mauritz of New York, where he has lived for 33 years, sailor, deposes 26 March, 1692, aged 47.

Gilbert Bant of Boston in New England, where he has lived for 8 years, sailor, aged 34, deposes 31 March, 1692, that the *Mahitable*, of which he is master and part owner, was built at Boston about 4 years since. Thomas Cooper of Boston, Gabriel Bernone of the same, and William White, formerly of Boston, now of Mounserat, merchant, are also owners.

John Bant of Boston in New England, where he has lived for 4 years, aged 21, deposes 31 March, 1692, that he is apprentice to Gilbert Bant.

Jacob Teller of New York, where he was born and has lived from his birth, sailor, deposes 4 April, 1692, aged 37.

Isaac De Riemer (or Derimer) of New York, where he was born and has lived from his birth, deposes 4 April, 1692, aged 26.

Robert Sinclar of New York in America, where he has lived for 14 years, sailor, deposes 7 April, 1692, aged 34.

Jacob Leisler of New York, where he was born and has lived from his birth, merchant, deposes 12 April, 1692, aged 27.*

James Ashley of New Providence, where he has lived for 3 years, theretofore of Carolina for 6 years, shipwright, deposes 23 April, 1692, aged 34.

Micajah Perry of St. Catherine Creechurch, London, where he has lived for 10 years, merchant, born in New England, deposes 25 April, 1692, aged 51.

Robert Marshall of St. Saviour's, Southwark, where he has lived for 6 months, born in New England and resident there from his birth, sailor, deposes 12 Oct., 1692, aged 25.

Robert Marshall of St. Mary Magdalen, Bermondsey, where he has lived for 9 months, theretofore of Boston in New England, where he has lived mostly from his birth, born near the same place, sailor, deposes 3 Dec., 1692, aged 25.

* Son of that Jacob Leisler who, in 1689, assumed the government of New York. He had a re-grant of his father's estates by Letters Patent dated 15 April, 1693.

Daniel Updick of Ratcliff in the parish of Stepney, where he has lived for 3 years born near New York, sailor, deposes 29 August, 1693, aged 38.

Edward Anketill (or Antill) of Richmond, co. Surrey, where he has lived for one year, theretofore of New York for 6 years, merchant, deposes 20 Jan., 1693-4, aged 34.

Joseph Dudley of Roxbury in Suffolk county in New England, where he was born and has lived from his birth, Esq., deposes 23 Jan., 1693-4, aged 46.

George Farwell of Enfield, co. Middlesex, where he has lived for a year and a half, theretofore of New York, gent, deposes 23 Jan., 1693-4, aged 30.

Thomas Wenham of St. Mildred, Bread Street, where he has lived for one year, theretofore of New York, where he lived for 8 years, merchant, deposes 24 Jan., 1693-4, aged 30.

John Pitts of Boston in New England, where he has lived for 14 years, sailor, deposes 19 Feb., 1693-4, aged 38.

David Waterhouse of St. Mary Hill, London, where he has lived for three months, theretofore of Boston in New England for 7 years, merchant, deposes 18 June, 1694, aged 35.

John Balston of Boston in New England, where he was born and has lived from his birth, sailor, aged 45, deposes 31 June, 1695, that the *St. Jacob* was brought a prize into the port of Boston this time three years, by the *Swan,* Thomas Gilbert, master.

Giles Shelley of the city of New York, sailor, now living at the house of John Young in Wapping, deposes 4 Oct., 1695, aged 31, that he has lived in New York for 7 years.*

William Kidd of New York in America, where he has lived for 6 years, born at Dundee in Scotland, mariner, deposes 15 Oct., 1695, aged 41.†

Ephraim Mickell of Carolina in the West Indies, sailor, deposes 16 Feb., 1695-6, aged 26.

Collin Cambell of New York, where he has lived for 14 years, sailor, deposes 2 March, 1695-6, aged 28.

Amos Wadland of Boston in New England, where he has lived for 27 years, sailor, deposes 23 June, 1696, aged 42.

James Conden of St. Paul's, Shadwell, where he has lived for 5 years, born at Boston in New England, sailor, deposes 17 Oct.. 1696, aged 28.

---

* He was a sailor and owned land on the west side of the Bowery Lane, a short distance south of Astor Place. On May 27, 1699, he wrote from Cape May to his principal, Stephen de Lancey, that the ship "Nassau," of which he was master, had arrived there with a valuable cargo from Madagascar. (*MSS. Col. Hist.,* Albany, 271.)—THE EDITOR.

† This deponent is Capt. William Kidd, who was executed for piracy in 1701. The *Dictionary of National Biography* states that he was a native of Greenock and lived for some time at Boston, N. E. His true birthplace is now first disclosed.

GENEALOGICAL NOTES FROM THE HIGH COURT OF ADMIRALTY EXAMINATIONS.

By J. R. Hutchinson.

James Sherley, citizen and goldsmith of London, Treasurer of the New England Company, who deposed 20 November, 1624, aged 33, was "borne vppon London Bridge, within the parish of St. Magnus, and hath for fourteene or fifteene yeares kept house and family in the parish of St. Michael's, Crooked Lane, and borne all offices there." He is now Renter-Warden of the Gold-Smith's Company.*

Richard Barnehouse of Bristol, sailor, aged 22, deposes 28 July, 1627, that he has lived at Bristol for two years, and before that was a captive in Algiers.†

Richard Hawes, sailor, deposes 7 February, 1627-8, aged 22, that he will be worth £100 after his mother's decease.‡

William Holman, mariner, deposes 13 Feb., 1628-9, aged 36.§

---

* John Norris, 27 April, Alexander Jackson, 28 April, 1631.

† Probably that Richard Barnhouse who gave bond, 1638, to William Pester of Salem.

‡ His age agrees with that of the Richard Hawes who came to N. E. in the *Truelove*, 1635, and settled at Dorchester.

§ His age agrees with that of William Holman of Cambridge, who died 18 Jan., 1652-3, age 59.

Thomas Dobson of Wapping Wall, mariner, deposes 24 Sept., 1629, aged 44. Is now master of the *Hope* of London, Holland built, burthen 200 tons.*

John Stratton of London, gent, deposes 27 Nov., 1629, aged 25.†

Matthew Avery of Wapping, mariner, deposes 25 January, 1629-30.‡

Thomas Shrive, sailor, deposes 2 Feb., 1629-30, aged 34.§

David Johnson, clothworker, deposes 30 March, 1630, aged 46. ‖

Edward Paine, mariner, master of the *Refuge* of London, deposes 3 April, 1630, aged 31.¶

Thomas Mathew of Marlow, Bucks, bargeman, deposes 7 May, 1630, aged 30.**

Stephen Reeks deposes 28 Oct., 1630, that John Wright, living in New England, is kinsman to Mr. Thomas Wright of Bristol, merchant.††

Thomas Hardy of Scotland, sailor, deposes 1 Nov., 1630, aged 24.‡‡

Christopher Winter, yeoman, deposes 17 Feb., 1630-31, aged 25.§§

George Bennett of London, tailor, deposes 28 April, 1631, aged 24.‖‖

James Grollier of St. Dunstan's in the East, merchant, aged 25, deposes 24 May, 1631, that he is son to James (also "Jacques" and "Jacob") Grollier, senior.¶¶

William Holmes of London, gent, aged 32, deposes 23 Jan., 1631-2, that in 1630 he traded at Todasack and Bonadventure, in the Gulf of Canada, on behalf of Capt. David Kirk and company, for elk and beaver skins to the value of £3000. He went purser,

---

* Probably the Capt. Dobson who set out from Boston, N. E., in 1646, to trade to the eastward, and was captured by D'Aulnay.
† John Stratton of Salem, gent, 1631. He was of Shotley, Suffolk. Genealogy by Miss Hesba Stratton, from data collected by the compiler of these notes.
‡ He was of Charlestown, N. E., 1638, but returned to Old England, where he died, 1642.
§ Perhaps that Thomas Shrive who was of Plymouth, N. E., 1643.
‖ May be the "Davy" Johnson who settled at Dorchester, N. E., in the same year.
¶ He commanded the *Anne* of London, 1631, and was of Charlestown, N. E., 1638.
** He is probably that Thomas Mathew of Boston who died there 1641 and whose wife, Margery, was a Clement of Wokingham, Berks.
†† Piscataqua is indicated as his place of residence.
‡‡ His age agrees remarkably with that of Thomas Hardy of Haverhill, N. E., who was 72 in 1677.
§§ He may be that Christopher Winter who was later of Marshfield, N. E.
‖‖ A George Bennett was at Charlestown, N. E., with wife Faith, in 1647.
¶¶ Like his father, he traded for many years to New England. The father, a French merchant domiciled in London, deposed 7 Sept., 1629, aged 53.

181

on that occasion, of the *Thomas* of London, Vincent Harris master. In the following year the trade in skins was spoilt by the interloping of the *Elizabeth* of London.*

Edmund Hall of Essex, gent, deposes 28 Feb., 1631-2, aged 28.†

William Hannam of London, merchant, deposes 21 April, 1632, aged 32.‡

Thomas Witherley (or Wetherley) of Horseydown, captain of the *John and Frances* of London, deposes 4 Oct., 1627 (no age stated), and 1 Oct., 1632, aged 30.§

Thomas Bredcake deposes 30 Aug., 1627, that he is master of the *Pleasure* of London; and 14 Feb., 1632-3, aged 42.‖

Augustine Lyndon of New England deposes 13 Feb., 1654-5, aged 35.

Thomas Hutchinson of Boston in New England, where he was born, merchant, aged 22, deposes 2 Feb., 1696-7, concerning the *St. Jago,* a ship purchased by deponent's late master, John Foster, of Lady Phipps, relict of Sir William Phipps, late governor of New England.

Benjamin Smith of Harford in New England, where he was born and has lived from his birth, deposes 8 July, 1697, aged 26.

Nicholas Lawrence of Dorchester in New England where he was born and has lived from his birth, deposes 20 Oct., 1697, aged 33.

---

* This deponent is almost certainly that Major William Holmes of Plymouth, N. E., who led the colonial forces in the Pequot war of 1637—an enterprise for which his acquaintance with the Indians, acquired in the course of trade, eminently qualified him. Kirk, his principal in the Canadian voyages, is the Capt. David Kirk who wrested Fort St. Lewis (Quebec) from Champlain, the French governor.

† May be that Edmund Hall, gent, who was of Boston, 1640.

‡ May be that William Hannam who was of Dorchester, N. E., 1635.

§ He is the Thomas Witherley, mariner, to whom such frequent reference is made in Lechford's "Note-Book." Savage confounds him with Wetherall. In 1630 he figured in a sea-drama which brought him into the H. C. A. in the capacity of defendant. Early in that year Sir Ferdinando Gorges, Mr. Isaac Allerton of New England, and Mr. Thomas Wright of Bristol, set out the *Swift* of Bristol, Stephen Reeks of Poole master, for New England, laden with passengers and provisions. These were in due course landed at "Sacho and Cuscoe," where Reeks reloaded with "fishe and trayne oyl" for St. Michael's, one of the Azores or Western Islands. He could speak a bit of French; so, in accordance with his owners' instructions, and in order to outwit enemy privateers, he called his ship the *St. Peter* and himself Phillip Alley. The ruse would doubtless have succeeded had not Capt. Witherley, then in command of the *Warwick* letter of marque, swooped down upon him, while he still lay in Damerell's Cove, on the New England coast, and made him a prize. On reaching London Reeks confessed his deception in Witherley's presence, at the house of Capt. John Mason in Fenchurch Street, but whether he recovered his ship is not apparent. (*James Nicholls,* 18 *Oct., Stephen Reeks,* 30 *Oct., Thomas Millard,* 1 *Nov.,* 1630.)

‖ Probably that Thomas Bredcake who had a commission from the General Court of Massachusetts, 1644, to take Turkish pirates. A John Bredcake, perhaps this deponent's father, had a command in the fleet set forth in 1614 by the Fellowship of English Merchants for the discovery of New Trades.

William Phillipps of Boston in New England, where he was born and has lived from his birth, sailor, deposes 15 Nov., 1697, aged 30.

John Smith of Boston in New England, where he has lived for 15 years, sailor, deposes 29 Dec., 1697, aged 48.

Joseph Jackson of Boston in New England, where he has lived for 20 years, sailor, deposes 29 Dec., 1697, aged 43.

Peter Machell (Marchill or Marshall) of New York, where he has lived for 6 years, deposes 17 March, 1697-8, aged 27.

William Pease of Newport in Rhode Island, where he has lived for 4 years, sailor, deposes 2 Aug., 1698, aged 25.

John Scott of Newport, Rhode Island, where he has lived for 20 years, born in the isle of Providence (Bahamas), deposes 2 Aug., 1698, aged 34.

Humphrey Parking of (Long Island next) New York, where he has lived for 8 years, sailor, deposes 9 Sept., 1698, aged 30.

Richard Sampson of Piscataway in New England, where he has lived for 16 years, fisherman, deposes 9 Sept., 1698, aged 23.

John Lawrence of Long Island next New York, where he was born and has lived from birth, sailor, deposes 9 Sept., 1698, aged 17.

Stephen Gisberts of New York, where he was born and has lived from his birth, sailor, deposes 25 Oct., 1698, aged 23.

Philip French, junior, of New York, where he has lived for 12 years, merchant, deposes 8 Nov., 1698, aged 31.

John Narramore of Boston in New England, where he was born and has lived from his birth, shipwright, deposes 8 Nov., 1698, aged 21.

William Bowditch of Salem in New England, where he has lived for 20 years, sailor, deposes 14 July, 1699, aged 34.

Richard Symms of Salem in New England, where he has lived for 5 years, sailor, deposes 14 July, 1699, aged 20.

David Robertson of Boston in New England, shipwright, deposes 25 Jan., 1699-00, aged 38.

Epaphras Shrimpton of Boston in New England, where he has lived 16 years, merchant, deposes 27 Jan., 1699-00, aged 46.

Joseph Palmer, now living at the house of Joseph Grove in Fanchurch-street, London, born at Westchester near New York in America, sailor, deposes 5 May, 1701, aged 32.

Daniel Honan of New York, where he has lived for 7 years, merchant, deposes 9 Feb., 1701-2, aged 33.

Samuel Burges of New York, where he has lived for some years, master of the *Margaret,* deposes 27 June, 1702, aged 33.

Joseph Wheeler of Boston in New England, where he was born, sailor, deposes 3 Aug., 1702, aged 32.

Thomas Ransford of New York, where he has lived for some years, sailor, deposes 4 Aug., 1702, aged 30.

Arnold Viele of New York, where he was born, sailor, deposes 30 Jan., 1702-3, aged 22.

William Thornton of Limehouse, where he has lived for 3 years, theretofore of Salem in New England, where he was born sailor deposes 2 March, 1702-3, aged 28.

Nathaniel Pickman of Boston in New England, where he has lived with his wife and family for 7 years, born at Salem, sailor, deposes 31 May, 1703, aged 27. He is master of the *Newport Galley*.

Thomas Beard of Boston in New England, where he was born and has lived from his birth, sailor, deposes 23 Dec., 1703, aged 34. He is master of the *Return* of Boston.

Thomas Taylor of Shadwell, where he has lived for 11 years, born in New England, sailor, deposes 29 July, 1704, aged 30.

John Davis of New York, sailor, deposes 22 Sept., 1704, aged 30.

Thomas Farmer of New York, sailor, deposes 14 January, 1704-5, aged 29. He married Capt. Christopher Billup's daughter. His wife and family are at New York.

John Corney of Boston in New England, where he has lived for 6 years, sailor, deposes 25 July, 1705, aged 32.

John Charnock of Boston in New England, where he has lived for 7 years, sailor, deposes 25 July, 1705, aged 32.

Thomas Holland of Piscataqua in New England, sailor, deposes 27 July, 1705, aged 35.

Jonathan Belcher of Boston in New England, merchant, deposes 27 July, 1705, aged 23.

William Waine of Boston in New England, sailor, deposes 15 Feb., 1705-6, aged 34.

Philip Davis of Boston in New England, sailor, deposes 23 Feb., 1705-6, aged 32.

John Jerman of Salem in New England, sailor, deposes 23 Feb., 1705-6, aged 55.

Joseph Candish of Boston in New England, where he was born, sailor, deposes 27 May, 1706, aged 27.

Thomas Dudley of Boston in New England, where he was born, sailor, deposes 30 April, 1707, aged 27.

Edward Rainsford of Boston in New England, sailor, deposes 13 Sept., 1708, aged 39, *re* the father and mother of Stephen Waters of Charlestown.

John Evans of New York, gent, deposes 17 Feb., 1710-11, aged 18. Is a midshipman on board H. M. S. *Burford*, Capt. John Evans commander.

Joseph Bickner of Boston in New England, sailor, deposes 8 July, 1715, aged 27.

Thomas Pike of Boston in New England, sailor, deposes 14 July, 1715, aged 61. Has lived at Boston for 40 years.

John Caffy of Boston in New England, born at Brazil in the West Indies, deposes 9 July, 1720, aged 25. *Niger.*

Joseph Bickford of Piscataway in New England, sailor, deposes 27 April, 1721, aged 24.

William Allen of Boston in New England, mate of the *Adventure,* whereof Alexander Foresight of Boston is master, deposes 11 July, 1724, aged 28.

John Browne of Boston in New England, seaman of the *Adventure,* born at Boston, deposes 14 July, 1724, aged 19.

Benjamin Jeffrey of Boston in New England, seaman of the *Adventure,* born at Boston, deposes 15 July, 1724, aged 21.

John Bridges of Charlestown in New England, sailor, deposes 8 May, 1728, aged 21. He has heard the producant, Joseph Hunting, shipwright, say that he is a native and inhabitant of New England, and has his mother and brother living there. Deponent is apprentice to John Soley of Charlestown.

Benjamin Norwood of New York, sailor, deposes 8 May, 1728, aged 26.

Michael Nowel of Boston in New England, shipwright, deposes 17 May, 1728, aged 29.

David Crawford of Maryland, merchant, deposes 26 Nov., 1728, aged 30.

Robert McArthur of Boston in New England, sailor, master of the *St. Luke,* deposes 25 Feb., 1729-30, aged 28.

Joshua Winslow of Boston in New England, merchant, deposes 23 Aug., 1731, aged 36.

Nathaniel Fletcher of Boston in New England, merchant, now dwelling in the parish of St. Bartholomew near the Royal Exchange, London, deposes 4 Jan., 1731-2, aged 33.

Philip Norman of Boston in New England, mariner, deposes 26 Jan., 1735-6, aged near 40 years.

William Hutton of Boston in New England, mariner, deposes 25 Jan., 1736-7, aged 26.

Thomas Sherborne of Marblehead in New England, mariner, deposes 5 Nov., 1737, aged 40.

Edward Hopkins of Portsmouth in New England, mariner, deposes 12 Dec., 1737, aged 45.

William Bendall of Boston in New England, mariner, deposes 14 May, 1745, aged 23.

John Searl of Marblehead in New England, mariner, deposes 6 Dec., 1745, aged 70. He was born and has always lived at Marblehead.

Henry Wethered of Boston in New England, merchant, deposes 12 Feb., 1746-7, aged 30.

SOME NOTABLE DEPOSITIONS FROM THE HIGH
COURT OF ADMIRALTY.

By J. R. Hutchinson.

(i) Andrew Hume of the Precinct of St. Katherine, aged 32,
William Forde of Limehouse, aged 36, William Deeping
of St. Mary Monthawe, aged 27, John Johnson of St.
Botolphs Aldgate, aged 45, respectively master's mate,
gunner, surgeon and cook of the *William* of London, and
Jacob Jacobson Elkins of Amsterdam, aged 42, factor for
the merchants freighting the said ship, severally depose on
the 5th, 6th and 7th of November, 1633, that William Clo-
berry, David Morehead and John Delabarr, merchants of
London, did in December, 1632, lade the *Willam*, whereof
William Trevore was master, with divers goods to be
transported to Hutson's river, between Virginia and New
England, there to be traded and trucked away to the
natives for beaver skynns and other skynns and furrs.
Having called at Plymouth in New England to land divers
passengers, the shipp, about the 13th of April last, arrived
at Hutson's river, where was a fort belonging to the Dutch,
called Fort Amsterdam, or Munhaddon's Fort. Here
Deeping, the surgeon of the shipp, was sent on shoare to
entreat the governor, Walter Vertrell, to come aboard; who
refused so to do, insisting that the Englishmen should

186

come to him, and bidding Deeping ask them: "Did they know the Prince of Orange?" The whole ship's company, led by Elkins the factor, accordingly went ashoare, excepte one boye, who was left to minde the shippe. The governor demanded wherefore they had come. "To goe vpp further into the river," replied Elkins, "there to trade with the natives, for the lande was the King of England's lande, and they would trade there; and if the governor would not suffer them to passe, yet would he goe vpp the river though it cost him his life." This the governor forbade him to doe if he valued his necke, at the same time commanding his gunners to shoot off three pieces of ordnance for the Prince of Orange, and to spreade abroad the Prince's colours vppon the castle; whereupon Elkins, going on board the *William* again, spread the English colours, shot off three pieces for the honour of the King of England, and weighing anchor proceeded vpp the river some fortye leagues. Here, to his dismay, he found a second Dutch fort, called Fort Orania or Orange, Hance Jorison Houton governor. Fearing to passe it, yet bent on accomplishing the purpose of his coming thither, he made a landing a mile below, set up a tente, and began to truck with the Indians. He had previously lived amongst them for fower yeares, and knew their customs, wants and language. Could he stay but one moone, the salvages assured him, a nation called the Maques would come down and bring with them fower thousand beaver skynns, and another nation called the Mahiggins would bring three hundred skynns more.

At this interesting juncture, just when the factor and ship's company—each of whom carried some small adventure in his cheste to helpe out his wages, as was customary—were congratulatimg themselves upon the fact that everye merchantable beaver skynn was worth twenty shillings at the leaste in London, up the river came a pinnance, a carvell and a hoye laden with Dutchmen armed to the teeth with halfe pikes, swords, musketts and pistols, while from the vpper forte there dropped downe vppon the traders a shallop, similarly manned and armed, whose occupants, after the approved Dutch fashion, did drincke a bottle of strong waters of three or fower pints to whet their courage, whilst their trumpeter sounded his trumpet in a triumphinge manner over the English. Uniting forces, the two parties landed, threw down the tent, beat the Indians who had come to trade, drove or carried the interloping English aboard their shipp, and there hove up her anchors, so that to keepe her from driving on shoare her company were faine to putt her under saile and sayle downe the river, the Dutch remaining with them untill they reached the open sea and there passed beyond the governor's jurisdiction. The voyage of the *William* was thus wholly overthrowne, and the merchants that sett her forth sustained losse and damage to the value of fower thousand pounds sterling.

(ii) Comfort Starr of Ashford in the county of Kent, chirurgeon, aged 45, deposes 11 February, 1634-5, that about the latter end of November last John Witherley of Sandwich, mariner, did buy at Dunkirk a certain Flemish built shipp lately called the *St. Peter*, now the *Hercules* of Sandwich, for the sum of £340 the first penny, which shipp now lies at Sandwich, and is of the burthen of 200 tonnes. Examinate, being noe seaman, cannot tell of what length, breadth or depth she is, but he guesseth her to be about twelve foote broad above the hatches, fowerscore foote longe, and sixteene foote deepe. She belongs to this examinate. John Witherley, Nathaniel Tilden and Mr. Osborne, and William Hatch is to have a parte in her with this examinate.

The above deposition, taken on the eve of the *Hercules'* departure for New England, incidentally corrects Pope who dates the voyage 1634, and confirms Savage, who assigns it to 1635. Starr, Tilden and Hatch, with their respective families, all crossed in the ship whose purchase is here described.

(iii) Thomas Harrison of Redriffe in the county of Surrey, mariner, aged 50, deposes 7 March, 1636-7, that he was sent to Dunkirk, on the 6th of January last, by Mr. George Price of London, merchant, to buy a ship for his use. He bought of the officers of the Admirality of Dunkirk, by publique outcry, a Holland-bottom shipp then called the *Lambe*, burthen two hundred and threescore tonnes, and paid for her 7,000 guilders the first penny. He arrived with the shipp in the river Thames, neere Redriffe church, on Sunday last, being the fifth of this present month. The shipp, now called the *Successe* of London, is to be sett forth for Danzick in Prussia, there to lade masts. Deponent's son, Thomas Harrison, is to goe master of her, if hee come from Holland before the shipp be ready; but if hee come not, then deponent's brother in lawe, Daniel Paule of Ipswich, shipwright and mariner, is to goe master.

Daniel Paul next appears at Boston, N. E., where 24 August, 1640, he formally empowers John Cole of Ipswich, shipwright, to sell his lands, tenements and personal possessions in Ipswich, England, and to pay over the proceeds to Elizabeth his wife. In 1643 he is of New Haven, Conn., and later of Kittery, Me. (*Lechford's Note-Book, p. 293*.) In face of this evidence connecting him with Ipswich, it is remarkable that no trace of him can be found in the Apprenticeship Indentures or Freemen's Rolls of that ancient borough, records of which the writer possesses a complete abstract. He may, however, have been a son of that John Paul who was baptised at St. Mary Key, Ipswich, in 1584.

His association with Kittery is doubtless explained by the allusion, in Harrison's deposition, to the Dantzig mast-trade. The supply of masts and spars for the British navy and the British mercantile marine had from time immemorial been drawn from Norway, Prussia and Muscovy, a precarious source of supply in time of war. The settlement of New England, and the subsequent exploiting of the northern forests of that diffuse territory, introduced white pine as a desirable substitute for the heavier, less resilient and more easily barred product of the Baltic provinces. In Paul's time the trade was yet in its infancy. A generation or two later it had grown to such proportions that it became necessary, in the interests of the royal navy, to restrict its ravages upon the forests of Maine and New Hampshire.

The charter of William and Mary accordingly reserved all white pine of a certain diameter for naval uses, while an Act of Parliament of later date expressly forbade, under heavy penalties, the cutting down of King's Woods. The inhibition was the first seed of the American Revolution. Logically regarding the felling of timber as a natural right, the colonists resented bitterly this unwarrantable interference with their liberties. Elisha Cook, a somewhat truculent member of the Massachusetts Bay Council, acting as the people's spokesman, in a caustic letter addressed to the Speaker of the House of Representatives roundly declared that "the King had no woods there;" a piece of plain speaking for which the General Assembly publicly thanked him. Bridger, the first Surveyor General of the King's Forests, escaped public odium and personal injury only because he "seldom visited the woods, but often sold 'em;" whilst David Dunbar, the irascible Scotsman who succeeded him, incurred both in full measure for enforcing the law, as he did on frequent occasions, "with a crow-barr." The people clamoured for his recall, but Dunbar sat tight. So tenacious was he of the sweets of office, indeed, that Gov. Belcher, his inveterate enemy, maliciously said he would believe Dunbar had really gone when some inward-bound skipper reported having sighted him "to the eastard of George's." (*Colonial Office Papers, passim.*)

(iv) John Tarleton, of the parish of St. Olaves in the Borough of Southwark, brewer, aged 46, deposes 30 December, 1631, that in July last he, at the entreaty of Susan Hooker, wife of Thomas Hooker of Waltham in the county of Essex, preacher of God's word, now resident at Delph in Holland, did lade abord the *Jacob* of London, Robert Jacob master, one small truncke of apparrell contayninge, as he hath bene informed by the sayd Mr. Hooker's wife, one stuffe gowne, one stuffe cloake, one cloth cloake, three shirts, twelle handkerchiefs, seaven white capps, three ruffe bands, two falling bands, three payre of ruffes, one payre stockins, one payre of garters, one payre of shooes and one or two sutes of apparrell, and two letters, wch truncke of apparrell this deponent, by the direction of the sayd Mr. Hooker's wife, did consigne to be delivered to one Mr. Peters, a minister dwelling at Rotterdam for the accompte of the sayd Thomas Hooker. And he also sayeth that the said Hooker went into Holland in or about the month of June last, and his wife and family still dwell within the parish of Waltham in Essex.

189

Apart from the allusion to Hugh Peters, Tarleton's deposition is noteworthy as fixing the date of Hooker's flight into Holland. They who fled from the wrath of Laud stood not upon the order of their going. He therefore travelled light, and the trunk, with its delightfully simple contents, was sent after him. It never reached its destination. Some accident of the sea claimed it, and Mistress Hooker sued the owners of the *Jacob* for its value. Of Tarleton we know nothing more than is told in the caption of his deposition; but the name is found in Leicestershire, Hooker's native county.

(v) 12 Martij, 1643—(4), Heugh Peters of London, minister, aged 41, yeares or thereabouts, sworne before the Judge of his Ma[ties] Highe Courte of the Admirality, sayeth & deposeth vppon his oath That about fourteene dayes since this exam[te], beeing at the Brill in Holland, saw the shipp called the *Signett ffriggott*, comanded by Capt: Whetstone, rideing at an anchor below the Pitts, about fower miles from Brill, and about a Cables length from her there lay a Scarboroughe shipp of the burthen of about 70[ty] tonns, newly runn a grounde vppon the shoare, & hearing that the M[r] of that vessell had complained to the Burgimaster of the Brill against Capt: Whetstone, this exam[te] went to that Burgimaster, who is alsoe Comissary of the shipps, and advised him to doe nothing in that matter without very good order, and that since they would doe the Parliam[t] noe good, that they should doe them noe hurt, & theruppon that Burgimaster tooke a boate and went downe to Capt: Whetstone, towrds the *Cignett ffriggott*, & by the way mett Capt: Whetstone & spake with him, & this exam[te] alsoe tooke another boate & went aboard Capt: Wetstone & lookt vppon his Comission & Instruccons to see how farr hee might thereby bee borne out in that action, w[ch] Capt: Whetstone then related to this exam[te] to bee thus, vizt. That hee, seeing the Scarboroughe vessell at sea, & not beeing able, as the winde then was, to goe out with his shipp to her, sent out his boate, who haling her, & expecting a roape from her to haue gon aboard her, shee perceiving them to bee in the Parlim[t] service, tackt about & rann herselfe a shoare in the place weere this exam[te] saw her w[ch] was not farr from the first tonn, w[ch] was about five English miles from the Brill, where shipps doe not Vse to harbour or ride except yt bee for a tide or soe, to goe forth or vppon extreamity; and thervppon the next tide the said said Whetstone sent his menn aboard the said Scarboroughe vessell, as shee lay agrounde in the place aforesaid, & fetcht her off & moored her neere his owne vessell, there beeing then aboard her (as yt was said) fower thousand pounds in money, wooll, cloth & ledd to the value as yt was said of fower thousand pounds more, consigned to S[r] Heughe Cholmly, to S[r] William Davenett at Rotterdam, & the proceed thereof to bee returned in armes to the North of England, as partly appeared by letters in that vessell wch this exam^te saw & pervsed; & forthwith this exam^te, returning to the Brill, founde two of the States shipps of 30 or 40 peeces of Ordnaunce each making ready, & the next day they went off from the Brill & rodd by the *Cignett ffriggott*, & vppon the Lords day followeing Admirall Trumpe came to this exam^tes lodging in the Brill & brought with him Capt: Whetstone, whom hee had brought ashoare, & told this exam^te that he was carrying him to the Hage; but with much importunity the said Trumpe gaue Whetstone leaue to goe to church at the Brill with this exam^te, yet in the middle of the Sermon sent for him out of the Church; but Whetstone staying out the Sermon, this exam^te, after the Sermon was done, went with him to Van Trumpe, then standing in the Streets at the Brill with multitudes of people about him, & Trumpe then expressed much anger for the long stay of Whetstone; and then this exam^te demaunding of Trumpe his Comission for the stay of Capt: Whetstone & his shipp, soe much to the preiudice of the Parliam^t, they hauing but one shipp then in the Maze, the s^d Trumpe gaue him thereto noe aunswere, but asked him yf hee did not know what hee was, to wch this exam^te replied that hee knew him well when hee was Deacon of the Church at Roterdam, but was afraide that his preferment had much changed him; vppon wch the said Trumpe grew much in passion, & this exam^te then in the name of the Parliam^t requiring to know of him whether hee came by the order of the Prince of Orange, the States, or the Admiralty at Roterdam, or of himselfe, the said Trumpe gaue noe other aunswere thereto, but said You know what I am; I am vppon Holland grounde, & yf Whetstone will not goe, I will presently goe fight with his shipp, for that is my order; & soe carryed Capt. Whetstone away with him to the Hage, & the Skarboroughe vessell was fetcht into the haven of the Brill by the Dutch, & the Thursday following in this exam^tes sight they carried the *Cignett ffriggott* into the Brill haven alsoe, & hee hath since bin advertised from thence that her sailes were taken from the yard & Capt: Whetstone detained at Roterdam, soe that there is now noe shipp in the Maze to hinder any body goeing in or out there, notwithstanding to his knowledge there is great store of amunition lyes ready at Roterdam to bee shipt for the North of England. And this exam^te further sayeth That at this departure from Holland hee was informed by very good hands that thus they intend to deale with Capt: Zachary, who lyes at the Texell wayting vppon Brocome Bushell, who was then comeing from thence with tenn thousand armes, 26 brasse feild peeces and other amunition for the Earl of Newcastle. And this hee affirmeth vppon his oath to bee true.

For a man of precision, as he undoubtedly was, Hugh Peters here states his age with singular looseness. As a matter of fact he was in his 46th year when he deposed, having been baptized on the 11th of June, 1598, in the parish church of Fowey, Cornwall, where he is registered as the son of Thomas Dickwood, an opulent merchant of that borrough, who most commonly passed under the alias of Peter or Peters. His mother, Martha Treffry, was a daughter of John Treffry of Fowey, Esq.; and at Place, the ancestral home of the Treffrys, a contemporary portrait in oils of the famous divine is still to be seen.

The deposition now first given to the world is eminently characteristic of the man. It is egotistic, theatrical, meddlesome, the quintessence, in short, of Hugh Peters, the evil genius of the Commonwealth. In it we see him playing with a high hand the game that later on made him the most cordially hated, the most vilely execrated man in all England—the game of audacious intermeddling in matters that did not concern him. The scene between the choleric Dutch admiral, livid with passion and outraged dignity, and the cool, hectoring little busybody of a parson, is worthy to live in history. Peters was not slow to perceive the possibilities of the encounter. He no sooner reached England, which he did with all speed, than he proceeded to use it as a means of currying favour with the Parliamentarians, thus laying the foundation of that sinister influence which ultimately brought both his king and himself to the scaffold. He began his disastrous political career by plucking Van Tromp's beard. He finished by plucking straws, fatuously, from the hurdle whereon he rode to judgment.

A DIGEST OF ESSEX WILLS.

WITH PARTICULAR REFERENCE TO NAMES OF IMPORTANCE IN THE AMERICAN COLONIES.

By WILLIAM GILBERT,

Corresponding Member of the New York Genealogical and Biographical Society, Member of the Essex Archaeological Society, etc.

FOREWORD.

It has been observed that wills are the backbone of pedigrees and it is now generally admitted by the genealogist that, of all the sources of information available to him, they stand absolutely first in respect of importance, as they enlighten him more than any other class of document as to the habits, possessions, occupations and relations of his ancestors, as well as informing the antiquary and topographer of the names of estates, farms, fields and houses long since vanished and forgotten. Previous to the commencement of our Parish Registers (A. D. 1538), and subsequently where the early register has been lost or destroyed, wills are of a value that cannot be overestimated in rescuing names and circumstances from oblivion, and recovering somewhat from the ever engulfing stream of time. I propose in the following series to give a digest of the wills of Essex families proved in the 16th and 17th centuries, more especially those whose names are now to be found in America. If any period is important to the American genealogist it is from 1560 to 1625. Comparatively few, in the first instance at any rate, require wills of a much earlier period, while those whose ancestors emigrated later, will, I hope, find the present series a useful basis for further research. This period in England embraces the reigns of Queen Elizabeth and King James I, and the country was calm and peaceful compared with the earlier time of the Reformation and the later time of the civil wars. We therefore find many people of quite a humble station of life exercising testamentary powers to dispose of their little properties; frequently only a few personal things. The wills were usually drawn up either by the parson or the parish clerk—a busy person in those days, frequently combining the duties of schoolmaster, singing master, sexton and verger. There is a great uniformity of expression—the majority commencing "In the name of God Amen," then the date, both the year of the Lord and the year of the reign being given, then the name, abode and occupation of the testator, usually recounting the fact that he is "sicke in bodye but of good hole and pfect mynde and memorie" and thanks Almighty God for it. It is possibly sentiment, but it appeals to many as being a more picturesque procedure than our modern practical method. The wills also frequently contain other religious sentiments and quotations from the Scriptures, which were held in the highest esteem. One reason for this "packing" perhaps lay in the fact that the scribe was remunerated according to the length of the will, and it is not an uncommon circumstance to find moral sentiment and religious hope occupying a good half of it. We however, as genealogists, while deriving a pleasure from this reading leave it to the student of contemporary religious thought and busy ourselves mainly with the earthly relatives and possessions of the deceased; so the digests which follow do not as a rule trouble about the religious clauses except where the fabric of the church is mentioned, or where there is something unusual, curious, or likely to be of service to the antiquary.

The Archdeaconry of Essex had a wide testamentary jurisdiction within the county and the wills date from the year 1400. This was one of the chief courts of Probate for Essex but is far from being the only one, as, without including the Prerogative Court of Canterbury, there were at least fifteen others having powers over various portions, the principal being the Commissary and Consistory Courts of London, the Peculiar of the Dean and Chapter of St. Pauls, and the Commissary Court of Essex and Hertfordshire. I hope to draw upon the vast stores of informotion in all these repositories.

It must be borne in mind that prior to 1752 the year commenced on March 25th (subsequently it commenced on January 1st), otherwise it will appear that a number of wills were proved before they were written which, as Euclid would say, is absurd.

The sign x after witnesses names signifies "his mark," and that he (or she) was unable to write.

It now only remains for me to say that I have a great pleasure in presenting these notes to my American friends (several of whom have corresponded with me at different times, and a few of whom I have personally seen), and I hope that, should anyone be able to throw further light on any of the wills, he will contribute such explanatory details as he may have to this magazine, which will thus become a store-house of no little value, to the antiquary and the genealogist.

1. MOOTTE, THOMAS, of Rochford, Essex, 31 Aug., 1547. To wife Christian my tenement and lands called Bevers for life after to Thomas my son and his heirs, in default to son John and his heirs, in default to remain amongst my daughters by equal portions. To my wife 3 kine 4 sheep and half a seame of wheat. "Yf that my sonne and she breke howssehold" she to have half of household except my best cawdron and two silver spoons the table and form the which I give to son Thomas. Also to him 4 draught bullocks and a young bullocke of 3 years old. To son John two kine—To Johan Hydde and Johan Wrighte a cow each. To Johan Hydde the younger a sheep. To John Shettyl a lamb. Res. and Ex. son Thomas. Overseer John Edward of Rochford—he to have 3/4. Witnesses—Robert Wolball, John Pycke "with others." (Arch. Essex. Bastwicke.)

2. MOTTE, EDWARD, of Downham, Essex, 6 July, 1552. To be buried in churchyard there—To poor mens box 8^d. To my uncle John Motte half my tools at the discretion of Thomas Edwarde. Res. and Ex. wife Kateryne. Overseer Thomas Edwarde he to have my "crusys." Witnesses William Hardye, Clarke; Myles Abarowe "with others." Proved 5 Oct., 1552, at Great Burstead. (Arch. Essex. Thonder.)

3. SWALLOWE, RICHARD, of Hare Street,* 18 Nov., 25 Eliz. Husbandman. To be buried in the South Side† of St. Edwards in Romford. To four of the poor folk 16^d. To my sister Margery a bed etc. To my son-in-law‡ John Burton my greatest colt. To my son-in-law‡ Richard Burton one of my best sheep. To my daughter-in-law‡ Mary Burton my youngest colt. Res. and Ex. My wife Jone.§ Overseer My brother-in-law John Maule of Gubbens‖ and to him 12^d. Witnesses Averye ffrythe, William Maule of the Almshouse, William Maule of Gubbendee‖ and John Payne of Dagenham. Proved 15 Jan., 1582.

4. BAKER, THOMAS, of Woodham Ferris, Co. Essex, 3 Oct., 1521. To be buried in the chapell of Saint Nicholas in the church of Woodham aforesaid, 5/- to the High Altar, £6-13-4 to make the high way betwixt Woodham Church and Halstrete "where moost nede is." Item I bequeath to the "brothren ffreres of the Crossed freres of Colchester 12^s amonge them." To son Thomas £6-13-4. To daughter Kateryn Spyser £3-6-8. To daughter Agnes Peters £3-6-8. To Margaret my wife my land in Hall Strete for life then to my sons John, William and Henry. Res. and Ex. William and Henry my sons. Overseer William Sandys 20/- to him. Wit. Thomas Athaye of Retingdon Hall, John Camp of Yelgers, John Camp of Strotts, John Petche, John Benson, William Baker, Henry Baker "and other." Pr. 25 Aug., 1524. (P. C. C. Bodfelde 25.)

5. GLASCOCKE, JOHN, of Moreton, Essex, 24 Oct., 1559. To my brother Angell my best coat. To daughters Mary, Joan, and Agnes £6-13-4 each at marriage "and I wyll that the gyft of my brother George Glascocke wch was given to Agnes my daughter shal be part of the £6-13-4." To son Thomas £5 at the age 21. To Katheryne Barlye my servant 20/- at age 23 or marriage.

---

* A hamlet near Romford within the Liberty of Havering atte Bower.

† For many centuries there was, in England, a strong prejudice against being buried on the north side of the churchyard, and that portion was usually reserved for the reception of suicides, excommunicate persons, unbaptized infants and those who had been executed. The place of honor was at the east end against the chancel wall (see will No. 6). This prejudice is mentioned by Arnot in his *History of Edinburgh*. In the "Wise and Faithful Steward" (1657) it relates "he requested to be buried in the open churchyard on the *North* side to cross the received superstition as he thought of the constant choice of the south side."

‡ Step-children.

§ Richard Swallow and Joana Burton were m. at Romford in 1580.

‖ There are farms known as Great and Little Gubbins at Laindon, not far from Romford, at the present time.

Res. of personal estate to Jone my wife also to her my houses and lands in Moreton until son Thomas is 21. Wife to have tenement called Blackhall in occupation of John Parker, a croft lying at Villgate and a piece of ground called Fakeners for life. Eexecutors my uncle Robert Thurgood of Magdalen* and Thomas Angyll my brother in lawe of Aytroppe Rothinge 3/4 to each of them. Overseer John Glascocke of Stanford† 3/4 to him. Witnesses Robert Throwgood of Magdalen. Thomas Hosgen "clarke wrytar hereof,"‡ John Borume, Sir Thomas Glascocke Priest,§ Wyllyam Kynge and Wyllyam Dowsett.

Debts wch are owing to me. Thomas Kynge of Aslyns 46/8. Wyllyam Dowsett for shepe 55/4. Burrell 16/-. Mr Becoke 13/4. Wyllyam Doughtye 4 marks. John Kynge £6-6-8. Hollgatt of Ongar 22ᵈ. Polly of Ongar 23ᵈ.

Debts that I owe. To William Dowsett of Magdalen £11-6-8. To my cousin John Lutar‖ £5. To Glascocke of Brendishe 23/4. More to sᵈ. Wyllyam Dowsett 6/8.

Pr. at Chipping Ongar, 3 April, 1560. (Arch. Essex. Randoll.)

6. GRAY, JOHN, of Gosfield, Co. Essex, 20 Aug., 1521. Yeoman. To be buried in the churchyard, at the east end of the said church. To the High Altar there 3/4. To the Ch'wardens 10/-. To do of Belchamp William 3/4. Ditto Belchamp Otten 3/4. Ditto Poslingforth 3/4. To Anne my wife my tenements in Gosfield for life—after to Giles Gray my son and his heirs In default to son William—In default to be sold and the money equally divided between my daughters. John Gawge my son-in-law and Anne his wife to have their free dwelling for 5 years. Res. wife. Ex. wife, John Gawge and James Dundebend. Wit: Sir William Hochekynson "pishe preest of Gosfeld" Harry Parker gent. William Coksall, John Golding, Thomas Loveday, William Tyler "and other." Pr. 5 Feb., 1521, by relict. (P. C. C. 20 Maynwarying.)

7. GILBERT, WILLIAM, of Pitsea, Essex, 13 April, 3 Eliz. To be buried in Pyttesey churchyard. To poor of Pyttesey 6/8. To wife Joane 8 best Kine 30 best sheep all the corn in barn 8 acres of wheat 10 acres of oats growing where I now dwell; all my household goods, a gray ambling nag etc. She to bring up my two young children. To daughter of Agnes 6/8 at age 20. Sons

---

* Magdalen Laver.

† Stanford Rivers.

‡ Rector of Magdalen Laver, d. in 1588. Will proven by Margery, his relict. He was probably also Rector of Lambourne.

§ Rector of Bobbingworth, 1528–1582, when he resigned. His will was proved March 27, 1585, and will be, I hope, given later in this series.

‖ The Luther family who were seated at Suttons, a manor near Ongar, and afterwards at Kelvedon and Doddinghurst, bore Argent two bars sable in chief three round buckles azure. I have an unpublished pedigree of them and also copies of inscriptions, etc. Various unsuccessful attempts have been made to associate them with the celebrated Martin Luther. Thomas Luther baptized at Greensted, 20 Sept., 1579, m. Bridget, dau. and heiress of Thomas Glasscock of Doddinghurst.

Isaake* and Abraham† under 21—Brother John Gylberts 4 children—John Walker—To John Carre of Basildon 4 sheep—To brother John my black gearkin and best hose—My sisters children To brother Newton my cloak. Ex. Thomas Holke of Pitsea and Harye Doore of same—20/- each. Res. My two sons—Overseer John Harrys of Basildon. (signed) William Gealbert. Wit: Walter Elyot—Peter Balyeff—Richard Venables—John Harrys and Richard Newton. Proved at Brentwood, June 17, 1561. (Arch. Essex. Randoll.)

8. FREER, JOHN (Calendared as Fryer‡ but signed Freer), of Clare, Co. Suffolk, 20 June, 1585. To poor of Clare 40/-. To Bridgett wife all my freehold in Essex. Also my mansion house in Clare with two crofts of land called Bryans and Tyle Croft. To Robert Payne son and heir of Thomas Payne of Wilberton in the Isle of Ely two tenements in Northgate Street Clare. To Henry Campion my servant one tenement in Nethergate Street now in the occupation of his father William Campion. I bequeath to Mr. Lynsey my father-in-law my black gelding. To my cousin Thomas Payne of Wilberton £10. Res. and Ex. wife and cousin Thomas Payne of Wilberton. Wit. Edmond Lee, Thomas Reynold, William Byshopp. Pr. 16 July, 1585. (P. C. C. Brudenell 36.)

9. KINGE, THOMAS, of East Ham, Essex (mutilated), 23 July, 1580. Yeoman. To be buried in East Ham Churchyard. To four men to bear me to the church 12ᵈ. To poor of East Ham 10/-. To Nicholas Snare 40/-. To Katherin ffollintyne £3. To Alice daughter of John Browne of East Ham 50/- at age 21. Son John Wasse. Christian daughter of Richard Raynoldes. To each godchild 16ᵈ. To William Woodlande of Barking my best cloke and my russett cote. Res. and Ex. wife Emme. Overseer my son John Wasse. Witness Edmund Hartley. Proved 8 March, 1582. (Arch. Essex. Draper.)

10. OWTRED, MARSCELM, of Romford, Co. Essex, 8 Oct., 1582. Commences "My helpe is in the name of oure lorde who hathe made bothe heaven and yearthe." To the poor of Romford 40/-. My tenement in Romford. My cousins Mr. William Owtred and Mr. John Owtred. Anne and Elizabeth sisters of my cousin Johh Owtred. My brother Richard Bowers. My aunts daughter Margery Holman. To Mr. Pytte minister of Allhallows in the Wall London§ 20/-. To Mr. Richard Atkys minister of Romford

---

* His will will follow later on.

† An administration of the estate of Abraham Gilbert of Corringham, Essex, was granted on 15 Jan., 1583, to his relict Agnes.

‡ Fryer family—I have in my collection of Essex deeds an original indenture dated 1 Jan., 1696, between Andrew ffryer of Bassledon, Co. Essex, gentleman, and Hester, his wife, and Henry Claris of Theobalds, Co. Middlesex, yeoman, of the one part; and William Woodroffe, citizen and brewer of London, of the other part—being a lease for 32 years of premises in Thames Street, London.

§ John Pitte, minister there 1571-1593, when he d.

40/–. Executors Richard Adkys and Robert Dickenson. Overseer—Francis Ramme.* Witnesses John Greene, Randall Hall.(x) Proved 9 March, 1582. (Arch. Essex. Draper.)

11. WRITE, JOHN, of Purleigh, Essex, 2 May, 1606, husbandman. To be buried in the churchyard. To eldest son John £20. To second son Thomas £20. To Johane Prentice 40/– at marriage and to Sarah Prentice 40/– at age 21. To John and William Prentice 20/– each at age 21. Res. & Ex. wife. Witnesses Thomas Trastell John Levitt. Proved 27 May, 1606, by Florence, relict. (Arch. Essex. Neville.)

A DIGEST OF ESSEX WILLS.

WITH PARTICULAR REFERENCE TO NAMES OF IMPORTANCE IN THE AMERICAN COLONIES.

BY WILLIAM GILBERT,

Corresponding Member of the New York Genealogical and Biographical Society, Member of the Essex Archaeological Society, etc.

NOTE.—The Probate reference to Will No. 3 (see RECORD, Vol. XL, No. 1, p. 6), was inadvertently omitted—it should be: "Arch. Essex. Draper."

12. ADKYNSON, ANNYS, of Purleigh, Essex, 8 April, 1589, widow. To be buried in churchyard. 12^d to poor mens box. To son Nathaniel 10/–. To son William "the cowe with the white face" and the bed he lyeth on &c. My son in law John Kempe and his son John.—William Kempe. John & Thomas Eastwood. Res. & Ex: son in law John Kemp. Wit: Robson(x) and John Anger(x). Johnannem Hewytt "clericum ac Scriptorem." Pr. 1589 (day and month blank). (Arch. Essex. Maynard.)

13. BAKER, WILLIAM, of Toppesfield, Essex, 9 Oct., 1558. To poor at Burial 6/8. To sister Rose Ede 13/4; to her children 20/. To each godchild 12^d. To John Pollarde (my godson) my best coat. Robert Towne. Jone Pollarde (widow)*. Jone Bygge. Rychard Hull. Residue to be disposed in deeds of charity. Ex.: John Madge Vycar of ffinchingfelde† and Rychard Yekam‡ of Toppesfelde, 10/– to each. Wit: Robert Pollarde and John Heymas, John Gage "prest." Pr. 26 April, 1560. (Com. Essex & Herts-Westwood.)

14. BALDWIN, THOMAS, of Upminster, Essex, 16 Nov., 34 Eliz. To son Thomas at 21, £40. To son John at 21, £30. To three

* 1580, Nov. 1. Buried—Joane Pollarde, widowe (Register). The early registers of Toppesfield have many entries to the name of Pollard.
† He was vicar from 1532 to 1562, when he died.
‡ Probably Yeldham, there being many of this name in the parish down to the present day. Yeldham is also a place name in Essex. A Richard Yeldham was buried at Toppesfield on Nov. 27, 1581.

* Francis Ramme was an important personage at that time, being Bailiff of the Royal Manor of Haveringe atte Bower. I have the original Manor Rolls of 1583, etc., bearing his name.

daughters Margaret, Joan and Hester Baldwin, £20 each at 21. Res. and Ex. Wife Agnes. Overseer Gyles ffarrlowe my bro-in-law. Wit: Gyles ffayrrlowe, George ffayrelawe, John Barker. Pr. 11 Dec.. 1592. (Arch. Essex. Stephen.)

15. BARNES, FRANCIS, of Finchingfield, Essex, 9 Sept., 2 Eliz. To be buried in chapel of St. John the Baptist in parish church of Finchingfield. To church for tithes forgotten 20ᵈ. To poor at burial £4. To poor of Much Barfelde, Wetherfelde and Topp-felde, 10/– each parish. To eldest son Francis my chain of gold and plate, &c., he to pay his three brothers Arthur, John and William, £20 each at 21. To Francis, aforesaid, my manor of Dyves and Petches and my manor of Justice situate in Wethers-felde Toppsfeld Maplestead and Hawstead in tail male. Res.: wife Barbara. She to remain at manor of Petches. Ex: wife and son Francis, Supervisor Humfrie Cornewell, Esq., he to have 20/– and a grey colte. Wit: William Eterell, Thomas Walford, Henry Hyslette, Richarde Spenser and Richard Emerie. Pr. 23 Jan., 1560. (Com. Essex & Herts. Westwood.)

16. BISHOPPE, AGNES, of South Weald, Essex (nuncupative), 12 July, 1599, widow. All her goods to her daughter-in-law Denis Bishop, widow, of parish aforesaid. Wit: William Reynolde John Ford. Pr. 7 Nov., 1599, by Dionisie Bishopp. (Arch. Essex. Stephen.)

17. BROWNE, WILLIAM, of Little Wenden, Essex, 28 March, 1577. To be buried in churchyard. To William Kinge, Bayliffe, my best shirte of the thre, a pair of bates and a pair of spurres. Res. to Agnes, daughter of Henry Searson of Gt. Wenden. Wit. Nicholas Yorke,* rector of Wenden pva, John Rombolde, John ffelsted. Probate not given. (Arch. Colchester. Roote.)

18. COLE, JOHN,† of Ardleigh, Essex, 8 Feb., 1517, "the elder." To be buried in the church. To the high altar 3/4. Son John Cole of Dedham to have my house called Hunte-of-the-Wode. Son Walter Cole to have the house he dwelleth in and Fordwell fylde. Son Young John to have his house called Walles and cer-tain fields—he to pay his brother John of Dedham 40/–. To dau. Christian 40/– and a cowe. Res. and Ex: John Cole of Dedham. Wit: John Baldwyn now of Ardlegh, Harry Perpaynte and John Pache. Date of Probate not given. (Arch. Colchester. Francys.)

19. COLE, WALTER, of Ardleigh, Essex, 8 May, 1528. Weaver. To be buried in churchyard. To the high altar 6ᵈ. To Pauls Pardon 2ᵈ.* To dau. Margaret a calf. To son John a bullock.

---

* Rector from 1572 to 1583, when he died.
† I contributed extended digests of this will and the succeeding one to the *Ardleigh Parish Magazine* and they appeared in this year's January and Feb-ruary numbers respectively. The name Cole still flourishes in that vicinity—one of the descendants suggests a connection with King Cole (frequently styled "Old King Cole"), the British King of whom Colchester (only a few miles from Ardleigh) is proud. It is not impossible.
‡ Pardon was the old English word for indulgence, and it was applied more specifically to an Indulgenced Altar or Shrine, viz.: a place at which so many days indulgence could be gained by the faithful who would devoutly

To eldest son Thomas my house and lands in Ardleigh on condition that he keep his mother Alice. Res. Son Thomas he to pay 13/4 to each of my other children. Wit: Raffe Lee, "prest," John Wente, Richard Wace. Date of Probate not given but not much later. (Arch. Colchester. Francys.)

20. EDWARDE, JOHN, of Little Thurrock, Essex. To be buried in churchyard. To poor of Lt. Thurrock £10, namely to Whyttfeild 6/8, Hicks 6/8, Tymothe Tybolde 6/8, Peche 6/8, Rowlye 3/4, Crose 3/4, Chalke 3/4, 3/4 towarde a Byble. To William Holidaye, clarke, 6/8. To Nicholas Greene 6/8. To the 3 children of James Humfrye, my predecessor, according to their fathers will, £11. I owe Henry Devenish £14, widow Edlynne of Oesedde * £10, William Humfrye of Thundersley 48/- & William Castle 6/-. William Castle owes me 13/-. John Slaterford of Stanford, butcher, hath received of me for hides £11-7-8 whereof I have received 9 hides and an halfe, four at 5/- apeece and five and a halfe at 5/2 apeece. Lewes Jonsonne of Horndon owes me 20/-, Thomas Cardye of Laindon Hills 5/-, Edward Austen of Greens End 20/-, Lucas of Greens End 7/10, William Standbace of London, curryer, 20/-, Duffeild of West Thoroke 4/4. I bequeath to my servant Henry Devenish my mill—Ollyfe the wife of Timothy Tybolde. To Agnes Humfrye a bed &c. To Elizabeth Humfrye 20 marks† besides her father's gift which is 11 nobles.‡ To James Humfrye 20 marks. To Margaret Savage 20 marks. Ex. William Humfrye of Thundersley. Overseers William Holydaye, clarke, and William Hickes. Res: equally between my Ex. and my overseers. Wit. Nicholas Greene(x) Timothie Tybolde(x). Pr. 1 March, 1593. (Arch. Essex. Stephen.)

21. FLETCHER, THOMAS, of Barking, Essex, 8 March, 1582. Tanner. To be buried in churchyard§ near late wife Jane‖ —. My wife Agnes. My four children Thomas, Matthewe,¶ Jane & Joane. To son John** 40/-. To my wifes dau. Dorothy Meadowes 20/-. William Wright of Matching to have the custody & education of my daughter Jane. John Poole of Little Waltham shall have ditto of dau. Joane. Res. & Ex. wife Agnes. Overseers Robert Comyns and Thomas ffisher. Wit: Thomas Newton, "minister,"†† Willm Prebell, Thomas ffyssher & Gryffin Goose.‡‡ Proved 23 March, 1582. (Arch. Essex. Draper.)

---

pray there. In the cloisters of old St Pauls (in London) there was a chapel, and in it an indulgenced altar, which was called Paul's Pardon—this is the reference in the above will. The offerings to it went to the support of the church. Both the cloister, chapel and pardon were taken down and the material used to build Somerset House. "Item the x day of Aprill (1547) was pullyd downe the cloister in Powles that was called the Pardon churchyard with the chappelle that stode in the myddes to bylde the protectors palace."
  * Orsett.   † A mark=13ˢ. 4ᵈ.   ‡ A gold coin, value 6ˢ. 8ᵈ.
  § Buried 17 March, 1582-3.   ‖ Buried 20 Sept., 1582.
  ¶ William and John, sons of Matthew Fletcher, bap. 1597 and 1600 respectively.
  ** Simon, son of John Fletcher, bap. 1596.
  †† Probably curate. His son Zachariah was buried at Barking, 11 Oct., 1852.
  ‡‡ Buried at Barking, 22 Sept., 1583.

200

22. GILBERT, ISAAC,* of Rayleigh, Essex, 24 April, 1597. To be buried in Churchyard. To poor 20/-. To Mother-in-law Margerie Brodwater 5/-. To each of her children 12ᵈ. To godson Henry Livinge 5/-. To my sister Livinge 5/-. To each other godchild 2/-. My sister Anne, wife of Thomas Meredithe,† of North Benfleet.‡ John Lake of Benfleet. To my eldest son Nicholas Gilbert £60 at 24. Ditto to son Isaac Gilbert. Children of my son Uncle John Gilbert, late of Layndon. My Kinsman Thomas Plommer of Basildon. My wife Anne to bring up son Isaac and apprentice him to a tailor and draper. To wife my houses and lands in Rayleigh and Pitsea for life after to son Isaac. To wife my house and land in Hawkwell after to son Nicholas. Ex. wife. Overseers brother-in-lawe Henry Lyvinge and John Lake 6/8 each. Wit. William Catly,(x) Thomas Blakemore,(x) John Waters,(x) Thomas Meredithe. Pr. 28 May, 1597. (Arch. Essex. Stephen.)

23. GLASCOCK, JOHN, of Hatfield Broad Oak, Essex, 10 June, 1579. Yeoman. To be buried in churchyard. To poor 10/-. To Nicholas Grene, my daughters son, my tenements in Hatfield where John Bromehead dwells with the shops which "sometyme weare the ould Geldehall." My land called Hales Land (after decease of Katherin my wife) to John Glascock of Roxwell, gent. He to pay my Executors £40. My three daughters viz. Olive Wright, Joan Bate, & Audreye Bromeholl. Brother John Wright. Res: wife. Ex: John Wright of Hatfield and Rychard Pechye of Gelsson Yeoman, 20/- each. Overseers John Wilkenson and Christofer Somner both of White Roding, 10/- each. Wit: Johem Meade, Willm. Lovedaye, John Lovedaie, John Wilkinson, James Thompsatt, John Bromehead. Pr. 19 Oct., 1580. (P. C. C. Arundel, 36.

24. GRIFFIN, JOHN, of Barking, Essex (nuncupative), 26 Aug., 1590. Husbandman. To his master Thomas Barnes gent. his naggs and 40/-. To John Barnes 20/-. Res. to be equally divided between his sisters (not named). £3 to be bestowed on his burial. Wit. Thomas Myller, Robert Robient "and others." Pr. 27 Aug., 1590. (Arch. Essex, Maynard.)
An administration of further goods of testator was granted to his brother Edward Griffin on 1 Nov., 1590.

25. HEDGE MATTHEW, of Gingmountney,§ Essex, 26 Dec., 1590. To wife Alice all my cattle and goods for life, after to son Matthew, he to be Ex. and to have 20/- which is owing to me by Ambrose Blackney of Ingatestone. Wit: Anthony Brasier,‖ Thomas Amott.(x) Pr. 20 Feb., 1590. (Arch. Essex. Maynard.)

---

* Son of William Gilbert of Pitsea (see Will No. 7).
† He was Rector of North Benfleet, 1581–1612.
‡ Their marriage licence was dated Jan. 28, 1589–90. From them, through their daughter Anne, descends Lord Raymond.
§ Mountnessing.
‖ He was Vicar of Mountnessing from 1562 to 1605 when he resigned. He was also Rector of Ingatestone from 1566 to 1609, when he died.

26. HUNT, THOMAS, of Boreham, Essex, 26 Sept., 1592. Labourer. To dau. Thomerzon my household goods at 18 (or marriage). My lands & tenements in Boreham to son John at 24. To dau. Alice £4 at 18. Ex. John Hayward of Westham. Wit: Edward Stanes, Thomas Tendringe, Roger Bramstone. Pr. 20 Feb., 1592. (Arch. Essex. Stephen.)

27. JOHNSON, ROBERT, of Stapleford Abbotts, Essex, 17 Jan., 1581. Husbandman. To be buried in churchyard. To son William £8 at 21. To dau. Christian 40/-. To dau. Elizabeth 33/4. To each of my other daughters 10/-. Res. & Ex. wife Jane. Overseer Clemente Stonarde.* Wit: Richard Reynoldes,† clarke. Pr. 9 March, 1582. (Arch. Essex. Draper.)

28. KYNGE, RICHARD, Parson‡ of Nettiswell, Essex, 26 April, 1524. To be buried within the church of Aldermary. 20/- to that church. To children of my brother Gilbert Howell, viz. Thomas, James, Mary and Cuthbert.—My sister's children, viz: Robert Patenson and Paronell. My sister Margaret. Residue to father Thomas Kynge and my mother (not named, but see probate), they to be Ex. with my brother Gilbert Howell. Supervisor John ffawyden of Southflete. Wit. Robert Tolle, Willm. Johns, Thomas Peercy, Richard Boydon and Sir John Reed, parish preest of Aldermary. Pr. 24 Oct., 1524, by Thomas Kyng (Executor named), power reserved for Katerine Kyng and Gilbert Powell. (P. C. C. Bodfelde, 26.)

29. KYNGE, JOHN, of Althorne, Essex, 18 April, 15 Hen. VIII (1524), "named John Kynge by West." To be buried in the churchyard. To the high altar 20/-. To Powlys pardon§ 12ᵈ. My tenement and lands called Rawlyns lying in parish of Mayland to son William. My tenements &c called Jacomyns and Sayers in the parish of Purleigh to son Robert, also to him my tenement &c called Skryvyns and Crowche Hill in parish of Lawing. My Ex. to have my farms called West Newland and Barkhams, to pay my debts, and keep my son Robert until he cometh to age of 21, when he is to have the farms. My Ex to have my Wyk‖ called Donmers Wik in Burnham to keep my son

---

* He was the representative of an ancient and well placed family, being the son of Francis Stonarde of Stapleford Abbotts and Lucy, dau. of Sir Clement Higham, the Lord Chief Baron, after whom he was named. When noting the memorial in Stapleford Abbotts Church in 1904, I observed (and copied) the one to his parents which bears the arms of Stonarde quartering Higham. His will was proved in 1612.

† Rector from 1568 to 1606 (when he died) and also at the same time Rector of Lambourne.

‡ Rector from 1522 to 1524 when he died. Respecting the term *parson* Blackstone says it is the "most legal beneficial and honourable title that a Parish priest can enjoy." Cripps says: "The Parson is the Rector of a church Parochial. Such an one, and he only, is said '*vicam seu persomam ecclesiæ gerere.*'" Others derive the title from the French '*paroissien*' (parochial) because he was the resident priest of the Parish, and not sent out from a monastery, as a vicar would be.

§ See note to Will No. 19.

‖ Wick, a bay, a small port or village on the side of a river (Halliwell's *Dictionary of Archaic Words*).

John till age 21, when he is to have it and pay to the lord ffitz-water £26-13-4 yearly. My father in lawe William Slynge and Alice his wife to have my Wykes called Redward and Calfe Cope in Burnham to keep son William till age 21 to pay the lord yerely £16-13-4 and to deliver to William when of age. My Ex to have the house I now dwell in called Robert Kynges and also that called Countys bredge for six yeres to pay debts &c and then son John to have it. To daughter Emme £40. To daughter Elynor £40. To our Lady Yelde* in Althorne £20. To church of Althorn to buy a cope and vestment 20 marks. To brother Richard Kyng 6/8. Res to be divided between children. To Thomas son of William Kynge £8. My Ex. to put my house and lands called Culverhouse for a perpetual obit in church of Althorn. An honest priest to sing for me for six yeres. Ex Wm. Harryes of Cold Norton and John Coker of Purleigh. Supervisors William Slyng of Mayland and John Smyth of Cold Norton. Wit: William Baker vicar of Althorne,† William Kyng "and other." Pr. 15 June, 1524. (P. C. C. Bodfeld, 22.)

30. KINGE, EDWARD, of Purley, Essex, 19 Nov., 1591 (non-cupative). To poor 40/-. Debts forgiven to Myles Thornet. Residue to brother Christopher Kinge. Wit: Thomas Hastler, Miles Thornett. Pr. 11 Feb., 1591, by brother George Kinge. (Arch. Essex. Stephen.)

31. KING, ELLEN,‡ of Halstead, Essex, 14 Jan., 1627, widow, late wife of Edmund King, gent, deceased. My son in law Crowche oweth me £40 to be divided equally between his children (not named) £10 each. To my son John Chambers £40 and various household articles. To my grandchild Anne Rowley a bed &c. To my daughter Katherine Lewes 20/-. To my daughter Clarke 5/-. To son-in-law John Rowley 20/-. To my grandchild John Rowley 20/-. To Mathewe Rowley daughter (?) to my son John Rowley 2 pr. of sheets &c. Servants—Sarah and Mary Raven & Edward Briggs. If my Executors are vexed in law by Peter King, or Thomas King, for any of my goods, then my son John Chambers to bear part of the charge. Res and Ex: my son Felix Chambers & my daughter Elizabeth Langham. Wit: William Bramstoon, Charles Owsold. Pr. 29 Dec., 1628, by Ex. named. (P. C. C. Barrington, 110.)

32. MOTTE, JONE, of Much Badowe, Essex, 24 Nov. (year blank). To father my beast and a young horse. To brother

---

* *I. E.*, Guild—at this time nearly every parish had its guild, which were voluntary associations established on a religious basis for mutual help and prayer. Their funds were formed by annual subscriptions and bequests. These guilds were suppressed at the Reformation because at them prayers were offered for their deceased members.

† Vicar from 1518 to 1532 when he died.

‡ There is an original will of an Edmund Kinge of Halstead, Essex, preserved in the British Museum Library, Mss. Room, dated 19 Jan., 1624, which mentions a wife Helen, sons Thomas, Robert, Barnabas, Abraham, Bartholomew, Peter and Edmund; grandchildren Elizabeth and Susan Kinge, daughters of son Barnabas, and Elizabeth Kinge, sister of Thomas Kinge.

John a cowe and a bullocke. To my sisters daughter a mark at
18 (or marriage). To Andrewe Byles my sword and buckler.
To Humphrey 20ᵈ. To Randall Bykarton 20ᵈ. To 3 godchildren
20ᵈ. each. Ex: John Cornish & Robert Cowp. Overseer father.
Wit: William Paschall, Thomas Paschall and John Motte. Pr.
1545. (Arch. Essex. Bastwicke.)

33. OSBORN, RICHARD, of Bradwell next the Sea, Essex, 31 Jan.,
34 Eliz. To be buried in churchyard. To my sister Mary Os-
borne a bed &c. My sisters Joan Osborne and Eme Osborne.
To brother John my apparel. Res: son John at age 21. Ex.
John Medcalfe of Bradwell and my brother John Osborne. Wit:
Robert Pecke, John Wakein. Pr. 23 April, 1593. (Arch. Essex.
Stephen.)

34. SMYTHE, THOMAS, of Blackmore, Essex, 12 Feb., 1590.
Gent. To be buried in Blackmore Church where grandfather
and grandmother are buried. Sole Legatee & Ex. mother. Wit:
Margaret Smeth, Thomas Smethe father to testator. Pr. 30 Oct.,
1592. (Arch. Essex. Stephen.)

35. STEVENS, CHRISTOPHER, of Stanford le Hope, Essex, 15
Nov., 1582. To my dau. Helen's eldest living son William
Clemente two sheep. To son John all my land except one yard
with one barn and sufficient timber to make the same a house to
dwell in, this to dau. Johan. To Edward Denton £6.13.4. To
Edward Dentons sister 40/–. The two sons of my cousin Jone
Banke. Res. & Ex. Dau. Johan. Overseer, friend Eugeny
Gatton. Wit: Thomas Somerfielde, Eugenye Gatton. Pr. 17
Jan., 1582. (Arch. Essex. Draper.)

36. WRIGHT, JOHN,* of Barking, Essex, 20 June, 1584. To be
buried in the church near my first wife. To poor £3. To sister
Alyce Stevens 20/– and the little house that Richard Ince
dwelleth in for life and after to Joane Stevens and her heirs.
To John Buckland 2/6. Thomas Fyssher 2/6. Grace Barber
10/–. To cosen Foote 3/4 and his wife 3/4. To sister Baker 5/–.
To Andrew and William Gravelinge 3/4 each. Res. & Ex: wife
Elizabeth.† Overseers William Walgrave & Henry Wilde. Wit:
William Nutbrowne, Christofer Myers, Henry Wilde, William
Squyer. Pr. 2 July, 1584. (Arch. Essex. Draper.)

37. WRIGHT, JOHN, of Little Laver, Essex, 12 Sept., 1585, "the
elder." To be buried in churchyard. To poor 3/4. To wife
Joanne my tenement called Castlyne in Lt. Laver & Moreton.
To dau. Jane £20. To son Bennet £30. To Dennes my son
£30. Sons John & Thomas, my five daughters Johane, Adrey,
Agnes, Jaine & Rose. Res. & Ex: Wife. Overseer son John,
Wit: Thomas Hoskin, John Hanson the younger. Pr. 11 Nov.,
1585. (Arch. Essex. Draper.)

---

* He was churchwarden and was buried on June 23, 1584. (Register.)
† Elizabeth Wright, widow, m. Thomas Powncett, gent., Aug. 14, 1589.
(Register.)

A DIGEST OF ESSEX WILLS.

WITH PARTICULAR REFERENCE TO NAMES OF IMPORTANCE IN THE AMERICAN COLONIES.

By WILLIAM GILBERT,

Corresponding Member of the New York Genealogical and Biographical Society, Member of the Essex Archaeological Society, etc.

38. BAKER, JOHN, the elder, of Ardleigh, Essex, 28 March, 1530. To be buried in churchyard. To high awter 12^d. To mayntayne the light of the church of Ardleigh a cow value 10/-. To Poullis p'don 4^d. To wife Margaret my howse & landes that y dwelin. Property in Ardleigh called Croyles. Eldest son Thomas, youngest son Thomas, son John. Res. & Ex. wife. Witnesses:—John Lowunt,* Thomas Lambe, John Nevers,†

---

* Lowunt should probably be Loueron or Loveron, a common name in Ardleigh. John Loveron was churchwarden about 1555 and put his cross on every page of the oldest register to testify to its accuracy (though he could not read!).

† Nevers is probably identical with Nevard, a very old local name spelled in former times Nouert, Neuert, etc.

Richard Wace.* (No probate mentioned.) (Arch. Colchester. Francys.)

39. BARNES, HENRY, of Rayleigh, Essex, 19 January, 1638. Yeoman. To son Henry my copyhold tenements called Pikes, and Wards, in Rayleigh. To son John my tenement in Hanfield. To Susan Camber, my daughter, £10. To Anne Allen, my daughter, £30. To Mary Barnes, my daughter, my tenement wherein John Scarcroft now dwelleth. 20/- each, to my grandchildren Elizabeth, John and Anne Allen; and Jeffery, Thomas and Jane Mitchell. To poor of Rayleigh 20/-. To Humphrey Plumb, William Boade and Margaret Brockes 5/- each. Res. and Ex. son Thomas. Overseers:—Isaac Gilbert† and John Pinson. Wit.:—George Deresley, William Brewster, John Packwood(x). Proved at Ingatestone, 12 Feb., 1638. (Arch. Essex. Whitehead.)

40. BROWNE, JOHN, of South Weald, Essex, 11 Nov., 1637. Yeoman. To son Matthew £20 & my tenement now in the occupation of Edward Waterman, blacksmith. To dau. Rebecca £40. To son John £80. To son Henry after decease of Olave my wife my house I now dwell in. Res. & Ex. wife, Olave. Wit: Gabriel Cawood, Walter Gittens, Henry Lucas. Proved 2 Feb., 1637. (Arch. Essex. Whitehead.)

41. FOSTER, THOMAS, of High Laver, Essex, 22 Sept., 1631. Yeoman. To poor 20/-. My wife Dennys to have my freeholds in High Laver. Joseph and Andrew the sons of my brother Michael Foster deceased. My Kinswoman Mary, wife of John Fann. To my maid servant Grace Kinge £5. Cousin Robert Wood the elder, of Harlow. The children of my sister Marie, late wife of John Carver. My brother Thomas Foster. Res. & Ex. wife. Wit: John Foster, John Gladwyn, Robert Wood, Prudence Harrison, George Harrison. Proved 5 Feb., 1637, by relict. (Arch. Essex. Whitehead.)

42. GLASCOCKE, JOHN, of Stanford Rivers, Essex, 12 March, 1574. To be buried in churchyard. My wife Bennett shall have in satisfaction of her dower or thirde my farm called Bridges for 6 years if she remain unmarried after to Mathew and Laurence my sons they delivering to my wife yearly one quarter each of wheat barley and oats. If both sons die without issue then to my youngest son Richard. If my tenement called Morrells which I have by the will of my father shall happen to come to my son Matthew by or after the death of my son Andrewe without heirs of his body then Laurence to have Bridges aforesaid. My wife to have my tenement and lands called Reydons in Bobbingworth and a yearly rent of £5 out of my tenement called Morrells for life, after to son Richard. To my daughters Maryon and Katherine £20 each at 21 or marriage. My three daughters already married viz. Joane, Ellyne and Clemence. To sons Laurence and Mathewe my lease in Holingesorth Wodde wch. I

---

* He was the parish clerk.
† Son of Isaac Gilbert of Rayleigh. See will No. 22.

have by lease from Mr. Ellyot.   To dau. Joane, dau. Hogge, and dau. Tanner 3/6/8 each.   Res. Andrewe, Laurence and Mathewe my sons.   Overseers:—My brother John Glascocke of Roxwell and my Bro-in-law Xpofer Summers.   Wit:—William Atkinson, Thomas Glascocke, Richard Glascocke.   Proved 19 May, 1575. (Arch. Essex. Gyll.)

43. GRUB, JOHN, of Thornewood Hamlet, North Weald Basset, Essex,* 27 May, 1644.   Weaver.   To my grandchild John Grub my house wherein I now dwell and the shopp and the medowe behind the shoppe—to him and his heirs for ever—he paying to his grandmother 40/ a year in lieu of her thirde.   To him also my great draught lome at Rumforde.   To my wife Sarah the parlour buttery etc. & the use of the kitchen to brue and to bake in—also linen etc.   Res. & Ex. wife and son John. To son John my copyhold land & 1 acre of freehold land that lyeth in Penny Meade.   Wit:—William Piggott† and Richard Spranger. (P. C. C. Fairfax, 166.)

44. HUNT, JOHN, of Shenfield, Essex, 3 Jany., 1649.   Husband-man.   My eldest daughter—Dorothy Bullithorp.   My dau. Sara. My grandchildren Dorothy, Robert, John and Sara Bullithorp. My grandchildren John and Sara Goodman.   My dau. Mary.   My grandchild Mary Kinge.   Res. and Ex. wife.   Wit:—George Parker, Robert King.   Proved 24 Jany., 1649, by Dorothy Hunt, relict. (Arch. Essex. Whitehead.)

45. ISAACK, WILLIAM, of Alphamstone, Essex, 17 Sept., 1584. Yeoman.   To be buried in churchyard.   To son John my three messuages known by the name of fflegge Crokes or Wolsees with the lands of the same lying in Alphamstone, Lamarsh & Bures. to him & his heirs—in default to son William.   To son James £140 to purchase a house which shall be bought for him by my brother Thomas Isaack and my cousin Peter Isaack.   To wife Elizabeth my tenement called Angurs for life after to son William.   To my three daughters Joane, Elizabeth and Marye £30 each at age of 21.   My brother Christopher.‡   My brothers in law Geffery Sidey and Robert Nicholl.   To cosen Martin 28/6. To my cosen & godson Robert Sidey 20/.   Res. equally between wife and son William.   Ex. son William.   Supervisors.   Thomas Isaack (brother) Peter Isaack.   Witnesses: John Allen and William Polly.   Proved 5 Nov., 1584. (P. C. C.   35 Watson.)

[NOTE.—I contributed an extended digest of the above will, together with some notes on the family of Isaacke to the *Alphamstone Parish Magazine* for October, 1908, and March, 1909.]

---

* Extracts from Parish Register: 1606, John Grubb and Sarah Pope married ye 11 September.   1607, John the sonn of Jhon Grubb was baptized ye 16 August.   1626, John Grubb married Anne Shelton ye 21 November.   1644, John Grubb buried ye 1st July.

† 1606, William Pickett married Joan Goody ye 7 July. (Register.)

‡ A marriage license was granted by the Bishop of London on Sept. 5, 1589, to Christopher Isaacke of Gaines Colne (a neighboring parish) and Frances Prentice, widow of same parish.

46. KING, JOHN, of Shelly, Essex, 16 October, 1517. I bequeath my soul to Almighty God and St. Mary His Moder. To be buried in the Churchyard. To the High Altar 2/. To my eldest son John at age 20 my tenement called Glorywyks in Bobbingworth, in default to my son Thomas, in default to my two daughters Alys and Jone. To Thomas my son, and to each daughter, 26/8. To Laurenc of Chelley* 3/16/-. To my brother John 20/. My wife Jone to be Ex. with my brother John. She to have residue of goods. Wit:—Laurenc aforenamed and my gostly fader Rawffe Hardgrave pson. Proved 17 Nov., 1517. (Arch. Essex. Sell.)

47. KINGE,† JOHN, of Althorne, Essex, 17 May, 1576. Yeoman. To be buried in church of Althorne by the place where Margaret my wife was buried. To poor 20/-. For a sermon 6/8. To the reparation of the Church 10/-. To Anne my wife my house etc. called Cliffordes wherein I now dwell and also Westwoods and East and West Wellmers for life after to the lawful issue of myself and Anne. In default to my son William Kinge and his heirs. Margaret Aylife mother of my said wife (Anne). Wife to have lease of the parsonage of Luckendon. To each child of my sister Dorothie and James Harrys 40/-. Cousin Margaret Boyton. My uncle William Kinge of London. Son William to have the lease of Burnham Hall. Res. and Ex. son William. Overseer:—Peter Osburne of London Esq. Wit:—Roger Preston Robte Chafer citizen and merchant tailor of London. Proved 22 Nov., 1580. (P. C. C. 46 Arundell.)
He owned land in Althone, Burnham, Sydminster and Lachenden, Essex.

48. KNAPP, JOHN, of Lawford, Essex, 2 Oct., 1535. To the High Altar 12d. My wife Agnes to sell my lands called Prylands and Veselands holden by fee and conteyning X acres in Lawford and with the money thereof to pay my debts funeral and legacies. To my said wife my tenement called Roots for life after to be sold and the money to be divided between my children begotten between the said Agnes and me. To my eldest son John Knapp 40/- to be paid in money when he cometh to the age of 26. Res. and Ex. wife Agnes. Wit:—John Clerk of Dedham, Robert Kertche of Lawford. (Probate not mentioned.) (Arch. Colchester. Roberts.)

49. KYNGE, JOHN, of Burnham, Essex, 19 Feb., 1566. (Nuncupative will.) Yeoman. To son William Kynge his best bedde after his mothers decease. Residue of his goods and also his lease, and term of years, in Burnham Hall, and other lands which

---

* *i. e.*, Shelley.
† A John Kinge of Althorne, Co. Essex, married (license of Bishop of London) 19 August, 1574, Anne Sulyard, fourth daughter of Eustace and Margaret (Foster) Sulyard of Flemings in Runwell, Co. Essex. He bore arms: "Azure, a bend ermine between two eagles displayed, or." A Pedigree of Sulyard appears in Visitation of Essex, Harleian MSS., and Eustace Sulyard left a will in which a large amount of goods, furniture and silver are mentioned. Runwell Church contains many monuments of Sulyard.—*Editor*.

he held of the yerle of Sussex he gave to his wife Margerie. She
to be sole Executrix. He left nothing to his other children (not
named) but left it to his wife's discretion to give them what she
thought fit. Wit. John Felton (in whose house he died) & his
wife Ellen, Cicilye Harris, widow, —— Holden, widowe, Katherin
Eton, & other of the said master Felton's servants. Probate
states he died in the diocese of Winchester. Proved 21 Feb.,
1566. (P. C. C. Stonarde, 5.)

50. MILBOURNE, THOMAS, of Stanford-le-Hope, Essex, 4 July,
1639. Singleman. To my two sisters Mary and Joane Milbourne
£18 each. To my two cousins living at Ramsden Crays one a
son of John the other the son of Samuel Milbourne 40/- each.
To my Master Thos. Dennis of Stanford farmer 20/-. To poor
13/4. To John Andrew and Francis, children of Mr. Dennis a
sheep each. Thomas son of Thomas Dennis. Mary Skinner
servant. To Isaac Hunter, my fellow servant, 5 lambs. To
Thomas Osbourne and Sarah Petchie, servants, a lamb each. Ex.
Nathaniell Darby of Stanford, farmer. Overseer Mr. Dennis.
Wit:—Caleb Wood, Thomas Hammond(x). Proved 18 July, 1639.
(Arch. Essex. Whitehead.)

51. MORE, THOMAS, of South Weald, Essex, 11 July, 1637.
Yeoman. Wife, Elizabeth. Daughters, Sarah, Elizabeth, Grace
and Anne. Sons, John and Thomas. My brother Symon More,
living at Baddow, to be overseer. Wit:—John Ewen, William
Fuller. Proved 3 May, 1638. (Arch. Essex. Whitehead.)

52. MOTT, JOHN, of High Ongar, Essex, 26 March, 1640.
Husbandman. My kinswoman now the wife of Edward Merells,
and their children John and Elizabeth. My kinswoman Joane
dau. of John Barker. My sister Mary wife of John Barker, and
her dau. Mary. My kinswoman Anne Holbrooke, Isaac Holbrooke. Res. and Ex. Brother John Barker. Overseers Richard
and John Petchie. Wit:—Ri. Petchy and John Petchie. Proved
23 June, 1640. (Arch. Essex. Whitehead.)

53. SMYTH, GREGORY (no place), 29 Feb., 1647. To my wife
the house called Panners* for life and after to my son Humphrey
Smyth. Richard the son of Robert Greene. Wit:—Benet Wright,
William Wright. Proved 16 Aug., 1648. (Arch. Essex. Whitehead.)

54. TURKE, WILLIAM, of South Weald, Essex, 9 June, 1591.
To son John £10 at 21. To son William £10 at 21. To son
Humfrie £10 at 21. To daughters Martha and Anne £10 each
at 18. To the poor dwellinge in Weald Lordship and Broke
Street 5/-. Res. and Ex. my wellbeloved wife Dorothie she to
see my children brought up to a convenient age. Overseers
Humfrie Bowland George Frith Averie Frith and John Waylett.
Wit:—John Waylett and George Reynolde. Provd. 13 Sept., 1591.
(Arch. Essex. • Stephen.)

* There is no house or farm of this name in Essex now.

A DIGEST OF ESSEX WILLS.

WITH PARTICULAR REFERENCE TO NAMES OF IMPORTANCE IN THE AMERICAN COLONIES.

BY WILLIAM GILBERT,

Corresponding Member of the New York Genealogical and Biographical Society, Member of the Essex Archaeological Society, etc.

55. BARKER, MARY, of East Ham, Essex, 11 March, 1596 (1595?). To be buried in the churchyard. To Allen my brother Edwards eldest son £5. To his youngest son Edward £5. To Mary his youngest daughter £5. To Margaret Barker £5. To my sister Mercy Barker gentlewoman linen etc. Res. & Ex. Brother Edward Barker of East Ham gentleman. Wit:—Tobye Chalfont,* vicar, goodye Herton, widow Batterye, Elizabeth Oliver, Richard Steede, Sara Miller, Elizabeth Band. Pr. 30 March, 1596. (Arch. Essex. Stephen.)

56. BARNES, RICHARD, of Corringham, Essex, 25 May, 1596. Husbandman. To brother Richard Barnes 12/. To sister Ellen 12/. Res. & Ex. Joyce Biffin. Overseer:—William Tery 12d. to him. Wit:—Lawrence Boyton, Henry Humfrey. By me Robert Savage. (No probate given.) (Arch. Essex. Stephen.)

57. BARRET, JOHN, of Hornchurch, Essex, declared his will nuncupative on Saturday the second of February, 1638. Husbandman. All his goods to Anne Lake of Alveley and he did deliver to John Cooper of Hornchurch miller a leather purse and a key the said John Cooper to deliver them to Anne Lake at their next meeting. Wit:—John Cooper and Nathaniell White. Pr. at Romford 17 July, 1639. (Arch. Essex. Whitehead.)

58. BONDE, THOMAS, of Much Stambridge, Essex, 28 Dec., 1593. 10/- to poor of Much Stambridge. 3/4 to poor of Packellsham. To sons Thomas and Nicholas and daughters Anne, Sarah, Marie, Elizabeth and Rebecca £15 each when sons are 21 and daughters are 20 years of age. Cosin William Cripes. 12d. to each servant. Res. & Ex. wife Mary. Overseers:—Nicholas Bounde, Edmund Ballard and Jasper Kingsman. Wit:—Edmund Ballard(x) William Cripes(x) Jaspr. Kingsman. Pr. 2 March 1593. (Arch. Essex. Stephen.)

59. BROWNE, JOAN, of West Ham, 12 Dec., 1595, widow. To be buried in the churchyard, next to where my daughter ffraunce lyeth. To son Henry Browne £60. Son-in-law John Grubb. To dau. Alice £20. My daughter Elizabeth and her children Mary, ffraunce, and Elizabeth. 12d. each. to twenty poor people. Res. & Ex. son Henry. Wit:—Richard Ley. Pr. 10 June, 1596. (Arch. Essex. Stephen.)

* Vicar, 1589–1600.

60. CLARKE, JOHN, of Rayleigh, Essex, no date (nuncupative). Labourer. To my uncle Charles my mare. Res. to wife (not named) and son (not named but under age) equally they to be Ex. Wit:—Thomas Rawlins and Humfrie Hart. Pr. 15 Sept., 1591. (Arch. Essex. Stephen.)

61. COCKMAN, WILLIAM, of Burnham, Essex, 26 July, 1591. Sole Leg. and Ex. my wife Alice. Wit:—Richard Neale, Thomas Westbrooke, Benjamin Harris. Pr. 20 Nov., 1591. (Arch. Essex. Stephen.)

62. COLE, EDMUND, of Dagenham, Essex, 21 May, 1638. To be buried in churchyard. To dau. Margaret various household things. Res. & Ex wife and son George Cole. Overseers, John Siggins and Henry Cole. Pr. at Romford, 14 January, 1638. (Arch. Essex. Whitehead.)

63. FOSTER, PHRYSWITH, of Harvard-Stock, Essex, 6 May, 1582. Servant to John Best. To be buried in the churchyard. To John Buntlng 20/-. My sister Twed. Elizabeth and Dennys Palmer daughters of Humphrey Palmer. John and Thomas sons of Thomas Charvell. Arthur Perryns wife. William Stonards wife. Res. & Ex. Humphrey Palmer. Wit.:—Robte Boninge, Thomas Lenseye and Alexander Garrett. " Item she confesseth her Mr. oweth unto her XXXs." Proved 29 May, 1582. (Arch. Essex. Draper.)

64. FROSTE, ANDREW, of Much Horkesley, Essex, 1508. To be buried in the churchyard. To the high altar 20d. To wife Jane tenement called Sewyns for life after to Alis my daughter and her children for evermore. Daughters to have tenement called Vedis. Ellyn my wifes daughter to have my tenement called Bukks. Ex. wife Jane. Wit:—the parson,* and Richard Horspit and others. Probate not given in Register. (Arch. Colchester, Clerke.)

65. GLASCOCK, ROBERT, of Bobbingworth, Essex, 15 Feb., 1636. Singleman. My house in High Laver to my Mother for life after to my sister Joane she to pay brother Richard £20. To brothers John and Bartholomew £3 between them they to pay Joane Glascock our maide 5/-. Ex. mother, Elizabeth Glasscock. Wit:—Richard Chapman, Joane Glascock. Pr. at Romford, 14 January, 1638. (Arch. Essex. Whitehead.)

66. HART, WILLIAM, of Upminster, Essex, 9 May, 1591. Blacksmith. To be buried in the churchyard. To Robert Heard the elder of Stifford Cleyes the Lease of my shop. To Julian my wife the Lease of the house wherein I dwell and residue of my goods. Ex. Robert Heard. Overseer Thomas Wright of Upminster. Wit:—Ralph Wassall George Heathe Robert Hawke. Pr. 15 June, 1591. (Arch. Essex. Stephen.)

---

* The parson of his parish at that date was Ranulph Daniel who continued in the living until his death in 1549.

67. HILLS, WILLIAM, of Rochford, Essex, 21 Feb., 39 Eliz. Linen draper. To Edward the son to James England my brother my messauge in Rochford in occupation of John Sturgion. Cosen John Hills of Much Badow. Res. & Ex. father-in-law James England. Wit:—Ezechiell Reymer, Edward Kent William Richardson. (No probate given.) (Arch. Essex. Stephen.)

68. JACKSON, ROBERT, of South Ockendon, Essex, 7 Feb., 1644. Yeoman. To sister ffrancis wife of William Smith of Croydon Surrey yeoman £10. Her children William and Jane. My sister Agnes wife of John Best of Croydon and her son John. James Waters, William Waters and John Waters, sons of James Waters, the former husband of my wife Elizabeth. My brother in law Richard White and his sons Richard and George White. Ex. wife Elizabeth. Wit:—John Pratt, Robert Hey, Richard Barlow, Susan Barlow. Pr. at Brentwood, 30 Dec., 1647. (Arch. Essex. Whitehead.)

69. KINGE, JOHN, of Moreton, Essex, 30 April, 1593, yeoman. To be buried in the churchyard.* My house called Spencers to son Richard at age 21 and also one piece of land called Darksdalle. To son Samuel £40 at age 21. To my three daughters Agnis, Catheren and Joane £10 each at ages 21. To son John £5 at 21. To mother 10/- per annum for life. To poor 8/-. My other lands in Moreton and Little Laver to wife Catheren† for life. Res. & Ex. wife. Overseers Thomas Kinge senior and William Jennings. Wit:—Andrew Jenaway, Thomas Kinge, William Jennengs and Thomas Kinge, junior. Pr. 6 June, 1593. (Arch. Essex. Stephen.)

70. KINGE, THOMAS, of the Lea in the parish of Elmdon, Essex, 25 Aug., 1603. Yeoman. All copyhold lands in Elmdon to wife Isabell for life after to son Thomas. To dau. Anne now wife of Daniell Porter £30 etc. To dau. Agnes wife of Robert Clarke £6/13/4. To daus. Mary and Mathye £30 each and various articles. Res. & Ex. son Thomas Kinge. Wit:—Samuell Sewster, ffrancis Ilger, John Lucas, Symon Clerke. Pr. 13 Feb., 1603. (P. C. C. Harte, 20.)

71. KING, WILLIAM, of Skote in Moreton, Essex, 26 May, 33 Eliz. To be buried in Moreton Churchyard.‡ To son William various household articles. To son Thomas £3. To son Robert £5. To son John £5. To daughters Clemence and Jone 40/ each and various articles. To daughter Mary £3. To son Richard various articles. Ex. William & Richard. Wit:—Andrew Kinge, Edward Pecocke(x) "with others." Pr. 12 April, 1595. (Arch. Essex. Stephen.)

---

* Burial Register:—1593. John Kinge sonne of Andrewe Kinge of Spencers buried the third of maie aº. pd.

† Baptismal Register:—1593. William Kinge sonne of Katharine Kinge widowe the first of Novembre aº. pdco.

‡ Burial Register:—1594—Willm Kinge sometime of Scotts buried the xxi of August anno pdco.

72. KIRBYE, JOHN, of Corringham, Essex, 20 May, 1582. Smith. To be buried in the churchyard. To poor 10/-. To wife Margery the mansion house at Fobbing that Richard Davies dwelleth in for her life and after to my daughter Joane. To dau. Joan £4. To dau. Mary £4 and one cow and two sheep. Res. & Ex. wife Margerie. Wit:—Robte Draper* pson of Corringham who was the wryter hereof. Proved, 1582. (Arch. Essex. Draper.)

73. MOTTE, WILLIAM, of the Newe Heythe within the towne of Colchester, Essex, 10 May, 1585. Mariner. To dau. Elizabeth Motte £4 at age 20 a bed and bedstead a brass pot and two pewter dishes. My youngest son Thomas Motte (other son or sons not named or mentioned). Res. & Ex. wife Dorothy. Wit:— William Deane, William Twede, Robert Browne. Proved 10 Dec., 1585. (P. C. C. 58 Brudenell).

74. NOTH, JOHN, of Mych Horkesley, Essex, 20 Dec., 1500. To be buried in the churchyard. To the reparacons of St. Powles† 1d. To the high altar of Horkesley 12d. "to the makynge of an iron werke to ber the light brenning before the sepulture of our Lord God at Ester tyme" 6/8. There shall be rehersed in the bederol‡ every Sunday the names of my father and mother that is to say William Noth and Margaret his wife. To my dau. Cristian Damon 40/-. To wife Margaret my house for life after to son John. Res. & Ex. son John. Supervisors Henry Smyth and John Danon. Wit:—William Rowe, Henry Smyth and Thomas Bayley. Pr. at Colchester 10 March, 1500. (Arch. Colchester. Clerke.)

75. OSBORNE, EDWARD, of Stanford le Hope, Essex, (nuncupative) 20 Oct., 1638. Howsholder. Estate to be equally divided between my wife Thomazine and my two children Edward and Richard Osborne. Overseers:—John Wood and Thomas Dennys. Wit:—Caleb Wood,§ minister, John Wood(x) Thomas Thresher. Proved 15 January, 1638. (Arch: Essex. Whitehead.)

76. PYKMAN, JOHN, of Lambourn, Essex, 10 April, 1520. To be buried in the church of Lambourn. To the high altar 20d. For a trentall‖ of mass for me and my friends 10/-. To Lambourne churche XXs. for a cope. To Roger my son my house in Abridge and a piece of land called Delall and also a piece called Longlands. To son John the house he dwelleth in in Abridge and also land in Lambourne and Theydon Bois. To

---

* Rector from 1578–1596. He was licensed Feb. 26, 1578–9, to marry Ellen Cotton, spinster of South Weald, Essex.

† St. Pauls in London, the mother church.

‡ A list of persons to be prayed for. Beadrolls were prohibited in England in 1550.

§ Rector, died in 1660.

‖ An office for the dead consisting of thirty masses said on thirty consecutive days.

dau. Alis 3/4 yearly. To each godchild 4d. Res. and Ex. John and Roger they "to bryng my bodie to the churche to the holyngrownde and to do for my soule." Wit:—Gyls Dewhurst.* Pr. 2 June, 1525. (Arch. Essex. Sell.)

77. SMITHE, JOHN, of Rayleigh, Essex, 31 March, 1582. To poor 2/–. To son Saunder Smithe 20/– and my tools at age 21. To daughters Alice and Jane various articles and 20/– each at age 21. To brother Thomas Smithe 5/– and a dublett. To William Somer a round tub. To Roger Foster my arrowes. To Thomas Knightsbridge one hundred hoops. My house in Rayleigh to my wife Margery for life after to my son Saunder. Res & Ex wife. Overseers brother Thomas Smithe and William Somer. Wit:—Richarn Blackwell, (minister) John Haryson, Edward Ireland. Pr. 28 May, 1582. (Arch. Essex. Draper.)

78. WAREYN, ALS BAKER WILLIAM, of Sudbury, Suffolk, 4th. Nov., 1506. Grocer. To be buried in the churchyard of St Gregory Sudbury next my mother Johan. To the high altar of St. Peters Church there 6/8. Other bequests to the church including a "tapyr of wax of VI poundes." To my daughters Johan and Agnes 20/– yearly for life. To each child of my brother Robert Wareyn 6/8. To Robert Bawd and his wife Katherine my daughter a piece of silver and 20/–. My son John. Property in Alphamstone, Essex to the church there to maintain a lamp there during divine service etc. Res. & Ex. wife Johan and son John. Supervisor Sir Thomas Gech 20/– to him. Wit:—William Herold, Robert Wolston, John Person. Pr. 31 Jany., 1506. (P. C. C. Adean, 18.)

79. WRIGHT, THOMAS, of Much Stambridge, Essex, 7 March, 1591. To be buried in the churchyard. To Repentance Luce £5 at 21 William Haslewood oweth me 59/–. I forgive him 19/– of it. To John Austin 10/–. To Hugh Hitchcock 3/–. To William Burton and Christopher Permeter 3/– each. To Alice my maide 3/–. To John Nevell 10/–. To John Rule the younger 10/. To Steven Larence 10/–. To widows Benefield, Heminge and Crippe 20d. each. Res. & Ex. wife Mabell. Overseers Steven Lawrence and John Rule the younger. Wit:—Edward Salmon and John Langer. Pr. 21 March, 1591, by Mabell Wright, relict. (Arch. Essex. Stephen).

80. WRIGHT, THOMAS, of Dunton, Essex, 23 Feb., 1639. Yeoman. To be buried in churchyard. Sole legatee and Executrix— mother Martha Wright (goods include three carthorses "two whereof browne and the thirde grey coloured" and five cows and three wennells.†) Wit:—John Norton, John Parker, Edward Spender and Richard Lake. Proved at Brentwood 16 Sept., 1641. (Arch. Essex. Whitehead.)

---

* Curate.

† Calves recently weaned.

A DIGEST OF ESSEX WILLS.

With Particular Reference to Names of Importance in the American Colonies.

By William Gilbert,

Corresponding Member of the New York Genealogical and Biographical Society, Member of the Essex Archaeological Society, etc.

81. ADAMS, ROBERT, of Hadstock, Essex, 29 Aug., 1566. To my eldest son Harry Adams (under 21) my lands both free and copyhold. My son George. My daughter Elizabeth (under 21). Res: wife Anable. Ex: wife and son Harry. Supervisor my brother George Adams. Wit: Robert Smyth, clerke,* George Willowes and William Rande. No probate mentioned. (Arch: Colchester. Hore 3.)

82. ATKINSON, WILLIAM, clerke,† parson of Nevendon, Essex, 14 Nov., 1570. To be buried in the middle of the chancel. To the reparation of the steeple 5 marks. 4d. to each of the poor. 4d. to Mr. Ockley for a burial sermon. Godson—William Gosbie. To Barnabie Wright a pair of hose & a jerkyn. To John Cox curate of Ranessedowne Bellows‡ my Elliotts Dictionary. To Robert Freman, parson, of Ashen "not far from Stocke" my booke called concordantie bibie. Ex: James Gosbie. Overseers: John Hawley & Rowland Whalehead. Wit: John Cox and John Sellwin. Proved 12 April, 1571, by Ex. named. Arch. Essex Driffall, 44. Act Book, II, 1.)

83. BALDWIN, JOHN, of Hornchurch, Essex, 1 Oct., 1589. Husbandman. To poor s. ¾. Jone Ayres of Upminster, widow. Agnes, wife of Edward Veare of Cranham. Martha & Joane Soame, sisters of William Soame. William, son of John Marden & Alice his wife. Ex: William Soame. Wit: John Skeale, Samuel Soame. Proved: 20 Nov., 1589, by ex: named. (Arch. Essex. Maynard, 21, and Act Book, III, 87.)

84. BANKS, ROBERT, of Moreton, Essex, clerke,§ 11 July, 1590. To be buried in the chancel‖ of Moreton Church. To poor 20/-. To my son Robert 10/-. To my three daughters: Marie Gilder, Katharine Bill¶ and Johane Shepperd 10/- each. To my servant

---

* Probably Curate. Simon Napp was Rector at that time.
† Rector from 1565–1571.
‡ Ramsden Belhouse.
§ Rector from 1548–1554, and 1559–1591. He was deposed during the reign of Queen Mary.
‖ 1591, Mr. Robert Bancks, parson, buried the ix of August (Parish Register).
¶ 1574, Oct., 10. Nicholas Bills & Katharin Bancks, the daughter of Robt. Bancks, were married by Mr. Shipton (Parish Register).
The two following entries also occur in the Parish Register:
1561, George, son of Robert Bancks, parson, buried xi August.
1571, Helen, daughter of Robert Bancks, parson, buried xx Sept.(?)

Margarett Bankes, daughter to my sister Margarett Bankes, 40/-
and a "cowe bullock." Res: & Ex: wife Johane & son Thomas.
Overseer son Robert. 20/ to him for his pains. Wit: William
Keyester, Thomas Cheston, John Jeyle. Proved at London, 23
Aug., 1591, by the Ex: named. (P. C. C. Sainberbe, 64.)

85. BANKES, WILLIAM, of Little Wenden, Essex, 16 Nov., 1571.
Labourer. To be buried in the churchyard. To John Banks the
elder, my son, the mansion house wherein I dwell. My daughter
Jone Bankes. My son John Bankes the younger to be supervisor
& John the elder to be Ex: Wit: George Nitingale, Robert
Driver, John Arbiston, Marke Roper. Memorandum: The said
Jone to pay yearly six pence to the chief lord for the premises to
her bequeathed (*i. e.*, the premises were copyhold). No probate
mentioned. (Arch. Colchester. Hore, 394.)

86. BARKER, HENRY, of Gt. Dunmow, Essex, 19 March, 1592.
Yeoman. To poor 6/8. To wife Alice for life my land called
Tantrilles Croft with the cottage upon it. My brother William
Barker of Writtle. To my son Thomas a brass posnett.* To
daughter Praxada Barker the use of said croft for eight years
after wife's death, after which my son Abdia & his heirs to have
the same for ever. Res: & Ex: wife. Wit: William Longe,
Nicholas Harrington, Thomas Moore. Proved at Dunmow, 12
Sept., 1592. (Consistory Court of London. Sperin, 53.)

87. BARNES, KATHERINE, of Childerditch, Essex, 17 March,
1567. To be buried in churchyard. To the church 2/6. To
the Poor Men's Box 2/6. My cosen William Balye. Residue of
goods to be equally divided between my three daughters Margery, Jone & Rabage. Ex. daughter Jone. Overseers: Thomas
Peke & Adam Shaller.(?) Witnesses: Richard Ballard, John
Wittam & Adrian Scheale, vicar of Childerditch. Proved 6 April,
1568. (Arch. Essex. Loffyn, 16, and Wyndover, 57. Both copies
examined.)

88. BARRETT, JOHN, of Conewdon, Essex, 8 May, 1545. To be
buried in churchyard. To Powles Church 12d.† To the High
Altar s. 6/8. To the reparation of the great bell of Canewdon
£10. To Dorothy, Margaret & Joan Bell the daughters of my
sister £15 each. Margaret, Mary & Jone Peeke. Robert Peeke.
Katerine & Robert Mootte. My godson John Telemer. To the
poor £10. My daughters Elizabeth & Katrine Barrett. My
godson John Barrett, the elder, to have my lands. Res: & Ex:
my brother Robert Barrett & John Barrett the younger. Supervisor: William Harrys. Wit: Sir Jamys Brodnesworth, Robart
Peeke, John Boryes, John Tyler. (No probate mentioned.)
(Arch. Essex. Bastwicke, 46.)

89. BAWDEN, RICHARD, of Upminster, Essex, 3 Feb., 1567.
Yeoman. To be buried in churchyard. Sons, Henry, Robert,
William & Richard (all under 21). Daughters Joan and Eliza-

---

* A little pot.
† St. Pauls in London, the mother church.

216

beth (both under 21). Res: & Ex: wife Allse. Overseers: Richard Frithe of Upminster & Harry Egget of Swanstom Kent. Wit: William Wassher, parson,* & Thomas Elyet of Alveley. Proved 15 Feb., 1567. (Arch. Essex. Wyndover, 100.)

90. CLARKE, PETER, of Stapleford Tawney, Essex, 15 Sept., 1595. Husbandman. To my wife Catherine† 12 years of the lease of my house called Saveres which I hold of master Elliotte. The residue of the term to my son Peter. Overseers: My brother Thomas Clarke of Stanford Rivers and Thomas Bradley of Theydon Bois. Residue: one half to wife, the other between my children (not named)‡ at ages 21. To Alice Jones 3/- at age 18. Ex: wife. Wit: William Nicolsonne§ & Thomas Clarke. Proved 22 Oct., 1595, by relict. (Consistory Court of London. Sperin, 114.)

91. GRAYE, "MR.," of Barking, Essex. "Preeste or clerke." 28 Aug., 1546. To be buried in the middle alley of the church of St. Margarette Virgin & martyr of Barking "ageynste the pulpytte afore the roode." To the High Altar s. 5/-. Sir John Sturdye to syng for my soul at St. Johns Altar "where the newe ile ys " and to that same altar a vestment of gold and of silk & curteynes of the same, an altar cloth, etc. A settle with two locks to put in the vestments, a masse booke wrytten. To Mr. Gregill vicar of Barking‖ my frock furred with conye. Gowns to the vicar of East Ham & the parson of Little Ilford. My godson Richard Bovington. Ex: Mr. John Gregill vicar & Mistres Susan Sulyard. Supervisor: Mr. William Pownsette. Wit: John Eden, Edward Baker. No probate mentioned. (Arch. Essex. Bastwicke, 104.)

92. GRAY, MARGARET, of Canewdon, Essex, 19 Nov., 1590. To Katherin Maunsell widow my customary tenement called Purrmans alias Oberes and my copyhold land called Southfield in Fingringhoe in said county for life & after to her son John & his heirs for ever. The children of Tobias Makin. My cousin Steven Graye. 10/- to Poor. My cosen Rose the wife of John Richman. Joane the daughter of Thomas Stone. Res: & Ex: Katherin Maunsell. Overseer: Jeromy Phippe of Little Stambridge. Wit: Nathaniel Cawston, John Busshe, George Marchen. Proved 16 Dec., 1590, by Katherine *Mansefild.* (Arch. Essex. Maynard, 73, and Act Book, III, 101.)

93. HUNT, RICHARD, of Horndon on the Hill, Essex, 12 May, 1573. Smith. To be buried in the churchyard. My sons William & Robert. If wife come home again she to have half of my

---

* Rector from 1562 to 1609, when he died.
† 1589, May 6, Peter Clarke married Katheren Boram (Register).
‡ 1590, Jan. 24, Baptized Katharyne d. to Peter Clarke (Register).
 1595, Oct. 2, Buried Peter Clarke (Register).
§ Rector from 1572 to 1596, when he died. See his will, No. 102 of this series.
‖ John Gregyll, A. M., Vicar from 1524 to Dec., 1559, when he died. His will P. C. C., 4 Mellershe. He is named in the will of Bishop Kyte in 1537.

goods—the other half to be equally divided between my three* children when they attain their ages of 16 years—the goods to be divided by Robert Godwin the smith and Robert Lilley. If wife come not home then children to have her share. Ex. son Robert. Witnesses: Robt. Godwin, Willm. Davy, Willm. Kyne. Proved 18 June, 1573, by Ex. named. (Arch. Essex. Gyll, 16, and Act Book, II, 41.)

94. HUNT, WILLIAM, of Upminster, Essex, 28 March, 1568. Carpenter. My two sons Richard & John to have my tools. Res. & Ex: wife Christian. Wit: Thomas Marshall, William Wassher, pson of Upminster.† Proved 10 May, 1568. (Arch. Essex. Loffyn, 23, and Wyndover, 49. Both copies examined, the only discrepancy being that Loffyn dates the will *18* March.)

95. KINGE, RAYMOND, of Harwich, Essex, 7 Oct., 1600. Merchant. To poor of Harwich £5, to poor of Dovercourt 20/-, to poor of Ramsey 20/-. To Helen wife of John Shrive & daughter of James Barker,‡ my son-in-law, my house in Harwich. Susan, Grace, Christian, Jone & Anne, daughters of said James Barker; James & William sons of said James Barker. John & Raymond sons of John Scrutton deceased and Grace his late wife, my daughter. Robert Goodfellow son of my said daughter Grace. Anne daughter of said John Scrutton. My son John Kinge & Anne his wife. Thomas their son & Josan & Anne their daughters. The three children of my kinsman Christofer Kinge. William, son of my brother Arthur Kinge, William son of my sister Mary Kinge, Raymond son of my cosen Wm. Kinge, My ship called the *Anne Fraunce* of Harwich now on a voyage. Residue to be divided into four equal parts—1 to wife, 1 to son John, 1 to daughter Christian, 1 to daughter Grace Goodwyn. My small ship called the *Phenix* of Harwich. The marriage portion promised my son John by Thomas Twyt with his daughter Anne. Ex: son in law James Barker & son John King. Witnesses: Hugh Branham, clerke, Michaell Twyt, George Eastricke, John fforber. *Codicil.* Further bequest to William & Raymond Kinge. 7 Jan., 1600. Wit: John Kinge, John fforber. 30 Oct., 42 Eliz: Raymond King surrendered the lands to the Manor of Dovercourt in the customary manner. Proved 23 Jan., 1600, by James Barker & John Kinge. (P. C. C. Woodhall, 2, and Probate Act Book, 1598–1601.)

96. KINGE, THOMAS, of Purleigh, Essex, 8 August, 1588. Yeoman. To be buried in Churchyard. To Anne my wife the

---

* The name of the other child is not mentioned.

† See note to No. 89.

‡ *Note by Editor.* Jamee Barker who m. Barbara Dungan, dau. of Wm. and Frances (Latham) Dungan, and was of Newport, R. I., in 1639 came from Harwich, Essex, and in view of this fact this will of Raymond King should be of peculiar interest to the Barker, Clarke and Latham families of Rhode Island. John King of Weymouth, Mass., who had issue: Mary, b. 15 June, 1639; Abigail, b. 14 May, 1641; had a second or third wife, who in her will, dated 14 June, 1641, mentions her son Joseph Barker, and dau. Sarah Hunt.

lease to the house I dwell in. My landlord John Bennett. To my eldest son Christopher my " flocke of cattell." My son Edward who was prenticed to Christofer Horwod of Brancklery. To son George the money which is in the hands of his master Mr. Ralph Pudsey* of Gray's Inn. To Thomas Hasker, my son in law £5. Edward Kinge the son of John Kinge, late of Burnham, deceased. My goddaughters Elizabeth Freake and Ellen Burles. I will that my tenant Thomas Carter be abated of his rent 40/-. To the poor of Purleigh 20/-. Residue equally between my three sons—they to be executors. Supervisor: Mr. Freake. Wit: John ffreake.† Edmund Burles (x), James Brett (x). Proved 4 Sept., 1588, by the Ex. named. (P. C. C. Rutland, 56, and Probate Act Book 1586-90.)

97. MILBOURNE, ALLES, of Stamford Rivers, Essex, widow, 2 Nov., 1574. To be buried in the church or churchyard. Sons, Thomas and John. Son-in-law John Dunstone. Ellyn Dunstone. Bartholomew Milbourne. Son William. Res: & Ex: son Thomas. Witnesses: John Moris, Morgan Williams. Provod, 13 Jan., 1574, by Ex. named. (Arch. Essex. Gyll, 86, and Act Book II, 78.)

98. MOORE, THOMAS, of Much Haddam, Herts., 14 January, 1571. Horsemaster. Son: John. Daughters: Margerye & Agnes. Residue & Executor son William. Wit: Richard Atkys, John Nettelton, Arthur Oyler. Proved 24 Jan., 1571, by the executor named in the will of Thomas More " of Romford" (so in Act Book). (Arch. Essex. Driffall, 45, and Act Book, II, 15.)

99. MORE, THOMAS, of West Ham, Essex, 2 Sept., 1569. Tailor. To be buried in churchyard. To Sudbury More my daughter £4. Res. & Ex. wife Agnis. Overseer: Thomas ffolantine. I forgive William Lover my brother-in-law 5/- that I lent him. Wit: Mylles Reeder, Thomas ffolantyne. Proved 15 Nov., 1569. (Arch. Essex. Loffyn, 54.)

---

* Mr. Ralph Pudsey of Gray's Inn, m. Anne Wiseman, widow of Wm. Fitch, of Little Canfield, and sister of Sir Ralph Wiseman. Wm. Fitch d. 1578. I have the wills of Wm. Fitch and Sir Ralph Wiseman. See Vis. of Essex. See Foster's Yorkshire Pedigrees.—WINCHESTER FITCH.

† Rector from 1575 to 1604, when he died.

A DIGEST OF ESSEX WILLS.

With Particular Reference to Names of Importance in the American Colonies.

By William Gilbert,

Corresponding Member of the New York Genealogical and Biographical Society, Member of the Essex Archaeological Society, etc.

100. MOTT, MARK, of Braintree, Essex, gent., 1 March, 1636. To the poor of Braintree £5. To the poor of Bocking 20/-. To my son John £100. The Manor of Shimpling Hall county Norfolk belonging to Alice wife of the said John Mott. My daughter Sara Woolrich. To my cousin Collyns' minister of Braintree* £3.6.8. and ditto to my cousin Wharton† minister of Felsted. To each of my children 20/- to buy a ring. To Mark son of Alice Draper my grandchild £5. My son Adrian Mott to have residue of goods & to be executor. Wit: Thomas Jekyll, Richard Cuting, Nicholas Jekyll. Proved at London, 7 May, 1638, by Ex. named. (P. C. C. Lee, 60.)

101. MYLBORNE, JOHN, of Wanstead, Essex, 26 October, 1570. Yeoman. To be buried in the church or churchyard. Goods to be equally divided between Margery my wife and Edward my son (under 21) they to be joint Ex. Wit: Mrs. Yale, John Turnor, curat of Wanstead, Griffith Vahan. Proved 15 March, 1570. (Arch. Essex. Driffall, 45.)

---

* Samuel Collins appointed 15 Feb., 1610, to the living and continued till May 2 1667.

† Samuel Wharton, who married (1614) Martha, daughter of Edward Gutter, late Rector of St. Peters, Colchester. He was at that time Vicar of Farnham, Essex.

[Rev. Samuel Wharton m. 1614, Martha, dau. of Rev. Edward Gutter. Rev. Edward Gutter m. Margaret, dau. of Richard Fitch, Churchwarden, at Bocking, who died in 1603. I have will of Richard Fitch naming Edward Gutter. Margaret Fitch, widow of Rev. Gutter, m. 2d Rev. John Smith, Curate of Bocking.—WINCHESTER FITCH.]

102. NICHOLSON, WILLIAM,* of Stapleford Tawney, Essex, 3 Oct., 1596. Clerke. To be buried in the church. To poor 20/-. To wife Agnes for life my house called Bellowes & all other lands & tenements; after to son Thomas† & his heirs, in default to son William. Residue to be devided in two parts—one for wife & the other equally between my two sons. Ex: wife. Overseers: Richard Luther & Anthony Luther‡ & my brother Thomas Nicholson. Wit: J. Wood, Thomas Nichollsonne, Chriscofer Nicholsonne, John Cassies(x). Proved 27 Nov., 1596, by relict. (Consistory Court of London. Sperin, 146.)

103. OSBORNE, GEORGE, of Much Lyes,§ Essex, 2 Nov., 1552. To be buried in the Churchyard. To Elizabeth my wife my tenement at Gubans for life, after to my son John. Servants Elyn Reed & John Pepper. Res: & Ex: wife. Supervisor: William Thayers. Wit: Robert Ferrer. Henry Rochester, John Pulleyn. Proved at Great Baddow, 7 Feb., 1552. (Arch. Essex. Bastwicke, 157.)

104. OSBORNE, JOANE, of Little Wakering, Essex (place not mentioned in will but supplied by Act Book), 27 July, 1571, widow. Daughters Margaret & Agnes (both under 21). John Hounter to have the bringing up of Agnes. Residue equally between my two daughters. Ex: John Heuyard (Brewar in Act Book) & Richard Dandie. Overseers: Thomas Rawllyn. Wit: Thomas Galwarne, John Marshall. Proved 8 Sept., 1571, by Ex. named. (Arch. Essex. Driffall, 73, and Act Book, II, 7.)

105. PYNCHON, HENRY, of Chignal St., James, Essex, 19 Maye, 1587. Husbandman. To be buried in the churchyard. My three daughters Clemence, Rose & Grace. My sons Harry & Isaake. Res: & Ex: wife (not named in will). Overseer: brother-in-law Richard Freeman. Proved 23 June, 1587, by Marthe the relict. (Arch. Essex. Draper, 166, and Act Book, III, 58.

106. SPARLING, CHRISTIAN,‖ of Gt. Horkesley, Essex, 25 July, 1592 (nuncupative). "did ordaine and make by word of mouth upon her death bedd her daughter Elizabeth Sparling to take all her goodes and to pay all her debtes & to be her sole executrix in that behalfe." Wit: Thomas Parker, John Warner, Robert Tarver. Proved at Colchester, 9 Sept., 1592, by Ex. named. (Consistory Court of London. Sperin, 45.)

107. TOWNESEND, MARGARET, of West Ham, Essex, 14 Aug., 1592. Widow. To be buried in the chyard. My son Daniel to

---

* Extracts from the Parish Register:
  1573 Dec. 25 Bap. Thomas son of William Nicholson.
  1575 Sep. 18   "   Joan daughter of   "   "
  1575 Sep. 30 Bur. Joan   "   "   "
  1576 Oct. 28 Bap. William son of   "   "
  1584 July 19 Bap. Agnes dauʳ. of   "   "
  1596 Oct. 12 Bur. Willm Nicholson clarke & pson of this pryshe.
† He succeeded his father in the living. His will will appear later in this series.
‡ They lived at a house called Suttons. See my note to will No. 5.
§ Great Leighs.
‖ 1592, July 20, Mother Sparling Buried (Parish Register).

have £20 at age 25. "Yf that ever he do come home againe." My sons William, Thomas & Nicholas to have £20 each at ages 23. Daughter Susan to have £20 at age 21. John Wilson to bring up my children till they reach the age of 16. Res: & Ex: John Wilson. Overseers: my friends Richard Stanton, Miles Ledes & Richard Burle. They to have 12d. each. Wit: Richard Stanton, Miles Ledes, Richard Beuerle(x), John Milbancke(x). Proved at Barking, 4 Sept., 1592, by Ex. named. (Consistory Court of London. Sperin, 23).

108. BARRETT, RICHARD, of Brentwood, Essex, 15 June, 1553. Fishmonger. To be buried in the churchyard. To Agnes daughter of John Swane s. 53/4 at age 20 or marriage. Said money to remain in the hands of Edward James als. Pynner. If she die the money to remain to Agnes Quicke her mother, my sister. My godson Richard Barrett dwelling with Alice Marden widow. To Alice Marden of Brentwood s. 3/4. To Edmund Quicke s. 3/4. To brother Henry Barrett my bow and quiver with arrows. To William Barrett tanner my black cloth jacket "gardyd with veluett." To Richard Barrett of Squerells Hethe my "doublett of yeolowe sylke" and residue of goods he to be Ex. Overseer: Edmund James. Witnesses: Richard White (Vicar), Edmund James, John Colbett, William Haman, Willm. Lewes, Edmunde Quicke. Date of Probate not given. (Arch. Essex. 166 Bastwyck.)

109. BAWLDEN, JOHN, of Hornchurch, Essex, 27 March, 1552. To be buried in the churchyard of Saint Andrew in Hornchurch. To my son Justinian £10. Res: & Ex: wife Elizabeth. Wit: Jamys Harrys, John Willett, John Cordye. Proved at Romford, 9 Aug., 1572. (Arch. Essex. 156 Bastwyck.)

110. GRAVE, LAWRENCE, of Barking, Essex, 29 August, 1541. To be buried in my parish church of Seynte Margarett virgyn and martyr of Berkynge. To high altar 3/4. To the reparation of said church 3/4. To my two daughters Jane and Margery after the decease of my wife my house in Padnall Corner. My daughter's daughter Agnes Woodland. Servants Johan Wylkinson, William Fysher. Res: & Ex: wife Elizabeth. Overseers: Rauffe Tracye, Edward Fullam. Wit: William Cleypoole, Richard Fysher. Proved 9 March, 1544. (Arch. Essex. 25 Bastwyck.)

111. KING, WILLIAM, of Malden, Essex, 2 Sept., 1599. To poor 5 marks. To son Benjamin (under 21) my copy lands in Southminster & Brightlingsea and to his heirs, in default to son Peter (under 21) and his heirs. To son Peter & his heirs lands in Althorne. To son James (under 21) lands in Canewdon and to his heirs in default to son William (under 21) & his heirs. To son William and his heirs lands in Paglesham in default to son James & his heirs. Should all sons die without issue then all the *freehold* lands to my daughter Dorothy (under 21) & her heirs, in default to my daughter Elizabeth (under 21) & her heirs; and all the *copyhold* lands vice versa. The child my wife goeth with. Various moneys to children. Household stuff one half to wife

(not named) rest to two daughters. My cousin Lees and her children. My wife's sisters (not named). My brother Benjamin Harris and his children Benjamin & Dorothy. Overseers: My brothers Thomas King & Benjamin Harris & Mr. Hanworthe, and they to "sett forthe the accompte thereof for euerie yeare in the Christmas hollidays." Resid: & Ex: son Benjamin King. Witnesses not mentioned. Proved 18 May, 1602, by Thomas King & Christopher Hanworth supervisors named, they to administer during minority of Benjamin the son. Proved 18 June, 1605, by Benjamin King, son and Executor, he having attained his full age. (P. C. C. 48 Montague.)

112. KINGE, WILLIAM, of Ashen Als Essee, county Essex, yeoman, 3 March, 1611. To the poor of Stoke next Clare 5/– ditto of Ashen 5/– ditto of Wixoe 3/4 ditto of Birdbrook 5/– To Barbarie Lambert 6/8 To Martha Mortclocke dau. to Robert Mortclocke of Wixoe 6/8 To Alice wife of said Robert M. 10/– and 20/– per annum To eldest son John Kinge £20 Arthur Coe and his wife Susan my daughter and their children (all under age) My daughters Sara and Ann Kinge Elizabeth Donnell (under 21) daughter of Alice Donnell my daughter deceased Res: & Ex: my sons William and Samuel Overseers: Robert Rowse of Birdbrook, Martin Sparrow of Wixoe and Reynold Bridges of Stoke next Clare. Wit: Thomas Donnell, Robert Bentley(x), William Sydaye. Proved 8 April, 1612, by William and Samuel Kinge, son of deceased. (P. C. C. 29 Fenner.)

113. MILBURNE, LEONARD, of Wanstead, Essex, husbandman, 5 November, 1554, "and in the fyrst yere of oͬ Soferaigne Lord & Lady Philippe & Mary by the Grace of God King & Quene of Ingland Fraunce Jerusalem Naples and Ireland defenders of the faithe princes of Spayne & Cicill Archedukes of Awstriche dukes of Myllane Burgondi & Brabant countyes of Aspurge Flaunders & Tyroll." To the reparations of the church 12ᵈ. To son John the Lease of the house which I have of Mr. Barker To Besse Hochinson a sheep. Residue of goods equally between wife Johane and son John they to be executors. No witnesses named. Proved 12 November, 1554, at Barking. (Arch. Essex. 184 Bastwyck.)

114. MOTT, JOHN, of Braintree, Essex, 8 July, 1596, yeoman. To poor £6.13.4. My Inn called the Cock in Braintree and tenements called Friers in Bocking My dau Marie Mott (under age) My brother Mark Mott To Margerie Vnglie my keeper 10/– Res: & Ex: Marie my wife Overseers my brother in law Sir Robert Gardiner and my brother Mark Mott Wit: James Hille,* Joseph Manne, John Smartley, Erasmus Sperhawk, Samuel Winterfludd. Proved 11 Feb., 1596, by relict. (P. C. C. 10 Cobham.)

NOTE.—This John Mott appears in the Visitation of 1634, where it states that Mary, his daughter and sole heiress, married John Church of Stanton in County Suffolk.

---

* Vicar 1585–1608. Probate granted May 19, 1608, to his relict Elizabeth. He is incorrectly styled *John* Hill by Newcourt.

A DIGEST OF ESSEX WILLS.

WITH PARTICULAR REFERENCE TO NAMES OF IMPORTANCE IN THE
AMERICAN COLONIES.

BY WILLIAM GILBERT,
Corresponding Member of the New York Genealogical and Biographical Society, Member
of the Essex Archaeological Society, etc.

115. OSBURNE JOHN, of Havering, Essex, 11 December, 1556.
To be buried in the churchyard of the Chapel of Romford. To
wife Johane my house at Havering at Bowre called Powltys for
her life, after to be sold and the money divided between my
children then living. My house at Stratford Langthorne called
Ascus. My son-in-law William Sawnder. My daughters Isabell
and Alice. Res: & Ex: wife. Overseer: Steven Cox. Wit: John

224

Bett, Reignold Godfrey, John Sawnder.   Proved at Romfodr 10 March, 1556.   (Arch. Essex.   212 Bastwyck.)

116.   ADAMS JOHN, of Terling, Essex, 9 August, 1607, Husbandman.   To be buried in the churchyard   To the poor 20/–   To my father (not named) for life £4.6.8. per annum   To my sister Kateryn Addams £10   To sister Margaret Cornewell £6.   To sister Alice Fooks £10.   To sister Phillipp Tomson £13   To George Jackson 20/–   To my Goddaughter Agnes Gay 20/– at age 20 or marriage.   Res: & Ex: Thomas Dagnet and William Tomson.   Overseer: Arthur Reding.   Wit: Robert Wood, John Bellest, Arthur Reding.   Proved 14 October, 1607, by William Tomson.   (Consistory London.   Sperin, 349.)

117.   BARKER, JAMES,* of Harwich, Essex, Merchant, 28 February, 1620.   To poor 20/–   To Mr. Innes† to preach a funeral sermon 20/–   My house etc. in Roydon Suffolk to my son William he to pay £10 per annum to my son James.   My house wherein I dwell in Harwich to be sold.   To my daughter Grace £20   To my daughter Anne the small Spanish bedstead.   Residue equally between my four daughters Susan Christian Johane and Anne.   Executor son-in-law Thomas Cowper   Wit: John fforber William Russell senr. Samuel Clarke.   Proved 28 May, 1621.   (P. C. C. Dale, 33.)

118.   BARKER, WILLIAM, of Shalford, Essex, 8 April, 1606, Husbandman.   My wife Cicely to have her dwelling with John Barker, my son, for her life.   To son William a table.   My son James and daughter Mary.   Res: & Ex: son John.   Wit: James Barker, James Thorpe, Edward Raymond.   Proved 8 Sept., 1612, by the Executor named.   (Consistory London.   Hamer, 117.)

119.   BONDE, ELIZABETH, of Hawkwell, Essex, 26 Feb., 1602, widow.   To be buried in the church or churchyard of South Fambridge Essex   All my goods etc. and the Lease of my house to be taken by Mr. Adam Wintropp he to keep my children with the profits until they come to the age of 20 years then they to equally divide the goods etc.   Executor my friend Mr. Adam Wintropp of Gretton Suffolk gent.   Overseer: friend Jonathan

---

* James[1] Barker m. a dau. of Raymond Kinge of Harwich, Essex (see will No. 95), and his dau. Christian Barker m. (1) Thomas Cooper of Wapping, who left her a freehold estate in Harwich, Essex.   She m. (2) Thomas Beecher and went to New England about 1630 with her said husband who was captain of the ship *Talbot*, 1629–1637, and resided at Charlestown, Mass., until he d. in 1637.   She then m. (3) Nicholas Easton, b. 1593; d. 15 Aug.. 1675.   She d. 20 Feb., 1666, at Newport, R. I.   James[2] Barker, the son of the above testator, left Southampton on 24 March, 1634, in the ship *Mary & John* with his young son James, and Nicholas Easton and his sons Peter and John among the passengers.   He is said to have died on the voyage, leaving an only son James to the care of his aunt, Christian Beecker.   James[3] Barker, b. 1623; d. 1702; m. 1644, Barbara Dungan, dau. of William and Frances (Latham) Dungan, and was the first American ancestor of the large Barker family of Rhode Island.

(G. A. M., JR.)

† William Innes, A.M., Vicar of Dovercourt and Harwich, 1618–1638. Probate March 11, 1638–9.   Son "Gerberetes" Innes.   A *de bonis* grant, Jan. 5, 1641–2, to the use of Robert and Aquila Innes, sons of deceased, "Garbarrett" being dead.

225

Clemence. Wit: Jonathan Clemence, Robert Sansham, Nathaniel Newman.

On the 30th. January 1602 Administration of the goods of Richard Bonde* clerk late Rector of South Fambridge Essex which was granted to his relict Elizabeth is now, together with the administration of the above will, granted to Adam Wintropp during the minority of Zachariah Bonde, John Bonde, Ezechiel Bonde, and Elizabeth Bonde. (Consistory London. Sperin, 284.)

120. BROWNE, JOHN, of Horndon upon the Hill, Essex, 11 October, 2 James I, Yeoman. £10 each to my four children viz: Anne Sara William and Mary at their several ages of 21, or marriages. Res: and Ex: wife Joan. Overseer: my father in law William Howlden of Great Burstead Essex gent. Wit: Edward Byrchley, John Potter, Charles Charvyle. Proved 31 Jany 1604 by relict. (Consistory London. Sperin, 393.)

121. CHAUNDELOR, WILLIAM, of South Ockendon, Essex, 13 April, 1582. To be buried in churchyard. To Christian my wife my lease of Hamptons in South Ockendon To John and George the sons of Paul Chandler my eldest son 40/– each To Thomas son of my son Peter 40/– To William son of John Cotsall 40/– To Johan my daughter wife of John Cotsall £5.† Res: and Ex: wife. Witnesses: Thomas Lewes, curate, Thomas Longe, Amos Lewes, "with others." Proved 29 May, 1582. (Arch. Essex Draper.)

122. CRAWLEY, THOMAS, of Grays Thurrock, Essex, 20 February, 1577. Sole Legatee and Executrix my wife Alice. Witnesses: John Williams clarke goodwyfe Downy "with others." Proved 24 April, 1582. (Arch. Essex. Draper.)

123. CURTES, JOHN, of Bocking, Essex, 4 March, 1599, Yeoman. To be buried in the churchyard of Gosfield, Essex. To poor at burial 20/–. To my nephew William Quodwell my best gelding etc. To my niece Marget Springe a cow and a bullock. To my servants Christopher Pigget and John Harlow a bullock each. To niece Elizabeth Curtes 6/8. To niece Anne Clere 6/8. To my "littell boye" John Thornton 40/ at age 20. To my maide Marget Hamonde a bullock. To my wife Jone the Lease I hold of my good master the Rt. Worshipful Sir John Wentworthe Knight in lands called Alewards in Bocking and Gosfield for her life and after to my brother John Curtes John Reve the younger and nephew William Quodwell The Manor of Cornish hall in Finchingfield Essex mine by an Indenture between me and my good friends William Wilford and his wife and John Wentworthe Esq bearing date the 20 Feby 2 Eliz. Saunder Walford shall have the preferment of the said Lease upon condition that he pay my wife and brother and John Reve the younger £100. Res: wife Ex: wife and John Reve the younger Supervisor: nephew William Quodwell Wit: Henry Hunt Thomas Lepar John Taylor

---

* Rector from 1586 to 1601, when he died.
† Married at South Okendon in 1575.

226

Thomas Starling.   Proved 13 June, 1560, by John Reve.   (P. C. C. 35 Mellershe.)

124. FITCH, NATHANIEL, of Prittlewell, Essex, 15 August, 1648, being in good health etc.   All my rights in my lands and tenements lying in Birch Essex unto my loving mother Anne Fitch widow of Gosfield for her life and after to my brothers Samuel and Joseph and their heirs for ever.   Res. and Ex. mother. Wit: John Reeve.   Proved 8 May, 1649, by the Ex. named. (P. C. C.   72 Fairfax.)

125. JACKSON, HUGH, clerk vicar of Brightlingsea, Essex, 19 May, 1608.   Sole legatee and Executrix wife Francis* she to bring up children (not named) till they come to ages 21   Wit: James Havell Robert Tye.   Proved 21 March, 1608, by relict. (Consistory London, Sperin, 409.)

126. KING, JOHN, of Inworth, Essex, 20 August, 1610, nuncupative.   Sole Legatee and Executrix: wife Jane.   Witness: William Foord.   Proved 8 Sept., 1610, by relict.   (Consistory London.   Hamer, 84.)

127. KINGE, WILLIAM, of Harwich, Essex, 13 March, 1625, Fisherman.   To poor 20/-   To daughter Joane wife of Richard Cocke of Bucklie Suffolk 10/-   To grandchildren Richard, William, Thomas and John Cocke 40/- each at ages 21.   To grandchild Jeptath Kinge the son of Alice Brassen 40/-   To Mary Dalby of Orford Suffolk widow 40/- and to her daughter my granddaughter Frances Mome 20/- at age 15, and to her younger daughter Mary 20/- at age 15.   To my grandson William Harrison and his heirs for ever my house etc. in Orford he to be sole executor and residuary legatee.   Supervisor: John Osborne. Wit: Nicholas Skoole Richard Whitwell Symon Sewell.   Proved 5 Feb., 1626, by the Ex. named. (P. C. C.   17 Skynner.)

128. MASON, JOHN, Parson of South Fambridge and Assingdon, Essex, 6 Novr., 1559.   To be buried in the chancel of South Fambridge church   To Johan Hutton 20/- a seame of wheat a seame of malt a "blacke bullocke withe a broune backe of the age of two yeres" also a hog a pair of blankets a coverlet a wicker chair.   To Sir John Ayrepst my foxfurred gown etc.   To Sir Robert Thomson priest my best short gowne   To Jane Greene 20/-   To Grace Gerrard 20/-   To Ellen Mason 17 old angells and four double ducketts at age 20 also linen pewter furniture etc.   Sole executor Raffe Mirshe Raffe Mason (so in will) he to be bound to Edmund Tirrell Esq for due performance. To John Platt of Hawkwell three bushels of wheat to Ellen Savage one bushel of wheat.   Supervisor Edmund Tirrell Esq. Wit: Anthony Grantham John Battyll Thomas Luteman.   Proved 22 June, 1560, by Radulphe Mershe the executor named in the will.   (P. C. C.   37 Mellershe.)

---

* Bishop of London's Marriage License:—Hugh Jackson, clerk vicar of Bricklingsey co. Essex and Frances Roade Spinster now of London daughter of James Roade late of Roade co. Chester gent. deceased.   To be solemnized at St. Michael Queenhithe London, 25 April, 1594.

227

129. NICHOLSON, THOMAS, of Stapleford Tawney, Essex, Clerk,* 28 January, 1647, "being aunciant and sickley" etc. To be buried in the chancel. To poor 40/– My tenement called Bells wherein I dwell with the lands etc. to my son John and his heirs. My messuage called Stewards† in Stanford Rivers in the occupation of William Glascock to my son John. My messuage called "Saveryes" with lands etc in Stapleford Tawney and Stanford Rivers in the occupation of William Yong to my son John. I have resigned unto my son Richard my parsonage of Stapleford Tawney.‡ My son George to have various moneys and articles also £10 per annum for life. My tenement called Stones in Harlow in the occupation of Thomas Hubbard to my daughter Jane Biggins. My tenement called Andrew Finches in Stanford Rivers in the occupation of Robert Hutchin to my son John. To my son Thomas £10 per annum for life. My tenement called Colliers Hatch§ with lands etc. in parishes of Stanford Rivers Stapleford Tawney and High Ongar in the occupation of Henry Orgar to my son John. To my daughter Mary Chambers £40. Ditto to my daughter Maud Glascock‖ £5 to grandchild John Burton¶ ditto to grandchild John Glascock** at age 21 ditto to grandchildren Agnes, Jane and Elizabeth Glascock†† at ages 18. To Thomas son of my brother William Nicholson a ring. My grandchild John Nicholson. Res: & Ex: son John. Overseers: brothers-in-law John and Nicholas Searle. Wit: John Cornelius, Thomas Browninge. Proved 12 Sept., 1649, by son John. (P. C. C. 132 Fairfax.)

---

* He was baptized at Stapleford Tawney, 25 Dec., 1572, his father being Rector there (see will No. 102). He succeeded his father in that living in 1596 and was sequestered in the Rebellion of 1642. He was licensed 10 Jan., 1597–8 to marry Dorothy Barfield, widow, of High Roding, Essex (she was aged 24). She was the relict of Lewis Barfield, M. A., Vicar of Great Dunmow, Essex, 1593–97. She died in 1598. Thomas Nicholson afterwards m. —— Searle.
Extracts from Stapleford Tawney Register:

1598 Jany 28	Bap Agnes dau of Thomas Nicolson.	
1598 Jany 30	Bur Dorothy wife of "	"
1599 April 5	Bur Agnes dau of "	"
1606 Oct 19	Bap John son of "	"
1608 Nov 13	" Mary dau of "	"
1610 Mar 25	" Maud " "	"
1611 Mar 1	" Richard son of "	"
1613 Feb 27	" Thomas son of "	"
1615 Mar 10	" Margaret dau of "	"
1618 April 19	" Jane dau of "	"
1620 April 23	" William son of "	"
1623 Sept 29	" George son of "	"

† This is still extant.
‡ Richard Nicolson, Rector from 1647 to 1661, when he died. Admon granted on July 31 in that year to his brother John Nicolson, LL.D. He is not mentioned by Newcourt.
§ This still exists and stands at the junction of three parishes.
‖ She was the wife of William Glascock of Stanford Rivers who was the fourth son of John Glascock and Elizabeth Stanes. William Glascock died in 1662 and in his will mentions his brother in law John Nicholson, LL.D.
¶ Son of his daughter Margaret.
** Baptized at Stanford Rivers in 1638.
†† Baptized at Stanford Rivers, 1637, 1642 and 1646 respectively.

130. SAMPSON, THOMAS, of Wethersfield, Essex, 27 April, 1560, Husbandman. To be buried in the churchyard of Bocking Essex To poor of Wethersfield 20/– and to poor of Bocking 40/–. To poor of Shalford 20/–. To son Thomas £40 at age 22. To my two daughters Sara and Agnes £30 each at ages 18 or marriage. If they all die then legacies to be parted between my brother Robert Sampsons children my brother in law John Marches children my sister Maynards children and my sister Myltons children. To my kinsman John Currye 10/– To Henry Bounde a bullock A calf each to Thomas Dorge, Thomas Elye my servant, John Osborne and William Choote. Res: wife Jone. Ex: wife and brother Robert Sampson Supervisor John Marche. Wit: John Sheppard, John Overed, John Curtis, Robert Goodfelowe, John Rice. Proved 13 June, 1560, by Ex. named. (P. C. C. 35 Mellershe.)

131. SKINNER, THOMAS, of Collier Row,* Essex, 1 June, 1582, Husbandman. To be buried in the Churchyard of St Edward in Romford. To the poor mens box 3/4 To daughter Margaret my field. To daughter Olyve my lease that I have in reversion she paying my daughter Joane £3 To wife Barbara the bedstead bedding and clothing and also the cow she brought with her and £15. To daughter Susan £5 and a further £5 at age 21 To John Harrolde a dublet etc. To Richard Jones a coat. Residue to my three daughters, if they all die then to Margery Collins. Executors: my brother John Collins and Nicholas Hearde. Overseer: Marselyn Hearde, "and if Nicholas Hearde, who now lyeth verye sycke, do dye" then brother Marselyn to be Executor, and Anthony Heard Overseer. Wit: John Coxe and John Harrowlde. Proved 27 June, 1585, by Nicholas Hearde. (Arch. Essex. Draper.)

132. SORRELL, THOMAS, of Great Waltham, Essex, 1 June, 1582, Yeoman. To be buried in the Churchyard To my brother William Sorrell my messuage that I dwell in with the lands etc. till my son John is 21. William to pay my wife Anne £10 per annum till that time and the residue of profits to bring up my children My tenement called Rowland Taylors in Waltham. My tenement called Fullers† My two daughters Mary and Alice. Ex: brother William Wit: Thomas Edwarde Robte Haywarde and Edmunde Marrian. Proved 21 March, 1582, by sentence of Court. (Arch. Essex. Draper.)

133. STACEY, THOMAS, of London, 23 June, 1559, Mercer. Sole Executrix wife Katherine Goods etc. to be divided in two parts one for wife and the other equally between children (not named). Overseers: brethren, John Cosoworthe, Anthony Hickman, Richard Hill, George Nedam, mercers each to have a blacke gowne and a ring of the value of four marks. Wit: Stephen Hales, Henry Lok, —— Northropp, Allyn Hill. Proved 26 Feb., 1559,

---

* A hamlet still flourishing near Romford.
† There is a place named Fuller Street, close to Gt. Waltham at the present day.

by John Castlin of the city of London, mercer, the relict renouncing. (P. C. C. 18 Mellershe.)

134. STEVEN, WILLIAM, of Sandon, Essex, August, 1610, nuncupative. To his children Thomas Elizabeth John and Mary £4 each at ages 14. Executrix wife Frances Wit: William Pond, John Pond. Proved 12 Sept., 1610, by relict. (Consistory London. Hamer, 42.)

135. THURGOOD, EDWARD, of Great Walden, Essex, 22 Marcn, 18 Eliz. To be buried in the church or churchyard of Great Walden To son John five milch neate after decease of Anne my wife, and half my household stuff. To Elizabeth Wilkinson my maid a featherbed etc. To my son John all my lands and tenements (not named) To my wife £50 upon condition that she allow son John to quietly enjoy the house and lands he now occupiuth Residue to sons John and Thomas. To son Thomas the lease I have of a farm called Michells of Henry Bretton. Ex. son Thomas. Supervisor: Ferdinando Parys Esq. Wit: Ferdinando Parys. Proved 2 Decr., 1578. (P. C. C. 45 Langley.)

136. THURGOOD, JOHN, of Manuden, Essex, 26 Novr., 1577. To be buried in the Churchyard of Manuden To son Robert £20 To sons John and Jeffrie £10 each To daughter Agnes £40 and a number of articles. To daughters Margaret and Edeth £5 each To my childrens children 6/8 each To each Godchild 10/-. To son Robert 10/- per annum out of a meadow lying in Southmead for ten years next after my decease To Nicholas my son the said meadow and a close of pasture called Eves Mychell and a piece of land of ten acres called Allyng. Res. & Ex: son Nicholas. Wit: Thomas Thurgood Thomas Phillipps. Proved 27 Feby, 1577, by the Ex. named. (P. C. C. 7 Langley.)

A DIGEST OF ESSEX WILLS.

WITH PARTICULAR REFERENCE TO NAMES OF IMPORTANCE IN THE AMERICAN COLONIES.

By WILLIAM GILBERT,

Corresponding Member of the New York Genealogical and Biographical Society, Member of the Essex Archaeological Society, etc.

137. ARCHER, FRANCIS, of Bocking, Essex, clothier, 25 Nov., 1578.* To poor £3. To the re-paration of Bocking church 10/. To the poor weavers and fullers of Bocking £3. 10. o. To wife Amie in recompense of her dower my messuage wherein I dwell and my two messuages in the occupation of John Fuller, and my six messuages lately purchased of Thomas Brokeman gent. The children of my son Robert viz: Robert,† Thomas,‡ Richard, Frances, Johan,§ Margaret ‖ and Mary. George Clarke and his wife, my daughter, Priscilla.¶ Their children Edmonde, Annie, Francis and Mary. To said son-in-law the messuage in Bocking he lives in and one other messuage there in the occupation of Agnes Wickham widow. To my son Robert the messuage I bought of John Panier. To my son Timothy messuage in Halstead, Essex. My two servants John Goodwin and Jacob Hartt £3, to the children of John Cawston of Lomysse beside Maldon. Bequests to servants. Household stuff to wife. Res: George Clarke. Ex: wife and George Clarke. Overseers:—Edward Golding and Roger Debnam. Wit: Thomas Gilbert,** Thomas Bacon, Edward Chissed, John Fuller, John Sparhawk, "and other Edwarde." Proved 24 Oct., 1759, by George Clarke, power reserved, etc. (P. C. C. 41 Bakon.)

138. AYLETT, JOHN, of Cranham, Essex, 30 Aug., 1595. To be buried in churchyard. To brother Gilbert Aylott 10/– To brother Harrys 10/– To brother Thomas Aylott 10/– and I forgive him the 10/– he oweth me. To my sister Ann the wife of Francis Lea 10/– To my sisters Agnes and Ellin Aylett 10/– each. To my maid Elizabeth Thackwell 20/– To my maid Johan Dickensonne 10/– To my man Thomas Cumbers 6/8 To my father William Aalatt a leade of cheese, Res. to daughter

---

* 1579, Franciscus Archer sepultus est 30 Junius (Register).

† Bap. 26 Aug., 1565.

‡ " 7 Sept., 1566.

§ " 28 Aug., 1569.

‖ " 19 Nov., 1570

¶ She introduced this Christian name into that branch of the Clarke family and it was handed down for generations.

** Buried 25 March, 1610. His son Thomas married Anne Bretten in 1621, and Triphena Ussher in 1634.

Elizabeth Aylett at age 18. Ex. Robert Cominge parson of Doddinghurst * and Richard Godfrye also of Doddinghurst. Overseer: brother Gilbert Aylott. Wit: John Mudge, John Younge,
John Hart, Robert Cominge, scriptor. Proved at West Ham 1
Oct., 1595, by ex. named. (Consistory London, Sperin 107.)

139. BAKER, HENRY, of Great Burstead, Essex, husbandman,
23 Jany, 1594. To wife Marie for 20 years my tenement and
lands in Mountnessing holden of Sir John Peter Knt.† as of his
Manor of Cowbridge Grange ‡ she to bring up my three children
viz: Margaret Mary and Judith Baker, and one other child
wherewith she now is great, until their ages of 16 years. After
the term of twenty years the croft in the occupation of Thomas
Symon of Billericay to come to the child yet unborn and the rest
of the lands to be sold £10 of the money to remain to wife
and the rest to be equally divided between my three daughters
but if the unborn child be a daughter then all the lands etc. to
be sold and divided. Res: and Ex: wife. Wit: Jo. Payne,
Joseph Smithe, William Clarke. Proved 13 Sep., 1595, by the
relict. (Consistory London. Sperin, 324.) On 22 Feb., 1605, administration of the goods etc. of Mariam Gun alias Baker who
while she lived was relict of Henry Baker of Great Burstead was
granted to Margaret Butcher alias Baker wife of William Butcher
of St. Leonard Foster Lane London, daughter of said Henry
Baker.

140. BRADFORD, JOHN, 8 Oct., 1580. To brother Thomas Bradford junior 20/– 20/– each to my brothers Randall, William and
Morris and sisters Margaret, and Johan. Brother Morris to also
have my trunk sword and dagger. To Mr. Richard Frampton
10/– To Randall's wife and her two eldest daughters 10/–. To
my clark of the kitchen 3/4. To William Henley 3/4, and ditto
to Richard Mathewe, John Lookye and Thomas Tannerdyne.
3/4 to be divided among the rest of the yeomen waiters in
the house. Wit: Thomas Winterbourne, Richard Frampton.
On the 25 Oct., 1581, commission issued to Maurice Bradford
brother of deceased to administer the above estate. (P. C. C.
36 Darcy.)
   Note.—The Probate Act Book states the testator was servant
to the Archbishop of Canterbury and died in Dublin, Ireland,

141. FAUNCE, JOHN, of Purleigh, Essex, 31 May, 1582. To the
poor 3/4. One half of my goods equally between my three sons
John, Robert and Jonas. To Alice Reinolde a sheep To Alice
Corsye a lamb. To John Webbe a lamb Res: & Ex: wife Mar-
garet. Overseer John Gaywood Wit: Daniel Carrington Henry
Hurrell, Thomas Twiste. Probate not mentioned. (Arch. Essex.
Draper.)

---

* Instituted 7 May, 1584; died in 1610, leaving relict Mary.
† Died Oct. 8, 1613, aud buried at Ingatestone.
‡ Near Billericay, Essex.

142. FYCHE, RICHARD, of Steeple Bumstede, Essex, 27 Oct., 1490 (in Latin). To be buried in the Churchyard of the Parish church of the Blessed Mary of Bumstede aforesaid. A number of religious bequests, mentioning the churches of Finchingfield and Pentlow. To Isabella my wife eight cows. To Richard my son 8 cows, 3 horses, pieces of pewter etc. To John my son 6 cows, 3 horses, 20 measures of corn, pewter, etc. To my wife for life my tenement in Finchingfield, after her decease to my son John. To wife a tenement called Setewellys and other tenements and lands. Mentions Thomas Fych of Birdbrook. Res: & Ex: wife and son Richard. Overseer John Green of Little Sampforth. Wit: John Hempsted senr. John Hempsted junr. Richard Chime and John Panell. Proved 18 Nov., 1494, by ex. named. (P. C. C. 16 Vox.)

143. GAUNTE, ELLEN, of Rochford, Essex, 16 Nov., 1580. To be buried in the churchyard. To Margaret Abblott my daughters child my house and orchard and all the household stuff within the same and I make her sole executrix. Wit: Johane Beryman Willm. Richardson et alijs. Proved 28 April, 1582. (Arch. Essex. Draper.)

144. GLASCOCK, WILLIAM, of Great Dunmow, Essex, 27 Nov., 1579. A number of bequests to the poor of various parishes. My wife Phillippa to have my Park etc called Hatfield park and my lease of the tithes of Hatfield and Dunmow My sons Philip, Richard, Robert, George, Andrew and Charles My daughter Marie. My house wherein I dwell called Mynchons. Tithes of Downhall to son Richard. My brother John Glascock of Roxwell. John, one of the sons of my late brother in law Thomas Everedde deceased My kinsman William Glascock the younger. Overseers: my brother-in-law Mr. John Wyseman and my brother-in-law Mr. Richard Everedde To my mother a ring. To my servant Katherine Glascock 20/-. Ex: wife and brother John Glascock of Roxwell. No witnesses mentioned in Register. Proved 29 Feb., 1579, by relict, power reserved, etc. (P. C. C. 5 Arundel.)

145. GOLDING, JOHN, of Beauchamp William, Essex, gent, 10 Dec., 1551. To poor 20/- To repair the highways 40/- To my son Robert all tenements and lands in Framesden Gretyngham and Goham county Suffolk which I lately purchased of Robert Gosnold Esq and John Roydon. My copyhold lands at Shelley and Leygham county Suffolk to my wife Johan until my son John comes to the age of 21. To son John lands in Otley. To son Roger lands in Olyngton and Ashen county Essex. To wife for life a messuage in Sudbury and land in Beauchamp William after to son Roger. My four daughters: Alice Ursula Katherine and Thomasin To son John the copyhold lands in Otley that I have lately purchased of my uncle Edmund Gosnold. To my god-daughter Margaret Potter 20/-. Detailed bequests of goods to wife and children. Bequests to servants. Res: son Robert Ex: wife and son Robert. Supervisors: my brother-in-law Rob-

ert Gosnold and my brother Thomas Golding. Wit: Thomas Golding, Richard Golding of Sudbury, Roger Golding of Calendyshe and Edward Alston of Bulmer. Proved 30 Jany, 1551, by the relict and the son Robert in the person of Thomas Golding the brother of deceased. (P. C. C. 3 Powell.)

146. KINGE, BENJAMIN, of Maldon, Essex, gent, 30 Nov., 1613. Bequests to the poor of Southminster, All Saints Maldon, and St. Peters Maldon. To eldest son Benjamin my messuage called Wrastlers in Southminster etc. My brother Edmond Kinge of Halstead Essex. To Robert my son two tenement at Lyhethe etc. To sons Thomas and Samuel freehold lands etc. called Awstans in Southminster equally between them. Also to them the messuage wherein I dwell at Maldon. To son Edward various goods he to be in the charge of my brother Edmond. To sons Benjamin, Robert and Bartholomew farms etc. My sons Thomas and Samuel to have my term of years in Asheldam Hall. To my three daughters-in-law viz: Elizabeth wife of son Benjamin, Elizabeth wife of son Robert and Sarah wife of son Bartholomew 40/– each John, Elizabeth, Susan and Edmond, the children of my son Benjamin. Edmond and Thomas children of my son Robert. Abraham and Bartholomew children of my son Bartholomew. To Sir John Sams Knt.* and my Lady his wife 20/– each. To my cousin Christopher Hanworth my best cloak. To his son Christopher 20/– and the same to his daughter Alice my goddaughter. To John Lorde "my heire at the Moore" 10/–. To my sister Shawe a ring. To Jane Gaywood my sisters daughter £6. 13. 4. To my cousin Johan now wife of Abel Death £6. Various money bequests one to Mr. Wilson preacher at Maldon. To Edward Hayes my last wive's sister's son at age 24, £20. To Bethsephora Dove who lately dwelt with me £10. Ex: sons Benjamin, Robert and Bartholomew. Overseers: my friends, Mr. Culverell of Lincolns Inn, Mr. Raffe Hawden, Edward Herrys Esq., John Soan, and Christopher Hanworth gent, my brother Edmond Kinge, Edward Hasteler† my son in law, and Thomas Cheese. My Executors to provide a strong chest with two locks to keep my deeds and indentures in. Wit: Benjamin Kinge, Christopher Hanworth, William Francis, George Purcas, and Thomas Cheese, the writer hereof. Proved 29 Jany, 1613, by the ex: named. (P. C. C. 46 Lawe.)

147. KINGE, JAMES, of Little Wakering, Essex, husbandman, 26 Sep., 1604 To my wife Joan for her life all my copyhold lands called Hoppity Hales, Missing Hall, and Cranes Acre in the Parish of Little Wakering and held of the Manor of Little Wakering Hall. After her decease to remain to Robert son of my brother Henry Kinge To wife my house and land called St. James in

---

* I have an original indenture signed by this Sir John Sams bearing date 1 Feb., 1615, leasing two acres of land called Awdy Hopes, in Witham, Essex, to Richard Barnard.

† Edward Hasteler of Maldon whose will was proved 4 Oct., 1622 (P. C. C. 92 Saville), also appoints John Soan as one of the Overseers.

Little Wakering for life, and after to Robert King aforesaid. To my goddaughter Dorothy Norman a cow   To my brother Henry King two hives of bees and to his son Henry a bedstead etc., and to his son John a cupboard. Res: and Ex: wife. Overseer: brother Henry. Wit: Richard Crayford John Sutter, John Keep, Christopher Tyffin. Proved 21 Dec., 1604, by relict. (Consistory, London. Sperin, 395.)

148. MOTT, RICHARD, of Little Horkesley, Essex, 11 Nov., 40 Eliz. To be buried in the churchyard. To my brother Robert Mott and to his son Robert and to my brother Bartholemew Mott and his son Richard the whole years profit of the house and lands wherein I dwell immediately after the decease of my wife Joane equally between them. Res: & Ex: wife. Wit: Jonas Lovell, Thomas Bramstall, Thomas Josselyn. Proved 5 May, 1599, by the relict. (Consistory, London. Sperin, 203.)

149. OSBORNE, WILLIAM, of Castle Hedingham, Essex, yeoman, 10 July, 1592. To poor 10/-   To Anna Tyler my daughter £13. 6. 8. and ditto to daughters Judith, Mary and Margaret Osborne at their ages of 21. To my maid Elizabeth Codwell £10. To my son William £20 at age 21. To my son John all my houses lands and household stuff, he to be ex. Sup: William Francis alias Puckle and Thomas Christmas the younger. Wit: Christofer Langton,* minister, Thomas Christmas, Isaacke Osborne and Anthony Hudson. Proved at Braintree, 11 Sep., 1592, by the ex. named. (Consistory, London. Sperin, 25.)

150. PITMAN, MARGARET, of Corringham, Essex, 17 June, 1582. My husband John Pitman. Jone the daughter of William Pitman. To my brother Blower two loads of wood and to his eldest daughter "a new white russett cassocke" etc. Susan and John Blower and their mother Ursley Foster, Susan Warley. My brother John Pytman and Christofer his son. Res: & Ex: my father Thomas Skandle.† Witnesses: Philippe White, John Seymor, John Hamon and William Brode. Probate not mentioned. (Arch. Essex. Draper.)

151. ROWE, AVIS, of Horndon, Essex, 26 March, 1581. Widow. To daughter Tacye at age 20 a bedstead and various articles. Res: & Ex: son John. Overseer: John Stonarde of Horndon. Witnesses: John Stonarde, George Stonarde. Proved 28 April, 1582. (Arch. Essex. Draper.)

152. STRACHIE, JOHN, of Walden, Essex, draper 9 April, 1589. To wife Emme all those my lands and tenements called Kelkes for ever towards paying my debts and bringing up my children (not named) and she to have all my other goods both real and personal, and to be sole Executrix. Wit: James Crofte, William

---

* His will was proved 27 April, 1620. He left sons Thomas and Richard.
† Spelled Skanbee in another place in the will.

Malyn, and Agnes his wife, Amable Goodwyn, widow, William Strachie. Proved 16 July, 1589, by relict. (P. C. C. 63 Leicester.)

153. THEYER, WILLIAM, of Great Wigborough, Essex, husbandman, 13 Feb., 1560 To be buried in the churchyard. To wife Amie for life my house and land called Brookmans in Woodham Ferris etc. after her decease to my son Thomas. To my son William my land called Carters Ridden in the Parish of Norton after my wifes death To wife all cattle sheep etc. upon condition she pay to sons Thomas and William £5 each and ditto to daughters Joane, Annes, Rose, and Audrie at their ages of 18 years, or days of marriage. Household stuff to wife for life after equally between children. If wife remarry then she to be bound to William Reignolde of Chelmsford draper to perform this testament Ex: wife. Supervisor: William Reignold of Chelmsford. Wit: William Reignolde, Robert Rowe of Tolleshunt Knights, John Ekynn, Rychard Lambe the wryter. Probate not mentioned. (Arch, Colchester. Puckle, 3.)

154. TURCKE, WILLIAM, of Romford, Essex, 24 July, 1582 To the Church 5/- To the poor 3/4. My apparel to be divided equally between my nearest relatives To Stephen Turke that dwelleth with Quicke 10/- To Jane one of Quickes daughters 10/- To cousin Turke of Hornchurch 10/- To George Owtred* 20/. To Elizabeth Owtred* 10/- To John Comports wife 20/- To my two keepers 3/4 each. To my Master Owtred* £4 part of the money he oweth me. To Willott my fellow my chest. To Margarett our maid my other chest. Res: & Ex: my good Master William Owtred Witness: John Comporte. (Probate not mentioned.) (Arch. Essex. Draper.)

155. TYLER, RICHARD, of Rochford, Essex, yeoman, 17 Feb., 24 Eliz. To wife Lucy for her life lands in Rochford and after to sons Edward and Francis My eldest son Thomas. Res: & Ez: wife. Wit: Thomas Scott, Richard Eve, Robte, Montaigne, Jeremye Norton "and others." Proved 31 May, 1582. (Arch. Essex. Draper.)

---

* See will of Marscelm Owtred (No. 10 of this series).

A DIGEST OF ESSEX WILLS.

WITH PARTICULAR REFERENCE TO NAMES OF IMPORTANCE IN THE AMERICAN COLONIES.

By WILLIAM GILBERT,

Corresponding Member of the New York Genealogical and Biographical Society, Member of the Essex Archaeological Society, etc.

156. ADDAMS, THOMAS, the elder of Harlow, Essex. Bone setter,* 4 Feby., 1605. To be buried in the Churchyard. To my son Thomas 2/–   To son John my freehold land in Hendon Middlesex to him and his heirs for ever upon condition he pay my son George and daughter Joyce Addams £16 equally between them and my daughter Joan Turner 10/– and Thomas Wood my daughter Turner's son 20/– at his age of 21. If my son John die without issue then the said land to come to my son George and his

---

* Surgeon.

heirs he paying to his sister Joyce £8. To my son Roger and his heirs the tenement wherein I dwell in Harlow aforesaid with the orchard and garden thereto belonging. To son John my biggest brasse pott one pewter platter and a pewter dish. To son George my biggest brasse kettle etc. To son Roger my brasse three legged kettle etc. To Thomas Wood my daughters son one latten* candlestick with a square nossell etc. To daughter Turner a warming pan. Res: daughter Joyce. Ex: son John. Overseer: John Gladwyn of Harlow yeoman, 2/– to him. Wit: Nicholas Graygoose and George Harrison. Probate not mentioned. (Consistory, London. Sperin, 342.)

157. AYLETT, MATTHEW, of Much Totham, Essex, Yeoman, 2 Oct., 1604. To be buried in churchyard. To Elizabeth my wife all my lands and tenements now in the occupation of Peter Payse situate in Tolleshunt Tregoose† Essex Also to her all my goods whatsoever and she to be sole Executrix. Wit: Robert Manninge, James Manninge. Proved 23 March, 1604, by relict. (Consistory, London. Sperin, 303.)

158. BAKER, ROBERT, of Cressing, Essex, 27 March, 2 Eliz. To the poor 6/8. To wife Margaret my house and land in Cressing for her life and after to my son John and his heirs he to pay my son Richard £5 and Ellen my daughter 40/– and Joan my daughter 6/8. To Joan my sons daughter one old angel‡ and a bullock sheep and lamb and a new hutch with a lock and key. To son John all such goods as he hath of mine noted in a bill dated 27 October 1559 he to pay out of said goods unto Joh Thorpes wife of Lyes (Leighs) being now widow 46/8. To each of Harry Bacon's sons a sheep and a lamb. Res. & Ex. wife. Wit: John Daynes Richard Deynes Fraunce Rawe and John Walford. Probate not mentioned. (Arch. Colchester. Puckell, 5.)

159. BARNES, JOHN, of Stanford, le Hope, Essex, Husbandman, 21 March, 1585. To be buried in the Churchyard. To the poor 20/– Various articles to sons John Richard and Robert. To daughter Ellen "all my wifes apparrell" and pewter, linen etc. Res. & Ex: Thomas Barnes of Bowers Gifford. he to bring up my children, and provide sureties to Lawrance Gilman and John Slaterford (who are to be Overseers) for the due performance of this my will. Wit: William Tery, Robert Drywood. Proved 10 April, 1585, by the Ex. named. (Arch. Essex. Draper, 136.)

160. BARRETT, JOHN, of Little Thurrock, Essex, Husbandman, 5 July, 1600. To be buried in the Churchyard. To my eldest son John £12 at age 20 and my Bible. Also to him my great

---

* Brass.

† The old name for Tolleshunt Darcy. The family of Tregoz held this Manor of the Honour of Peverell in the time of Stephen. It is called Tolleshunt Tregoz on a brass dated 1419 in the church. The Darcy family held it later.

‡ A gold coin having on the obverse St. Michael and the Dragon, hence its name. The current value of the angel in the time of Mary and Elizabeth was ten shillings, but previously it was only eight shillings, hence I suppose the signification of the term " old."

brass pot that was my fathers etc. To son Robert £12 at age 20.
and the great brass pot that was his Aunt Katherines etc. To
my daughter Martha £12 at age 20 or marriage and pewter etc.
Res. & Ex. wife Martha she to give to John Haman my sisters
son a sheep and a lamb or 10/– in money at his choice. Overseers: John Beda* and Robert Herde† of Stifford they to each have
eight bushels of rye. Wit: Lewes Jones, Richard Prior. Proved
2 Aug., 1600, by the Ex. named. (Arch. Essex. Stephen, 298.)

161. FINCH, WILLIAM, of Braintree, Essex, Clothier, 13 Sept.,
1604. To the Poor 6/8. To son William £40 at age 21. Res. &
Ex. wife Editha. Overseers William Baldwyn and Robert Myres
of Braintree Clothiers, and to each of them 6/8. Witnesses:
James (blank) John Corke, Robert Reeve (X). Proved at Braintree, 10 Oct., 1604, by relict. (Consistory, London. Sperin, 298.)

162. FRENCH, ELYAS, of Little Stambridge, Essex, husbandman, 1 Oct., 1611. To be buried in the Churchyard. To son John
£35 at age 21, the said sum to be meanwhile held by John Freeborne of Prittlewell. To Abigail my daughter £30 at age 18 or
marriage, the said sum to be meanwhile held by Thomas Burnet
of Rochford. Res. & Ex. Wife Bridgitt. Wit: Thomas Burnet,
John Freeborne, John Prisly (x). On the 31 Oct., 1612, administration of the above will was granted by William Pasfeild Rector
of the Parish Church of Chelmsford,‡ to Edward Jeppe, late the
husband of Bridgitt, the Executrix named in the will—she now
being also dead. (Consistory, London. Hamer, 141.)

163. FRENCH, THOMAS, the elder of Wethersfield, Essex, gentleman, 23 July, 1599. To poor of Halstead 40/– Ditto of West
Wratting Cambridge 20/– Ditto of Snettisham Norfolk £3. Ditto
of Much Bardfield 40/– Ditto of Little Bardfield 20/– Ditto of
Whethersfield 40/– Ditto of Arkesden 20/–. To my daughter
Mary now the wife of John Collin £20, and to her children John,
William, Mary and Elizabeth Collin £20 each to be paid them "in
the South Porch of the Parish Church of Much Bardfield." To my
daughter Elizabeth now the wife of John Meade £20 and to her
children Edward, Elizabeth, John and Agnes Meade £20 each to
be paid as before. To the children of my son Thomas French
(not named) £10 each. To Thomas Girton one of the servants
of my said son 10/– To John French son of my son Thomas a
silver bowl. To my wife Bridgit £5 and such goods as I had
with her and possessed at the time of our marriage. Res. & Ex.
son Thomas. Wit: Thomas Reynoldes, William Younge, William
Purcas. Proved 31 Oct., 1599 by the Executor named. (P. C. C.
Kidd, 73.)

---

    * This John Beda was sometime Rector of Horndon on the Hill, Essex.
He was buried at Stifford, 10 April, 1610, and his will was proved 14 May, 1619.
    † "Memorandu that Robert Herd of Stifford did giue vnto the poore of
Stifford Xs. to be distributed amonge them by his laste will wc. tene shillinges
was distributed amonge them the fifte day of ffebruary in the psence of John
Beda and Robert Herd and other Ano Regni Jacobi primo 1603." (Entry in
Stifford Parish Register.)
    ‡ Instituted 23 May, 1604.

164. GOLDINGE, EDMOND, minister of Birdbrook, Essex.* 21 Novr. 15 Eliz. Sole Legatee and Executrix Sara "My trewe and lawfull wyef". Supervisor my brother William Golding of Tilbury. Wit: John Mortlacke, Thomas Coo and Wyllyam Fytche. Proved 29 Jan., 1572, by relict. (P. C. C. Peter, 4.)

165. GOLDING, HENRY, of Little Birch, Essex, Esquire. 20 March, 1575. To the poor of the Parish where I happen to be buried 20/- To the poor of Great and Little Birch and Estropp (Eastthorpe) 60/- equally between them. To my wife Alice all my household goods, corn, cattle etc. She to suffer the heirs of John Freelove quietly to enjoy the moiety of the Manor of Harsted, County Suffolk, which I sold to the said John Freelove. Whereas there is owing unto Mary Waldegrave by Nicholas Mynn £400 and by myself £160 my Executor to pay the same to my wife and my cousin William Ayloff to the use of the said Mary and she to be allowed £10 of every hundred towards her living. Mentions that Mr. Robert Waldegrave stands bound to him in a pair of Indentures for the performance of certain covenants touching the said Mary. To my wife for her life in consideration of her dower my Manor of Little Birch and other lands in little and Great Birch Copford Stanway and Layer de la Haye. After her death to my brother Arthur Golding for his life† and after to his son Henry Golding and his heirs. In default of issue to my brother George, in default to my brother Willian and in default to my right heirs for ever. To Elizabeth daughter of Mary Waldegrave £100. To my nephew Thomas Becke £20. The moiety of my Manor of Estropp‡ and Great Birch§ and one tenement in Great Birch which I lately bought of one Waynewright and his wife to descend to my brother Arthur. In consideration of the payment of my debts my executor to have the lease of Campes (which I hold of the Right Hon. the Earl of Oxford) for a term ten years, and the residue of the term to my brother George he to be my executor. Wit: Nycholas Mynne, Thomas Aglionby, John Myners. On the 12 Feb. 1576 George Golding personally appeared and renounced probate. Administration granted to Arthur Golding brother of the deceased. (P. C. C. Daughtry, 8.)

166. HEDGE, HENRY, of Rayleigh, Essex, Husbandman, 21 July, 1596. To the poor 20/- to be distributed by the Parson and Churchwardens. To William Harte the elder £10, now in his hands and a further £3. which William Jackson of Roxwell oweth me. upon a bond. He to pay William Harte his son 20/-. To George Brett all my wearing apparel. Ex. William Hart the elder. Wit: Radul Howghe, Benjamin Burie. Proved 2 Aug., 1596, by Ex. named. (Arch. Essex. Stephen, 177.)

167. KINGE, ANDREW, of Arkesden, Essex, 24 Novr., 1584. To Thomas my son at age 18 twenty shillings and ditto to daughter

* Instituted 21 Feb., 1571.
† Arthur Golding sold this Manor to John Lord Petre.
‡ Arthur Golding sold this Manor in 1577 to Richard Atkins, gent.
§ Arthur Golding sold this Manor to Edward Ellyott, Esq.

Sarah at similar age.   Residue to wife she to be sole Executrix.
Wit: John Brownridge, (Vicar) John Lucas, George Hidon alias
Yonge.   Probate not mentioned.   (Arch. Colchester.   Root, 271.)

168.   KINGE, LETTYS, of Much Leighs, Essex, widow, 10 June,
1584.   To be buried in the Churchyard.   To William Kinge my
son-in-law one year old cow bullock, a kettle of brass of four gal-
lons "wth. an hole betwene the brasse and the bande", a coverlet,
a blanket and a pair of canvas sheets.   To my daughter Lettice
two gowns, a kirtle etc.   To Joane Hulke my own brothers
daughter a half sleeved gown.   A pewter dish to each of my godchildren viz: Mary Bronde, Joane Ingrame and my godson
Hulke.   Residue equally between son John Kinge and daughter
Lettice Kinge.   Ex. Thomas Cornishe and my brother John
Hulke.   Wit: Mr. Fitche, Thomas Cornishe "with others".   Proved
7 Novr., 1584, by Ex. named.   (Arch. Essex.   Draper, 28.)

169.   KINGE, WILLIAM, of Harwich, Essex, Mariner, 1 Oct., 1627.
To the poor 40/-   To my wife Elizabeth the house wherein I
dwell and all my household stuff and shipping for her life; after
her decease the said house to come to my grandchild William
Heard eldest son of John Heard and his heirs.   In default to his
brother John Heard.   My tenement at the Town Gate in Harwich wherein John Hart butcher lately dwelt to my wife for life
after to my grandchild John Heard and his heirs.   For want of
such heirs the said house to come to the Church or Chapel of
Harwich for ever the rent to be applied to the repair of the
Church.   To my goddaughter Mary the daughter of Richard Renoulds 20/-   Ex: wife.   Wit: Richard Renoulds and Frances
Butcher.   Proved 11 Feb., 1627, by relict.   (P. C. C. Barrington, 10.)

170.   MOORE, SAMUEL, Clerk, Parson of the Rectory of Little
Oakley, Essex,* 13 Oct., 1605.   My body to be buried in the Chancel of the Church of Little Oakley under that grave stone that
Sir William Atkins† sometime Parson of the said Church lyeth.
To the poor 20/-   To my successor the next Incumbent the
herbs in my garden one hive or stock of bees the glass locks han-
dles etc. at the Rectory also my book of rates and tithes collected,
on condition that he deliver to my Executrix a discharge of all
dilapidations.   To my brother Nicholas my book of Josephus his
Antiquities in English.   To my brother Edward my tenement
called Milles lying in Walton in the Sooke in the county of Essex
on condition that he acquit my Executrix of £30 that I owe him
and pay my nephew Samuel son of my brother Enoch £40 at his
age of 24.   Mentions goods bought of "my sister Anne Hensen
when she was the widdowe of Brice Smith."   To Margaret my
wife and her heirs my cottage and land in Little Oakley called
Borroughs als. Bramlies upon condition that she the said Margaret and her son George Wilson release the said tenement called

---

* Date of presentation not known.   He was succeeded by Jeremiah
Burgess who was instituted 16 Nov., 1609, " per mort Moore."
† William Atkins, Rector from 1491 to 1515.   Will dated 10 Oct., 1515, and
proved 15, same month.   He desires to be buried in the Chancel and leaves
bequest for a window to be made in the south wall of church.

241

Millers to my brother Edward and pay her goddaughter Sara the daughter of Mr. Branham 40/– and to Sara the daughter of my brother Enoch £5 at her age of 21. Res. & Ex. Margaret my wife. (Witnesses not named.) Proved 12 Feb., 1609, by relict. (Consistory, London. Hamer, 50.)

171. MOTT, GEORGE, of Bradwell juxta, Mare, Essex, Single-man, 20 March, 1583. To the poor 40/–. To the Church 40/–. To my brother William Thorne all legacies and debts bequeathed me to be paid by him. To Gregory London of Tillingham husband-man 10/– and a similar amount to George Sydaye, married. Robert Buttler, singleman, Henry Farrin, Taylor, John Phillipp, Josias Osborne. To my Godson George son of George Maulden 10/–. To my brothers Henry and Richard Mott my wearing apparel. Residue equally between Henry and Richard Mott. William Thorn and Mary George. Ex: William Thorne. Supervisor: John Maul-den. Wit: John Maulden, Josias Osborne John Phillip. Proved 15 April, 1584, by executor named. (Arch. Essex. Draper, 55.)

172. MOTTE,* WILLIAM, one of the Aldermen of the Town of Colchester, Essex†, 16 Aprill, 1562. To the poor 40/– To wife Joan a number of household articles twenty loads of wood yearly £6 and a mylche Bullock. Also to her a little more (i. e. moor) I have by lease and a piece of land adjoining same which I bought lying under the Town walls by the Rye Gate for her life. Also to her for her life the house wherein widow Cowbridge dwells. After her decease the said house shall come to my son Robert‡ and his heirs he to pay 40/– to each of my daughters' children at their ages of 21 viz: John, Katherine and (blank) Tytley, Priscilla and Nathaniel Meryll and John Clayton. I give to Thomas Wood £3. To my daughter Dorothy Tytley £5 her husband John Tytley to deliver to my son Robert Mott "a generall release and acquytaunce" of all matters. To John Spisall a lamb. A lamb each to my servants viz: Alice Raynold, John Church, Giles Sew-ell, Macute Snowe and Russell Pie. To my son-in-law Richard Clayton my scarlet gown. Ex: son Robert and John Pickasse. Res: son Robert Motte. Supervisor: Mr. Robert Lambert§ one

---

* The family of Motte was of importance in Colchester for more than three centuries. The following are notes from the early Town Records:
  - 1334   William son of Thomas de la Motte. Free Burgess.
  - 1421   Richard Motte of Bergholt Sackville.
  - 1460   John and Helen Motte.
  - 1461 & 1468   Robert Mott.
  - 1472 & 1481   Richard Mott.
  - 1472   William Mott.
  - 1481   Geoffry Motte.
  - 1534   Richard Mott of Lexden.

† The testator occurs with his wife Joan in various deeds, 1532, etc. He was a Common Councillor in 1538, a Senior Assistant in 1548, an Alderman in 1551, etc. Bailiff in 1551, 1558 and 1559.

‡ He was Bailiff in 1574, 1579 and 1584.

§ Robert Lambert was a stock fishmonger and a Free Burgess in 1542, Common Councillor in 1548, Alderman and Bailiff, 1562, 1568 and 1576. He died in 1592.

A Samuel Mott was Mayor of Colchester in 1686 and 1693. He married Elizabeth Criffield.

of the Aldermen of the Town of Colchester. Wit: Edward Strachie, John Fludd, Nycholas Wilbore, John Evered and John Paynter. Proved 26 Oct., 1562, by Robert Mott. John Pickasse renouncing probate. (Arch. Colchester. Puckell, 75.)

173. OSBORNE, RICHARD, of Little Waltham,* Essex, Labourer, 3 Feb., 27 Eliz. My goods and chattels, and the lease of Little Peverells (the house wherein I dwell) and croft adjoining and the lease of Great Peverells I give unto Katherine my wife she to be sole Ex. "trusting that she will be a good mother to all our children" To John and Mary Osborne 13/4. Overseer: my brother Robert Osborne. Wit: Edmonde Griffyne, Thomas Cooke, Elizabeth Griffine, Margaret Tyrry, Joanne Porter, Joan Cooke. Proved 30 March, 1585, by relict. (Arch. Essex. Draper, 106.)

174. REEVE, GILES, of Finchingfield, Essex, Yeoman, 31 May, 1649. To the poor of the Parish of Finchingfield where I was born £5. To my mother Dorothy Reeve £20. To my brother Joseph Reeve and his heirs for ever my cottage in Finchingfield which I late purchased of Luke Bird chapman† and now in the occupation of Thomas Chalis and Daniel Shed. Also to him £10 and wearing apparel. To my brother Thomas Reeve £40. To my kinsman William Chesill who now dwelleth with me £10 at his age of 21. To my servant Anna Wakering 5/-. Res: & Ex; brother John Reeve. Wit: Will. Tym and Thomas Heard. Proved 9 Novr., 1649, by the Executor named. (P. C. C. Fairfax, 154.)

175. REEVE, WILLIAM, of Colchester, Essex, Clothier, 2 Nov., 1610. To wife Anne my Geneva Bible, household goods, 20 marks in money, a sow "greate with pigg" etc. To son Daniel various articles. To son Nathaniel 20 marks to be paid him on

---

* The Parish Register of Little Waltham from its commencement in 1538 to 1585 (which is as yet unpublished), yields the following information about this family:

1540	May 2	Bapt. Robert son of Richard Osburne.			
1542	June 10	"	Anne dau. of	"	" ye younger.
1544	May 11	"	Colet	"	" "
1560	Aug 18	"	John Osborne.		
1560	Aug 21	"	Joan Osborne.		
1562	Nov 25	"	Marie Osborne.		
1562	Jan 5	"	Thomas Osborne.		
1563	Nov 5	"	Richard son of Richard Osborne.		
1569	Feb 27	"	Em daughter of	"	"
1547	Oct 30	Mar.	John Sawen & Agnes Osborne.		
1554	Nov 4	"	Richard Osborne & Kateren Kynge.		
1557	July 24	"	John Osborne & Audre Panett.		
1558	Jan 15	"	Thomas Osborne & Annes Barnard.		
1559	May 28	"	Edmund Osborne & Agnes Lampson.		
1545	June 20	Bur.	Anne dau of Richard Osborne.		
1557	Octr 11	"	Richard Osborne.		
1557	Octr 14	"	The wife of Richard Osborne.		
1559	May 13	"	John Osborne.		
1585	Feb 17	"	Richard Osborne.		

† A merchant or seller. Shakespeare refers to it:
"Beauty is bought by judgment of the eye
Not uttered by base sale of chapmen's tongues."
Loves, L.L., II, 1.

the first of May next after my death and if my son Nathaniel do not happen to come home by then the money to be delivered to John Badcocke of Colchester Clothier for the use and behoof of my son until he do come home. The said John Badcocke to pay at the rate of eight pounds in the hundred for the use of it and enter into a bond with Mr. John Waylett and Mr. Henry Cleaveland both of Colchester for the true payment of the Legacy. To my son Joseph £20 etc. "Willm. Reeve my nephew and Anne Reeve my neece the children of Willm. Reeve my sonne deceased." To Thomazin Reeve my daughter in law 40/– To Margaret Orums 10/– To Mary May my wifes sister 10/– and to William Cooke clerk 10/–. Res. & Ex my son Daniel. Wit: William Cooke, John Waylett, junior, Robert Wyniffe (X). Proved at Colchester, 4 April, 1611, by the Executor named. (Consistory, London. Hamer, 70.)

176. TERLINGE, THOMAS, of Bobbingworth, Essex, 17 Feb.ʼ 1597 (*sic*.). To be buried in the Churchyard.* To Weston Terlinge my son a cow. Ditto to Ellen Terlinge my daughter. To son Christopher a bullock and to son George a cow. To Thomas Jone† and Christian‡ Terlinge a sheep each. Residue to be equally divided between my said children. Ex: my two sons John (not elsewhere mentioned in will) and Weston. Wit: John Poole, the writer hereof), and Richard Poole.§ Proved 14 March, 1596, by the Ex. named. (Arch. Essex. Stephen, 182.)

177. WOODCOCKE, JOHN,‖ of Harfordestocke.¶ Essex, 21 Aprilʼ 1595. To the poor 40/– My copyhold land called Jemes in Margaretting to my wife Clemence** until son John comes to age 21, then to him and his heirs for ever. In default of issue to Thomas Shory my son-in-law and his heirs for ever. Res. & Ex. wife. Overseer: Mr. Thomas Whitebreade. Wit: Robert Hawkens, Edward Wittam William Croxon. Proved 27 May, 1595, by relict. (Arch. Essex. Stephen, 149.)

---

* Thomas Terlinge was buried the 16 March, 1596. Jone Terlinge the wife of Thomas Terlinge was buried 11 April, 1596 (this was nearly a year before her husband).

† William Waylett, son of Robert Waylett of North Weald Bassett, and Jone, daughter of Thomas Terlinge of Bobbingworth, mar. 13 Oct., 1588. (Jone was probably the eldest child and Christian the youngest.)

‡ Christian, daughter of Thomas Terlinge, bap. 27 Feb., 1577. Richard Hatche and Christian Terling married 10 Oct., 1608.

There is a number of entries to the Terling family in the Registers, but when I noted all the memorials both in the Church and Churchyard some years ago, I found none extant to the name. It was a place-name as there is a parish called Terling in Essex at the present day.

§ The family of Poole was a large one in this neighborhood and is still flourishing.

‖ Extracts from Parish Register:
    1571 July   1 Mar. John Woodcocke and Alice Wilson.
    1583 July 25 Bur. Alice wife of John Woodcocke.
    1589 April 27 Bap. John son of John Woodcocke.
    1595 April 23 Bur. John Woodcocke.
¶ Now called Stock.
** Apparently his second wife.

A DIGEST OF ESSEX WILLS.

With Particular Reference to Names of Importance in the American Colonies.

By William Gilbert,

Corresponding Member of the New York Genealogical and Biographical Society, Member of the Essex Archaeological Society, etc.

178. Wright, Mabel, of Great Stambridge, Essex, widow, 5 Feb., 1596. To the poor widows of Great Stambridge 5/– Ten shillings to each of the six children of Peter Lawrence of Barking and I forgive the said Peter the debt he oweth me To the two children of John Rule of Barking ten shillings each. To Elizabeth Nevell the daughter of Elizabeth Bennett of Paglesham 10/– at her age of sixteen. To my maid Alice Durman 3/–. Res. & Ex. my son William Burton. Overseers: John Langer and John Rule. Wit: Ezekiell Culverwell,‖ John Langer. Proved 23 March, 1596, by the Ex. named. (Arch. Essex. Stephen, 183.)

179. Adams, John, of Little Laver, Essex, Husbandman, 6 February, 1573. To be buried in the Churchyard. To my wife Johane all my household stuff My son Raynolde to keep her and provide for her. To my three sons George John and Edward 40/– each and corn cattle etc. To my two daughters (not named)

‖ Ezekiel Culverwell, Rector of Great Stambridge, 1591 to 1609, was licensed Oct. 20, 1598, to marry Winifred, widow of Edward Barefoot of Hatfield Broad Oak. She was buried at All Hollows, Barking, 19 Nov., 1613. He was buried at St. Antholins, 14 April, 1631.

a bushel of wheat and a bushel of malt. To Elizabeth Skotte a pewter platter candlestick etc. Res. & Ex. son Raynolde. Supervisor: John Collen of Little Laver. Wit : John Collen, Thomas Asser. Proved 30 October, 1574 by Ex. named. (Value £13. 16. 4). (Arch. Essex. Gyll 77.)

180. AYLETT, WILLIAM, of Rivenhall, Essex, Yeoman, 27 July, 1581. To be buried in the churchyard of Rivenhall or Kelvedon. Bequests to the poor of a number of parishes. To wife Margaret for her life copyhold land called More Land in Kelvedon. Also to her £100 and cattle &c. half of household stuff and the occupation of a tenement called Graces. To my eldest son Richard my lease in Cressing. To son Leonard my copyhold closes in Rivenhall called Elmesfield and Sewerland and other copyhold lands held under same Manor, and a lease called Little Rivenhall and my lease in Black Notley which I late had of George Raymond of Braintree. To son Robert my lease in Coggeshall. To son William my lease in the moiety of a tenement in Mayland called Bovells and all my tenements in Mayland Southminster and Steeple which I late had of Henry Luckyn of Roxwell.* To son Thomas lease of a meadow in Rivenhall I bought of Thomas Burgess, a copyhold tenement in Rivenhall·called Black Mere and a meadow called Bayes. To son John the other half of my household stuff by the dividing of my brothers Robert & Thomas Aylett and George Raymond and also the lands bequeathed to wife, after her death, and £100 at age 21. My executors to have my lands held of the Manor of Kelvedon Hall for the better performance of this my will. To my daughter Susan the wife of Edward Sammes £20. and each of her children (not named) to have £6. 13. 4. To John, Thomas, Edward and Susan Lambe, the children of my daughter Elizabeth, deceased, late the wife of John Lambe £6. 13. 4. each. To Judith the daughter of my brother Thomas Aylett £6. 13. 4. at age 21. To each of my servants 3/4. Res. & Ex. my six sons. Supervisor: my brothers, George Raymond and Thomas Aylett. My free messuages and tenements in the hamlet of Stansted in the parish of Halsted which I bought of Robert Noke, gent, and Dorothy his wife to remain to the uses declared in a pair of indentures dated the 25 July 23 Eliz. between myself and wife on the one part and George Raymond of Braintree, Grocer, (my brother-in-law) and Thomas Aylett of Leaden Roding (my natural brother), on the other part as in the same more plainly doth appear. And whereas I have taken up by copy of Court roll of George White, Esquire, one parcel of the waste ground of his Manor of Rivenhall and thereupon have builded one house, being now two tenements for the poor of the parish of Rivenhall, my sons to have the appointing of such persons to dwell therein. Wit: Thomas Hunt, gentleman, John Upcher, John Binded, William Piggett. Proved 7 May, 1583, by the ex. named. (P. C. C. Rowe 26.)

---

* The Visitation of Essex, 1612, states that Henry Lukyn of Roxwell married Alice, dau. of Richard Pullestone of Bardfield Hall, Essex.

181.   BALDWIN, WILLIAM, of Upminster, Essex, Yeoman, 26 November. 1574. To be buried in the Churchyard. To ten poor householders on the day of my burial 6 pence each.   To wife Johane all my copyhold lands and tenements in the Southend of Upminster held of the Manor of Gaynes for her life.   To son Thomas £6. 13. 4. at age 21.   To son John £10 at age 21.   To the child my wife goeth with £10 at age 21.   To my daughter Thamer Baldwin £10 at age 21.   To William Baldwin, my brother's son my best coat.   To Richard Baldwin my next coat.   To John Baldwin that dwelleth with me my best hosen and best hat.   To sister Alice half a seam of rye.   To my brother John Baldwin my spanish leather jerkin, and my satten nightcappe.   A kercher clothe of 20 pence a piece cach to John Baldwin's wife, my sister Samford, Thomas Heynes wife and the widow Wright.   Res. & Ex. wife.   Overseers: Thomas Herde, George Herde, John Baldwin my brother and John Skeele.   Wit: William Soane, Robert Herde, Humfry Benton.   Proved 18 December, 1574 by the Ex. named.   (Value £111. 10. 0.)   (Arch. Essex.   Gyll, 83.)

182.   GLASCOCKE, JOHN, of Rayleigh, Essex, Carpenter, April, 1638 (nuncupative)   To his eldest daughter Sara Glascocke £5, her mother's gown and a blue silk girdle.   To his daughter Mary Glascocke £3 and a silver spoon.   To Jonas his manservant his wearing apparel and tools.   Residue to his two sons John and Henry Glascocke.   His brother John Hamond of Harlow to have the bringing up of John, and his sister-in-law, Mrs. Elizabeth Waylett, to have the bringing up of Henry.   Wit: Edward Pond, William Julian.   Administration of the above will was granted on 17 July, 1638, at Great Baddow, to Henry Liveing and Henry Barnes, overseers of the poor of the parish of Rayleigh during the minority of John, Sara, Mary and Henry, children of the deceased.   (Arch. Essex.   Whitehead, 16.)

183.   GREEN, THOMAS, of Brentwood, Essex, 15 November, 1610.   Gentleman.   To be buried in the parish church of South Weald.   To the poor of Brentwood 20/–   To Mr. Weston 10/– to preach at my funeral.   To wife Thomazine two thirds of goods.   To children (not named) the other third.   Cousin John Green.   Servants Joane Wooddall and Henry Smith.   To Mr. Marwood 20/–.   Res. & Ex. wife.   Overseers: Edward Marwood and cousin Charles Green of London, Goldsmith.   Wit: Edward Marwood, Thomas Tabor, George Bowdishe "and his wife."   Proved 19 March, 1610, by the relict.   (Arch. Essex.   Blunt, 58.)

184.   HANCHETT, THOMAS, of Berden, Essex, Yeoman, 20 June, 1666   To the poor of Arkesden 40/–   To wife freehold land called Bledlews comprising 24 acres.   Sons George and Samuel.   Lands to son Edward.   Lands in Arkesden and Elmdon.   To son William copyhold lands held of Dodenloe *als* Dudnall Grange.   Youngest son Thomas.   Son Richard.   My grandchildren Thomas and Edward, the sons of Edward Hanchet, and James, Richard and William, the sons of Richard Hanchet.   My daughter Susan, the wife of William Morrice.   Res. & Ex. wife Elizabeth.   Wit:

John Beard and Thomas Hagger. Proved at Henham 1 March, 1678, by the relict. (Arch. Colchester. Polley, 276.)

185. HANCHETT, WILLIAM, of Arkesden, Essex, Yeoman, 10 September, 1681. To wife Grace my copyhold ground known as Millfield containing 30 acres in Elmdon until my son John arrives at age 21 and then he to have it. Also to wife for her life my messuage wherein I dwell with the two closes adjoining containing about 11 acres, and also 7 acres in Elmdon called Dawsfield, and 6 acres called Pishedge Croft, and 3 acres in Larkesfield. After her death (or marriage in case she remarry) to my son William. To my eldest daughter Elizabeth £30 at age 21. Ditto to daughters Sarah and Anne. My son William to have my 9 acres of land in Elmdon and Wenden Lofts on condition he pay the above legacies. Residue to wife for life and after equally between children. Ex: wife and son William. Wit: John Wright, Mary Wright, Tho. Patson. Proved at Walden 24 April, 1682, by Ex. named. (Arch. Colchester. Collin, 90.)

186. HILLS, WALTER, of Ramsey, Essex, 6 April, 1560. To Ramsey Bridge 6/8. To Agnes my wife and her heirs all my houses and lands in Much Oakley on condition she pay to five of my kinsfolk £6. 13. 4. each. viz: John Hills, Peter Hills, a poor wife sister of said John and Peter, dwelling in Writtle, John Hills the younger and William Hills. I have surrendered into the hands of John Gillot in stead of the bailiff and in the presence of three of the lords tenants viz: Richard Herriche, James Hewet, and Nicholas Smythe. the said lands. 6/8 to each of my three servants. Res. & Ex. wife. Agnes. Wit: Thomas Richmond, John Callyn, Thomas Porter. Probate not mentioned. (Arch. Colchester. Puckell, 187.)

187. HOWLAND, JOHN, of Wicken Bonhunt, Essex, Yeoman, 16 July, 1607. To Collett, my wife, for her life a piece of arable land in Wicken called Little Field between the land belonging to the Parsonage of Wicken on the South and the land late of John Bell on the North and containing by estimation 2 acres. After her death the land to come to Thomas Thurgood one of the sons of my son-in-law John Thurgood and his heirs for ever. To Collett my daughter, the wife of John Collyn, £10. To my daughter Margaret, the wife of Daniel Peverley, £12. To my daughter Agnes Westrawe, widow, £10. To Elizabeth Cosin, my daughter, a basin; and to John Cosin, her son, 6/8 at age 21. To Martha Westrawe, daughter of my said daughter Agnes, £3. 6. 8. at age 21 or marriage. To each child of my three daughters Margarett, Barbara and Agnes 6/8 at their ages of 21. Res. & Ex. the above named John Thurgood. Wit: John Langham, Richard Spiltimber. Probate not mentioned. (Not Registered. Original will examined. Archdeaconry of Colchester.)

188. HUNT, ROBERT, of Beaumont, Essex, 27 Jan'y., 1561. To William Wade, my father-in-law, and his heirs, my house called Crowche House, and my land called Durches, on condition that Jane Wade, my mother, have her dwelling there and have the

profit of the said lands during her life; and the said William Wade to pay to William Hunt, my brother, £6. 13. 4., and to my brother Richard Hunt, £20 and to my sister Jone Bayninge £6. 13. 4., and ditto to sister Elizabeth Hayle. To my brother John Wade the elder my sword. To my brother John Wade the younger my coffer. Residue of goods to be sold and distributed at the discretion of my Executors. Ex. William Wade my father-in-law and Robert Payne my uncle by-the-law. Wit: John Grene, John Coke. Probate not mentioned. (Arch. Colchester. Puckell, 192.)

189. KINGE, EDMUND, of Tillingham, Essex, 18 August, 1646. I give my house and lands in Maldon called Winterslade now in the occupation of Goodman Fledger (which I have in reversion after my mother's decease, given me in will by my father Bartholomew Kinge) to my son Thomas Kinge and his heirs for ever. If he die without issue then to my wife Elizabeth and her heirs for ever. All my goods etc to wife and she to be ex. Wit: Francis Parfe, Mary Parfe, Mary Gellenwater Thomas Nicholson. On the 27 June, 1650, a commission was issued to Joseph Ellistone the Executor of the will of Elizabeth Kinge deceased who while she lived was the executrix named in the above will to administer the same. (P. C. C. Pembroke, 95.)

190. KINGE, ELIZABETH, of Tilllingham, Essex, Widow, 26 February, 1646. To be buried in the Church of Tillingham. To the poor twenty shillings. To Susanna the daughter of my brother Thomas Nicholson deceased £20 at age 17. If she die before then the legacy to be equal divided between her two brothers Thomas and Rowland. To the said Thomas and Rowland £40 each at ages 21. To Augustine Hill, clerk, 11/- to preach my funeral sermon. Res. & Ex. Joseph Ellistone of Dengy Gentleman. To my sister Susanna Nicholson 40/- a year for each of her three children to bring them up and educate them. Wit: Augustine Hill, James Noble, William Harrison. Proved 4 March, 1646, by Joseph Ellistone. (P. C. C. Fines, 62.)

191. KINGE, THOMAS, of Harlow, Essex, Husbandman, 30 November, 1646. To be buried in the Churchyard. To Katherine my wife my tenement in Church-gate Harlow for her life and after to John Kinge my brother for his life and after to his son John Kinge and his heirs on condition 10/- each be paid to my brother John's children and 10/- each to my brother Powton's children. and my brother to discharge my executrix of a bond of ten pounds wherein I stand bound with him to Mr. Edmund Skoles of Calton. To wife my tenement in Harlow Market in the occupation of Samuel Jennings, for her life and after to Andrew Kinge my brother for his life he to pay ten shillings to each of his two children Joane and Thomas, ten shillings to each of my brother William's three children, and ten shillings each to three other of his own children After the death of the said Andrew I give the tenement to his son Andrew and his heirs for ever. To Jeffery my brother my copyhold tenement in Morton Essex. he to pay ten shillings to each of my sister Elizabeth's

children. and ten shillings to my sister Dennis. To Judith Haver my daughter-in-law, all my household stuff. Res. & Ex. wife Katherine. Wit: Edward Spranger. Proved Jany. 5, 1647, by relict. (P. C. C. Essex, 11.)

192. MOTTE, JOHN, of Layer Marney, Essex, Yeoman, 16 March, 1560. To wife Agnes my house and lands in Much Wigborough, Essex, called Hidde for her life she to pay to my executor 40/- a year and to discharge a bond between Robert Brodocke that married the wife of Audley and me. After her decease the house and lands to go to John the son of William Motte in satisfaction of a legacy of £30 given to him by his father's last will, and he to pay to Mary Motte such residue of the £30 bequeathed her as has not been paid. To Anne Hithe a bedstead etc. To wife £40, residue of household stuff and cattle. She to have two thirds of the corn growing at Wigborough and my brother Richard the other third. To John Hithe a colt and a silver spoon. Silver spoons to Stephen Hithe, Elizabeth Hithe and John Pignet. To Prissitt Motte an old ryall and a silver spoon. To my brother Richard Motte 3 kine and 10 hoggs. To my brother John a tyke that I had of him being fifteen sticks in ye tike. I deliver the surrender of my said house and land into the hands of John Alleyne, Thomas Harvye, and John Graunte. Res. & Ex. brother John Motte. Wit: Robert Camocke, John Graunte, Cristopher Ayleward, Edward Mutton, Thomas Gage. Probate not mentioned. (Arch. Colchester. Puckell, 8.)

193. MOTT, JOHN, of Hawkewell, Essex, 15 March, 1558. To be buried in the parish churchyard at Forrest. To wife Alice all goods and moveables within house and without to bring up my three children (not named). She to be sole Executrix. Overseer: William Dedin. Wit: William Hewes, Thomas Glaskok, Robert Hankin. Proved 4 April, 1559, by the relict. (Arch. Essex. Randoll, 7.)

194. OSBORNE, ROBERT, of Layer Bretton, Essex, Husbandman, 24 July, 1592. To the poor of Layer Bretton viz: father Daulton 5/- Richard Gilder 5/- mother Clarke 5/- Thomas Garland 3/4. Robert Cooper 3/4. Mother Living 3/4. To Alice my wife seven beasts three of them at this farm and the other four at the Moore at Salcott Verley. To Edward Skinner my son-in-law 40/- cattle hay etc. To Richard Osborne my brother's son a bason. To Sarah Southey my daughter-in-law £3 and a black bullock. To Mary Kibbate my sister 30/- To William, Jane and Joane, the children of my brother John Osborne 10/- each. To Anne Francis my sister 30/- To John and Joan the children of my sister Vintner, 10/- each. To John, Jone, Mary and Emme, the children of my brother Richard Osborne, 10/- each. Ten shillings to be divided between Mother Howe, Father Goddard, Mother Bitson and Jeremy Goddard. To William Teele of Salcott Wigborough £10. to be paid out of a bond of twenty pounds which Matthew London of Wigborough standeth bound to me. Res. & Ex. wife Alice. Supervisor William Teele. To my

daughter Katherine Taseler £3. To Clemence Skinner my son-in-law 20/– To Leonard Skinner my son-in-law 20/– To John Skinner 20/– To Elizabeth Ricarde, my sister's daughter, 10/–. Wit: John Lucas, clerk,* William Bearde. Proved at Colchester 8 Sept., 1592, by the relict. (Consistory London. Sperin, 43.)

195. PARTRIDGE, JOHN, of Navestock, Essex, 1 October, 1652, To be buried in the chancel of the Parish Church. To the poor of Navestock £5. To my daughter Margaret Hudson £100. To my grandchildren Thomas & Jane Lake at their ages of 18 the £100 that my son-in-law John Lake oweth me. To my servants Mary Corter, Elizabeth Elkin and Elizabeth Scarlett 20/– each To my cousin John Combers 40/– Res. & Ex. wife Jane and son John. Wit: Thomas Hayward John Combers. Proved 27 June 1663, by relict. (Dean & Chapter of St. Paul. F. 67.)

196. QUINBE, JOHN, of Much Wakering, Essex, Husbandman, 21 May, 1630 To Elizabeth my wife all my corn and implements To John Richardson the younger, my wife's son, £5 at his age of 21. To John Richardson, the other of my wife's sons, 40/ at his age of 21. To Henry Harmon, my wife's brother, 10/– To William Quinbe my brother £6. To Thomas Quinbe my brother £3 at his age of 21. To Richard Abraham my kinsman 40/– To Mary Arkersen my sister the wife of John Lannce shoemaker 50/– To the poor of Much Wakering 10/– To Elizabeth Brette my wifes god-daughter 5/– to buy her a coat. To Ellinn Ellmur my god-daughter 5/–. To Alles Cooke my maide 3/4. Res. & Ex. wife. Overseer: Henry Brette. Wit: Thomas Dranne, Henry Brette, Henry Harmon. Proved 20 July, 1630, by Ex. named. in the Court of the Archdeacon of Essex. (Not registered, Original Will examined.)

197. QUINBE, WILLIAM, 3 January, 1632. To Richard Abraham of Lee, county Essex, smith 30/– To the Widow Bedman of Little Wakering 10/– and my cloak. To John Dynam 5/– My trusty friend Thomas Mayers to be Executor, to him 20/–. To my brother Thomas Quinbe the residue or my money and goods to be paid him at the time his apprenticeship shall come out. Wit: John Dynam, Robert Chapman. Proved in the Court of the Archdeacon of Essex on Feb. 18, 1632, by the Executor named. (Not Registered. Original Will examined.)

198. TABOR, JOHN, of Burnham, Essex, 27 September, 1609. To be buried in the Churchyard. To my father Henry Tabor of Wickford £20. If both my father and mother die before me then sister Elizabeth to have the money. To sister Annys, wife of Richard Glover, £15. To brother Richard Glover £5. to repair a little cottage now in the occupation of my father. To Anthony and John Edwards my ten chaldrons of coal in the malthouse. To the wife of Gregory Wicken 20/– To the wife of Owen Towlton 20/– To Annes Arnold 10/– To my godson

---

* Rector of Layer Bretton. Instituted 12 Dec., 1588.

John Taylor 5/- To my cousin Annis Gilder widow 20/- To my cousin John Tabor a pair of blue Jersey stockings. Res. & Ex. cousin Edward Tabor of Fryerning. Overseer: Ambrose Pettiwell, of Fryeringe 5/- to him. Wit: John Thompson, John Hawke, Andrew Simson. Proved at Great Baddow, 24 Oct., 1609. by Ex. named. (Arch. Essex. Blunt, 42.)

199. TABOR, ROBERT, of Margaretting, Essex, 21 February, 1608. Tailor. To Jesse Tabor (son) my best bedstead feather bed etc. after my wifes decease. To daughter Grace my next feather bed, etc. To daughters Sarah and Joan various household articles. To James Ketch the younger a round table. To Cytus Preistland a little posnett etc. Res. & Ex. wife Dennys. Supervisors Thomas Freeman and my brother John Tabor. Wit: Thomas Freeman and Jeremy Bird. Proved 11 April, 1609, at Great Baddow by relict. (Arch. Essex. Blunt, 15.)

200. WENLOCKE, STEPHEN, of Much Bentley, Essex, 5 July, 1687 Very aged but in good health To son Nathaniel* lands in Much Bentley called Riches and Savores. In default of issue to Elizabeth, my daughter, wife of James Minter and her heirs, she to pay to my daughter Mary, the wife of Edmund Blowers, and her heirs for ever £6 a year; and whoever shall enjoy the said lands shall pay my wife Elizabeth £8 a year during her widowhood. To Martha Wenlocke my daughter and her heirs all my copyhold land called Edwards and a piece of freehold land now occupied by the widow Woodward. In default to the heirs of my son Stephen according to the custom of the Manor of Much Bentley. To Thomas Porter my grandchild £5. My wife to be guardian to Nathaniel and Martha until their ages of 21. Res: & Ex: wife. Wit: David Siday, William Martin, Sarah Siday. Proved 3 May, 1693, by the Ex. named. (Arch. Colchester. Hayward, 39.)

201. WRIGHT, JOHN, of Wright's Bridge within the Liberty of Havering, in the County of Essex, Esquire, 2 April, 1644. To be buried in the North Chancel of the Parish Church of South Weald. To the poor of Noke Hill 40/- To the poor of South Weald 40/- To sister, Mrs. Martha Delbridge, an annuity of £12 for her life out of my lands belonging to my mansion house of Wright's bridge. Also to her my diamond ring. To daughter Elizabeth £400 at age 21. To daughters Martha, Frances and Annett £300 each at ages 21. To my son Laurence Wright three tenements in Noke Hill in the occupation of Giles Siser, Henry Sands and Richard Andrewes. And if my eldest son John Wright desire to redeem them he to pay to his said brother £300 at his age of 21. To sons William and Henry £200 each at ages 21. To brother Nathaniel Wright, Doctor† in Physic, 40/- for a

---

* The Will of this Nathaniel Wenlock was proved 2 Oct., 1716, and mentiones wife Mary, sons Nathaniel and Stephen, daughters Mary and Martha.

† In the Will of Edward Sammes of London, Grocer, (proved 1685 P. C. C. Pile, 21,) mention is made of my brother-in-law Doctor Wright and his wife and

ring. To my brother Robert Wright ditto. To my brother William Atwood my black mare. The rest of my household stuff together with my lease of the Manor of Maunsis which I have assigned over in trust to my honoured and respected uncles Sir Thomas Cheeke Knight* and Laurence Wright Doctor in Physic† to the uses of this my will I leave to my wife Mary for the education of my children and raising of their portions for them. If the portions of my younger children cannot be raised from my personal estatate etc. by the time they are due, then my eldest son John to join with his mother in the sale of the house and land in Romford in the occupation of William Grafton; or else I charge them upon my freehold lands that are to descend to my son John. Ex, wife. Overseers: Sir Thomas Cheeke and Doctor Wright. Wit: John Johnson, Thomas Atwood and Robert Wright. Proved at London, 8 October, 1644, by the relict. (Arch. Essex. Whitehead, 146.)

202. WRIGHT, LAURENCE, of Kelvedon, near Ongar, Essex, Gentleman, 17 Novr., 1638. To the parishes of Kelvedon and White Notley 50/- each. To my brother John Wright the elder in the County of Essex gent. my lands in Shenfield Essex. To my nephews and nieces as follows: To Richard, Stephen and Anthony Wright, Katherine and Mary Wright, and unto John and Edward White, and my Godson Richard White £5 each; and to my nieces Anne and Margaret 50/- each. and to Margaret Burton and Mary White my goddaughters 50/- each. To my sister Mary £20. To my cousin John Wright of Stanfield in White Notley £5. To my cousin Richard Wright of Wealdside £10. To my honourable friend John Petre, Esquire, a younger brother unto Richard Lord Petre, £350 Res. & Ex. my brother John Wright, the elder. Wit: Richard Wright, Thomas Heywood. Proved at London, 6 December, 1638, by John Wright, senior, the Ex. named in the will. (P. C. C. Lee, 175.)

203. WRIGHT, RALPH, of South Weald, Essex, Yeoman, 12 February, 1641 To the poor 10/- To my eldest son Ralph copyhold land in South Weald named Quicks. To son William freehold land in Morton and copyhold lands in Cranham after death of my wife. To daughter Elizabeth Clemens £20 To daughter Sara Wright £60 and a feather bed. etc. Res. & Ex. wife Overseers: my brother Symon Jenings. Wit: John Sond. Thomas Gill. Symon Jenings. Proved at Brentwood, 17 June, 1642, by Elizabeth Wright the relict. (Arch. Essex. Whitehead, 115.)

---

my brother-in-law Nathaniel Wright and his wife. This Edward Sammes married Bennet, daughter of John Wright of Wrightsbridge, the grandfather of the present testator.

* This relationship requires a little explanation. The testator's wife was Mary, daughter of John Mole of York, and her mother was Elizabeth, sister to Sir Thomas Cheeke, Knt.

† He was his half uncle, being the son of John Wright by his second marriage, while the testator was grandson of the same by his first marriage.

A DIGEST OF ESSEX WILLS.

WITH PARTICULAR REFERENCE TO NAMES OF IMPORTANCE IN THE AMERICAN COLONIES.

BY WILLIAM GILBERT,

Corresponding Member of the New York Genealogical and Biographical Society, Member of the Essex Archaeological Society, etc.

204. CARTER, JOHAN, of Audley End, Essex, widow, 16 Jany 29 Eliz. To be bur. in Walden churchyard. To son Thomas household articles. To Susan the daughter of Bennet Carter my son 10/- at age 12. To Margaret and Elizabeth Mathew daughters of my son in law Martin Mathew various household articles at ages 21. My son Martyns servant Jane Croft. To Adam and Thomas sons of my son Martyn Mathew 10/- each at ages 18. Res. & Ex. Martyn Mathew. Wit: Thomas ffrancklyn, John Hennyngton, John Reade. Testator makes mark. Probate not mentioned. (Not registered, original will examined.) Archdeaconry of Colchester.

205. CARTER, ROBERT, senior, of Earls Colne, Essex, 6 April 7 Jac I, Husbandman, To my wife Johan my cottage and garden in Earls Colne called Clovers for her life she to bring up Robert and Mary Carter my grandchildren till their ages of 21 years. After her death the said cottage to go to my grandchild Robert Carter. Res. & Ex. wife Johan. Supervisor, Rober Rookes senior. Wit. Robert Rookes William Dashe. (seal a talbot passant) Proved 29 Nov., 1610. (Not registered, original will examined.) Archdeaconry of Colchester.

206. COLE, HUMPHREY, of Tillingham, Essex, Clerk, 4 November, 1623. To be buried in the Chancel. To poor 4 marks. To son Robert (Student of Emanuel College Cambridge) books, wearing apparel etc. To wife Hester corn etc. My perpetual advowson of the Rectory of Great Oakley Essex to be sold and the money divided between my sons. My freehold land in Tillingham commonly called Hodgwatts to be sold and the money divided as follows: my wife Hester to have the use of £80 for her life and the residue and also the £80 after wife's death to be equally divided between my sons William, Thomas, Robert and John Cole, or such of them as are living. To William Cole now in Virginia (if he be living) my three acres of freehold land with a new barn built upon it called Sewders Head in Tillingham and next adjoining to a cottage and two acres of copyhold land called Finches which doth belong to his brother Robert Cole, and if my said son William be not living at the time of my decease I bequeath the said land and barn to my second son Thomas. My wife to have for her life all my plate, household stuff etc. by virtue of a deed of gift made by me to Sir John Sams Knight and Mr. Blunt gent. Sole Ex. wife, if she refuse then son Thomas to

to be ex. Overseers my two sonnes in law Micaiah Wood parson of Great Oakley and John George yeoman of Writtle. Wit: John Draske, John Moody. Proved 17 May, 1624, by relict. (Dean & Chapter of St. Pauls, D. fo. 232.)

207. HALL, RICHARD, of Ardleigh, Essex, 9 May, 1590, Tailor. To Ann my wife my land in Merse Street Lane by estimation four acres for life and after to my cousin Robert Hall of Ardleigh for his life and after to his son Samuel Hall and his heirs for ever. Res. to wife An for her life and after to be divided between my brother Downes and his children, the said Robert Hall, and the two John Bondes ye younger. Ex. wife. Supervisor, Brother William Downes. Witness Lawrence Lyde, William Downes. Probate not mentioned. (Not registered.) Original will examined. Archdeaconry of Colchester.

208. KINGE, THOMAS, of Heybridge, Essex, Yeoman, 8 March, 1609. To my daughters Mary and Grace £15 each at their ages of 15 years, also to them certain household articles, after decease of my wife. Res. and Ex. wife Grace Kinge. Overseers: Richard Freshwater and Thomas Wells of Maldon baker. Wit: William Bennett, John Townesin, Thomas Wells. Proved 28 May, 1610, by relict. (Dean & Chapter of St. Pauls, D. fo. 25.)

209. MAULE, GEORGE, Rector of Vange, county Essex, 23 Sept., 1667. To be buried with or close to my wife Mary in the chancel. Bequests to poor of Vange and Fobbing. To Clerk or Sexton of Vange five shillings a year till the year 1700 to keep the memorial to wife clean.* House and land in Vange called Lunsees alias Mopses. House and land in Canvey. Mentions brothers (in law) Richard Champneis† (now or late of Biddenden Kent clothier), Samuel Hare of Leigh (and Elizabeth his wife) Richard Hare (Jane & Elizabeth his daughters) Justin Hare. Mentions sisters, Susan Emerson, Mary Jones, (John Jerome and Mary her children), sister Drywood of Brentwood, Elizabeth & Anne Hare of Leigh singlewomen sisters of my late wife Mentions cousins, Mary Hewit and Justinian Champneis her brother, Robert Tucker and Susan his of Stanford le Hope, Samuel Brett of Romford. The ring my mother Camden gave me. Library to be sold to defray expenses of funeral which is not to exceed £50. To Mr. Rogers rector of Laindon Hills a gown and other vestments. To Mr. Gale Vicar of Horndon £20, and vest-

---

* When I visited this Church in 1908 I noted this memorial which is of black marble in a frame embedded in the North wall of the Chancel, Arms above: Champneis impaling Darell. It states she died 4 Sept., 1659, and was the daughter of Justinian Champneis of Wrotham, and Sarah, daughter of John Darell of Calehill Kent. She had an only child Charles, who died an infant.

Near this memorial is one to George Maule, S. T. B., for 33 years rector of Vange, died 1667, aged 64. This has the Arms of Maule viz: Argent on a bend sable three dolphins naiant embowed or.

The will of Elizabeth, widow of Francis Scott, rector of Fobbing (an adjoining parish) mentions her brother George Maule clerk. (Arch. Essex, 1660.)

† John Champneis, clerk of Digswell, Herts., in his will dated 1645, mentions his "loving brother in law Mr. George Male of ffange Essex clarke." (P. C. C. 130 Rivers.)

ments. To his son my godson Andrew Gale 20/-. Sole Ex: my kinsman, Justinian Champneis. Wit: Joane Hearde, Clemence Stoners, Thomas Wakefield. Proved 28 Feby., 1667-8. (P. C. C. Hene 10.)

210. QUYNBY, JOHN, of London, servant with Thomas Goodman of the same City, 28 July, 1556. To poor 40/- To Jane Goodman £20, three rings, my chest etc. To the five children of my brother Roberd 20/- each and ditto to the four children of my sister Catherine, and ditto to the child of my sister Elizabeth. To my sister Audrey a pearl set in gold etc. To my brother Anthony 40/- etc. Various articles to my brother Roberts wife, my sister Katherine; my sister Elizabeth. To my mother £4 to buy her a gown etc. I forgive Thomas Champion 20/- of the 40/- he oweth me, the other 20/- he to pay to my father. To Joane Stell in Farnham four nobles. To Robert Bell my crossbow. To my master and mistress my two chests of apparell as well in Spain as here. To Alice Mathew 10/- To Ursula Godman my signet of gold. Res. & Ex, my father and he to have my two lewtes. Witnesses not named. Proved 3 May, 1557, by John Quynby of Farnham. On 1 December, 1557, administration granted to Jane Quynby, John Quynby being dead. (P. C. C. 12, Wrastley.

211. WARNER, WILLIAM, of Great Horkesley, Essex, Yeoman, 11 Sept., 1612. To be buried in the churchyard. To the poor of Great Horkesley 40/- To do. of Stondon, 20/- To Hellén my wife my house and land in Stondon for her life in lieu of Dower. After her death the house and lands to pass to Steven the son of my brother Steven Warner he to to pay his sister Agnes Warner £10. and also to give £6. 13. 4. unto two sons of my brother Samuel viz: Samuel and William Warner. To John son of my brother Samuel Warner £10. To the children (not named) of my brother John Warner 20 nobles each. Ex. my brother John and I give him all my houses both free and copy in Great Horkesley. Wit: William Ball, Thomas Dynes. Proved 21 October, 1612, by John Warner, brother and executor named in will. (Consistory, London. Hamer folio, 192.)

212. WRIGHT, JOHN, the son of George Wright of Hornchurch, Essex, 24 April, 16 Eliz. My brothers William and George Wright and my sister Margery Wright (all under 21) To my brother Thomas Gill 20/- at age 21. To my brother William one acre of land in Havering Marsh. Ex: Thomas Gill "my father" Wit: Ralph Wreight and William Awlger. Proved 9 June, 1574. (Arch. Essex. Gyll, 53.)

213. WRIGHT, JOHN, of Hornchurch, Essex, 20 Decr., 1582, Husbandman. Sons: John and William. Wife Angis. My sister Thornedon and her two children (not named) Brothers, William and George Wright Res. to wife. Ex: wife and brother George. Overseers: Henry Humfrey, William Augar. Wit: Henry Humfrey, Thomas Gill, William Awger, Richard Harroware and John Hodsonne. Proved 23 March, 1582. (Arch. Essex. Brewer, 286.)

Billopp, Joseph 127
  Middleton 128
Bills, Katharin
  (Bancks) 215
  Nicholas 215
Billup, Christopher 184
Binded, John 246
Bird, Jeremy 252
  Luke 243
Birkett, Edward 21
Birling, Joshua 18
Biscoe, Johan 30
Bisell, William 116
Bishon, Edw. 99
Bishop, Denis 199
  John 174
Bishopp, Dionisie 199
  John 37, 173
Bishoppe, Agnes 199
Bitchnoe, Robert 103
Bitson, --- (Mother)
  250
Bitts, Daniel 143
Blackburn, John 131,
  153
Blackman, Jeremie 38
Blackmoore, Annis 80
  William 80
Blackmore, George 80
Blackney, Ambrose 201
Blackshaw, --- 176
  David 176
  Rachel 176
  Rachel (Jenner) 175
  Samuel 175, 176
Blackwell, Francis 6
  Hettie 144
  Miriam (Hart) 144
  Montague 144
  Richarn 214
  Robert 66
Blakemore, Thomas 201
Blancks, Abraham 130
Blangdone, Barbara 115
Blanure, Thomas 163
Blau, Eleanor 142
  Richard 142
  Uriah 142
  Waldron 142
Blinman, Sarah 87
Blisset, Joseph 158
Blomefeild, John 107
Bloom, --- (Miss) 121
Bloome, Peter 152
Blower, --- 235
  John 235
  Susan 235
Blowers, Edmund 252
  Mary (Wenlocke) 252
Bludworth, John 83
Blunt, --- (Mr.) 254
Bly, Giles 11, 12
  John 11
  Mary 12
  William 11
Blyer, Sarah
  (Timberlake) 22
  Timothy 22
Blyhton, John 85
Boade, William 206
Bolderson, John 133
Boldston, Edward 96
Bolter, Alice 75
Bolton, Anne 140
  Stephen 166, 171

Bonbonons, --- (Mr.)
  121
  --- (Mrs.) 121
Bonde, Anne 210
  Elizabeth 210, 225,
  226
  Ezechiel 226
  John 226, 255
  Marie 210
  Mary 210
  Nicholas 210
  Rebecca 210
  Richard 226
  Sarah 210
  Thomas 210
  Zachariah 226
Bones, Thomas 96
Boninge, Robte 211
Booker, Roger 37
Booth, Elizabeth 81
  Hannah 161
  John 81
  Judith 81
  Marie 81
  Richard 11, 52
  Robert 81
  Susanna 81
Boradile, Margaret 67
Boram, Katheren 217
Borroughe, --- (Widow)
  86
  Agnes 86
  Margery 86
  Walter 86
Borume, John 196
Boryes, John 216
Boswall, Edward 72
Boucher, --- (Mr.) 110
  Frances 110
Boudinot, Elias 159
  Mary 159
Bough, William 11
Bound, Robert 32
Bounde, Henry 229
  Nicholas 210
Bourdett, Judith 129
  Samuel 129
Bourn, Thomas 114
Bourne, Christopher 69
Bovin, Jo. 157
Bovington, Richard 217
Bovyatt, John 42
Bowdishe, George 247
Bowditch, William 183
Bowers, Richard 197
Bowes, William 45
Bowing, Edward 162
  Elizabeth 162
Bowland, Humfrie 209
Bowles, --- (Mr.) 4
Bownd, Gersham 177
Boxe, Tobias 58
Boyce, Francis 79
Boyd, --- 136, 151
Boydon, James 166
  Richard 202
Boyes, Joseph 68, 69
Boyles, Catherine 110
  Philip 110
Boys, Joan 68, 101
  John 68, 101
  Joseph 68, 101
  Mary 68, 101
  Sibylla 68, 101
  Thomas 68, 101
  William 68, 79, 101

Boyse, Alice 78
  Luke 78
Boyton, Lawrence 210
  Margaret 208
Brackford, Samuel 126
Bradbank, Anne 26
  William 26
Bradford, Alice 35
  Elizabeth 35
  Grace 35
  Johan 232
  John 35, 232
  Margaret 35, 232
  Martha 35
  Maurice 232
  Morris 232
  Moses 35
  Randall 232
  Robert 35
  Thomas 232
  William 232
Bradley, Thomas 217
Bradshaw, Richard 169
Bradstock, William 54
Bradstreete, Margaret
  85
  Samuell 85
  Symon 85
Bragg, Sara 95
Bragge, Elizabeth 95
  Marie 95
  Richard 94, 95
  William 95
Bramstall, Thomas 235
Bramstone, Roger 202
Bramstoon, William 203
Branch, Christopher 11,
  12
  Peter 11
  Thomas 12
Brand, John 19
Branham, --- (Mr.) 242
  Hugh 218
  Sara 242
Brapple, Thomas 141
Brasier, Anthony 201
Brassen, Alice 227
Bratheridge, Thomas 54
Brayfield, William 88
Breach, Samuel 22
Bredcake, John 182
  Thomas 182
Bredstreete, Margaret
  85
  Simon 85
Breesleda, John 137
  Rebecca (Onckelbag)
  137
Breete, Henry 251
Bremell, John 49
Brent, Giles 173
Brett, George 240
  James 219
Brette, Elizabeth 251
  Henry 251
Bretten, Anne 231
Bretton, Henry 230
Brewerton, George 144
Brewin, John 24
Brewster, John 86
  William 206
Bridge, Katherine 91
  Ramsey 248
Bridger, --- 189
Bridges, Eliza 128
  Jane 36, 128

261

Byrne, Mary (Hughes) 154
Byron, John 175
Byshopp, William 197
Byvanck, Evart 100
Cable, John 143
Cade, Anthony 52
 James 177
Cadman, James 30
Cadmas, Abraham 139
Caffy, John 185
Cage, Daniel 58
 Phil. 58
Calley, Francis 26
Callis, William 91
Callowhill, Thomas 115
Callyn, John 248
Calthorp, Ambrose 168
Calvert, Leonard 168, 169
Caly, Francis 26
Cambear, John 59
Cambell, Collin 179
Camber, Susan (Barnes) 206
Camden, --- 255
Cameron, Charles 164
Camocke, Robert 250
Camp, John 195
Campion, Clement 171
 Henry 197
 William 197
Candish, Joseph 184
Canning, Robert 141
Cannon, Anne 17
 Elizabeth 18
 Joanna 18
 John 17, 18
 Nathan 18
 Philip 18
 Robert 18
 Timothy 17, 18
Cardye, Thomas 200
Carew, --- (Rev. Mr.) 118
 Esther 118
Carey, John 27
 Judith (Bryn) 124
Carie, Elizabeth 40
 James 40
Carleton, --- (Gen.) 54
Carre, John 197
Carrington, Daniel 232
 Jane 21
 Robert 21
Carter, Anne (James) 3
 Bennet 254
 Edward 118, 119, 122
 Johan 254
 John 14, 22
 Mary 254
 Olyver 107
 Robert 152, 254
 Susan 254
 Thomas 219, 254
Carver, John 206
 Marie (Foster) 206
 William 9
Cary, James 41
 Jane 127
 Miles 41
 Richard 127
 William 41
Casamajor, --- (Mr.) 121
 --- (Mrs.) 118

Casamajor, Ann 117, 118, 119
 Betty 121
 Elizabeth 118, 119
 Henry 120, 121
 Maria 118, 119, 120
 Mary 118, 119
Casamajors, Ann 121
 Elizabeth 121
 Mary 121
Cason, Abigail 172
 Robert 172
Cassies, John 221
Castle, Gregory 166
 William 200
Castlin, John 230
Catherwood, John 110
Catlin, Henry 19
Catly, William 201
Catter, John 98
 Mary 98
Caunt, Edward 43
Causey, Thomas 108
Cavalier, Henry 149
 John 149
 Mary 150
Cawood, Gabriel 206
Cawston, John 231
 Nathaniel 217
Chaddocke, Charles 14
Chadwick, Charles 15
Chafer, Robte 208
Chafyn, --- (Mr.) 87
Chalfont, Tobye 210
Chalis, Thomas 243
Challoner, Francis 166
 Thomas 166
Chamberley, Anne 26
 William 26
Chambers, Elizabeth 88
 Felix 203
 John 203
 Mary (Nicholson) 228
 Sergeant 153
Champion, Thomas 256
Champneis, Justinian 255, 256
 Richard 255
 Sarah (Darell) 255
Chandler, Daniel 128
 George 226
 John 226
 Nat. 142
 Paul 226
Chaplin, Alice 49
Chaplyn, --- (Ensigne) 63
Chapman, Dorothy 106
 John 23
 Joseph 72
 Martha 72
 Richard 81, 211
 Robert 251
 Samuel 72
 Thomas 63
 William 17, 72
Chappell, Alice 25
 Francis 25
 John 25
 Margaret 25
 Stephen 25
 Thomas 25
Charlton, John 142
Charnock, John 184
Charvell, John 211
 Thomas 211

Charvyle, Charles 226
Chauncy, Isaac 110
Chaundelor, Christian 226
 Johan 226
 Peter 226
 Thomas 226
 William 226
Cheeke, Elizabeth 253
 Mary (Mole) 253
 Thomas 253
Cheese, Thomas 234
Cheeseman, Margarett 90
Cheesman, Anna 89
 Edmond 89
 John 89
 Margarett 89
 Thomas 89
Chelwarde, John 43
Chesill, William 243
Chesman, John 90
Chester, John 54
 Thomas 106
Cheston, Thomas 216
Cheyne, Robert 59
Child, Francis 152, 156, 161
Childe, Richard 90
Chime, Richard 233
Chisman, John 90
Chissed, Edward 231
Chitter, Anne 30
Cholmly, Heughe 190
Choote, William 229
Chorley, Matthew 114
Christmas, Thomas 235
Christopher, Christopher 81
Church, John 223, 242
 Mary (Mott) 223
 Robert 99
 William 38
Clapham, Jeremiah 45
 John 45
 Samuel 45
 Thomas 45
Claris, Henry 197
Clark, --- (Mr.) 104
 Edward 21
 Ellen 21
 Richard 21
Clarke, --- 126, 203, 250
 Agnes (Kinge) 212
 Annie 231
 Catherine 217
 Charles 211
 Christo. 66
 Edmonde 231
 Ellen 20
 Francis 231
 George 231
 Joan 88
 John 177, 211
 Jonathan 142
 Katheren (Boram) 217
 Mary 231
 Nicholas 42
 Peter 217
 Philip 4
 Priscilla (Archer) 231
 Robert 212
 Samuel 225
 Thomas 144, 217
 William 232

Cosserat, Nathaniel 117
  Nathaniel Elias 117,
  119
Cotchett, John 84
  Mary 84
  Oliver 84
  Richard 84
  Thomas 84
Cotsall, Johan
  (Chaundelor) 226
  John 226
  William 226
Cotton, Elizabeth 15
  Elizabeth (Harcocks)
  16
  Ellen 213
  Johannes 16
  John 15
  Makepeace 15
  Mary 15
  Roland 15
Coughland, John 20
Coursey, Elizabeth 108
  Henry 108
  Mary 108
Courtland, Frances 118
  James 118
Courtlandt, Jacobus V.
  144
Courtney, Thomas 132,
  133
Coutts, --- (Mr.) 136,
  150
  T. 151
  Thomas 136, 137, 150,
  153, 154
Cowbridge, --- (Widow)
  242
Cowp, Robert 204
Cowper, Edmond 42
  Henry 126
  John 42, 43
  Matthew 126
  Thomas 225
Cox, --- 136
  John 215
  Lewis 151
  Sarah 45
  Steven 224
Coxe, Daniel 135
  John 229
Coxon, John 14
  Margaret (Bellers) 14
Coyny, --- (Mr.) 27
Cradock, Elizabeth 43
  Francis 44
  George 44
  John 44
  Jorden 43
  Mary 43
  Mathew 43, 44
  Richard 44
  Samuel 43, 44
  Thomas 44
  William 44
Cradocke, Alice 41, 43
  Anne 41
  Dorothie 42
  Dorothy 43
  Elizabeth 41, 43
  Emme 41, 42, 43
  Francis 41, 42
  George 41, 42, 43
  Jane 43
  Johan 42
  Katherine 41, 43

Cradocke, Mannering 41
  Margaret 43
  Mary 41, 43
  Mathew 41, 42, 43
  Richard 41
  Sara 41
  Sarah 42, 43
  Thomas 41, 42
  Walter 41, 42
  William 41, 42
Craford, John 150
Crane, Francis 71
  Hester 71
  Joseph 130
  Josiah 130
Crawford, David 185
Crawley, Alice 226
  Thomas 226
Crayford, Richard 235
Creek, Richard 115, 148
Crego, Margery 110
  Stephen 110
Cren, John 99
Creye, Elizabeth 106
Criffield, Elizabeth
  242
Cripes, William 210
Crippe, --- (Widow) 214
Cripps, Jane 36
  Richard 36
Croft, Jane 254
Crofte, James 235
Crofts, Dno. 148
  Dud. 156
  Edward 94
  Elizabeth 94
  William 94
Croke, Fran. 61
Crommelin, Charles 148
  Daniel 149
Cromwell, Anne 26
  Thomas 27
Crony, Daniel 165
Crookes, Elizabeth 135
  John 135
Crookston, Ann 162
  John 162
  Samuel 162
Cropton, Zach. 95
Crosse, --- (Mr.) 61
  William 166
Crouch, George 39
  John 84
Crowche, --- 203
Crowell, Agness 153
  Catherine 153
  Edward 153
  Joseph 153
  Sarah 153
  Thomas 153
Crowther, William 167
Croxon, William 244
Crugar, Jacob Minor 112
  Valentine 112
Cruger, Abraham 132
  Elizabeth 124
  Henry 123, 124
  Jacob Minor 132
  Jacob Myna 132
  John 124
  John Harris 123, 124
  Mary 123, 124
  Nicholas 124
  Valentine 132
Cubben, Thomas 71
Cuerin, Maynard 110

Cullen, Elizabeth 135
  Katherine 135
  Luke 135
  Nicholas 135
  Thomas 135
  William 135
Cullenben, Thomas 18
Culverell, --- (Mr.)
  234
Culverwell, Ezekiell
  245
Cumbers, Thomas 231
Cumins, Pheba 133
Cunney, Anne (Cradocke)
  41
Cunningham, Waddell 100
  William 7, 139, 140
Cunningham(e), Margaret
  139
Currie, David 154
  Isobel (Findlay) 154
  James 149
  John 154
  Lucy (Wallace) 149
Curry, David 154
Currye, John 229
Curtes, Elizabeth 226
  John 226
  Jone 226
Curtis, John 229
  Thomas 88
Curtisse, Richard 79
Curtys, Audry 88
  Thomas 88
  William 88
Cushman, Robert 171
Cuting, Richard 220
Cutting, John 175, 176
D'Aulnay, --- 181
Dagge, --- 118
  --- (Mrs.) 118
Dagnet, Thomas 225
Dalby, Mary 227
Dale, Catherine 98
  Christian 44, 45
  Francis 44, 45
  John 44, 45
  Samuel 44
  Sarah 45
  Thomas 45, 63
Dally, Edward 140
Dalrymple, Robert 111
Daltera, James 118,
  120, 121, 122, 126
  Joseph 120
Dalzell, Da. 123, 148
Damon, Cristian (Noth)
  213
Danby, Thomas 4
Dancas, Joan 77
  Nicholas 77
Dandie, Patience 94
  Richard 221
Dandy, Patience 94
Daniel, Edward 158
  Joseph 121
  Ranulph 211
Daniell, John 110
Danon, John 213
Danson, Mary 20
Darby, Nathaniell 209
Darell, John 255
  Sarah 255
Darnell, Richard 28
Dartnall, Jasper 22
  William 22

ºfryer, Andrew 197
  Hester 197
ºfrythe, Averye 195
ºido, --- (Mr.) 120
  --- (Mrs.) 120
ºile, Richard 48
ºinch, Anne 18
  Editha 239
  Isaac 18
  John 143
  William 239
ºinche, William 48
ºindlay, Isobel 154
ºinley, Samuel 152
ºish, Augustine 62
  Isabella 62
  John 61
  Jonathan 61
  Susanna 62
  Thomas 61, 62
  William 62
Fisher, John 83, 162
  William 30
Fitch, Anne 227
  Anne (Wiseman) 219
  Joseph 227
  Margaret 220
  Nathaniel 227
  Richard 91, 220
  Samuel 227
  William 219
Fitche, --- (Mr.) 241
  Thomas 42
Fittar, James 161
Fitter, William 168
FitzHughes, Francis 20
FitzJames, Ralph 87
Flamand, Honora 135
Flavell, Chr. 96
Fledger, --- (Goodman)
  249
Fleet, Simon 140
Fleming, James 149
Flesher, William 19
Fletcher, Agnes 200
  James 38, 77
  Jane 200
  Joane 200
  John 200
  Matthewe 200
  Nathaniel 185
  Simon 200
  Thomas 200
Flier, Edward 42
  Mathew 41
Flinte, James 35
Fludd, John 243
Flyer, Mathew 42
Flynton, Pharao 5
Folliott, George 141,
  145
Fooks, Alice 225
Foord, William 227
Foote, --- 204
  Cales 33
  Daniel 33
  Elizabeth 33
  Hannah 33
  John 33
  Joshuah 33
  Leonard 33
  Mary 33
Ford, Jane (Thompson)
  53
  John 199
  Thomas 53

Forde, William 186
Foresight, Alexander
  185
Forrest, --- (Mr.) 115
  Ebenezer 114, 115
  Theo. 114
Forrester, George 158
Forty, Thomas 175
Fosket, Thomas 17
Fosse, Elizabeth 99
Foster, Andrew 206
  Anne 88
  Dennys 206
  Edward 88
  Elizabeth (Higginson)
    96
  Francis 88
  Henry 96
  John 182, 206
  Joseph 206
  Margaret 88, 208
  Marie 206
  Michael 206
  Phryswith 211
  Roger 214
  Thomas 206
  Ursley 235
  William 88
Fothergill, --- 165
Fouthery, Grace 104
Fowler, John 6
Foxcrofte, Anthony 4
Frampton, Richard 232
  Walter 83
  William 83
Frances, Mary 56
Francis, Anne (Osborne)
  250
  Elias Melchisedic 118
  Richard 56
  William 234, 235
Francklin, John 146
Francklyn, Judith 20
Frank, Tho. 161
Franklin, John 7
Freake, --- (Mr.) 219
  Elizabeth 219
Free, Thomas 19
Freeborne, John 239
Freek, John 7
  Katherine 7
Freelove, John 240
Freeman, James 115
  John 63
  Richard 221
  Thomas 252
Freer, Bridgett 197
  John 197
  Thomas 169
Freman, Robert 215
French, Abigail 239
  Bridgit 239
  Bridgitt 239
  Elizabeth 239
  Elyas 239
  James 71
  John 239
  Mary 239
  Philip 183
  Silvanus 21
  Thomas 239
Freshwater, Richard 255
Frier, Mary 20
Frith, Averie 209
  George 209
  John 19

Frith, William 19
Frithe, Richard 217
Frost, Anthony 149
  John 94, 177
Froste, Alis 211
  Andrew 211
  Jane 211
Fryer, John 197
Fullam, Edward 222
Fuller, John 231
  Thomas 31
  William 209
Fych, Thomas 233
Fyche, Isabella 233
  John 233
  Richard 233
Fysher, Richard 222
  William 222
Fyssher, Thomas 204
Fytche, Wyllyam 240
Gacomina, Jacob Minor
  112
Gage, John 198
  Thomas 250
Gailard, Alice 51
  John 51
  Samuel 52
  William 51
Gailerd, Agnes 49
  Alice 49
  Antonie 49
  Jefferie 50
  John 49
  Jone 49
  Julian 49
  Margaret 49
  Nicholas 49
Gaim, Hugh 145
Gaine, Hugh 140, 141,
  145
Gale, --- (Mr.) 255
  Andrew 256
Gallard, Geffrye 50
Galler, William 47
Gallopp, John 173
Galwarne, Thomas 221
Gamble, --- (Mr.) 100
Gamblin, Robert 82
Games, Edward 161
Ganger, William 99
Gardiner, Edmund 167
  Robert 223
Gardner, --- 127
  John 12
Garland, Thomas 250
Garner, John 79
Garret, Hendrick 130
Garrett, Alexander 211
  Robert 81
Garth, Catherine 53
  Robert 53
  Sarah 53
Gate, Anne (Morley) 27
  Judith 27
  Katherine 27
  Thomas 27
Gatehouse, John 110
  Richard 110
Gatton, Eugeny 204
Gaunte, Ellen 233
Gawge, Anne (Gray) 196
  John 196
Gay, Agnes 225
  Robert 50
Gaylard, Agnes 50, 51

268

Goosy, Robert 104
  Susan 104
  Thomas 104
Gordon, Augustine 164
  David 146
  John 160
  Margarett 164
  William 143, 164
Gore, Chr. 144
Gorges, Edward (Lord)
    170
  Ferdinando 182
Gorstich, Jane 128
  Thomas 128
Gorzen, Marianne 121
  Mary 121
  Sarah 121
Gosbie, James 215
  William 215
Gosnold, Edmund 233
  Robert 233, 234
Goudett, Peter 45
Goulden, George 95
Gourdon, Francis 149
Goven, Elizabeth 111
  John 111
Grafton, Joseph 174
  William 253
Graham, Lewis 152, 153
  Margaret 152
Grantham, Anthony 227
Graunte, John 250
Gravelinge, Andrew 204
  William 204
Graves, Roswell 133
  Thomas 173
Grawes, George 144
Gray, Anne 196
  Giles 196
  John 196
  Margaret 217
  Mary 14
  William 196
Graye, --- (Mr.) 217
  Elizabeth 222
  Jane 222
  Lawrence 222
  Margery 222
  Steven 217
Graygoose, Nicholas 238
Green, Charles 247
  John 233, 247
  Thomas 247
  Thomazine 247
Greene, --- (Widow) 75
  Henry 69
  Jane 227
  John 198
  Nicholas 200
  Ralph 170
  Richard 72, 209
  Robert 209
  Thomas 25
Greenewood, --- (Mr.)
    57
Greenfield, Joseph 60
Greenhill, John 95
  Tho. 22
  William 14
Greenwood, Nathaniel
    177
Greg, J. 141
  Thomas 100
Gregill, --- (Mr.) 217
  John 217
Gregory, Susan 75

Gregyll, John 217
Grene, John 249
  Nicholas 201
Grevill, Michael 33
Grey, William 45
Griffin, Edward 201
  John 201
Griffine, Elizabeth 243
Griffith, Evan 4
  Kewelin 131
  Mary 131
  Moses 44
Griffiths, Anthony 139
  Jane 139
  John 139
  Thomas 120
Griffyne, Edmonde 243
Grimditch, Eshew 111
  Thomas 111
Grollier, Jacob 181
  Jacques 181
  James 181
Grome, William 30
Groome, Fras. 142
Grove, Joseph 183
  Richard 167
Grub, John 207
Grubb, Anne (Shelton)
    207
  John 210
  Sarah (Pope) 207
Guinand, --- (Master)
    118
  --- (Miss) 118
  --- (Mr.) 118
Gullsonne, --- (Mr.) 57
Gumfield, Rebecca 84
  Rebecca (White) 83
Gun, Mariam 232
Gundy, --- (Mrs.) 118
Gunter, --- (Aunt) 61
  --- (Capt.) 61
Gutter, Edward 220
  Margaret (Fitch) 220
  Martha 220
Guy, Edward 64
  Richard 64, 65
  Susan 64
Gwatkin, Mary 118
  Sarah 118
Gwynn, Elizabeth
    (Gilliam) 171
  Thomas 171
Gylbert, John 197
Gyllett, Elias 52
  Habiah 59, 60
  Jeremiah 60
  Mary 59, 60
  Nathan 59
  Richard 60
  Thomas 59, 60
  William 59, 60
Haden, Joseph 164
Hadock, William 24
Hadocke, Elizabeth 15
Haggard, Catherine 127
  Sarah 127
Hagger, Thomas 248
Haifield, Ellen 20
Haines, Ralph 91
Hakewell, William 89
Hale, Robert 118, 119,
    120, 121, 122
  William 148
Hales, Stephen 229
Haley, Peter 99

Halhead, --- (Mr.) 61
  Henry 61
Hall, Ann 255
  Benedict 3
  Edmund 182
  Jarvis 42
  Richard 255
  Samuel 255
  William 7
Hallam, Elizabeth
    (Wannel) 77, 78
  James 78
Haman, John 239
  William 222
Hamar, Richard 137
Hambleton, William 100
Hammon, Anthony 93
Hammond, Abigail 55
  Abigail (Salter) 55
  Anne (Diggs) 92
  Anthony 92
  Elizabeth (Aucher) 93
  John 55
  Thomas 209
  William 92
Hammonde, Elizabeth
    (Ruggle) 57
  George 57
Hamon, John 235
Hamond, John 247
Hamonde, Marget 226
Hamor, Hester 166
  Ralph 5, 166
  Thomas 166
Hampton, Jonathan 124
Hanchett, Anne 248
  Edward 247
  Elizabeth 247, 248
  George 247
  Grace 248
  James 247
  Richard 247
  Samuel 247
  Sarah 248
  Susan 247
  Thomas 247
  William 247, 248
Hancock, Edith
    (Woodman) 107
  Leonard 107
Handforth, Robert 94
Hands, Thomas 61
Handson, Richard 38
Haninge, John 50
Hankin, Robert 250
Hannam, William 182
Hanninge, Alice 49
Hanson, John 204
  Robert 85
Hanworth, Alice 234
  Christopher 223, 234
  John 234
  Soan 234
Hanworthe, --- (Mr.)
    223
Harby, Katherine 70
  Thomas 70
Harcocks, Elizabeth 16
Hardgrave, Rawffe 208
Hardwick, Joane
    (Collcutt) 95
Hardy, Thomas 181
Hardye, William 195
Hardyn, Christopher 63
Hare, Anne 255
  Elizabeth 255

269

Hare, Jane 255
John 19
Justin 255
Mary 255
Richard 255
Samuel 255
Harlow, John 226
Harman, --- 84
Abra. 54
Abraham 141
Benjamin 84
Elizabeth 84
Hannah 84
Richard 84
Susanna 84
Susannah (White) 84
Harmon, Henry 251
Harper, Anne 76
Harris 77
Isabel 76
Joan 76
John 76
Richard 76
Russell 77
Thomas 76
William 76
Harrington, Nicholas
216
Harris, Benjamin 211,
223
Bridgett (Ruggle) 57
Cicilye 209
David 133
Dorothy 223
George 137
Henry 26, 89
John 57
Martin 57
Mary 132, 138
Nicholas 150
Richard 116, 132, 138
Vincent 182
William 26, 79
Harrison, --- 136, 151
George 130, 142, 206,
238
Jane (Nicholas) 142
John 57, 90, 140
Prudence 206
Ri. 97
Richard 137
Samuel 97
Thomas 6, 188
William 227, 249
Harroware, Richard 256
Harrowlde, John 229
Harryes, William 203
Harrys, Dorothie
(Kinge) 208
James 208
Jamys 222
John 197
William 216
Hart, Abm. 145
Charles 153
Elizabeth 28
Ester 140, 144
Henry 28
Humfrie 211
Jacob 144, 145
Jane 28
Jane (Joan) (Rossiter)
10
John 232, 241
Julian 211
Mary 28

Hart, Miriam 144
Moses 144
Nicholas 10, 38
Samuel 174
Susan 28
Thomas 28, 140
William 211
Harte, Nicholas 9
William 240
Hartford, --- (Mr.) 61
Hartley, Edmund 197
Edward 103
Jeremiah 20
Richard 104
Hartly, Anne (Sheppard)
67
Francis 67
Hartt, Jacob 231
Harvey, Anne 127
Margaret 127
Margaret (Long) 127
Martha 90
Mary 127
Symon 90
Harvill, Elizabeth 90
Ellinor 90
Harvye, John 168
Thomas 250
Harwood, Arthur 167
Haryson, John 214
Hasellwood, Thomas 96
Haselwood, Henry 75
Katherine 75
Hasholt, John 157
Hasker, Thomas 219
Haslewood, William 214
Hasteler, Edward 234
Hastler, Thomas 203
Hatch, William 188
Hatche, Christian
(Terling) 244
Richard 244
Hatfield, Eliza 120
Hatherley, --- (Mr.) 59
Hatt, Andrew 158
Robert 38
Hauknit, Mary 98
Havell, James 227
Haver, Judith 250
Hawden, Raffe 234
Hawerid, Elizabeth 15
John 15
Samuel 15
Hawes, Richard 180
Hawford, Thomas 12
Hawk, Matthew 33
Hawke, John 252
Robert 211
Hawkens, Robert 244
Hawker, Thomas 50
Hawkes, James 95
Mary 96
Mary (Torkington) 95
Hawkeswell, Mary 20
Hawkins, Peter 6
Thomas 173
Hawkritch, John 51
Hawley, Jeremy 168
Jerome (Jeremy) 169
John 215
Hay, Alexander 139
Hayens, Ralph 91
Hayes, Edward 234
Thomas 124, 146
Hayfield, Anne 20
John 21

Hayle, Elizabeth (Hunt)
249
John 67
Hayward, Francis 98
John 202
Simon 98
Thomas 144, 251
William 98, 99
Haywarde, Robte 229
Hazard, Joseph 125
Heacock, Jonathan 84
Healy, John 123, 148
Heard, John 78, 241
Robert 211
Thomas 243
William 241
Hearde, Anthony 229
Joane 256
Marselyn 229
Nicholas 229
Heathcote, --- (Widow)
128
Cuthbert 138
Elizabeth 111
Gilbert 128
Martha 111, 128, 138,
139
Mary 128, 139
William 111
Heathcott, George 144
Heathe, George 211
Heaven, Mary 20
Heckford, Thomas 44, 45
Hedge, Alice 201
Edward 107
Henry 240
Matthew 201
William 81
Heely, Dennis 156
Helena, Benwjna 130
Heminge, --- (Widow)
214
Hemmings, --- (Mrs.)
119
Margaret 122
Richard 119, 122
Hempsted, John 233
Henfield, Robert 174
Henley, William 232
Hennyngton, John 254
Henson, Anne 241
Herbert, Anna Maria 155
Edmund 155
Herde, George 247
Robert 239, 247
Thomas 247
Herinsole, Anne 140
Elizabeth 140
Hermitage, --- (Mrs.)
119
Herold, William 214
Herriche, Richard 248
Herring, --- (Mrs.)
119, 120
Mary 121
Richard 119
Susannah 121
Herrys, Edward 234
Herton, Goodye 210
Heuyard, John 221
Hewes, William 250
Hewet, James 248
Hewit, Mary 255
Hewtin, William 159
Hewytt, Johannem 198
Hey, Robert 212

Hunt, William 13, 14,
  217, 218, 249
Hunter, David 164
  Isaac 209
  Ralph 92
Hunting, Joseph 185
Huntington, Osias M.
  133
Hurrell, Henry 232
Hurst, Charles 141, 145
  John 31
  Margaret 80
  Mary (Brownejohn) 140
  Mary (Brownjohn) 145
  Timothy 140, 141, 145
  William 80
Hutchin, Robert 228
Hutchins, Henry 60
  Raynold 86
Hutchinson, Henry 169
  Thomas 182
  William 169
Hutton, Johan 227
  William 185
Hydde, Johan 194
Hyett, John 74
Hyne, Mary 140
Hynemanals, Elizabeth
  138
Hyslette, Henry 199
Ibell, Thomas 14
Ielees, Manuel 160
Ilger, Ffrancis 212
Ilot, Thomas 62
Ince, Richard 204
Ingham, John 44
Inglesby, Mary 70
Ingleton, William 175
Ingoldsby, --- (Capt.)
  70
Ingram, Anne 84
  Edw. 85
  Edward 90
  Hester 84
  John 84, 85
  Joseph 84, 90
  Mary 84
  Obadiah 90
  Richard 85
  Robert 84, 85
  Sarah 30
  Thomas 84
  William 84
Ingrame, Joane 241
Innes, --- (Mr.) 225
  Aquila 225
  Robert 225
  William 225
Ireland, Edward 214
Isaack, Christopher 207
  Elizabeth 207
  James 207
  Joane 207
  John 207
  Marye 207
  Peter 207
  Thomas 207
  William 207
Isaacke, Christopher
  207
  Frances (Prentice) 207
Ivatt, John 33
  Sarah (Feering) 32, 33
Iverie, John 49
Ivery, John 48
Ives, Thomas 88, 89

Ivie, John 20
Izard, Ann 150
Jackson, Agnes 82, 212
  Alexander 180
  Arthur 41, 42, 77, 78
  Elizabeth 77, 78, 82,
    212
  Elizabeth (Dunckley)
    82
  Ffranciis 212
  Frances (Roade) 227
  Francis 227
  George 225
  Hugh 227
  Joan 25
  John 41, 42
  Joseph 41, 183
  Mary 82
  Richard 82
  Robert 212
  Thomas 24
  William 240
Jacob, Andrew 39
  Henry 39
  John 177
  Katherine 39
  Robert 189
  Sarah 39
Jaffey, Mary 133
James, Anne 3
  Benjamin 130
  Edmund 222
  Edward 222
  Elizabeth 119, 122
  Jo. 37
  John 52
  Josua 92
  Katherine (Oxenbridge)
    70
  Thomas 3
  William 50
Jauncey, James 153
  John 153, 154
  Mary 153, 154
  William 153, 154
Jay, Ann 120
  Ann Maricha 125
  Augustus 120, 125
  Eve 125
  Fred 151
  Fred. 136
  Frederick 120, 125,
    126
  George 80
  James 118, 125, 126
  John 120, 125, 126
  Peter 118, 120, 125,
    126
Jeakins, Christopher 70
Jefferie, Robert 49
Jeffrey, Benjamin 185
  Michael 134
Jeffreyes, Nathaniel
  166
Jeffreys, Robert 165
Jekyll, Nicholas 220
  Thomas 220
Jemison, David 159
Jenaway, Andrew 212
Jenings, Symon 253
Jenkins, --- (Mr.) 57
  Walter 130
  William 32
Jenner, David 175, 176
  Ellen 176
  Jonathan 175

Jenner, Mary 175
  Rachel 175
  Rebecca 175, 176
  Thomas 175, 176
Jenneway, Richard 112
Jennings, Abraham 166
  Ambrose 166
  Anne 67
  Benjamin 14
  Edith 52
  Elizabeth 33
  John 14
  Samuel 249
  Sarah 14
  Thomas 33
  William 14, 212
Jeppe, Bridgitt 239
  Edward 239
Jerman, John 184
Jeuvrein, --- (Mr.) 149
Jeyle, John 216
John, Evan 131
  Robert 58
Johns, William 202
Johnson, --- 165
  Alice 79
  Ambrose 69
  Anne 41
  Christian 202
  David 181
  Elizabeth 94, 202
  Francis 30, 94
  Henry 168
  James 24
  Jane 94, 202
  John 76, 94, 136, 150,
    186, 253
  Luke 40, 94
  Margaret 80
  Mary 79
  Mary (Watts) 136, 150
  Nath. 28
  Priscilla 80
  Richard 79
  Robert 202
  Samuel 178
  Sarah 69
  Tho. 79
  Thomas 17, 80
  William 17, 160, 170,
    202
  Zonaberiah 94
Jollye, Thomas 42
Jones, --- (Mr.) 27
  Alice 217
  Anthony 169
  David 131
  Edward 17
  Ellinor 54
  Gilbert 4
  James 40
  Jerome 255
  John 54, 255
  Lewes 239
  Lewis 54
  Loure 54
  Mary 54, 255
  Mary (Maule) 255
  Richard 54, 144, 229
  Roger 54
  Samuel 134, 137, 138,
    146
  Sibill 14
  Thomas 54
  William 81, 86
Jonsonne, Lewes 200

272

Morgan, William 74
Moris, John 219
Morlace, Margaret 25
Morley, Anne 27
  Constant 28
  Cuthbert 92
  James 27, 28
  John 27, 28
  Katherine 27
  Katherine (Burnell) 28
  Thomas 28
Morrell, Henry 168
Morrice, Susan
  (Hanchett) 247
  William 247
Morris, Lewis 99
  William 175
Mortclocke, Alice 223
  Martha 223
  Robert 223
Mortier, Abraham 134
  David 134
  Martha 134
Mortlacke, John 240
Morton, Richard 41
Mosson, --- (Mr.) 100
Motier, John 114
Mott, Adrian 220
  Alice 220, 250
  Bartholemew 235
  Bridgett 111
  Edmund 111
  Elizabeth 111
  Elizabeth (Criffield)
   242
  George 242
  Henry 242
  Joane 235
  John 209, 220, 223,
   250
  Marie 223
  Mark 220, 223
  Mary 209
  Richard 235, 242
  Robert 235, 242, 243
  Samuel 242
  Sara 220
  William 242
Motte, Agnes 250
  Dorothy 213, 242
  Edward 195
  Elizabeth 213
  Geoffry 242
  Helen 242
  Joan 242
  John 195, 204, 242,
   250
  Jone 203
  Katheryne 195
  Mary 250
  Prissitt 250
  Richard 242, 250
  Robert 242
  Thomas 213
  William 213, 242, 250
Moulte, Dorothie 40
  Edmon 40
  Francis 40
  John 40
  Lince 39
  William 39, 40
Mountgomery, James 162
  John 162
  Joseph 162
  Margaret 162
  Samuel 162

Mountgomery, William
  162
Mowse, --- 76
  Elizabeth 76
  Mary 76
  Richard 76, 77
Moye, John 7
  Richard 7
Moyses, --- (Goodwife)
  167
Mudge, John 232
Mullard, Elizabeth 169
  Joshua 169
Munro, Eve (Jay) 125
  Harry 125
  Peter Jay 125
Murray, Joseph 130, 164
Mutton, Edward 250
  Robert 26
Myers, Christofer 204
Myhill, John 83
Mylborne, Edward 220
  John 220
  Margery 220
Myller, Thomas 201
Myners, John 240
Mynn, Nicholas 240
Mynne, Nycholas 240
Myre, Robert 110
Myres, Robert 239
Mytch, Barbara 30
Napp, Simon 215
Narramore, John 183
Nash, Anne (Cannon) 17
  George 126
  Richard 17
  Thomas 64
Natt, Thomas 115
Naylor, --- (Mr.) 15
  William 71
Neale, Joan 108
  Richard 211
Neate, Edmund 31
  William 164
Nedam, George 229
Nelson, Elizabeth
  (Smith) 152
  Margaret (Cradocke) 43
Nettelton, Joh 219
Nevell, Elizabeth 245
  John 214
Nevers, John 205
Nevet, Ann 115
  Elizabeth 115
  Susannah 115
Newcastle, --- (Earl
  of) 191
Newcomen, Matthew 56
Newman, Davies 153
  John 111
  Nathaniel 226
  Samuel 120
  Thomas 111, 172
Newton, Richard 197
  Thomas 43, 200
  William 34, 134
  Zachariah 200
Nicholas, Elizabeth 142
  Jane 142
  Mary 142
  Richard 142
  William Robert 142
Nicholl, John 137
  Robert 207
Nicholls, James 182
  Mary 114

Nicholls, Richard 109,
  110, 130
  William 131
Nichollsonne, Thomas
  221
Nicholson, Agnes 221
  George 228
  Jane 228
  Joan 221
  John 228
  Mary 228
  Maud 228
  Philip 148
  Richard 228
  Rowland 249
  Susanna 249
  Thomas 221, 228, 249
  William 221, 228
Nicholsonne, Christofer
  221
Nickolls, Edward 104
Nickolss, Francis 104
Nicoll, Andrew 109
  Elizabeth 109
  Francis 133
  George 109
  Helen 109
  James 109
  Susannah 109
Nicolson, Agnes 228
  Dorothy 228
  George 228
  Jane 228
  John 228
  Margaret 228
  Mary 228
  Maud 228
  Philip 123
  Richard 228
  Thomas 228
  William 228
Nicolsonne, William 217
Nightingale, Anne 96
  Robert 97
Nitingale, George 216
Niven, James 145
Noble, James 249
Noke, Dorothy 246
  Robert 246
Norborne, John 175
Norcross, Jeremiah 14
  Jeremie 15
  Marie 15
  Mary 15
  Nathaniel 15
  Richard 15
  Sarah 14
Norden, John 31
Norerosse, Jeremiah 14
Norman, Dorothy 235
  Philip 185
Norris, John 180
North, Thomas 10
Northropp, --- 229
Norton, Jeremye 236
  John 214
Norwood, Benjamin 185
Noseiter, John 94
Noth, Cristian 213
  John 213
  Margaret 213
  William 213
Nott, Mary 130, 131
  Randolph 130, 131
  Thomas 131, 148
Nottingham, Richard 86

Prigg, Robert 162
  Thomas 162
Prinderges, Thomas 94
Prior, John 84
  Richard 239
Prise, Howell 37
Prisly, John 239
Proby, William 127
Proctor, --- (Mr.) 63
  Daniel 83
Prowd, John 19
Puckford, Edward 144
Puckle, William 235
Puckmore, Thomas 74
Pudsey, Anne (Wiseman)
  219
  Ralph 219
Pugh, Da. 132
Pullestone, Alice 246
  Richard 246
Pulleyn, John 221
Purcas, George 234
  William 239
Pury, Adlard 15
Putnam, Ebenezer 123
Pycke, John 194
Pykman, Alis 214
  John 213, 214
  Roger 213, 214
Pynchon, Clemence 221
  Grace 221
  Harry 221
  Henry 221
  Isaake 221
  Marthe 221
  Rose 221
Pyner, Will 9
Pynner, Edward 222
Pytman, Christofer 235
  John 235
Pytte, --- (Mr.) 197
Pytts, John 51
Quick, Isaac 84
Quicke, --- 236
  Agnes (Barrett) 222
  Edmund 222
  Jane 236
Quinbe, Elizabeth 251
  John 251
  Thomas 251
  William 251
Quodwell, William 226
Quynby, Anthony 256
  Audrey 256
  Catherine 256
  Elizabeth 256
  Jane 256
  John 256
  Katherine 256
  Robert 256
Radford, Ralph 22
  Rebecca (Burrowes) 22
Rainsford, Edward 184
Raistone, Thomas 34
Ramme, Francis 198
Randall, Elizabeth 60
  Hannah 127
  James 127
  John 60, 61
  Margery 60
  Robert 60, 61
  Thomas 60, 61, 139
  William 60, 177
Rande, William 215
Randoll, John 61
  Thomas 61

Ransford, Thomas 184
Ranshawe, Francis 42
  George 42
  William 42
Ratcliffe, Agnes 22
Raven, Mary 203
  Roger 4
  Sarah 203
Rawe, Fraunce 238
Rawlin, Christopher 88
Rawlins, Thomas 211
Rawlinson, --- (Mr.) 14
Rawllyn, Thomas 221
Ray, John 45
Rayment, William 45
Raymond, Edward 225
  George 246
Raynall, John 49
Raynold, Alice 242
Raynoldes, Richard 197
Read, John 149
  Joseph 149
  Mary (Collier) 95
  Richard 95
Reade, John 31, 254
Reay, --- (Lord) 115
Reddinge, William 6
Reddish, Edward 94
Rede, Thomas 106
Reding, Arthur 225
Redish, William 43
Redman, Abraham 27
Reed, Elyn 221
  John 202
Reeder, Mylles 219
Reeks, Stephen 181, 182
Reeve, Anne 79, 97,
  243, 244
  Daniel 243, 244
  Dorothy 243
  Francis 97
  George 79
  Giles 243
  Jane 79, 97
  Joan 97
  John 79, 97, 227, 243
  Joseph 243, 244
  Judith 97
  Letitia 97
  Margaret 25
  Nathaniel 243, 244
  Richard 25
  Robert 79, 239
  Roger 25
  Sarah 25
  Susan 97
  Thomas 79, 243
  Thomazin 244
  William 79, 243, 244
  Wiltshire 96, 97
Reignolde, William 236
Reignsbery, William 91
Reinolde, Alice 232
Relph, John 154
Remington, William 156
Rems, Thomas 104
Renoulds, Mary 241
  Richard 241
Reve, John 226, 227
Rewe, Henry 48, 49
Reymer, Ezechiell 212
Reynold, Thomas 197
Reynolde, George 209
  William 199
Reynoldes, Richard 202
  Thomas 239

Rhinelander, Frederick
  152
  Jacob 146
Rhodes, Catherine 140
  Charles 116
Ricarde, Elizabeth 251
Rice, John 142, 229
Richards, John 174
Richardson, George 171
  Henry 63
  John 251
  William 212, 233
Richman, John 217
  Rose 217
Richmond, Thomas 248
Ridall, Richard 43
Ridgeway, Rebecca 34
Ridley, Alice
  (Cradocke) 41, 43
Riever, Joan 22
Rigby, Alexander 161
Rily, John 167
Rilye, John 166
Rimell, Johanne 106
  Mawde (Smith) 106
  Nicholas 106
Rittzema, Rudolphus 134
Rivington, James 124
Roach, --- (Mrs.) 120
Roade, Frances 227
  James 227
Robert, Ellen 238
Roberts, Henry 98
  Joseph 152
  Martha 152
Robertson, David 183
Robinet, Robert 201
Robinson, --- (Mr.) 20
  Beverley 160
  Isabell 43
  John 85
  Joseph 159
Roceter, Roger 50
Roche, James 10, 11
  Robert 11
Rochester, Henry 221
Roddam, Lucy 111
  Robert 111
Rogers, --- (Mr.) 57,
  255
  Anthony 127
  Catherine 127
  Ezekiel 108, 109
  George 118, 119, 120,
    121, 122
  John 58
  Peter 116
Rolfe, Thomas 155
  William 155
Rollo, Robert 123
Rolls, Robert 123
Rolt, Edward 70
Roman, Samuel 36
Rombolde, John 199
Rookes, Robert 254
Roome, John L. C. 130
Roosevelt, Elizabeth
  159
  Nicholas 159
Roote, Robert 88
Roper, Marke 216
  Randall 62
Rose, --- (Dr.) 133
  Agnes (Dunckley) 82
  Anne 82
  Isabella 133

Rose, John 82
 Margaret 82
 Thomas 82
 William 82
Rosier, John 169
Rosseter, Roger 50
Rossiter, Edward 10
 Jane (Joan) 10
Rouse, Phillippa 55
Rowe, Avis 235
 John 235
 Robert 236
 William 213
Rowely, Sarah (Wall) 98
Rowley, Anne 203
 Edmond 98
 John 203
 Mathewe 203
Rowlston, Lionell 58
Rowse, Robert 223
Roydon, John 233
Royse, Daniell 128
 John 128
Rudderford, Richard 168
Ruggle, Amos 57
 Anne 57
 Bridget 57
 Edward 57, 58
 Elizabeth 57
 Gefferie 57
 George 56, 57, 58
 Jefferie 57
 John 57, 58
 Mary 57
 Nicholas 57
 Phillip 57
 Richard 57
 Samuell 57
 Susan 57
 Thomas 57, 58
 William 57, 58
Ruggles, George 58
 Jeffery 58
 Jeffrey 58
 John 44, 58
Rule, John 214, 245
Rush, John 158
 Sarah 158
Rushton, John 59
Russel, Thomas 41
Russell, --- 76
 Daniel 53
 Hellen 76
 William 84, 225
Ryall, Nathaniel 83
Sabine, Robert 169
Sabyn, Robert 169
Sadler, --- (Mr.) 27
Sagar, Richard 59
Sallis, --- (Mr.) 57
Salmon, Daniel 56
 Edward 214
Salter, Abigail 55
 Elizabeth 55
 Hannah 55
 John 55
 Phillippa (Rouse) 55
 Samuel 55
 Theophilus 55
 Thomas 55
Saltinstall, Richard
 167
Salway, Jone 50
 Margaret 50
Salwey, Thomas 50
Samford, --- 247

Sammes, Bennet (Wright)
 253
 Edward 246, 252, 253
 Susan (Aylett) 246
Sampson, Agnes 229
 Jone 229
 Richard 183
 Robert 229
 Sara 229
 Thomas 229
Sams, John 234, 254
Sanders, Clement 6
Sanderson, --- (Mr.) 8
Sandes, --- (Mr.) 57
Sands, Henry 252
Sandys, Edwin 159
 William 195
Sansham, Robert 226
Sant, Edward 131
Saunders, Christopher
 31
 Martin 32
Savage, Ellen 227
 Margaret 200
 Robert 80, 210
Sawen, Agnes (Osborne)
 243
 John 243
Sawnder, John 225
 William 224
Sawyer, Dorothy 43
 Thomas 43
 William 14
Say, --- (Lord) 61
Sayer, --- (Mr.) 8
Saylett, John 244
Scamity, --- (Goodwife)
 26
Scanlan, Edward 114
Scarburgh, Edmond 175
Scarcroft, John 206
Scarlett, Elizabeth 251
 John 110
Scheale, Adrian 216
Schooling, Robert 44
Schutz, George 149
Schuyler, Angelica (Van
 Renssalear) 133
 Barbara 133
 Cortlandt 133
 Dirck 159
 Francis William 133
 John Cortland 133
 Philip 133
 Stephen 133
Scott, Bathshuah
 (Oxenbridge) 71
 Elizabeth (Maule) 255
 Francis 255
 Hannah (Troheir) 155
 James 155
 John 14, 183
 Martha (Bellers) 14
 Richard 71
 Thomas 236
Scriven, Elizabeth 20
 Mary 20, 24
Scrutton, Anne 218
 Grace (Kinge) 218
 John 218
 Raymond 218
Scudamore, Thomas 74
Seaborn, --- (Mr.) 56
Seabright, Anne 28
 William 28
Searl, John 185

Searle, --- 228
 John 228
 Nicholas 228
Searson, Agnes 199
 Henry 199
Sedgwick, --- (Mr.) 72
Sellecke, Charity 87
 David 87
 John 87
 Merab 87
 Nicholas 87
 Robert 87
 Simon 87
 William 87
Sellick, Daniel 87
 David 87, 176
 Elizabeth 87
 Joanna 87
 John 87
 Jonathan 87
 Nathaniel 87
 Susan (Kebby) 87
 Susanna 87, 176
Sellwin, John 215
Sely, Jone (Gaylard) 51
 Potter 51
 Sarah 51
Semple, William 114
Sephery, --- (Mr.) 57
Serieant, Winwood 139
Serjeant, Elizabeth 139
 Marmaduke Thomas 139
 Mary 139
 Mary Brown 139
Sewell, Giles 242
 Henry 92
 Symon 227
Sewester, Samuell 212
Seymor, John 235
Shaller, Adam 216
Shapleigh, Alexander
 174
 Jeffrey 173
 Nicholas 173
Sharpe, Henry 3, 4
 William 97
Sharwin, Richard 132
Shawe, --- 234
 Cicely 72
 Elizabeth 72
 Joan 72
 John 72
 Margaret 72
 Martha 72
 Martha (Chapman) 72
 Mary 72
 Sarah 72
 Thomas 72
 William 72
Shea, Patrick 54
Sheaf, Harman 69
Sheare, William 34
Shed, Daniel 243
Sheepard, John 115
Sheeres, Elizabeth 77
Sheers, Martha 77
 Susanna 77
Shelley, Giles 179
Shelton, Anne 207
 Edward 30
Shepard, John 66
 Thomas 67, 79
 William 79
Shepherd, Hannah 68
 Samuel 68
 Thomas 67, 170

Shepherd, William 68
Sheppard, Amy 67
 Anne 67
 Benjamin 12
 Daniel 67
 Elizabeth 67
 Ferdinado 170
 Frances 67
 John 67, 229
 Samuel 67, 173
 William 66, 67
Shepperd, Johane
 (Banks) 215
Sherborne, Thomas 185
Sherbrooke, Elizabeth
 145
 Miles 145, 146
Sherley, James 180
Sherrard, --- (Lord) 3
Sherwin, Ann 132
 Richard 132
Shettyl, John 194
Shipley, George 156
 Hannah 76
 Hannah (Lee) 156
Shipp, William 8
Shipton, --- (Mr.) 215
Shirley, James 171
Shomaker, Samuel 123
Shonke, James 44
Short, William Pitt 139
Shortland, Elizabeth 81
 Joseph 81
 Marie 81
 Thomas 81
Shory, Thomas 244
Shrimpton, Epaphras 183
Shrive, Helen (Barker)
 218
 John 218
 Thomas 181
Shurt, Abraham 26
Shute, John 48
Shyte, Robert 139
Sibley, Joseph 71
Siday, David 252
 Sarah 252
Sidey, Geffery 207
 Robert 207
Siggins, John 211
Simpson, Hannah 15
 Sampson 124
Simson, Andrew 252
Sinclair, Robert 132
Sinclar, Robert 178
Sion, Anthony 160
Siser, Giles 252
Sitwell, George 20
Skanbee, Thomas 235
Skandle, Margaret 235
 Thomas 235
Skeale, John 215
Skeele, John 247
Skiner, Judith (Leigh)
 99
Skinner, --- (Mr.) 165
 Barbara 229
 Clemence 251
 Edward 250
 James 165
 Joane 229
 John 251
 Leonard 251
 Margaret 152, 229
 Mary 209
 Mary (Billop) 161

Skinner, Olyve 229
 Susan 229
 Thomas 229
 William 161
Skirven, John 50
Skoles, Edmund 249
Skoole, Nicholas 227
Skotte, Elizabeth 246
Skrine, Robert 90
Slader, --- (Mr.) 60
Slater, Edmund 85
 Henry 132, 138
 John 7
 Margaret (Bradstreete)
 85
 Mary 132, 138
Slaterford, John 200,
 238
Sleigh, William 149
Sloane, Hans 45
Slococke, John 59
Slow, John 68, 101
 Thomas 68, 101, 102
Slyng, William 203
Slynge, Alice 203
 William 203
Smallay, Elizabeth 63
 Robert 63
Smart, William 96
Smartley, John 223
Smeth, Margaret 204
Smethe, Thomas 204
Smith, --- (Lady) 60
 Abraham 24
 Abraham L. 123
 Agens 106
 Ann 127
 Anne 36, 84, 241
 Anne (Ingram) 84
 Annis 80
 Bartlee 123
 Benjamin 182
 Brice 241
 Dorothy 152
 Elizabeth 56, 152
 Ffrancis (Jackson) 212
 Francis 36, 60
 George 39, 56, 92, 139
 Hayes 7
 Henry 247
 Isaac 63
 James 139, 148
 Jane 212
 Janet 139
 Jennison 118
 John 63, 97, 183, 220
 Joseph 62, 63, 152
 Judith 62
 Mary 63
 Maryann 118
 Mawde 106
 Peter 106
 Richard 7, 24, 44
 Robert 63, 153
 Thomas 62, 63, 73, 139
 Tobias 172
 W. H. 4
 William 62, 63, 80,
 139, 165, 212
Smithe, Alice 214
 Jane 214
 John 214
 Joseph 232
 Margery 214
 Saunder 214
 Thomas 214

Smyth, Gregory 209
 Henry 213
 Humphrey 209
 John 168, 203
 Robert 215
Smythe, Nicholas 248
 Thomas 204
Snare, Nicholas 197
Snowe, Macute 242
Soame, Joane 215
 Martha 215
 Samuel 215
 William 215
Soan, John 234
Soane, William 247
Soley, John 185
Sollam, Elizabeth 98
 Joseph 98
Somer, William 214
Somerfielde, Thomas 204
Somers, Anna 83
 William 83
Somerton, Robert 83
Somner, Christofer 201
Sond, John 253
Sonmaine, Simeon 130
Sorrell, Alice 229
 Anne 229
 John 229
 Mary 229
 Thomas 229
 William 229
Southey, Sarah 250
Spackman, Nicholas 172
Spademan, Anne (Reeve)
 97
 Thomas 97
Sparhawk, John 231
Sparling, Christian 221
 Elizabeth 221
Sparrow, Martin 223
Speede, George 97
Spencer, Mary 124
Spender, Edward 214
Spenser, Richarde 199
Sperhawk, Erasmus 223
Spiltimber, Richard 248
Spisall, John 242
Spooner, Henry 45
Spranger, Edward 250
Sprigg, William 60, 61
Springe, Marget 226
Springer, Richard 207
Springett, --- (Mr.)
 115
Springfield, Emanuel
 175
 Emmanuel 176
 Mary 176
Spursaie, John 48
Spyser, Kateryn (Baker)
 195
Squier, Daniel 141
Squyer, William 204
St. Quentin, Katherine
 (Cradocke) 43
St. Quyntyne, Katherine
 (Cradocke) 41
Stables, Keene 152
Stacey, Katherine 229
 Thomas 229
Staddier, George 52
Stafferton, Peter 78,
 79
Stafford, --- (Lady)
 168

282